MORVERN TRANS[...]

Eirich agus tiugainn, O,
Eirich agus tiugainn, O,
Eirich agus tiugainn, O,
   Farewell, farewell to Fiunary.
A thousand, thousand tender ties
Awake this day my plaintive sighs;
My heart within me almost dies
   At thought of leaving Fiunary.

(From a poem by Dr Norman MacLeod of St Columba's, written *c.* 1810.
The words at the beginning mean 'Get up and come along'.)

   Almost everyone who visits the
   Highlands and Islands returns.

(Peroration of MacBrayne's publicity leaflet *Enchanted Isles*, 1960.)

MORVERN TRANSFORMED

A HIGHLAND PARISH IN THE NINETEENTH CENTURY

BY

PHILIP GASKELL

FOR MARG
1948–1968–1980
ALL HAPPINESS

British Library Cataloguing in Publication Data
A catalogue record for this book is available from the British Library
ISBN 1-899863-09-5

Printed in Great Britain by BPC Wheatons, Exeter
for House of Lochar, Isle of Colonsay, Argyll PA61 7YR

PREFACE

This is a book about social and economic change in a Highland parish during the nineteenth century. Much has been written about the earlier stages of the Highland clearances—most of it by fervent partisans of the crofters—but practically nothing about the later stages of the same revolutionary process, when sheep-farming became unprofitable and many of the grazings were cleared again, this time for sport. Neither have the landlords, and especially the reasons for their agrarian policies, received much attention; yet they were on the whole reasonable men, as good and as bad as people generally are, and they deserve as much consideration as any other section of the population. I have therefore tried to cover here the process of change between the temporary equilibrium of the years around 1800 and the very different equilibrium that developed by 1900 after the stresses of the mid-century, and at the same time to avoid the customary over-emphasis on the misfortunes of the Highland peasantry.

Generalisation in this field is not yet possible—the detailed work must come first—but the parish of Morvern proved to be particularly well suited to the kind of investigation that can usefully be made. This is not only because it is large enough and sufficiently isolated to be considered by itself, but also because it has been possible to find and work on a considerable range of primary sources—estate papers, parochial registers, county records, census enumerations, diaries, memoirs, photographs and so forth—as well as to carry out field-work on the ground.

Much of the detailed evidence which follows the text as a series of appendixes is of the statistical and topographical sort that is intended for reference and, although I hope that historians will find it useful, others may safely skip it. This dispensation does not apply to Appendix E, however, and in particular the reader is urged not to miss the Astley Diary (transcribed on pp. 188–212), the lively and engaging record of the visits made by two mid-Victorian girls to a great sporting estate in the 1870s.

Anyone who writes a history book, particularly one that draws on manuscript sources, soon finds himself in debt to many people who, with patient generosity, have given their time and their skill towards helping the work on its way. This book, certainly, could not have been written at all had not Mrs Owen Hugh Smith first allowed me to become her tenant at Ardtornish, and then given me access to the Ardtornish Estate Papers; my gratitude to her (who, I should explain at once, is not related to the nineteenth-century owners of Ardtornish who were also called Smith) and to her daughter Mrs John Raven for their help and friendship is very great. Then there are my friends in Morvern: Mr Donald Lawrie, postmaster and local historian, who has helped liberally from the beginning; the late Donald Paton, formerly manager of the Lochaline sand mine; Mr Charles Ives, shepherd of Ardtornish, and Mrs Ives; the late Donald Cameron, also of Ardtornish, and Mrs Cameron; the late William Moffat; and Mr Iain Thornber. At Inveraray, His Grace the Duke of Argyll gave me, not only hospitality, but also the freedom of the superb Argyll archives and his expert guidance in examining them; and at Oban I had special facilities for working on the files of the *Oban Times* through the kindness of the editor, Mr A. E. Cameron. I also want to thank most sincerely Mrs John Lipscomb, Mr Peter Sinclair-Thomson, Miss Catherine Cameron and Colonel Arthur Gemmell for the loan of documents and for permission to copy them; Professor R. H. Campbell, Mr Eric Cregeen, Mr David M. Walker and 'North Argyll' for their help with a variety of special problems; Miss MacPhail of the County Clerk's Office, Lochgilphead, Dr Taylor of the Registrar-General's Office, and Mr Grant Simpson of the Scottish Record Office for their ready assistance whenever I bothered them; and many others who helped in a number of ways, especially Miss Joan Becher, Mr Robert Cowper, Mrs Mona Davidson, Dr R. W. Davis, Dr Horace Fairhurst, Superintendent James Farquharson, Mr Donald Grant, Miss Alice Horsman, Mr G. E. Langmuir, Dr Robert MacClements, Dr George MacLeod, the Reverend Hector MacSween, Mr H. A. Moisley, Mr Alex Morrison, Mr Charles Murray, Mr Keith Parkhurst, Mr W. G. Rawlings and Mrs Neville Temperley. My thanks are also due to Sir James Fergusson and Messrs Faber and Faber for permission to quote from *Argyll in the forty-five.*

PREFACE (1980)

The text of this reprint remains unaltered, but new photographs have been used for some of the plates. Further documents have turned up since 1968. The most important of these are:

(1) A substantial collection of Gregorson papers (see pp. 28–9), mostly of the late eighteenth and early nineteenth centuries; belonging to Mrs Hector Greenfield of Kilmartin, Argyll.

(2) A drawing of Lochaline House made before its conversion by Mrs Paterson (see pp. 30 and n., 169); belonging to Mrs Margaret Mason of East Grinstead.

(3) A report on the Tearnait copper mines (see p. 171), dated 1789, by the geologist (and author of *Baron Munchausen*) R. E. Raspe; in the Argyll Archives at Inveraray.

(4) The autograph manuscript of Miss Agnes King's Memoirs (see p. 223); lent me by Miss Ann Bircham of Swannington, Norfolk.

(5) The journal of a visit to Morvern made in 1900 by John MacCalman, a Morvern man who emigrated to America in the 1880s and became a Minister in New York State; belonging to Mrs Kenneth MacCalman of Nyack, N.Y.

It may be added that there are traces of houses in Inninmore at 728416 (remains, see pp. 131–2) and in Dubh Dhoire at 714487 (outline, see p. 141); and of shieling structures in Ardtornish/Inninmore at 713425 (750 ft, see p. 132), in Tearnait around 748455 (650 ft, see p. 132), and in Beach at 776531 (800 ft, see p. 159). Iain Thornber has established that Dr John MacLachlan, the Morvern physician (see p. 230 and n.), became a Licentiate of the Royal College of Physicians and Surgeons of Glasgow in 1830; that he was practising in Lochaline in the 1850s; and that he died in Tobermory in 1874.

I am very grateful to all those who have helped me with information since this book was first published; and especially to Iain Thornber, whose *Castles of Morvern* and *The sculptured stones of Cill Choluimchille, Morvern* were published privately in 1975. Mr Thornber has also published a number of articles in periodicals on the history of Morvern, and he has a book in preparation which will incorporate much of this material.

Finally, an apology. I was mistaken in 1968 in believing that the volume of the Astley Diary from which extracts were quoted in Appendix E belonged to Mrs John Lipscomb, and I am very sorry for this error. The Diary was and is the property of Miss M. J. Becher of Arisaig, by whose kind permission the extracts are reprinted here.

PHILIP GASKELL

Trinity College, Cambridge

INTRODUCTION (1980)

by R. H. CAMPBELL

Professor of Economic History, University of Stirling

Popular yet serious interest in the Highlands and their problems has grown since *Morvern transformed* was first published in 1968, partly through the appearance of a number of good studies, some of which have been aimed successfully at general and not only at specialist readers, and partly because the Highlands seem to possess so many of the characteristics of social problems which attract contemporary interest. Sympathy, even identification with the Highland problem can be explained in different ways. Some are the result of the way in which so many aspects of Highland life today seem to compare adversely with those in other parts of the country. The comparative tests may be the common statistical ones of the era of the welfare state, derived from the levels of unemployment or from various indices of the standard of social provision, or from less precise indicators of a degree of isolation from such conventionally accepted necessities of modern life as the standard of reception of television programmes. Other explanations of the concern with the Highlands are more complex because in many cases evidence of a similar degree of social deprivation can be found in other parts of the country. Why then should the Highlands absorb so much interest while similar problems in other areas are neglected? Some reasons are simple. The Highland area is large, easily identified and cannot be ignored, especially when promoted by a tourist trade much influenced by romantic interpretations of Highland life. There are also deeper-seated and more serious explanations. The modern propensity to engage in social protest does not imply universal sympathy with those who have suffered or whose standard or way of life does not measure up to conventionally accepted standards; nor has it led to any greater readiness to accept responsibility for providing remedies; but it strives to identify whatever agent is thought to have been responsible for the relative deprivation. That effort may lead to historical investigations which, as in the Highlands, have implications for current policy. If the modern concern with social amelioration is less marked by its own willingness to accept responsibility for providing remedies, it is marked by its insistence that responsibility be assumed by the agent identified as the cause of the social problem, even to the extent of visiting the sins and the responsibilities of the fathers on the children of the present day. If the Highland landlords of past generations are held responsible for creating the problems of social deprivation in the Highlands, then it is possible to place the blame on those of today, and so to transfer much, if not all of the social responsibility for action or inaction to them, and to take credit for doing so. The criticism of the landowners is an aspect of Scottish culture, deeply rooted and not easily removed by rational argument. It remains, even though the landowners' power had been drastically eroded through adverse economic conditions and through legislation applicable generally and to the Highlands in particular. Agitation about who owns Scotland attracts attention so long as it remains at a popular and emotional level, but it is not eliminated, nor is it much affected, by more serious investigations into the problem. As so often in the past, the landowners stand out as the favourite targets of social criticism, the wicked ogres, the scapegoats of the Highland scene. Perhaps there is nothing so stable in the interest in the Highlands as this criticism.

Dr Gaskell's study is a vital piece of evidence in this highly emotional debate. It cannot be dismissed as ". . . the epitome of sleekness, with an unusually open conflation of Highland landlords' sectional interests with the national interest".[1] Indeed its strength lies in its attempt to give the landowners' contribution to the wider interests of society a recognition which it is all too readily denied. Admittedly the world which Dr Gaskell portrays sympathetically and that of much other modern writing on the subject differ from each other. Today's social values are far removed from those of the autocratic landowners who changed the face of the Highlands, socially and physically, almost as effectively as afforestation does today, and nowhere is the gulf more evident than in the glimpse, so rarely available, which Dr Gaskell gives into the lives of those well-to-do Victorians who came in the late nineteenth century, when the day of sheep was waning, to seek the glamour of the Highlands and a contrast from their normal daily round in the sports it offered, especially deer-stalking.

Any critical evaluation of Highland history which ends in the identification of a scapegoat, whether landowners or others, normally depends on the acceptance of two propositions, one chiefly historical, the other chiefly speculative. The first is the belief that the history of the Highlands, especially its economic history, is a story of exploitation. The approach is evident in the work of Marx and has been followed by many others, even by those who do not always share his ideological presuppositions. Sometimes the allegation of exploitation may be specific, levelled directly against the landowners, as in their introduction of sheep or later when they turned to deer as the price of sheep fell, or the allegation of exploitation may be more general, when it is seen as the consequence of the relative economic backwardness of the Highlands

[1] I. Carter, *Farm life in Northeast Scotland 1840–1914* (Edinburgh, 1979), p. 223 n. 23.

compared with other parts of the United Kingdom, and in later years with other parts of the world. It then becomes possible to suggest that the Highlands were brought into a dependent relation with more advanced regions, that it supplied resources required for industrialisation, frequently the labour power, or more occasionally raw materials, such as kelp in the early nineteenth century or in more modern times certain facilities for the provision of oil. The danger of any such relationship is evident historically in the experience of kelp production and it is then easy to transpose the same danger to the present-day links with the oil industry. As soon as the economy or the industry to which the kelp was supplied obtained a more acceptable commodity, the sources of supply in the Highlands were abandoned. A similar fate may await developments in the oil and oil-related industries. As with other extractive industries, the end of the extraction can lead to the abandonment of the area of original development and so to dereliction.

The critical evaluation and the desire to find a scapegoat are intensified when the acceptance of the first proposition of historical exploitation is complemented by the second, that a different, independent form of economic development was open to the Highlands. Both propositions must be held together for the case to be fully effective. If another, and an independent form of economic development were not possible, it is difficult to sustain some of the charges of exploitation; then the Highlands could hardly have experienced any economic development other than a dependent one. To some a dependent economic relationship of some form was unavoidable quite simply because the Highlands did not have the diversified economic potential to enable it to compete against other better endowed regions. The adverse consequences of the dependent relationship may be deplored, but they are regarded as the price of any economic progress which must be paid by less well-endowed regions, and the only way of avoiding them would have been, and still is, for the Highlands to keep itself apart from the indirect and ephemeral benefit of the economic growth elsewhere. That policy of economic isolationism may seem an attractive course and one which would have had the benefit of retaining distinctive features of Highland life and culture, but is not easily accepted except by those already amply provided with the benefits of industrial societies. By contrast, though the hypothetical forms of economic growth may vary, the greater the degree of independent development which is considered possible, the greater the substance in allegations of exploitation. To those less pessimistic about the prospects for indigenous economic growth in the Highlands the dependent relationship was derived from the imposition of greater economic power from outside the Highlands, which set out to exploit the opportunities which were open to it. In that way the Highlands became the economic appendage of greater national or international interests, liable to be exploited to suit that power and to be neglected whenever it had served its purposes. The land-owners can become agents in such a process even if not its ultimate cause. Though different interpretations may be advanced, the answer to the hypothetical question of how far indigenous economic growth was possible is therefore a vital issue in the historiography of the Highlands.

The pessimists, those who doubt the possibility of independent economic development and so the extent to which exploitation might have been avoided usually begin their interpretation by stressing the exceptional nature of the challenge to any economic potential of the Highlands raised by the increase in population which was a persistent factor from the late eighteenth century, especially in the areas of most acute difficulty in the north and west. Even in areas from which tenants were forcibly removed, the overall population continued to rise, so that the peak in many Highland counties was reached only after some of the best-known clearances had taken place. The demographic explosion must occupy a central part in any examination of Highland history in the later eighteenth or early nineteenth centuries. The pessimists regard it as perhaps the single most important factor in Highland history, one which overshadowed many attempts at improvement and which had to be tackled if any was to be realised, but for which the only solution was the ultimate one of emigration. Others, the optimists, regard the demo-graphic challenge as something which could have been overcome and the increased population supported in the Highlands at a reasonable standard of living. Attitudes to the demographic explosion depend largely on the response to the vital question already posed, of the extent to which the Highlands are considered to have had the capabilities for independent and indigenous economic growth. The challenge made a successful response still more difficult to achieve. The potential for economic growth is then the answer not only to any threat of exploitation but to the additional challenge of the rising population.

An assessment of the extent of the economic potential is, of course, difficult because it rests on arguments of what might have happened but did not. Arguments are advanced on all sides. It may be suggested, as has often been done in modern times, that the Highlands did not need to reproduce the forms of economic growth of the Lowlands, and so the absence of many of the keys to the successful economic growth of the latter, such as the absence of adequate supplies of coal, need not have impeded economic growth. It can still be held that certain other vital features of industrialisation elsewhere were absent in the Highlands, notably the lack of those who in other societies provided the entrepre-neurial or marketing abilities on which so much economic growth de-pended. Since the issue is counter-factual, it must remain a matter of speculation and one in which it will be impossible to reach any consensus of opinion. But the issue leads to what is often considered the major determinant of interpretations of the economic potential of the Highlands. It lies in the attitudes adopted towards what may loosely be termed the social structure and the social rights and duties of those who held positions of influence in Highland society. All writers agree on the importance of this factor in any appreciation of Highland life and so on how it must be included in any interpretation of Highland social history, but the emphasis placed upon it varies. Those who are generally more optimistic about the possibilities which the Highlands offered of achieving some form of economic independence stress the failure of the social structure to adapt to changing conditions in their explanations. By contrast, those who are pessimistic about the possibilities stress the contribution of more strictly economic factors and their conspicuous absence in the Highlands. The nature of the change in the social structure which all accept and stress to differing degrees is the intrusion of a more commercial approach to rights and duties in Highland society and that especially among the landowners. Yet the change must be qualified in a number of ways. It is too easy to see the new attitudes in a simple and unqualified way as representative of those who were seeking their own narrow interests, their own narrow profits, at the expense of those who had no economic power to resist. In every society there have always been those with such objectives, but in the Highlands the criticism is directed particularly towards the landowners. The question which must always be considered is then how far they had such a narrow view of their interests. To the modern mind, especially to those seeking out the causes and especially the culprits of social ills as they see them, it is difficult to associate anything other than a narrow view of interest with the profit motive but in the later eighteenth and much of the nineteenth centuries at least it was possible for an individual to believe in all good faith that in following the maximisation of his own profit he was promoting the welfare of society at the same time. The combination of the two is less easily accepted today but their combination was the mark of much advanced social thought at the time the new values were being accepted in Highland society. The acceptance of the commercial values by the landowners did not therefore mean in theory at any rate such a rejection of old responsibilities as so often seems to be the case in retrospect. Admittedly private action brought public benefits only in the long run and sometimes not at all in practice, but even in the short run, whatever their basic beliefs and objectives, some Highland landlords still contradicted them by contriving to provide for their dependants, notably in the form of famine relief and then, especially later as is evident in *Morvern transformed*, in a modern form of social paternalism. The relationship had been transformed and the form of the aid changed but the extensive social provision for those who remained in the Highlands cannot be denied. It may have had certain characteristics which are unacceptable, even offensive to modern thought, but it was given in a way in which it was not given, often by the same individual, in the industrial society of the Lowlands or in England. To that extent the social structure of the Highlands remained very different. It was not necessarily the social structure which contemporaries wanted, still less the social structure which many present-day critics of the Highland scene think desirable, but it was a social structure which had elements of social responsibility, and was provided often at substantial cost to the proprietor. One irony of the entire Highland problem historically is that those who did most to try to tackle the difficulties on their estates, and who were more able and willing to devote resources from elsewhere to try to do so, have been the recipients of the most virulent criticism. By contrast those who may have succeeded, though on a modest scale, in dealing with the increase of population in a new social order on their estates have received virtually no notice, but, most interestingly of all, those who merely sold up, often when their way of life had so burdened their estates with debts that there was no other alternative, have escaped much of the criticism to which they were more entitled than some of those who have received it in full measure.

Such defence of the landowners may be considered yet another "epitome of sleekness", because their action is not considered conducive to the prevention of exploitation by external forces through the encouragement of indigenous economic growth, not even, and sometimes least of all, when they engaged in constructional activities which were remarkably similar to many of the schemes advocated to tackle unemployment in the twentieth century. In short, the discussion reverts yet again to the counter-factual issue of whether even another social structure, and one in which rights and duties were differently held and interpreted, could have led to economic independence in the Highlands. Those who stress the absence of many of the ingredients of modern economic growth in the Highlands consider their pessimistic view is confirmed by the futility of some of those efforts to build a new Highland society and continue to assert their doubt that it would ever have been possible to achieve an economic revolution by the adoption of any social structure. Instead then of basing a radical form of social criticism on the belief that it was possible, another more moderate form of social criticism, and one for which the evidence is well-presented in *Morvern transformed*, is more defensible, and that is again the way in which the nineteenth century witnessed the perpetuation of a dependent relationship of tenant and retainers to some occasional visiting landowner. But the critic must tread warily. The landlord's absenteeism was hardly his main fault in that the estates were not neglected, and indeed it was his absenteeism which often ensured the availability of the ready supply of funds from one source or another which enabled the dependent society of the Highland estates to exist. If a charge of exploitation has to be made against the absentee landlord, *Morvern transformed* shows that it might well be made against the landowner's activities in those areas out of the Highlands, which were exploited for the benefit of the Highland estates. The defect of the dependence was that it could lead easily to demoralisation and any attempt to induce independence in the Highlands was then doomed to extinction. Such a social structure was not harsh, but it was repressive of the possibilities of an independent way of life existing, so that, when the support was removed in consequence of modern social and fiscal policy, there was ultimately nothing left except for the state to take its place or dereliction was complete.

Morvern transformed gives a rare insight into this other world, its attitudes and its way of life, especially unusual being the insight into the activities of Octavius Smith and his family in the days of the sporting estates at the end of the nineteenth century. It shows a group which came to the Highlands not through any desire to exploit it in a commercial spirit. They had already ample funds derived from other sources and would not have considered the Highlands as remotely suitable as a good investment. By the second half of the nineteenth century the Highlands were opened up for the tourist and the sportsman and for a short period to 1914, and on a modified scale until 1939, the sportsman had his day, leaving a mark on social thought out of all proportion to reality. The sportsman did not exploit the Highlands except in so far as it is considered that he impeded the development of Highland potential, but, as has already been indicated, the extent of that potential must be a question of faith. At worst he demoralised the Highlands by inculcating a new and specially dependent relationship. Yet that relationship was not deliberately engineered by anyone, and, when it was, it was in the expectation that it would be perpetuated in a way which taxation, war and different social customs ensured did not take place. But that was not what the Victorian sportsman and landowner expected in the hey-day of his reign in the half-century before 1914. *Morvern transformed* shows the tightly-knit society of the wealthy of the day. They were not the great landowners of the past; they could not even aspire to rival them, but they were carving out for themselves a social order which they thought would be secure. It passed; whether it did any permanent damage to the Highlands; whether that had already been done; whether there were any alternatives—these are all issues about which opinions will differ and *Morvern transformed* will help to mould them. It throws light on a period which many, with very different social attitudes, might find even objectionable. But the nineteenth-century landowner needs the sympathetic interpretation of Dr Gaskell rather than the much more common caricaturing adopted by his more frequently encountered critics and enemies. And Dr Gaskell gives a fascinating portrayal of a way of life which, though only a century old, is already as different from the present as it was in its own day from the way of life another century before.

CONTENTS

Contents

APPENDIXES

Contents

LIST OF PLATES

(following p. 258)

Plates 5, 6 b, 8, 9, 12, 14 a, 15 a and 16 are from the nineteenth-century sources given in the captions; the rest of the plates are from the author's photographs.

MAPS

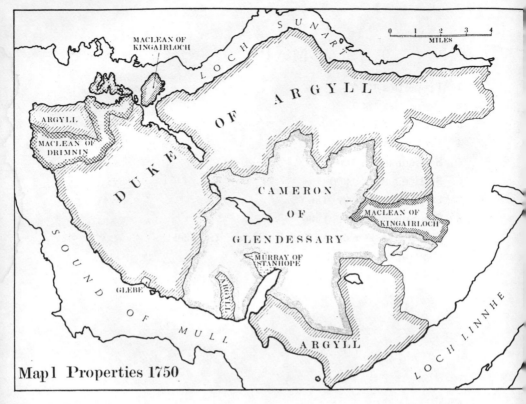

Map 1 Properties 1750

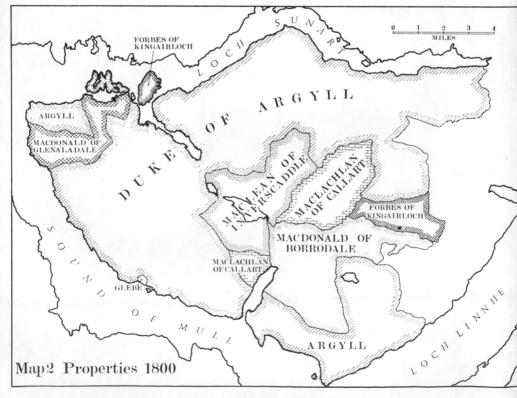

Map 2 Properties 1800

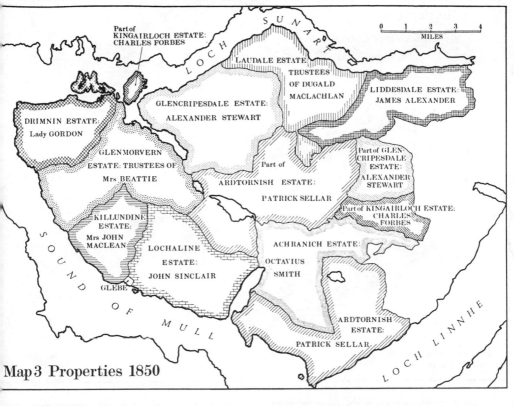

Map 3 Properties 1850

Part of KINGAIRLOCH ESTATE: CHARLES FORBES

LOCH SUNART

LAUDALE ESTATE: TRUSTEES OF DUGALD MACLACHLAN

LIDDESDALE ESTATE: JAMES ALEXANDER

GLENCRIPESDALE ESTATE: ALEXANDER STEWART

DRIMNIN ESTATE: Lady GORDON

GLENMORVERN ESTATE: TRUSTEES OF Mrs BEATTIE

Part of ARDTORNISH ESTATE: PATRICK SELLAR

Part of GLEN-CRIPESDALE ESTATE: ALEXANDER STEWART

Part of KINGAIRLOCH ESTATE: CHARLES FORBES

KILLUNDINE ESTATE: Mrs JOHN MACLEAN

LOCHALINE ESTATE: JOHN SINCLAIR

ACHRANICH ESTATE: OCTAVIUS SMITH

GLEBE

SOUND OF MULL

ARDTORNISH ESTATE: PATRICK SELLAR

LOCH LINNHE

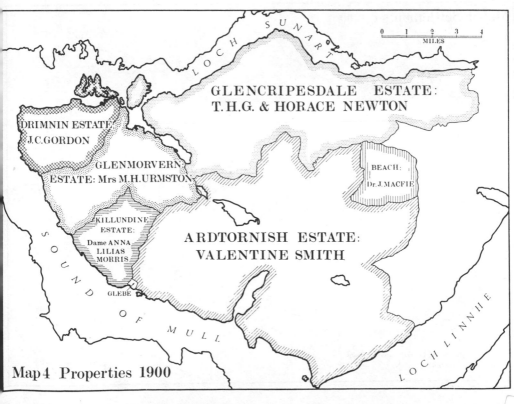

Map 4 Properties 1900

LOCH SUNART

GLENCRIPESDALE ESTATE: T. H. G. & HORACE NEWTON

DRIMNIN ESTATE: J. C. GORDON

GLENMORVERN ESTATE: Mrs M. H. URMSTON

BEACH: Dr. J. MACFIE

KILLUNDINE ESTATE: Dame ANNA LILIAS MORRIS

ARDTORNISH ESTATE: VALENTINE SMITH

GLEBE

SOUND OF MULL

LOCH LINNHE

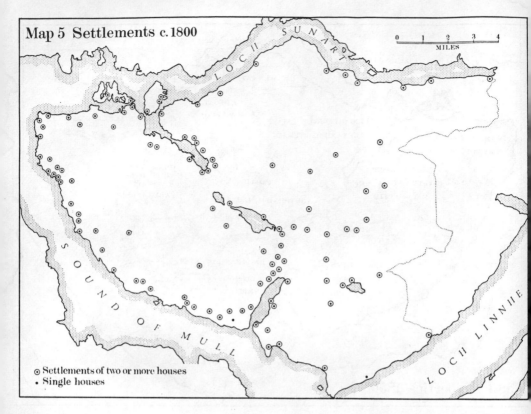

Map 5 Settlements c. 1800

0 1 2 3 4
MILES

LOCH SUNART

SOUND OF MULL

LOCH LINNHE

⊙ Settlements of two or more houses
• Single houses

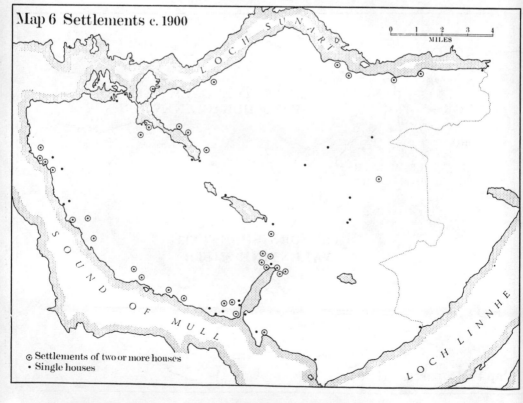

Map 6 Settlements c. 1900

0 1 2 3 4
MILES

LOCH SUNART

SOUND OF MULL

LOCH LINNHE

⊙ Settlements of two or more houses
• Single houses

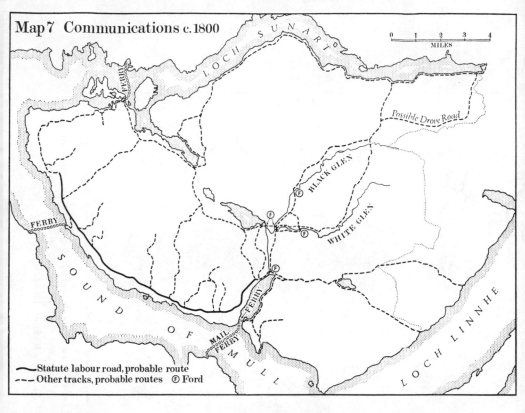

Map 7 Communications c.1800

LOCH SUNART

0 1 2 3 4
MILES

Possible Drove Road

BLACK GLEN Ⓕ

Ⓕ

WHITE GLEN Ⓕ

FERRY

FERRY

Ⓕ

SOUND

OF

FERRY

MAIL
FERRY

MULL

LOCH LINNHE

—— Statute labour road, probable route
– – – Other tracks, probable routes   Ⓕ Ford

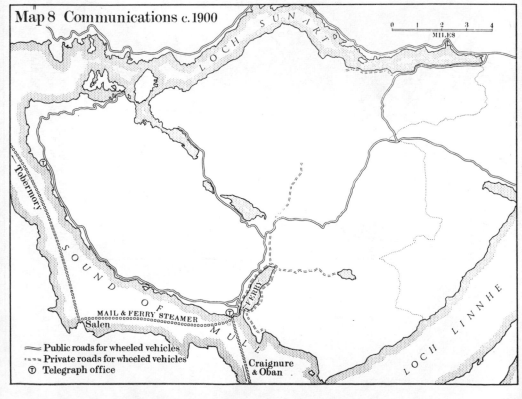

Map 8 Communications c.1900

LOCH SUNART

0 1 2 3 4
MILES

Tobermory

Ⓣ

SOUND

OF

MULL

FERRY

Ⓣ

MAIL & FERRY STEAMER
Salen

Craignure
& Oban

LOCH LINNHE

══ Public roads for wheeled vehicles
═ ═ ═ Private roads for wheeled vehicles
Ⓣ Telegraph office

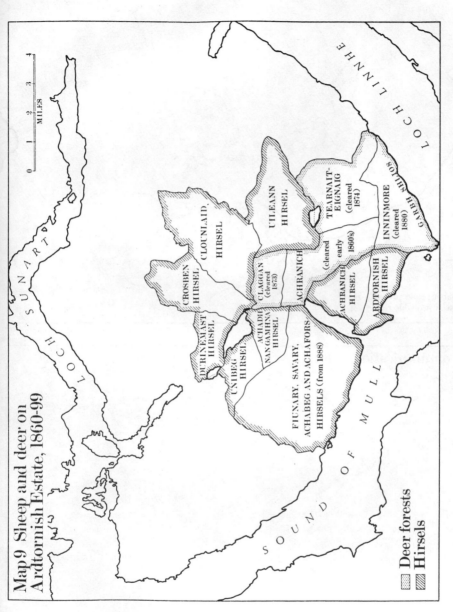

Map 9 Sheep and deer on Ardtornish Estate, 1860-99

Map 9. The boundaries between the hirsels, and between the areas cleared for deer-forest are approximate. The boundaries of the Lochaline hirsels are not known even approximately.

For Map 10 please turn to the back of the book.

Deer forests

Hirsels

KEY TO MAP 10
(see overleaf)

1 Ardtornish Castle
2 Ardtornish (1)
3 Ardtornish (2) and House
4 Caolas
5 Garbh Shlios
6 Inninbeg (1)
7 Inninbeg (2)
8 Inninmore
9 Rubha an t-Sasunnaich
10 Samhnach (Ardtornish)
11 Eignaig
12 Doire Dharaich
13 Leacraithnaich
14 Tearnait
15 Kinlochaline Castle
16 Fishing station
17 Achafors
18 Kinlochaline (1)
19 Kinlochaline (2)
20 (?) Achtidonile
21 Clounlaid (1)
22 Clounlaid (2)
23 Sron
24 Achnatuaisaig
25 Doire Leathan
26 Muicrach
27 Uladail
28 Achnatavishruskline
29 Achranich
30 Samhnach (Achranich)
31 Srath Shuardail
32 Ath Buidhe
33 Claggan
34 Torr a'Chall
35 Clais Bhreac
36 Dubh Dhoire
37 Uileann
38 Achadh nan Gamhna
39 Acharn (1)
40 Acharn (2)
41 Arienas
42 Crosben (1)
43 Crosben (2)
44 Crosben (3)
45 Durinemast (1)
46 Durinemast (2)
47 Larachbeg
48 Unibeg (1)
49 Unibeg (2)
50 Achabeg

51 Ardness
52 Ardness Port House
53 Achnaha (1)
54 Achnaha (2)
55 Dounanlui
56 Keil
57 Cuibheag
58 Cul a'Chàolais
59 Knock
60 Lochaline village
61 Fiunary
62 Lochaline House
63 Savary (1)
64 Savary (2)
65 Savary (3)
66 Gleann nan Iomairean
67 Killundine
68 Lagan
69 Salachan (1)
70 Salachan (2)
71 Ardantiobairt (1)
72 Ardantiobairt (2)
73 Baile Geamhraidh
74 Barr
75 Eilean nan Eildean
76 Gleannaguda (1)
77 Gleannaguda (2) and (3)
78 Torraneidhinn and
   Cnocandubh
79 Carnacailliche
80 Fernish (1) (Achnasaul)
81 Fernish (2)
82 Glenmorvern
83 Rhemore
84 Bonnavoulin
85 Druim Cracaig
86 Mungasdail
87 Mungasdail Mill
88 Unimore
89 Achleanan (1)
90 Achleanan (2)
91 Auliston
92 Auliston Point
93 Carraig
94 Drimnin (1)
95 Drimnin (2)
96 Drimnin Crofts
97 Doirlinn
98 Druimbuidhe
99 Glasdrum (1)

100 Glasdrum (2)
101 Oronsay (1)
102 Oronsay (2)
103 Oronsay (3)
104 Oronsay (4)
105 Poll Luachrain
106 Portabhata
107 Sruthain
108 Sornagan
109 Beach
110 Beinniadain
111 Glencripesdale
112 Innbhir Mor
113 Kinloch
114 Achadhcoirbte
115 Kinlochteacuis
116 Baile Brucaiche
117 Caol Charna
118 Camas Glas
119 Carnliath (1)
120 Carnliath (2)
121 Rahoy
122 Camas Salach
123 Camas na h-Airdhe
124 Glenlaudale
125 Laudale
126 Lurga
127 Achagavel
128 Achleek
129 Liddesdale
130 Loch-head
131 Altachonaich (1)
132 Altachonaich (2)
133 Achadhlic
134 Dailechreagain (1)
135 Dailechreagain (2)
136 Glensanda Castle
137 Killundine Castle
138 Drimnin Castle (site)
139 Keil Church
140 Killintag Church
141 Fernish Church
142 Airigh Shamhraidhe
143 Inninmore coal mine
144 Doire Dharaich copper
    mine
145 Lurga lead mine
146 Ardtornish Tower
147 Inninmore early settle-
    ment

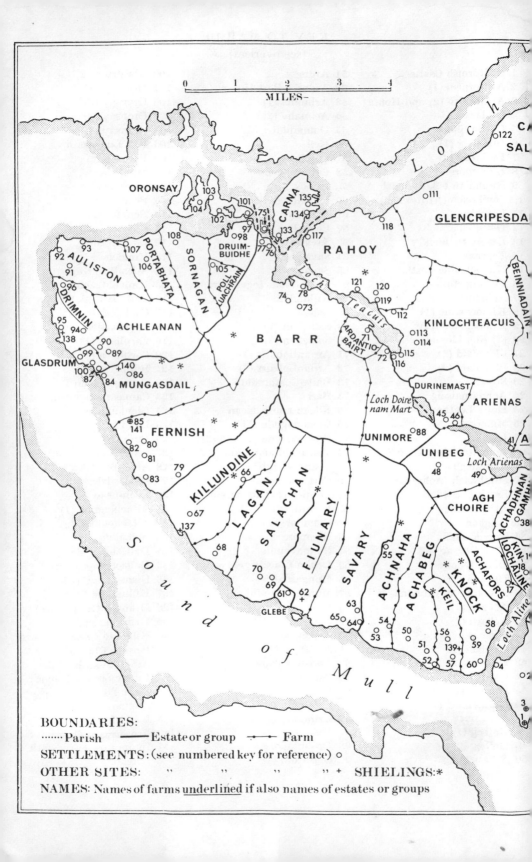

BOUNDARIES:
...... Parish ——— Estate or group ——•—— Farm
SETTLEMENTS: (see numbered key for reference) ○
OTHER SITES: "   "   "   + SHIELINGS: *
NAMES: Names of farms underlined if also names of estates or groups

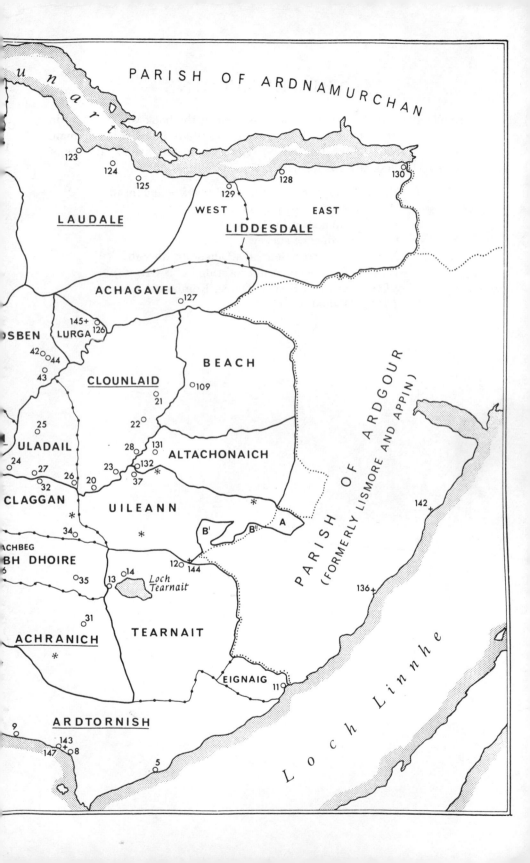

PARISH OF ARDNAMURCHAN

LAUDALE

WEST   EAST

LIDDESDALE

ACHAGAVEL

145+
LURGA 126

SBEN

42 44

43

CLOUNLAID

BEACH

109

21

22

25

ULADAIL

28   131

ALTACHONAICH

24

23   132

27   26   20   37   *

32

CLAGGAN

UILEANN

*

34

B'   B''   A

*

ACHBEG

BH DHOIRE

6

35   13   14
Loch
Tearnait

12   144

31

TEARNAIT

ACHRANICH

*

EIGNAIG

11

ARDTORNISH

9

143
147   +8

5

PARISH OF ARDGOUR
(FORMERLY LISMORE AND APPIN)

142+

136+

Loch Linnhe

ABBREVIATIONS

Explanations of all the abbreviations used in the book will be found in the various sections of the bibliography; they are indexed in the main section, Printed Books (pp. 254–8). Here meanwhile are expansions of some of the less obvious forms:

ACOL Argyllshire County Offices, Lochgilphead
AP Ardtornish papers
ICP Inveraray Castle papers
OS Ordnance survey
RGO Registrar-General's Office, Edinburgh
RSA Register of sasines abridgments (Argyll)
SRO Scottish Record Office, Edinburgh
VR Valuation roll

1

MORVERN IN 1800

BETWEEN THE DEVIL AND
THE DEEP BLUE SEA

THE BACKGROUND

At the end of the eighteenth century the people of Morvern[1] were poised between an unstable and often bloody past, and a future dissolution of the social order that would cause their descendants to look back even on this lean and uncertain time as to a golden age. Civil war and armed feud, they knew, lingered only in the memories of the old; a benevolent lord watched from a comfortable distance over the interests of his lands and his tenants; and men felt that they were members of an interesting and notable society, established on ground which they considered (however mistakenly) that they had a right to occupy. Poor they may have seemed, but poverty is relative, and they had been poorer before. The insecurity of their position was similarly difficult for them to grasp; they could not foresee what would happen when their landlords died or sold up, could not understand that the apparent strength of their economy was delusive, could not believe that the very size of their teeming families would bring their own downfall.

Such comfort and stability as the parish enjoyed in the later eighteenth century was largely due to the rule of the Argyll family. Morvern had been dominated by the MacLeans of Duart and their kinsmen for the whole of the sixteenth century and for most of the seventeenth, but in the 1670s Argyll brought a century of litigation and fighting to a head with an armed invasion of MacLean territory, whereby he fought his way into control of all the Duart estates, which included two-thirds of Morvern; and, although the people of Morvern at first hated both Campbells and agricultural reform, their new superiors brought a measure of peace and prosperity to a country which had hitherto known

[1] Here and throughout the book 'Morvern' means the civil parish of Morvern, Argyll, and does not include that part of the parish of Ardgour (formerly part of the parish of Lismore and Appin) which lies within the peninsula of Morvern and in which Kingairloch is situated; but it does include the area from Achagavel to the head of Loch Sunart in the civil parish of Morvern which was attached *quoad sacra* to the parish of Strontian. No boundary changes took place during the eighteenth or nineteenth centuries. See Map 10.

1

little of either.[1] But Argyll's ascendancy did not immediately lead to a new age. For half a century more the old, feudal ways persisted, the land being held by large tacksmen who were in effect middlemen in a military organisation, and who in turn let it out to sub-tenants who paid for it in produce, work and military service. It was the wildest outpost of the Argyll estates, in every sense remote from the civilised south, a land where all spoke a foreign tongue and were notorious as Jacobites and as non-jurant opponents of the established church. Two events, however, struck in quick succession at the roots of the old social order, causing it to wither and die in a generation: they were the agrarian reforms attempted by the second Duke of Argyll in 1737, and the Jacobite rebellion of 1745–6.

Considering that many of the large tacksmen acted as centres of disloyalty in his northern properties, and believing moreover that they did not all pay adequate rents for their land, Argyll sent his friend Forbes of Culloden as agent to his estates in Mull, Morvern and Tiree in order to effect the renewal of the leases then about to expire, and to re-adjust the conditions and rents of his tenants.[2] "Upon my arrival in Mull", Forbes wrote to his master in September 1737, "I called the tenants of that island and of Morvern before me, and acquainted them with your Grace's favourable intention of delivering them from the tyranny of taxmen, of freeing them from the oppression of services and Herezelds, and of incouraging them to improve their farms by giving them a sort of property in their grounds for 19 years by leases, if they showed themselves worthy of the intended favour by offering frankly for their farms such rent as honestly and fairly they could bear."[3] Argyll's aim was "in the first place, to let as many as possible of the farms to the sub-tenants themselves, holding directly from the proprietor;"—that is, with a prohibition on sub-letting—"and, in the second place, to abolish or limit services, and to convert the rents into fixed and definite sums of money, which were to be incapable of increase during a considerable term of years."[4] In Morvern the rents had been raised from £222 to £467, and services abolished, shortly before Forbes's visit, so here it was only a question of finding new and more acceptable tenants, but even this turned out to be harder than he and the Duke had expected. At first the tacksmen and sub-tenants combined in attempts to retain the old system,

---

[1] For the early history of Morvern, see *OPS* ii pt 1 (1854), 188–93; 'Information for Allan M'Lean of Drimnin, Pursuer; against John, Duke of Argyle, Defender' (1774), printed in Macphail, J. R. N. (1914), 245–50; and much unpublished material concerning the 'MacLean War' in *ICP*.

[2] Duncan Forbes's report is printed in full, with an interesting discussion, in *Napier Commission report* (1884), 380–94.

[3] *Napier Commission report* (1884), 387.

[4] The eighth Duke of Argyll writing in *Napier Commission report* (1884), 381.

but Forbes succeeded eventually in reletting the northern farms according to the new plan. The tacksmen he chose were still local people, not yet Campbells from the south, but they were smaller men than their predecessors had been, and their power in the district was proportionately less.

Any idea that the Duke may have had, however, that his Morvern people would give up their disloyal ways in gratitude for their emancipation was sharply disproved in 1745. Many of them were Camerons, owing allegiance to Lochiel, and amongst the rest were a number of MacLeans adhering to Drimnin—for the third of the parish of which Argyll was not actual proprietor was still in effect MacLean territory[1]— so that they were intimately involved in the rising from beginning to end. Lochiel made his vital promise of support to the Prince within a few days of the landing in July 1745, and it was the actual arrival of Lochiel with his Camerons that was the signal for the raising of the Jacobite standard at Glenfinann on 19 August. Lochiel, Drimnin and their followers served with the Prince's army throughout the rebellion —not one man from Morvern joined the loyalist Argyll Militia—but even before Culloden the government was to strike at the parish, in one of the first of the terrible reprisals directed against the families and possessions of the men who were 'out'.

In February 1746 Cumberland sent orders through General Campbell (later to become the fourth Duke of Argyll) for the wasting of Morvern as a prime centre of disloyalty. Captain Robert Duff R.N. was sent with the naval sloops *Terror* and *Princess Anne* to carry them out. He first destroyed every boat that he could find on the coast of Morvern and Loch Sunart, and then went on to report: "On the tenth instant [March 1746] at four in the morning I landed Lieut. Lindsay with the detachment of your regiment [the Scots Fusiliers], Captain Campbell with twinty men from Mingary Castle, a lieutenant and fifty-five men from my ship with orders to burn the houses and destroy the effects of all such as were out in the rebellion. They began with Drumnin M'Clean's town, and by six o'clock at night had destroy'd the Morven coast as far as Ardtornish, except a town belonging to the McDugals,[2] and the houses of those men who appeared and declared that they had never been out, which were very few. While the men marched along the coast I covered them with

---

[1] In Scotland all land was—and theoretically still is—held feudally; there is no such thing as absolute ownership of land or freehold. By 'proprietor' is meant the landlord who was in actual possession of the land. All proprietors held their lands from a feudal 'superior' (either the Crown or an intermediary), and were liable for 'feu duties', which by this time were paid in cash rather than in service. Thus MacLean was proprietor of Drimnin, but held from Argyll to whom he paid feus; while Argyll paid feu duties on the same land to *his* superior, who was King George.

[2] This was most probably Mungasdail, of which John MacDougal of Dunollie was tacksman (Rental of Mull and Morvern 1744, *ICP*).

my ship. This service was performed without the loss of a man on our side, although they were often fired at by parties of the rebels from behind the hills." Captain John Hay R.N. added the following details five days later: "near 400 houses [were wasted] amongst which were several barns well fill'd with corn, horse, cows, meal and other provisions were distroy'd by fire and fire-arms. As we had anchor'd on that coast the evening before landing the inhabitants were suspicious of some danger, that they had removed the whole of their linnens, woolens, and cloathing from there houses. Some small parcels of these were found by our soulders while the sailors were burning all doun. Six at night all the men return'd aboard without hurt, of the enemy one kill'd one wounded."[1] The burning was on a fearful scale: "According to tradition," John MacLeod wrote in 1843, "the parish was at one time covered with wood, insomuch that, from the line of [the old] road leading along the coast, only two views of the sea could be obtained. This statement may be somewhat exaggerated, but not extravagantly. So late as the year 1746, in the memory of persons but recently removed, who, according to their own graphic description, saw the country 'as one red ember;' great quantities of timber were, in enforcing the sad policy pursued at the time, consumed by fire";[2] and to this day the difference between the scanty, regrown woods between Drimnin and Lochaline and the natural forest under the cliffs from Ardtornish to Inninmore is very noticeable.

Argyll himself (the third Duke, who was at this time a member of the Pelham administration and was ultimately responsible for the Argyll Militia) was appalled both by the inhumanity and by the folly of the reprisal. Protesting officially a week later, he wrote: "I am mightily concerned at the order relating to burning houses and committing devastion [*sic*] of that nature...for militia to burn houses and possibly in the scuffle murder women and children is what I should be very tender of. ...the nearest rebels to Argylshire are my own tennants, the Camerons of Morven, and their houses are mine. I don't find any houses have been burned by the army on the east side of Scotland. I suppose these orders have been given in heat and time may be taken so as not to be hasty in executing them; besides as the Highland war may possibly be protracted some time yet before all is over, it's dreadful to think of the consequences that would attend each side burning everything they can come near to, for at that rate in a short time the whole country may be burnt, and the well affected suffer as much and even more than the rebels."[3]

Although the Duke's protest went unheeded, the atrocities that were committed in the Great Glen after Culloden reaching even greater depths

[1] Fergusson, Sir J. (1951), 118–19, 120.   [2] MacLeod, J. (1843), 176.
[3] Fergusson, Sir J. (1951), 124.

of brutality, Morvern itself got off relatively lightly in the summer of 1746, for it was disarmed by the Argyll Militia, not by Cumberland's regulars; and, although the process cannot have been pleasant, the Campbell commanders kept their troops from wanton killing. General Campbell wrote to Cumberland on 7 June: "[I] shall leave Colonel Campbell [his son John, later fifth Duke of Argyll] with about 200 men to scour up Morvern. But as they [the people of Morvern] are bringing in their arms very fast, I think it is advisable to give them some days longer, for as I told your Royal Highness before, this country which is chiefly the Duke of Argyle's property is intirely in my power and I have a scheme of banishing all the rebellious inhabitants of Morvern so as to have a new set of people here. I propose driving [away] all the cattle before Colonel Campbell leaves the country, for tho' the people have [been] and are delivering up their arms, submitting to His Majesty's mercy, yet I have a very just pretence for so doing, towards securing the Duke of Argyle's rents."[1]

In fact the rebellious inhabitants of Morvern were not immediately banished. Many of the tacks that had been held by both large and small tenants in 1744 were renewed in 1750, and it was not until 1754 that half the Argyll leases in Morvern were reset to Campbells; and even then the Duke is likely to have been influenced more by the economic than by the political reliability of his kinsmen. Likewise the ordinary people on the Argyll properties in Morvern in 1779 bore, with few exceptions, the surnames that had been commonest in the parish before the rebellion.[2] What the Forty-five did do in Morvern was to put the Duke of Argyll in full control of his properties—in the earlier part of the century the Duke's agents had occasionally been abused and even imprisoned in Morvern,[3] but now they commanded obedience—and it is much to the credit of the eighteenth-century Dukes that they laboured to rebuild the economy of the parish, as much on account of their genuine enthusiasm for reform as for the increase of their rents.

The Dukes of Argyll were actual proprietors of two-thirds of the parish, and feudal superiors of the rest. The Argyll properties were arranged roughly round the periphery of the peninsula (Map 1). The chief farm was Ardtornish (the seat of Donald Campbell of Airds, who was the Dukes' factor for Morvern from 1732 until 1775); then came the long, fertile strip along the Sound of Mull as far as Mungasdail; then a gap at Drimnin in the north-west (though even here the Dukes owned farms in the heart of MacLean's estate); and finally the huge area from Loch Teacuis round the north end of the parish beside Loch Sunart to

[1] Fergusson, Sir J. (1951), 217.
[2] Early rental accounts, *ICP*; Cregeen, E. R. (1963), 65–70.
[3] Unpublished early eighteenth-century correspondence, *ICP*.

Liddesdale and Loch-head—the whole totalling 58,000 acres. The remaining 31,300 acres of the parish, which were farmed by other proprietors, were split up into Drimnin in the north-west, Acharn and Kinlochaline (which then included Knock, Achranich and Clounlaid) around Loch Aline and two small properties belonging to Kingairloch; none of them was directly affected by the Argyll reforms, although none can have been uninfluenced by them.

Morvern's agricultural and demographic development after the Forty-five followed a pattern that was in large things common to the whole of the West Highlands. Most of the parish consists of hilly grassland, for there are no really high mountains—no ground above 2,000 feet, indeed, apart from that forming the border with Ardgour parish—and virtually the whole area is available for grazing; in the eighteenth century Morvern was "famous for Grass", and there is moreover some fine arable land on the basalt slopes that face south-west along the Sound of Mull from Loch Aline to Drimnin.[1] Until the 1760s Morvern was cattle country. Like their neighbours, Morvern people grew oats and bere, and kept a few sheep, for their own use; but cattle were the basis of their economy, supplying both the dairy products on which, before the introduction of potatoes, they chiefly subsisted and the cash to buy supplementary meal, to pay their rent and to purchase the necessaries which they could not make for themselves such as pottery and iron-ware. It was a way of life which had been followed for generations, and it must have seemed timeless. The seeds of change, however, were already sown: they were, first, a relentless increase in the human population, and, secondly, the discovery of the possibilities of farming sheep rather than cattle in the Highlands.

In 1755 the population of Morvern was about 1,200; by 1795 it was half as many again; and in 1801, when the first official census was taken, the number was over 2,000.[2] Many reasons for the rapid increase of the West Highland population at this period have been suggested, but no one of them seems convincing with respect to Morvern: improvement in food supplies, especially after the general introduction of potatoes around the 1760s (but large-scale sheep-farming appears to have deprived the people of as much food from arable land and of cash from cattle-raising as were supplied by potatoes and kelping); improvements in medicine (but Morvern had no doctor, and inoculation was not practised there until about 1785[3]); the rise of the kelping industry with its need for a large labour force (but Morvern was never more than a minor kelping

---

[1] The best general introduction to the geography of the region is in Darling, F. F. (1955), 27–32; for the detailed geology, see Scott, J. F. (1931), and for early farming Robson, J. (1794). The note on Morvern's grass was written by a government agent in 1749–50 (Lang, A. (1898), 70).

[2] See Appendix A.   [3] MacLeod, N. (1794), 273–4.

centre); and isolation as a deterrent to emigration (but there is the difficulty of explaining the relationship between the population-increase in
Morvern and the parallel increase that was taking place throughout much
of Europe—and especially elsewhere in Britain—at the same time). The
fact is that we do not know why there was a population explosion in West
Scotland in the later eighteenth century; the chances are that there was no
single reason but a complex mixture of a number of different influences.

There can be no doubt that the increase of population alone would
have altered the agriculture and society of Morvern in the end. But before
its full effect could be felt it was discovered that certain southern breeds
of sheep would thrive on Highland pastures, and this quickly led to the
imposition of an entirely new agricultural balance on the parish. The
story has often been told. Until the mid-eighteenth century Highlanders
had kept no more than a few small, fine-fleeced sheep (similar to the
surviving Soay breed) which were wintered indoors and even taken in at
night. It was then found on the Borders that hardy, coarse-woolled
sheep such as Cheviots and black-faced Lintons could live and grow all
the year round on pastures that had hitherto been grazed in the summer
only by cattle. This discovery offered a more productive use of Highland
grazings, which were increasingly let out as large sheep farms rather than
as small cattle farms and crofts. For the indigenous population the effect
was generally unfortunate and sometimes disastrous. The sheep-farming
tacksman or proprietor wanted *all* the land for his flocks, for he found
that his sheep on the old arable fields and cattle grazings made more
money for him than the people could afford in rent, and in pursuit of
this end he either reduced their already spare means of livelihood by en-
croaching upon their holdings, or took it away altogether by evicting them.

Large-scale sheep-farming was begun in Morvern by the 1770s, but
its full effects were postponed by the unwillingness of the landlords to
engage in comprehensive evictions for some decades more, and by the
development of a new cash crop—kelp—that supported the partially
displaced smallholders during the same period. "The method of uniting
farms began long ago," wrote the minister in 1794, when the ratio of
sheep to cattle in Morvern was already six to one, "and seems to be
gaining ground in proportion to the avidity for high rents, and the rage
for sheep stocks."[1] It has been shown how Argyll tried in 1737 to replace
the old, powerful class of tacksmen with a new class of small tenants
holding directly from the proprietor. Although apparently successful at
first—and permanently successful in breaking the power of the old tacksmen—the reform failed in the end because small units of land were not
able to support proportionately higher rents than had been paid for
larger units of the same land before the changes. Argyll's Morvern

[1] MacLeod, N. (1794), 265.

7

rents had been put up to £467 just before Forbes's visitation of 1737, but in 1744 they were reduced to £449, and by 1750 they were down to £396, in which year six farms were still taken by small tenants. In 1754, however, four of these six small-tenants' farms were let to large tacksmen, and four other pairs of farms which had hitherto been let separately were now set as single units; half of the new tacksmen were Campbells and the total rents went up again to £466. These new large tenants, not now military chiefs but "entrepreneurs in a system designed to realise the commercial value of the northern lands",[1] brought a new level of efficiency to their farming and it was they who began to introduce stocks of hill sheep into Morvern by about 1775; the degree of their success is indicated by the fact that their rents were more than doubled to a total of £975 when their leases were reset in 1772–4, after only nineteen years.

Satisfactory as were the returns from the sheep-farmers, the fifth Duke of Argyll—amongst the most admirable of eighteenth-century landlords—was nevertheless concerned as a humanitarian about the future of the still-expanding population of cottars and smallholders settled on the edges of the large farms, and as a landlord about the poor return they gave him. From 1786 he made another attempt to provide for them by dividing the smaller farms once again into yet smaller units,[2] and this time the scheme was more successful because the lack of grazing on the new smallholdings was partly balanced by income from the booming kelp industry.

Kelp, an alkaline ash obtained by burning the yellow sea-weed that grows between the tide lines on the west coast, was then essential to various manufacturing processes, especially to the bleaching of linen and to the making of glass and soap. Kelp-making was hard and disagreeable work—twenty tons of wet sea-weed had to be gathered and burned to produce one ton of kelp—but as the import of *barilla* (a cheaper kelp from Spain) became at first difficult and then impossible prices rose from £2 a ton in the middle of the eighteenth century to a peak of £20 a ton in 1810, and the coastal farms became for a time extraordinarily profitable. In Morvern kelping never became the major industry that it did elsewhere on the west coast, but such cash as it did bring in was nevertheless important to the smallholders in the absence of the money that they had obtained hitherto from the sale of cattle.

So, for the moment, the deluge was averted.

[1] Cregeen, E. R. (1964), xvi.

[2] For instance, Argyll wrote to his Chamberlain in 1786: "Give notice to Drimnin that he is not to have his lease [of Auliston, Portabhata and Poll Luachrain, which he had held since 1750] renewed and let his farms be given to ten small tennents including one or two of the best of the present possessors" (Cregeen, E. R. (1964), 142). The new smallholdings, which would have averaged 179 acres each, were presumably distributed when Drimnin's lease expired in 1788, although the new tenants did not get formal leases.

PEOPLE

The collapse of feudalism and the reform of agriculture had begun to change their outlook and their ways, but the people of Morvern entered the nineteenth century at a standard of living not much different from that at which their forebears had entered the eighteenth. It is hard to grasp, however, just how different it was from that characteristic of the later nineteenth and of the twentieth centuries. We can see back easily enough through some of the changes of the last 150 years: can imagine, for instance, what this patch of ground looked like before it was planted with trees, or how that group of ruins appeared when it was a settlement[1] of thatched houses. It is extraordinarily difficult on the other hand to think of people living in this empty land in such numbers that it seemed positively overcrowded; living moreover not in picturesque rural felicity but in conditions of penury and squalor that can fairly be compared with those of a famine area in contemporary India, and that were tolerable only because they were traditional and familiar.

A distinguished and sympathetic social historian of the Highlands concluded that in the later eighteenth century "the greater part of the population of the Highlands were living under conditions that would now be considered incompatible with a civilised existence, and that they were often on the very verge of starvation".[2] The evidence left by a succession of eighteenth- and early-nineteenth-century travellers fully bears out Dr Grant's view, and we hear repeated again and again a tale of a half-naked, hungry people living in mud-floored hovels, peat-smoke blackening their faces before it drifted through a hole in the dripping roof, the sole room shared all the winter through with starving cattle; a tale of intermittent famine and endless poverty. Perhaps Adam Smith's grim comment says as much as any of them: "It is not uncommon, I have frequently been told, in the Highlands of Scotland for a mother who has borne twenty children not to have two alive."[3]

Morvern was always off the beaten track and was not visited by any of the well-known travellers, but the following description of the people's houses in Morvern in the 1820s—written though it was forty years later in nostalgic evocation of the author's youth and with the intention of showing the life of the period in the most favourable and romantic light —is worth quoting for the shock of its last sentence: "When I was

[1] The neutral word 'settlement' is used here for any small group of Highland houses and farm buildings. The Gaelic *baile*—generally translated as 'town' in the eighteenth century and as 'township' in the nineteenth—implied a certain type of communal and agricultural organisation; *clachan*, preferred by some modern writers, could mean specifically a village with a church.
[2] Grant, I. F. (1924), 123.
[3] Smith, A., *The wealth of nations* (1776), bk I, ch. viii.

young, I was sent to live among the peasantry in 'the parish,' so as to acquire a knowledge of the language; and living, as I did, very much like themselves, it was my delight to spend the long evenings in their huts, hearing their tales and songs. These huts were of the most primitive description. They were built of loose stones and clay; the walls were thick, the door low, the rooms numbered one only, or in more aristocratic cases two. The floor was clay; the peat-fire was built in the middle of the floor, and the smoke, when amiable and not bullied by a sulky wind, escaped quietly and patiently through a hole in the roof. The window was like a porthole, part of it generally filled with glass and part with peat. One bed, or sometimes two, (with clean home-made sheets, blankets, and counterpane,) a 'dresser' with bowls and plates, a large chest, and a corner full of peat, filled up the space beyond the circle about the fire. Upon the rafters above, black as ebony from peat-reek, a row of hens and chickens with a stately cock roosted in a paradise of heat."[1] There is nothing romantic about fowls' dirt on an earth floor.

The people were strung out over the parish in agricultural settlements which varied considerably in size; their usual population was probably around thirty persons of all ages, but it might be as few as ten or as many as a hundred. Families averaged just under six persons each, and the average number of persons to a house was also about six[2]—the houses of course being tiny, sometimes measuring as little as seven by eleven feet inside, and seldom more than nine by twenty-two feet. These settlements were concentrated in areas which were both fertile and relatively easy of access, which meant along the south-west coast, especially from Auliston to Ardtornish; along both sides of the through valley Loch Teacuis–Loch Arienas–Loch Aline; and up the White Glen (Map 5). In the middle of the eighteenth century some 1,200 people were grouped in about fifty settlements and a number of detached houses; by the 1830s, with the population over 2,000, a further fifty settlements had grown up (and in some cases had already been abandoned). There was no town, or even any sizeable village, until Lochaline was founded in the 1830s.

The great majority of the people were engaged in agricultural work (of which more in a moment); but there were also a number of tradesmen serving the community, not grouped in any one place but spread out amongst the settlements. In 1794, when the male population of the parish between the ages of twenty and seventy numbered about 365, there were sixty-three tradesmen (not counting millers, retailers of spirits and female weavers), all of whom were producing goods and services for home consumption, not for export. There were twenty-four weavers, fifteen tailors, four broguemakers and a shoemaker, eight cowans

---

[1] MacLeod, N. (1863), 140.   [2] For more detailed figures, see p. 123.

(workers in dry-stone), three joiners, two wheelwrights, two boat-carpenters, two blacksmiths and two coopers.[1] The three corn mills of the parish were situated beside rivers at Acharn, Mungasdail and Savary; the millers were paid in kind at the rate of one pound in thirty-two.[2] There were also twelve 'dramhouses' in 1794, the locations of which probably included Caolas ferry (one side or both), Kinlochaline, Fernish ferry (Rhemore), Glasdrum, Doirlinn ferry and Kinlochteacuis.[3] The paupers of the parish at this time numbered between forty and fifty.

Foremost among the public functionaries was the minister, Norman MacLeod (1745–1824), a Skyeman who had been presented to the parish by the Duke of Argyll in 1775. A stout presbyterian and Hanoverian loyalist—which was why Argyll chose him for the charge—MacLeod probably did more than anyone to reconcile the people of Morvern to the final collapse of their Jacobite hopes, and to lead them from episco-palianism into the established church. MacLeod lived at Fiunary Manse, rebuilt for him in a situation of great beauty which he and his family fully appreciated, and served two parish churches eight and a half miles apart on either side at Fernish and Keil. In 1777 he married the daughter of the tacksman of Achnaha and they had sixteen children of whom nine survived, the start of a dynasty of distinguished churchmen, teachers and politicians which flourishes still. To supplement his stipend of £89 the minister farmed his sixty-acre glebe, and also Fiunary farm which he rented from his patron at a low figure.[4] He was succeeded in his ministry by his youngest son, their incumbencies together lasting for more than a century.[5]

If the minister was by no means a rich man, the parish schoolmaster, with a nominal £8 a year in 1794 (even though this was slightly increased by private charity), was a very poor one. Even a labourer, with £4–£5 a year and a house, was little worse off, while a shepherd, with £7–£10 plus house, maintenance and shoes, did distinctly better; no wonder that the schoolmaster also served as postmaster. Of the five-hundred-odd children in the parish between the ages of five and fifteen, fewer than fifty attended

[1] See below, pp. 121–2.

[2] Rate of payment from *MacKichan's memoirs*, p. 236 below; he refers to a rather later period, but the rate is unlikely to have changed.

[3] P. 122 below; locations inferred from the later positions of inns (e.g. as given in *Census*, 1841).

[4] The rent MacLeod paid for Fiunary is not known for certain as he did not have a formal lease, but it was probably £15. 15s. 0d., which was what had been paid by his predecessor Alexander MacTavish.

[5] See *Fasti* (Scott, H. (1915–28), IV, 117). The figure of sixteen children is given in MacLeod, N. (1863), 27; *Fasti* names fourteen of them. Only two sons reached manhood: Norman MacLeod (1783–1862) of St Columba's, Glasgow, prominent in the famine-relief organisations of the 1830s and 1840s, and father of Norman MacLeod (1812–72) of the Barony, Glasgow; and John MacLeod (1801–82), minister of Morvern. See p. 248 below.

the parochial school in the 1790s, while attendance at the only other school, which was run by the S.P.C.K., was probably even less.[1]

On a social level with the minister were the 'gentlemen tacksmen', who might be more or less well off according chiefly to the sizes of their holdings. On Argyll's estate in late-eighteenth-century Morvern there were generally a dozen tacksmen with holdings ranging from 1,500 to 10,000 acres, the larger units being the result of uniting two or three of the old farms. Far beneath these men in income (though not necessarily in social pretensions) were five groups of small tenants, also tacksmen, but holding no more than a fraction—from a half down to a sixteenth— of a farm that could measure as much as 2,000 or as little as 500 acres. These small tenants were resident on their holdings, but the larger men might employ a manager to run their farms for them while they lived somewhere else; in 1779, three of the largest of Argyll's Morvern tacksmen were non-resident.[2]

The houses in which the tacksmen lived varied enormously in size and comfort. Gregorson of Ardtornish lived in a substantial slated 'mansion house', probably a good deal better than the average proprietor's house (Plate 12), but the small tenants lived in houses that were scarcely better than those of the peasants, consisting often of 'a but and a ben'— a thatched, dry-stone cottage with a room at each end, a closet in the middle and bed-space on the roof-joists.[3] Even the houses of resident proprietors might have a remarkably rustic appearance. Acharn, where the Camerons of Glendessary lived from 1703 to 1775, was constructed of wicker-work between oak beams, completely covered with heather and turf outside and lined with wood within, the interior being "divided into several apartments, and finished in a style of taste and elegance corresponding with the enlightened refinement of the occupants".[4]

By 1800, however, there was probably not a single proprietor regularly resident in the parish. The MacLeans were gone from Drimnin and Kinlochaline after four centuries of ownership, and Argyll had never been more than an infrequent visitor. It is improbable that MacLachlan of Callart ever lived at Kinlochaline, MacLean of Inverscaddle at Acharn, or MacDonald of Glenaladale at Drimnin. Even MacDonald of Borrodale, who bought Achranich in 1800 and was certainly living there in 1824, is unlikely to have been resident so early. It will be observed, though, that all these proprietors were Highlanders of the landowning class, and included as yet no Lowland sheep-farmers or other foreigners.

The relationship between landlord and tenant was generally less personal than it had been: now it was the laird's agent who was in direct

[1] MacLeod, N. (1794), 271–3, 266–7 and n.
[2] *Book of Mull and Morvern tacks*, vols. '0', '4', *ICP*; Cregeen, E. R. (1963), 65–70.
[3] MacLeod, N. (1863), 177–80.
[4] MacLeod, J. (1843), 177; MacLeod, N. (1863), 177–8.

contact with the people, not the laird himself or the laird speaking through a tacksman of the same name as himself. While this arrangement was obviously liable to abuse—it enabled either the landlord or his agent to blame the other for any harsh or illiberal act—an able and humane agent such as James Maxwell, Argyll's Chamberlain for Mull and Morvern from 1787 until 1829, could successfully combine the service of his master with an amelioration of the tenants' lot.[1]

AGRICULTURE

Details of agriculture in Morvern at the turn of the century are hard to establish with certainty owing to the incompleteness of the surviving records, but there appear to have been two main types of farm in the parish at this time. One type was the co-operative farm of·small tenants holding directly from the landlord, with a mixed economy of arable and stock-raising, the stock being still mainly cattle but with an increasing proportion of sheep. This arrangement was especially characteristic of the Argyll estates where it resulted directly from the Dukes' agrarian reforms, although it may also have occurred elsewhere. The other main type of farm was the large stock-farm operated directly by the proprietor or his agent, or by a single tacksman, on which the peasantry still raised crops around the old settlement but were no longer able to keep more than a small number of beasts because of the loss of the hill grazings. Much the greatest part of Morvern was incorporated in farms of the second type by 1800, as indeed it had been since the 'seventies; most of them were sheep farms, although there was at least one large cattle farm (Rahoy). Both types were derived from the old feudally-organised, communal Highland farm, on which runrig agriculture and cattle-raising with transhumance were practised under a proprietor or tacksman who might have been a considerable military chieftain or a tenant who was no more than *primus inter pares*.

(It may be helpful to explain what 'runrig' and 'transhumance' mean here. *Runrig* involved the division of the arable land into strips which were allotted to those who were entitled to them and were redistributed at regular intervals, often every year. These strips were in two groups, the 'infield' and the 'outfield'. The infield, adjacent to the settlement, received all the available fertiliser and was kept in permanent cultivation, a crop of barley generally following two of oats, and so on with no fallow year. The outfield, poorer land which might be half a mile or more from the settlement, was not fertilised but was cropped by sections every year until the soil was exhausted, and the sections were then abandoned in turn for several years to allow natural

---

[1] See, for instance, Cregeen, E. R. (1964), 186 ff.

regeneration—the most primitive of all arable systems and much less effective than the technically remarkable feat of getting cereal crops from the infield every year without interruption. *Transhumance*, the seasonal removal of livestock to fresh pastures, is also an ancient device but, unlike agriculture by soil-exhaustion, is one specially well-suited to marginal hill country. The mountain pastures were not allotted to individuals but were grazed indiscriminately by everyone's cattle. Part of the community—women, children and old people—moved with the cattle in the early summer to the 'shielings' (favoured grazings, usually high up the glens) where they lived in small circular huts until it was time to return home in the autumn; the men meanwhile having remained at the settlement, cutting peats, working the land and repairing the houses.)

The farms of this period about which most is known are those which belonged to Argyll. In 1779 the fifth Duke made a census of the inhabitants of his estates, and the information which he gathered in Morvern, combined with figures for the areas and rentals of his farms at the same date (also deriving from the Argyll estate papers), gives us the best available picture of Morvern's agriculture in the later eighteenth century. It is summarised in Table 1.

Argyll's five small-tenants' farms were as a group the smallest in area (averaging 1,600 acres, or 285 acres per tenant) and the most densely populated (average 27·3 persons per square mile); their productivity per acre, to which the figures for 'rent as pence per acre' may be used as a rough guide, was relatively high at an average of 6·2, while their productivity per inhabitant (this time using 'rent as pence per inhabitant ÷100' as an index) was correspondingly low, averaging 1·4. It must be supposed that runrig agriculture and cattle-farming with transhumance was the normal practice on the small-tenants' farms until about 1820, when those that were not brought to an end by the Argyll and other sales of the period became 'club farms'[1] with increased emphasis on stock raising. They probably offered a pleasing way of life—at least such farms were intimately associated with an extremely vigorous culture—but the returns were meagre. "The small farmers", one observer wrote in 1813, "for nine or ten months of the year, make generally two, and sometimes three meals a day of potatoes, with herrings and milk. Such as can afford it salt a cow in winter, and kill a sheep or two in harvest. Oatmeal pottage, or oatmeal jelly (*sowens*), make commonly the third meal a day, with milk; and oaten or bear bread, when the potatoes fail, supply their place."[2] Argyll, who continued to believe that small indivual farms could offer a better living than overpopulated co-operatives, tried once more to introduce them in 1801, but again without much success. His existing small tenants were encouraged to divide their farms

---

[1] Club farms are described below, pp. 51–2.   [2] Smith, J. (1813), 61.

Table 1. Argyll's Ardtornish farms in 1779

Name of farm or group	Acres	No. of tenants	Tacksman resident or not	Population	Persons p.sq.m.	Rent	Rent as pence per acre	Rent as pence per inhabitant (÷100)
							Productivity	
I. SMALL-TENANTS' FARMS								
Auliston (Portabhata)	1,543	10	—	74	30.6	£51. 10s.	8.0	1.7
Fernish	2,336	5	—	88	24.1	£61. 1s.	6.3	1.7
Keil	550	2	—	51	59.4	£17	7.4	0.8
Savary	2,068	6	—	83	25.7	£49	5.7	1.4
Unimore	c. 1,500	5	—	45	c. 19.0	£26. 10s.	c. 4.2	1.4
II. TACKSMEN'S FARMS								
A. More than 10 persons per square mile								
Barr	4,224	—	R	72	10.9	£80	4.5	2.7
Fiunary	1,434	—	R	28	12.5	—	—	—
Killundine	1,741	—	R	43	15.8	£38	5.2	2.1
Lagan (Salachan)	2,681	—	R	73	17.4	£93	8.3	3.1
Mungasdail	1,459	—	R	85	37.2	£60	9.9	1.7
Rahoy (Ardantiobairt) (Beinniadain)	3,059	—	R	55	11.5	£70	5.5	3.1
B. Less than 10 persons per square mile								
Ardtornish (Eignaig) (Tearnait)	9,965	—	R	67	4.3	£105	2.6	3.8
Glencripesdale (Beach)	7,834	—	NR	33	2.7	£90	2.8	6.5
Kinlochteacuis	2,899	—	NR	26	5.7	£53. 5s.	4.4	4.9
Laudale (Camas Salach) (Lurga)	7,284	—	NR	34	3.0	£80	2.6	5.7
Liddesdale (Achagavel)	7,508	—	R	85	7.2	£120	3.8	3.4

Notes: The Auliston group was in tack to Drimnin, who subset it. Rent of Savary mill not included. See p. 155 concerning area of Unimore.

Notes: Fiunary was in tack to the minister at an artificially low rent. Rent of Mungasdail mill not included.

Sources: Areas: see Appendix B.   Population: Cregeen, E. R. (1963), 65–70.   Rents: Book of Mull and Morvern tacks, vol. 3, ICP.

15

into separate lots which were to be let to them on nine-year leases provided that each tenant built himself an adequate dwelling-house on his lot and had the whole enclosed. This would have been a radical reform indeed, but the Duke's Chamberlain reported in 1802 (and did not amend the report later) that it had not been carried out at Unimore, Savary, Keil or Knock, and there is no evidence on the ground that any of the Duke's small-tenants' farms in Morvern were in fact reformed in this way.[1]

Argyll's tacksmen's farms of 1779 may be considered in two groups, arranged according to the density of their population. The farms in the more densely-populated group (15·6 persons per square mile) were of moderate size, averaging 2,430 acres, and may not yet have gone far towards conversion into thorough-going sheep farms. One farm of the group, Rahoy, was certainly devoted to cattle until after the end of the century (it contained 475 acres of Argyll's carefully-preserved woods),[2] while another, Mungasdail, had a population-density which suggests co-operative agriculture. Nevertheless the rentals indicate that even the densely-populated tacksmen's farms were more efficient than those held by small tenants; using the same indices as before, their productivity per acre at an average of 5·6 was scarcely less than that of the small-tenants' holdings, but their productivity per inhabitant, averaging 2·3, was up by sixty-five per cent. Most of the farms in this group had gone entirely over to sheep by 1794, when the minister reported that seventeen of the thirty-two farms in the parish were in the hands of gentlemen-tacksmen, for the most part stocked with sheep, and that five others were in the hands of shepherds.[3]

The second group of tacksmen's farms, those that were less densely populated, were plainly different, even in 1779. With an average of only 4·4 persons per square mile, they were much larger—averaging 7,100 acres—and it is likely that it was these farms (three of the five with non-resident tacksmen) that were first turned into great sheep ranches. The 'productivity index' derived from the rentals is especially suggestive in this connection: while the productivity per acre of the farms in the group, at an average of 3·0, was only half that of the other farms in Argyll's Morvern properties, their productivity per inhabitant averaged 4·4, which was double that of the more densely-populated tacksmen's farms, and three times that of the small-tenants' farms. Argyll's rents were raised during the early 1770s, and it seems likely that sheep stocks were introduced on the larger tacksmen's farms at about the same time; a document at Inveraray indicates that Glencripesdale, Kinlochteacuis,

---

[1] Cregeen, E. R. (1964), 144–5, 196–9.
[2] Details of the Rahoy stock in 1807 are given below, pp. 125–6.
[3] MacLeod, N. (1794), 266, 270.

Laudale and Liddesdale were still primarily cattle farms in 1770,[1] and it is known that Angus Gregorson turned Tearnait wholly over to sheep when he took the tack of Ardtornish in 1773.[2]

The tacksmen's sheep farms—which were the dominant form by the 'nineties—were not at first sight very different from the small-tenants' farms: they had the same sort of settlements with patches of infield beside them worked by members of the townships in the traditional way, sometimes with the nearer outfield in cultivation as well. But here the similarity ended. The hills were entirely given over to the farmer's sheep with the result that the workmen's and cottars' cattle, no longer allo,ved to graze the shielings, were confined for the whole year to the grass immediately around the settlements and so had to be drastically reduced in numbers. It was estimated in 1807 that the tacksman of Laudale should be able to farm 2,200 sheep and 25 breeding cows; this indicated a density of three hundred sheep per 1,000 acres, a heavy stock for Laudale's north-facing slopes even without the cattle, and it can have left no room at all for township beasts.[3] The people were thus more completely the dependants of one man, and none of them but the shepherds and labourers he needed to run his farm could feel much security in their patches of arable and cows' grass. There were indeed removals in Morvern at this time—on the Argyll estate in about 1803, for instance, when some people were removed to Barr "to make room for sheep"[4]—although there were no wholesale evictions.

An excellent map of Achranich Estate made for the proprietor by Alexander Langlands in 1815 gives further details of land usage on a Morvern estate of the early nineteenth century.[5] Achranich was never Argyll property and therefore does not figure in the records at Inveraray, but Langlands gave so much detail that it is possible to deduce something of the recent development of the estate from the plan alone. Originally part of Kinlochaline Estate, and traditionally MacLean territory, Achranich had passed to MacDonald of Borrodale in 1800, in whose family it remained until 1838. Whether the proprietor himself was resident when the plan was made is unclear—the old farm-house which Octavius Smith occupied in the middle of the century does not appear to be marked—but he was certainly living there by 1824.[6] The estate comprised four old farms: Achranich with Srath Shuardail (3,027 acres),

---

[1] 'Contents of different farms in Mull and Morvern', 1770, *ICP*. Glencripesdale and Kinlochteacuis had 100 cows and 100 sheep each; Laudale, 160 cows and 200 sheep; Liddesdale, 151 cows and 130 sheep. These would have been total, not breeding, stocks; Rahoy (which was to have 35 breeding cows plus followers in 1807) had 160 each of cows and sheep in 1770.

[2] Cregeen, E. R. (1964), xix.   [3] See p. 126.

[4] *Napier Commission evidence* (1884), III, 2294.

[5] *Achranich plan 1815.*   [6] MacCulloch, J. (1824), II, 174.

Claggan (1,490 acres), Dubh Dhoire with Clais Bhreac (1,580 acres) and Uileann (2,706 acres), a total area of 8,803 acres. It was not particularly good land—its sheep-carrying capacity in the 1850s was only 233 sheep per 1,000 acres—but there are no high hills on it and it was all available for grazing. None of the settlements marked on the plan appear to have been very large. The most considerable of them were at Achranich (about eight houses), Claggan (five houses) and Uileann (nine houses); and there were also groups of two or three houses at Dubh Dhoire, Samhnach and Srath Shuardail. All these settlements have infield strips marked around them, but two other small groups of houses in the middle of the estate (Torr a'Chall and Clais Bhreac) have their strips marked as outfield only, indicating that they were no longer inhabited. The total number of buildings suggests that the population of the estate was between 125 and 150, giving a density of nine to eleven persons per square mile; taking the intervening population-increase into account, this is the equivalent of a density of seven to nine persons per square mile in 1779 (cf. Table 1). The proportion of arable land to pasture over the whole estate was small (it was four per cent of the total, again close to the equivalent figure for the large tacksmen's farms of the Argyll estate), and its distribution was uneven: three-quarters of the arable land was concentrated on only two of the four 'farms' (Achranich and Claggan), and more than half of all the outfield was situated on only one of these two, Achranich, the home farm. Shielings—referred to significantly as "Old Sheillins"—are marked at six points across the middle of the estate, but there is no indication of shielings still in use; there were, however, two large sheep-folds, one to the south of Uileann settlement and the other at Achranich. What the Achranich plan of 1815 shows us, then, is a centralised pro-prietor's farm, with the interior cleared for sheep but with a consider-able population still working arable strips at a number of peripheral settlements.

OTHER INDUSTRIES

The kelp industry, though never the major factor in Morvern's economy, was growing in importance by 1800, with kelp prices started on their climb to the spectacular but delusive peak of 1810. In 1796–7 the Duke of Argyll had wanted to take over the control of Morvern's kelp manu-facture from his tenants, after the fashion of some of his fellow landlords; but his Chamberlain, James Maxwell, persuaded him that it would be in the general interest to leave production and marketing in the people's hands, letting the shores to them on three-year leases separately from the land, at rents based on a fair estimate of their individual productivity. The most valuable kelp shores (to judge from contemporary squabbles over their ownership and from the amount of sea-ware on the beaches today) were probably Savary and Salachan bays and the Fiunary shore between them, and most of the coast from the Killundine river north-westwards to Auliston Point; but even the shores of Rahoy and Laudale, apparently poorer in the right sort of sea-weed, were thought capable of producing twelve and ten tons of kelp respectively in 1807. Although Morvern kelp was noted for its high alkali content, only about seventy tons were produced annually in the early 1790s, 0·04 tons per head of the population; in an area of intensive kelping, such as the Uists, production per head was nine times this figure during the same period.[1]

Although many of the small boats in the parish were used for fishing, the whole catch was consumed at home, no fish being exported. Fishing as a casual by-employment was characteristic of the whole west coast from Kintyre to Skye at this time; "a casual technique, an erratic catch and a commercial stagnation left agriculture here wholly predominant."[2] Loch Sunart occasionally enjoyed large runs of herring, but lack of salt—and probably also of organisation—prevented their exploitation. Fish were also caught on the coast in tidal fish-traps (there are the remains of five such traps along the shore from Inninmore to Oronsay Island) and by river trap: there was a salmon-fishing station with a corf house at the mouth of the only good salmon river, the Aline, where the fishing was let to a tacksman.[3]

In the context of the general timber shortage of the West Highlands, Morvern was well wooded. There were particularly fine stands of trees along the coast at Ardtornish, from Rahoy to Camas Salach, and at Liddesdale; these all belonged to Argyll, who took good care to preserve them, enclosing the most promising of them against the depredations of sheep in 1786–8. 'Wood leave' for his tenants was strictly limited so that the timber could be sold to the Lorne Furnace Company for fuel, oak bark to the tanners and hoops to the coopers.[4]

Mining for minerals had been attempted earlier in the eighteenth century at Lurga (where lead mines were operated in association with the Strontian mines in the 1730s by the Morvern Mining Company) and near Loch Tearnait (where copper mines had been worked around 1750), but both these enterprises had failed and been abandoned after only a few years; the Lurga mine was re-opened in 1803, but again without lasting success. Similarly, small outcrops of coal near the head of Loch

[1] MacLeod, N. (1794), 266; Cregeen, E. R. (1964), 185–94, 145, 182–3.
[2] Gray, M. (1957), 120.
[3] MacLeod, N. (1794), 268–9; *Sellar's plan (fishings) 1848*. See also pp. 180, 240 below.
[4] MacLeod, N. (1794), 267–8; MacLeod, J. (1843), 176–7; Cregeen, E. R. (1964), 120, 123–35, 165, 178–80.

Aline had been worked opencast during the eighteenth century, but the seams were small and soon exhausted, and scarcely more success attended an attempt to mine coal underground at Inninmore, probably around the turn of the century.[1] Quarrying did better; there are splendid exposed sections of limestone and sandstone around Loch Aline, from which stone was cut and exported from early times until about 1830.

COMMUNICATIONS

Poor communications result inevitably from a deeply-indented coastline and a mountainous hinterland, and Morvern with the rest of the West Highlands has always suffered from the lack of direct routes from place to place. The isolation of the parish relative to that of its neighbours, however, has steadily increased. In the feudal period, when virtually all traffic went by water, Morvern's command of the Sound of Mull gave it some local importance (Ardtornish Castle was at one time a major stronghold of the Lord of the Isles), but since the mid-eighteenth century, when the building of the Highland military roads got under way, Morvern has slipped more and more into the background. The nearest approach of a military road was to the far side of Loch Linnhe at the Corran narrows, in about 1750; then, half a century later, a 'Parliamentary road' was built from the near side of the Corran Ferry to Kinlochmoidart, coming within a mile of the parish boundary at the head of Loch Sunart (1804–14[2]). But neither in 1800 nor for half a century more were there any true roads either into Morvern or within it; there was nothing but a few miles of 'statute labour road', useless from lack of repair, a ring of pony tracks and footpaths, and a relatively unimportant drove road (Map 7).

The only official provision for road-making in 1800 was the system of 'statute labour', whereby tenants and cottars were required by an Act of 1669 to labour on public roads for a certain number of days each year, and to provide a horse and cart for the purpose. But by this time the Act was widely disregarded; at best the work was commuted for a disproportionately small money payment, and in Morvern the eleven-mile statute-labour road that ran from Mungasdail along the Sound of Mull and up to the head of Loch Aline was so broken and badly kept that it could be described only as "for the most part rideable"; it was quite impassable to wheeled traffic, only three of the ten large streams that it crossed being bridged. The seven-foot carriageway was reinforced with

---

[1] Further details of the early mines are given on pp. 170–1 below.
[2] *Highland roads and bridges reports*, 7th report (1815), 6. The Moidart road is the modern A 861–B 850.

stones thrown down in the boggy patches, but the road was not otherwise surfaced and it was not graded.[1]

Conscious of the disadvantages of being unable to use wheeled vehicles in the parish, the proprietors of Morvern and Kingairloch petitioned the Commissioners for making Highland roads and bridges in 1810 for a new road linking the Moidart road (then under construction) to the Sound of Mull, expressing their willingness to pay half the cost as required by the Act of 1803. In the summer of 1811 Hamilton Fulton surveyed a line for this road from Inversanda to Kingairloch, and thence via Torr na Caber (where the roads from Loch Sunart and Kingairloch now join up), the White Glen and Knock to Drimnin, a distance of just over thirty-five miles. The Morvern proprietors, who had been thinking of a much shorter line from the head of Loch Sunart to Knock, were taken aback by the estimated cost of Fulton's road—more than £10,000 —and declined to pay their half share, the more readily perhaps because they were non-resident and so were not much inconvenienced personally by the lack of roads. The Commissioners therefore abandoned the project when the time limit ran out on 19 March 1813.[2]

Thus most of the internal traffic of the parish continued to use the old footpaths and tracks. The best of the tracks were about five feet wide, and could accommodate pack ponies and pony sledges. They occasionally had supporting walls at steep places, but generally they avoided obstacles by going round them, following the contours where they could and fording the streams. A track of this sort was specially made by the Morvern Mining Company from Lurga to Liddesdale in the 1730s,[3] but most tracks appear to have followed traditional routes: the ring from Bonnavoulin round the north coast to the head of Loch Sunart, and the White Glen track, both shown on the early-nineteenth-century maps. There were linking footpaths from Fernish to Barr, and from Achranich to Eignaig and Glensanda (where a track came down from Kingairloch), parts of which can still be traced on the ground. Oldest of all, perhaps, and still easily visible where they have not been obliterated by forestry plantation, were the tracks leading up to the shielings overlooking the Sound of Mull, worn in places to deep hollow-ways by the annual passage to and fro of the township cattle.[4]

Most of the cattle going to market from Mull, Coll and Tiree reached the mainland via Grass Point, Mull, and Kerrera (near Oban), but a

---

[1] The length of the statute-labour road, 11 miles 118 yards, suggests that it ran from Killintag church to M.R. 688473, where there was a junction with a track to Agh Choire and another down to the Tree-root Ford by Kinlochaline Castle (*Statute Labour Trusts (Scotland): abstract of returns, 3 July 1848*).
[2] *Highland roads and bridges reports*, 5th report (1811), 6, 31; 6th report (1813), 7, 43.
[3] Murray, Sir A. (1740), 'A plan of Loch Sunart, &ct.'.
[4] See p. 172 below, for a note of early tracks which are still traceable.

few were ferried across from Fishnish to Knock in Morvern, to be driven through the parish to a main drove route that ran from Ardnamurchan through Glen Tarbert to Corran. The exact line of the Morvern drove road—which was not of course a made road, and was probably no more than a barely-perceptible track—is not known, but it presumably followed the White Glen track as far as Achagavel, and may then have branched north-eastwards towards the head of Loch Sunart.[1] It was never a major drove route, however, and some of the Morvern cattle were actually ferried the other way from Knock to Fishnish in Mull to reach the mainland via the Firth of Lorne.[2]

In the absence of more than rudimentary communications by land, boats had a particular importance in the economy and society of the parish. In 1794 there were "no fewer than 100 small boats...kept for the purpose of fishing, and carrying seaware as manure to their lands &c.; as also 12 or 14 barges of a larger size, well rigged, the property of the gentlemen tacksmen, for transporting themselves occasionally to the neighbouring islands, and for other purposes of usefulness and convenience".[3] All these boats, however, were essentially local craft, and there was no service by larger ships that might have made up for the lack of a link by road with the east and south. "Though a vessel, called a packet, runs at times between the Clyde and the Sound of Mull," the minister continued in 1794, "it has only been set agoing and continued by private adventurers for their own interest, and is subject to no rules calculated for the public good; no dependance can be had either on the time of its sailing, or the rate of freight."[4] There were at this time only two regular ferries to other districts, one from Fernish at Rhemore across the narrowest part of the Sound to Mull, and the other from Doirlinn to Glen Borrodale, Ardnamurchan; surprisingly there was not yet a regular ferry to Mull from the mouth of Loch Aline.

The mail came only once a week, the parochial schoolmaster eking out his miserable salary by acting as postmaster. Its precise route at this date is uncertain, but it was probably (as in the 1840s) "through two islands and over three ferries", that is, via Oban, Kerrera and Mull. "It contained only a few letters for the sheriff or the minister, and half-a-dozen to be delivered as opportunity offered to outlying districts in the parish...'Post haste' was unknown in those parts: the 'poste restante' being much more common."[5]

---

[1] This route is shown as an alternative to the Achagavel–Liddesdale–Loch-head track on *Argyll farms plan 1819*, and as the only track in *Thomson's atlas 1824*; air photographs show no trace of it on the ground, and it is hard to see what it can have been but the drove road, since there was a relatively good road from Achagavel to Lochhead via Liddesdale for ordinary traffic.

[2] Haldane, A. R. B. (1952), 86–7.   [3] MacLeod, N. (1794), 269.

[4] MacLeod, N. (1794), 276.

[5] MacLeod, J. (1843), 189; MacLeod, N. (1864), 282–3.

2

THE IMPACT OF EFFICIENCY
1800–1850

PEOPLE REMOVED, LAND IMPROVED

THE END OF THE OLD ORDER

At the end of the eighteenth century the chief proprietor in Morvern had owned land there for 125 years; there had been MacLeans in uninterrupted possession of their territories for more than twice as long; and no Lowland Scot or other *sasunnach* held an acre of land in the parish. Yet in the twenty-five years from 1813 to 1838 every single property in Morvern changed hands, and by 1844 there was scarcely a proprietor left who had any traditional or lengthy association with the parish, or (in most cases) with anywhere else in the Highlands either. Only the minister—now John MacLeod, who had succeeded his father in 1824— stayed on as a link with the old order, increasingly saddened as its last traces disappeared.

John, the enthusiastic, reforming fifth Duke of Argyll, died in 1806, and was succeeded by his infamous son George. The sixth Duke was a dandy, a rake and a spendthrift familiar of the Prince of Wales, whose only interest in his inheritance was to discover how much money could be squeezed from it to feed his pleasures and pay his debts. Rent alone proving insufficient, he soon proceeded to borrow upon the security of his lands; but even that was not enough and he was obliged to sell a considerable part of his inheritance (including all the Morvern property), which was put under trust for the purpose; altogether he is thought to have reduced the Argyll fortune by something like two million pounds.[1] How the ghosts of the seventeenth-century MacLeans of Duart must have laughed.

Duke George's memory is not revered. "It is the duty of every man who occupies such estates" (wrote his nephew, the eighth Duke, deploring Duke George's depredations) "to manage them for the best, not only for his own, but for the lives that are to come."[2] Perhaps the eighth Duke was thinking chiefly of the damage done to the family's fortunes, but the damage done to the people of Morvern was, in a different way,

---

[1] See Harriette Wilson, *Memoirs* (1825), for an account of where some of the money went.
[2] Campbell, G. D. (1906), I, 24, 28.

equally striking. The deluge could scarcely have been avoided altogether, but if Duke George had inherited his father's character as well as his lands its effects would certainly have been softened. As it was the Duke's trustees put all the Morvern farms on the market at the same time, in 1819, when they were offered as five separate lots: Ardtornish; Savary–Killundine; Fernish (Glenmorvern); Rahoy–Glencripesdale; and Liddesdale–Laudale. All were sold—though not all in these divisions—within six years.

Meanwhile similar troubles, the less spectacular but equally intractable effect of trying to make a Highland gentleman's income support a Lowland gentleman's expenditure, had been afflicting the MacLeans of Morvern. Even before the death of Allan MacLean of Drimnin in 1792 the Register of Sasines tells a complicated story of borrowing and re-borrowing, with debts shifted from one creditor to another and the Mac-Lean properties of Drimnin and Kinlochaline pledged as security. Allan's son Charles, who inherited the estate, was "a careless, imprudent and extravagant man"[1] who, far from putting the property to rights, sold it in bankruptcy in 1797–8. With the departure of the last of the old MacLean proprietors from Morvern, an era came to an end; there had been MacLeans at Drimnin since 1528, and around Loch Aline since 1390.

Another era came to an end in 1822 when the paddle-steamer *Highlander* arrived at Tobermory to begin a regular passenger and freight service between Glasgow and the Sound of Mull, with Loch Aline as a port of call.[2] She was only a little ship, built of wood and seventy-eight feet long—half the length and a quarter of the tonnage of the *Lochinvar*, the small motor-vessel that worked in the Sound during the first half of the present century—but the regularity of service which steam could provide and sail could not revolutionised the communications of the district. Previously, if there was a calm, travellers had had to be rowed the fifteen miles from Oban to Loch Aline; if there was a gale they had not been able to travel at all. Now the old isolation was gone for ever: information, supplies and above all people could be sure of getting to and from Morvern at predictable times. Compared with neighbouring districts Morvern remained hard to get at, but the way was nevertheless opened by the steamers for southern landowners and southern visitors to explore and colonise a country that had hitherto been beyond their reach.

[1] Sinclair, A. M. (1899), 440.
[2] The first steamer to visit the district passed through the Sound of Mull in 1818, when some of the old inhabitants of Morvern expressed "great surprise, that, during a long residence on the sea-coast, they had never seen another vessel of the same wonderful construction" (MacLeod, J. (1843), 189, who wrongly gives the date of the beginning of the *Highlander*'s service as 1821. See Duckworth, C. L. D. and Langmuir, G. E. (1950), *passim*).

Coincident with the changes of ownership there occurred a series of evictions of the inhabitants of Morvern which, in common with similar happenings all over the Highlands, caused suffering at the time, became a matter of general controversy soon after the middle of the nineteenth century, and have been widely condemned for their cruelty ever since. As we have seen, clearances began in Morvern not long after the middle of the eighteenth century when many small farms were united to make a few larger ones, the peasants being obliged to huddle together on the peripheries of the new properties or to leave the parish altogether and go to seek a livelihood elsewhere. "There has, indeed, " the minister wrote in 1794, "no emigration to America taken place from this parish as yet, but a yearly drain to the low country for service, &c. owing to the union of farms, and the general poverty of the country, where there are no manufactures to employ, and little produce to support the inhabitants."[1] It was a movement parallel to the enclosures of open farm-land that took place simultaneously in England, but, whereas the English small-holders had to be dispossessed by Act of Parliament and were ensured of at least some compensation, small tenants and cottars in the Highlands had no legal title to their land and could be deprived of it at will without compensation or redress. The number of evictions increased rapidly after the Argyll sales of 1819–25 and, until the last clearance of 1868, hundreds of Morvern people suffered unhappiness and distress as a result. To be expelled suddenly from a dearly-loved home with the alternatives of either starving in an overcrowded slum-village nearby or of leaving to seek work in a strange place with no knowledge of its language or its ways was the atrocious plight of these ordinary people who had done nothing to deserve it, and the thought of their misery can still move us deeply.

Nevertheless we must reject an emotional approach if the clearances are to be understood. This is difficult because they have attracted popular historians who have been interested chiefly in the propagandist or sensational aspects of the subject; and perhaps because few of us, in our guilt-obsessed century, can look back on the evictions without some feeling of responsibility for them, however mistaken, and a consequent urge to atone for it by coming out on the side of those who suffered. Therefore we must remind ourselves that the Highland clearances were the symptom of the inability of the old Highland economy to adapt to a changing world, and of the breakdown of the old Highland way of life, not their cause. The proprietors who cleared their farms for sheep were acting under severe economic pressure, and the fact that they did not suffer as the people did does not in itself make their actions wrong.

The economic recession which followed the end of the Napoleonic

---

[1] MacLeod, N. (1794), 266.

War led to a period of deflation in the West Highlands lasting approximately from 1815 to 1850. Kelp prices began to drop almost immediately and then, when protection was withdrawn in 1825, slumped to a level which brought kelp-manufacture to an end by 1830. At the same time cattle prices fell steeply, with results for many small tenants that were extremely serious, because it meant that they had to make up for poor returns from cattle by selling yet more cattle, thus depleting their primary capital resource. The larger sheep-farmers were doubly affected, first by falls of as much as a half in the prices of sheep and wool, and then by the inability of their remaining small tenants to pay their rent for lack of the cash previously earned by cattle raising and kelping.

It soon became clear that, if a proprietor could not afford to subsidise his small tenants, he could not afford to have them on his land at all. Even if he evicted them and so increased the efficiency of his sheep farm, he might still be hard put to it to break even; many farmers failed, as will be seen in Morvern. But, although it was a situation in which the rich and the ruthless had the best chances of survival, it would be mistaken to put the blame for the resulting clearances simply upon greedy or malign landlords, for they were really the result of impersonal forces beyond the control of either landlords or tenants, of "the total impact of the powerful individualism and economic rationalism of industrial civilisation on the weaker, semi-communal traditionalism of the recalcitrant fringe".[1]

Three basic points must be grasped. First, the west-coast climate—and especially its excessive rainfall—ensured that the land would not support even the eighteenth-century level of population at a nineteenth-century standard of living, let alone a population that continued to grow, so that the continuance after about 1820 of a substantial smallholding population at an acceptable standard of living was a plain impossibility; emigration on a large scale had to take place whatever the proprietors did. Secondly, the Morvern landowners cannot be blamed more than the owners of any other sort of property for objecting to losing money on it, or indeed for wanting a reasonable return from their investments, and sheep gave a better return than smallholders; as they saw it, clearance for sheep 'improved' their land and might well be the only means of avoiding bankruptcy. Finally, many responsible people at the time (to whom the first two points were obvious) honestly concluded that all the Highlanders would be better off if most of them were to emigrate without delay; and therefore that, since the Highlanders did not always see for themselves that this would result in the greatest happiness of the greatest number and emigrate voluntarily, it was necessary and proper to force them to go. The people who thought this may well have been right; at any

[1] Gray, M. (1957), 246.

rate, the facts that we in the twentieth century do not evict unprofitable crofters but subsidise them out of public funds, and that we are acutely conscious of the subjective difference to a displaced person between forced and voluntary emigration, are irrelevant to a judgment of what the Highland landlords did in the very different conditions of a century and more ago.

This is not to pretend that evictions were not too often carried out with a culpable disregard of people's feelings. Where a little sympathy, a little help and consideration might have gone some way towards easing the pain of those who had to leave their homes, the behaviour of a stupid or callous factor, arrogantly insisting on his employer's legal rights, would frequently have quite the opposite effect. Indeed, what could cause even more bitterness than the clearance itself was how it was done and by whom. If a tenant's holding did not return enough to pay the rent and he had to quit, he might accept the situation with some fortitude. Likewise, if an old-style Highland proprietor moved him across the estate to make room for sheep, he would grumble, but Highland proprietors had always treated their people like this, they understood one another, and again the situation might be accepted. But if a foreigner bought the land and promptly ordered him, through an underling, to leave the place that had been his family's home for generations, he was deeply unhappy and resentful.

So it went in Morvern. During the whole of the nineteenth century something like 3,250 people emigrated from the parish, but no more than about 750 people are actually known to have been evicted from their homes during the same period, and by no means all of those who were evicted left the parish;[1] the great majority of those who emigrated went simply because they could no longer make a living at home. Again, some of the evictions of the 1840s and 1850s were carried out by a proprietor of Highland origin, John Sinclair of Lochaline, and they do not appear to have caused much resentment. But the clearances ordered in the period 1824–68 by Miss Stewart, the Gordons, Patrick Sellar and Mrs Paterson (all of them foreigners) focussed the people's misery; they were remembered for decades in all their bitter detail, becoming the symbols of the frustration of folk who—for other reasons—had lost contact with their past.[2]

[1] For details see Appendix A, pp. 123, 128–9.
[2] Some unrecorded evictions are likely to have taken place in Morvern, probably on a fairly small scale, before 1824. It is most improbable that many evictions took place after 1868, even of individual families; see below, pp. 111–12.

THE NEW PROPRIETORS

See p. vii

The Gregorsons of Ardtornish

The tack of Ardtornish, which included the old farms of Tearnait and Eignaig (almost 10,000 acres in all), was taken in 1754 by Donald Campbell of Airds, who was Argyll's factor for Morvern from 1732 until 1775. When he first arrived, the settlement of Ardtornish was situated on the hillside south-east of Miodar Bay, but in the following year Airds brought in "a parcell of Low Country masons and dykers" and built himself a handsome mansion house (Plate 12) nearer to the ruined castle of Ardtornish, at the base of Ardtornish Point.[1] It was to this house, completed between 1755 and 1770, that Angus Gregorson (or MacGregor), Airds's successor as tacksman of Ardtornish, came in 1773. Gregorson was already a substantial tacksman on the Argyll estates in Mull, and he now became extremely prosperous; he indemnified Airds for improvements to Ardtornish to the value of £555, he paid the highest total rent of any of Argyll's tacksmen (£186 a year in the 1770s), and he purchased the estates of Durran, Loch Awe, in 1795 and of Acharn in Morvern in 1808, the latter for £14,500.[2]

In 1813 Angus Gregorson was succeeded in his holdings by his son John (born *c.* 1776), who stayed on at Ardtornish House in some style; with about twenty rooms, it was the grandest house in Morvern, and towards the end of his time Gregorson was Sheriff for the district, and employed a clerk and a tutor for his children.[3] When Ardtornish, with the rest of Argyll's Morvern farms, was put up for sale by the sixth Duke's trustees, Gregorson borrowed the purchase price of £9,000 on the security of the land and in 1819 became proprietor of the estate which he had hitherto rented. About six years later he sold Acharn for £15,650, and bought instead another Argyll estate, Liddesdale–Achagavel. Gregorson continued to borrow money on the security of his land during the 1820s, and then, in 1831, found it necessary to put his properties in trust while remaining in actual possession of them. Liddesdale was sold in 1840; and then in 1844 Gregorson left Morvern, Ardtornish being sold for £11,000. The reason for the apparent decline in Gregorson's fortunes

[1] Cregeen, E. R. (1964), xviii, 101 n.

[2] 'Notes on the lands and estate of Ardtornish...1938', *AP*; Cregeen, E. R. (1964), xix.

[3] The Gregorsons' tutor in 1841 was a 'student' of twenty-five (*Census*). Miss King believed that Thomas Campbell the poet was tutor at Ardtornish in the late 1820s (see p. 232 below), and there is a mid-nineteenth-century reference to Campbell's presence in the parish as a tutor at an earlier date (MacLeod, N. (1863), 41–2); but, although Campbell was indeed a tutor in Mull and in Kintyre in the 1790s, there is no suggestion in the very detailed *Life and letters of Thomas Campbell* (Beattie, W. (1849)) that he was ever employed by the Gregorsons, or indeed that he ever set foot in Morvern.

is now obscure; perhaps he had had to borrow too much to pay for his properties—1818 and 1819, for instance, were years of exceptionally high prices for sheep and wool—and then had failed to recover enough in the leaner years that followed to pay his debts. If so, his case was not unusual at the time. During the same period, Grant went bankrupt after eleven years at Kinlochaline (1825–36), and the Frasers sold Acharn after thirteen years (1825–38) at a loss of £4,400.

Throughout their tenure of Ardtornish, the Gregorsons seem to have behaved after the fashion of eighteenth-century tacksmen. They did not carry out evictions wholesale (except at the very end, when John Gregorson agreed to clear four smallholdings for his successor), but they understood the potential of the large sheep farm and deliberately kept the number of people on their estate down at a time of increasing population. Tearnait which, to judge from the eighteenth-century maps and from the remains of houses and of cultivation on the ground, once supported a sizeable population was turned over by Angus Gregorson entirely to sheep; in 1779 there were only two shepherds, one widow, and their families at Tearnait, a total of twelve persons. At the same date the Ardtornish end of the estate supported only thirty-nine persons apart from Gregorson and his family, making a total with Tearnait of fifty-one, precisely the same as the number of people living at Keil, a small-tenants' farm that was one-seventeenth the size of Ardtornish–Tearnait. The Gregorsons then succeeded in keeping their relatively sparse population at the same level throughout the period of greatest population-increase in the rest of the parish; Ardtornish and Inninmore had a population of 55 in 1779 and of 58 in 1841, while that of Tearnait remained unaltered at 12.[1] Since the Gregorsons never acquired a bad reputation for evictions, they probably did not more than move people about the estate and keep control of the number of dwelling-houses that might be erected on it; thus, even though 'surplus' members of the population had to leave the district to seek work, they left behind them a home to which they might hope to return, which was quite a different thing—even though the hope might in fact prove to have been vain—from leaving houses unroofed and all the people gone.

John Sinclair of Lochaline

Like the Gregorsons, John Sinclair was a Highlander, having been born at the top of Glen Kinglass, Loch Etive, in 1770; his forebears were tacksmen of Doire nan Saor, one of the many families of Sinclairs that claimed descent from the St Clairs of Rosslyn. John left home early to

---

[1] Cregeen, E. R. (1963), 69; *Census*, 1841. The *total* population of the estate had increased by 1841, when there were additional settlements at Eignaig (16 people), Samhnach (7) and Garbh Shlios (8).

make his way in the world, and settled at Tobermory—the village founded in Mull by the Duke of Argyll and the British Society for Extending Fisheries in 1788–9—where he became established as a merchant: he imported seed corn and other necessaries to the island, and exported its produce; he built up a fleet of trading vessels which ranged as far south as Glasgow and even Liverpool; and he owned the important Tobermory Distillery. In time he became rich, married Catherine MacLachlan—the eldest daughter of Argyll's tacksman at Rahoy—and looked round for land of his own. He found what he wanted over the Sound in Morvern, a fertile rectangle bordering the coast from the Savary river to Loch Aline, comprising the farms of Achnaha, Achabeg, Keil and Knock. He bought it in 1813 for £10,000 from MacDonald of Glenaladale, who had had it seven years earlier from Argyll; but for the time being Sinclair kept his base in Mull, just taking his young family over to Morvern for the summers where they stayed in one of the farm houses on the estate.

Then came the Argyll sales. In 1821 Sinclair bought Fiunary and Savary from the Duke's trustee for £7,500, with the result that he now owned all the coastal land from the Salachan burn to Loch Aline, a rich, homogeneous property of 7,650 acres; and he called his new estate Lochaline. All it lacked was a mansion house, and this Sinclair proceeded to build near the old boundary between Savary and Fiunary, a quarter of a mile along the road from the manse. What this new house—called originally *See p. vii* Lochaline House and later Fiunary House—looked like is now hard to determine, since it appears to have been considerably altered and enlarged by Mrs Paterson in the 1870s, and was then deliberately set on fire in 1910, so that little more than Mrs Paterson's façade is now standing (Plate 4). Well built of dressed stone blocks quarried on the estate, Sinclair's house was probably a 'regency' composition of a central block with two small wings and a stable yard at the back; but the two-storey central tower and the other italianate details added later have largely masked the original design.[1] With some twenty rooms, it was about the same size as Airds's eighteenth-century Ardtornish House, although it was perhaps more self-consciously a 'seat'.

Sinclair and his family were able to camp in their nearly-finished house in the summer of 1825, but during the following winter his wife died, and it was a sad move for the five children and their father into the permanent home that they had all looked forward to sharing together.

---

[1] The only description of the house in its original form appears to be Miss King's (see p. 225 below); it is mentioned in MacLeod, J. (1843), 170. The returns of windowed rooms in the *Censuses* of 1871 and 1881 suggest that the changes were made between these dates; Mr D. M. Walker is certain that the existing façade cannot be original. A 'Report on the Mansion House at Funary' of 1888 in *AP* speaks of "The original House, with the subsequent additions made to it...".

Sinclair did not give up, however, but threw himself into the management of his estate with the energy and ability that had made him a successful merchant. He "devoted his time to improving his property", his grand-daughter recalled. "He planted much wood.... built farm steadings, and kept the home farm in his own hands, as he believed in the landlord setting an example to his tenants. Whatever he did was thorough."[1]

Sinclair bought more land in 1836, paying £10,000 for a substantial part of the old estate of Kinlochaline, but the difficulty of administering the detached part of this property cannot have appealed to him—or perhaps he simply found it uneconomic—for he sold the Clounlaid group of farms five years later to Sellar of Acharn for £7,500. The net addition after all this of the adjacent farms of Kinlochaline and Achafors brought Lochaline Estate to its final size of 8,550 acres,[2] for which Sinclair had paid a total of £20,000. It was not a great estate, but its south-facing basalt slopes contained much of the most fertile land in the parish, land which was capable of carrying a greater density of sheep than anywhere else in Morvern but which had also attracted a relatively dense human population. The temptation to evict all the smallholders and make the whole estate—which from 1836 until 1860 was the highest-rated property in Morvern—into one great sheep walk must have been considerable; the experts advised this course, and most of his fellow proprietors were actually taking it, but Sinclair followed his own path.

The lack of full population-statistics for the period before 1841 makes it impossible to follow the pattern of Sinclair's early management in detail, but it is certain that when he bought the Knock and Fiunary groups of farms in 1813 and 1821 respectively they still supported substantial smallholding populations; a map of the Knock group made by Langlands in 1815 showed thirteen houses at Achnaha, twenty at Achabeg, twenty-nine at Keil and thirty at Knock.[3] By 1841, Achnaha and Fiunary (apart from Lochaline House and the manse) each had only twenty-two people in five houses, which indicates considerable reductions. At the same date Achabeg, Keil, Knock and Savary still had populations ranging from 59 to 109 people, though in rather smaller numbers of houses than before. Of these, Sinclair cleared the smallholders from Keil between 1841 and 1851, and from Savary during the following decade; he did not clear Achabeg or Knock, which reached peak populations in 1851 of 75 and 130 people respectively. Of his other two farms, Achafors was cleared before 1841, though not necessarily by Sinclair,

---

[1] *King's memoirs*, p. 227 below.
[2] The nineteenth-century owners thought that it contained 9,260 acres ('Particulars of the Estate of Lochaline', 1887, *AP*); exaggeration of this sort was not uncommon (see below, pp. 103–4, 180–1, 185).
[3] *Knock plan 1815*.

while Kinlochaline was not cleared until after his time. Thus Sinclair compromised: he cleared part of his estate after the modern fashion, but was content to allow numbers of small tenants to remain on the rest of it.[1]

The resulting 'mixed' estate was unusual, although apparently satisfactory to the proprietor and his tenants. Sinclair could live like a chieftain of old surrounded by a numerous family of relations, dependants and visitors in a stylish modern house, making a success of his farm and watching the value of the estate rising to more than double the price he had paid for it; while the co-operative smallholders' farms which were left undisturbed continued to support their inhabitants. The position of the people who had been evicted from the other farms, who certainly numbered more than 100 and may have been twice as many, was less satisfactory. To help with their resettlement, Sinclair founded a village in about 1830 near Knock which he called Lochaline after the estate.[2] In 1841 it already had 191 inhabitants, which had increased by 1851 to its maximum of 309, all crammed into forty-four inadequate houses. Neither was Sinclair an indulgent landlord. He always charged what he considered to be an economic rent for the very ordinary dry-stone, thatched cottages which were all that the estate provided for most of its inhabitants, and kept a 'comprisement book' in which damages and repairs to these cabins were scrupulously noted down. Nevertheless, although his treatment of the people could be high-handed, although he made no serious effort to raise their standard of living, he did not actually hound them out of the parish; he was a Highlander, speaking to them in their own language and behaving like an old-style Highland laird, which was something they understood and were grateful for.

Sinclair was always more an original than a mere anachronism. It was characteristic of him that he was the only proprietor in the district to 'come out' for the Free Church at the disruption in 1843; and he lived to a vigorous old age, blind but with a full head of white hair, a jolly old man of ninety-three who could still "crack nuts with his teeth when others waited for the crackers".[3] When he died in 1863 his heirs wisely put the estate up for sale—the sheep boom was at its height, the wool prices of 1864 being the highest of the century—and they got the remarkable price of £43,000 for it. As for the people, "the departure of the family from the house which had been for so long a blessing to the whole district, was a source of distress and lamentation to all".[4]

[1] It is possible that Sinclair also cleared the Clounlaid farms between 1836 and 1841, perhaps on Sellar's instructions; see below, p. 41.
[2] 'Missive letter', Allan Cameron to John Sinclair, 26 April 1830, *AP*; MacLeod, J. (1843), 189.
[3] *King's memoirs*, p. 232 below.   [4] *King's memoirs*, p. 233 below.

The new proprietors

Miss Stewart of Glenmorvern

Christina Stewart, a shadowy figure who had an estate in Morvern for only five years and who is unlikely ever to have resided there, was nevertheless notorious in the parish as the first proprietor to clear whole farms, settlements and all, for sheep. 'Glenmorvern' was the name she gave to the group of farms put up by Argyll as 'Fernish', consisting of Ardantiobairt, Barr, Fernish, Mungasdail and Unimore, a total of 9,510 acres; she bought the property in 1824 when she was a spinster of forty-seven, possibly on the advice of her cousins the Stewarts of Auch who had recently bought the Glencripesdale group of farms from Argyll. Miss Stewart proceeded immediately to evict all the smallholders from Mungasdail and Unimore, and a few from Barr and Ardantiobairt, about 135 people in all; and she let the land so cleared as two sheep farms based on Mungasdail (about 2,000 acres) and Barr (about 5,000 acres).[1] She did not clear Fernish and Rhemore, or Barr settlement, and she allowed a number of smallholders to remain on the coast at Bonnavoulin (where a terrace of houses was built for them in about 1840).[2] Miss Stewart's actions were thus very similar to Sinclair's: each of them bought a large estate from Argyll, each evicted between 100 and 200 people for the sake of their sheep farms (Sinclair more if anything than Miss Stewart), and each permitted a number of smallholders to remain undisturbed. But whereas Sinclair gained the people's respect and even love by living patriarchally in Morvern, Miss Stewart stayed away in Edinburgh and was remembered after her death in 1829 only for her vicarious cruelty to the peasants who were evicted, as the landowner responsible for the distress of 'Mary of Unnimore'.

Mary's story, told years later in Glasgow to the old minister's eldest son, is worth repeating both because it brings an actual eviction in Morvern to life, and because it was an important document, when it was published in an English translation in 1863, in the mounting controversy about the clearances.[3] The events she describes took place in 1824, when Unimore was a village of about fifteen houses under the 'Aoineadh Mor' south-west of Loch Doire nam Mart, with perhaps seventy-five inhabitants, most of whom were Camerons.[4]

"That was the day of sadness to many—the day on which Mac Cailein

---

[1] *Napier Commission evidence* (1884), see pp. 219–20, 221–2 below; *Census*, 1841, 1851.

[2] *Napier Commission evidence* (1884), III, 2297–8. One of the original houses of the terrace (consisting of a single room measuring fourteen feet by twelve) is still standing as a roofless shell, but the others were rebuilt on a larger scale in the later nineteenth century.

[3] Norman MacLeod's translation of his father's Gaelic text first appeared in *Good words*, and was reprinted in book form at least four times.

[4] See below, p. 155. In 1779 *all* the inhabitants of Unimore were named Cameron (Cregeen, E. R. (1963), 67).

(*Argyle*) parted with the estate of his ancestors in the place where I was reared.

"The people of Unnimore thought that 'flitting' would not come upon them while they lived. As long as they paid the rent, and that was not difficult to do, anxiety did not come near them; and a lease they asked not. It was there that the friendly neighbourhood was, though now only one smoke is to be seen, from the house of the Saxon shepherd.

"When we got the 'summons to quit,' we thought it was only for getting an increase of rent, and this we willingly offered to give; but permisson to stay we got not. The small cattle [sheep] were sold, and at length it became necessary to part with the one cow. When shall I forget the plaintive wailing of the children deprived of the milk which was no more for them? When shall I forget the last sight I got of my pretty *cluster* of goats bleating on the *lip* of the rock, as if inviting me to milk them? But it was not allowed me to put a *cuach* (pail) under them.

"The day of 'flitting' came. The officers of the law came along with it, and the shelter of a house, even for one night more, was not to be got. It was necessary to depart. The hissing of the fire on the flag of the hearth as they were *drowning* it, reached my heart. We could not get even a bothy in the country; therefore we had nothing for it but to face the *land of strangers*, (Lowlands). The aged woman, the mother of my husband, was then alive, weak, and lame. James carried her on his back in a creel. I followed him with little John, an infant at my breast, and thou who art no more, Donald beloved, a little *toddler*, walking with thy sister by my side. Our neighbours carried the little furniture that remained to us, and showed every kindness which tender friendship could show.

"On the day of our leaving Unnimore I thought my heart would rend. I would feel right if my tears would flow; but no relief thus did I find. We sat for a time on 'Knock-nan-Càrn' (Hill of Cairns,)[1] to take the last look at the place where we had been brought up. The houses were being already stripped. The bleat of the 'big sheep' was on the mountain. The whistle of the Lowland shepherd and the bark of his dogs were on the brae. ...

"What have you of it, but that we reached Glasgow, and through the letter of the saintly man who is now no more, my beloved minister, (little did I think that I would not again behold his noble countenance,) we got into a cotton work [mill]. ... "[2]

Glenmorvern Estate remained in Miss Stewart's family until the end of the nineteenth century, but the owners were never resident for any length of time; 'Glenmorvern Cottage' (built by 1841) was generally either let as a shooting box or occupied by servants.

[1] The party apparently took the extremely steep path leading up through the Bealach na Sgairn, an extraordinary feat in view of James's burden. The 'Knock-nan-Càrn' is probably the hill-top immediately to the east of the Bealach which has some large boulders perched on its south face.

[2] MacLeod, N. (1863), 393–6.

The Gordons of Drimnin

When Charles MacLean sold his family estates in bankruptcy in
1797–8, Drimnin went first to MacDonald of Glenaladale (a non-resident);
and then, with the addition of the Argyll properties of Auliston, Portabhata and Poll Luachrain, to MacLean of Boreray in 1817–18. These
MacLeans resided at Drimnin—John MacLeod the minister married one
of the girls—and it was from them that the Gordons bought the estate
in 1835. Here were more colourful proprietors than Miss Stewart. Sir
Charles Gordon, who derived from landed gentry in Banffshire, was
Secretary of the Highland and Agricultural Society of Scotland. As a
wealthy Roman Catholic settling in an entirely protestant area, he
promptly built a chapel near his house—scandalising the minister, who
was something of an antiquary, by demolishing the remains of Drimnin
Castle in the process—and installed a chaplain. "It is pardonable to
express regret", MacLeod wrote in 1843, "that so very unnecessary a
work of demolition should have taken place; but it is just to add, that,
in this expression of regret, the enlightened proprietor of Drimnin now
fully participates."[1] In 1845 Sir Charles died at the age of fifty-four. Of
his six sons, the first and third had died as children, the second joined the
army (he was killed in 1851) and the fourth became a priest (and
eventually Roman Catholic bishop of Jamaica), so that it was the fifth
son, Joseph Clement Gordon, who was eventually to inherit the estate;
but as he was only seven years old at the time of his father's death, Lady
Gordon, the strong-minded daughter of a Cowal landowner, had to
manage in the meanwhile on her own.

Her fortitude was tried when old Drimnin House was accidentally
burned down in 1849. "My Dear Charles," wrote Margaret Gordon, the
eldest daughter, to her brother (the one who became a priest) on an
appropriately black-bordered writing paper, "Mamma is so knocked up
that she cannot write to you but she told me to tell you that a most
dreadful accident has befallen us, last night Drimnin house was in
flames & nothing now remains except two or three broken ruins. It
began first at 8 oclock at night when we remarked that the chimney of
the kitchen was smoking we all went down but it could not be discovered
from whence it proceeded it continued till about 11 oclock after which
the noise ceased and it became pretty quiet & we all went to our beds   A
little while after that Mama saw that the drawing room was in flames
she immediately cried through the house *Fire—Fire* & she immediately
along with Margaret who was awake pulled us out of bed & by that time
the fire had reached your bedroom & John's one. When we all got [out]
not a single Man was to be found as it was 12 oclock at night so we sent

[1] MacLeod, J. (1843), 184.

35

for Jamie down at the Lodge who immediately arrived   by this time Mama was trailing all the boxes & trunks out of the bedrooms & we had not a single stitch of clothes on except our night-gowns   we immediately rung the *Gown* [*sic*] as loud as possible but no one could be found Mr Hood unluckily was at Tobermory & being alarmed by the sight of the flames he crossed the sound   after that we sent Peggy Thomson down to Mr Ramage & also to Glasdrum to procure as many men as possible who came up to assist us in getting the furniture from the house but the most valuable of it was gone   the large picture in the drawing room was ⟨the⟩ the greatest loss to Mama all the dining room furniture as well could ⟨not⟩ be got & the little that we managed to get was   all broken & smashed in ever so many pieces   The Fire continued for all the night & for the forenoon after which it was extinguished   for further particulars you must wait till Mama is able to give you them as I have not the time to do so at present. . ."[1] A new mansion house was built by 1861, a gawky pile rather bigger than Lochaline House, in a gothic style that attempted unsuccessfully to combine the charm of Rickmanesque fantasy with the solidity of Gilbert-Scott-ecclesiastical.

A map made for the new proprietor in 1836 shows Drimnin to have been largely uncleared when Gordon took possession,[2] but he did not immediately proceed to change things on a large scale. Achleanan and Drimnin Mains farms were 'improved', probably in the early eighteen forties, by the removal of six or seven families from each, those from the area of Auliston and Carraig being moved across the estate to Oronsay Island;[3] the people also disappeared from Portabhata and Sornagan during the same decade, but this may have been the result of the famine of 1846–7. It was not until some years after Sir Charles's death, when his widow may have felt poorer than she had done, and may also have been influenced by the disasters of the famine years, that the evictions were authorised which drastically depopulated the estate. The figures for the total population of Drimnin Estate in the nineteenth century are revealing: there were 306 inhabitants in 1841, and 269 in 1851; but in 1861 the number was down to 118, from which it declined steadily to 58 in 1891. In 1851 the great settlement of Auliston alone had 115 inhabitants, including twelve crofters, living in twenty-two houses; all were evicted together in 1855 (Plate 1), and during the same decade three of five families, including two crofters, left Druimbuidhe. Then, in about 1868, some of the same families who had been sent to Oronsay from the

---

[1] Margaret Gordon to Charles Gordon, 2 August 1849; MS at Drimnin.
[2] *Drimnin plan 1836.*
[3] The evidence concerning the Drimnin evictions is contradictory and cannot all be true. The summary given here is of the most likely facts, and is based on *Census*, 1841, 1851, 1861, 1871, 1881; *Oban Times*, 6 May 1882, 10 Feb. 1883, 20 Dec. 1884; *Napier Commission evidence* (1884), III, 2288–9, 2301, 2304, 2321–2. See also pp. 94–5, 213–15, 216–17, 220–1 below.

Auliston area twenty-five years earlier were evicted from their homes a
second time: they were few in number, but were sent away in circumstances which caused particular resentment and which were cited—
probably with some exaggeration—in the Land League controversy of
the 1880s. It was even suggested that this eviction was the result of a
plot made by the tenant-farmer of Druimbuidhe, unsurpassable "for its
diabolic malignity and cruelty", of which Lady Gordon might not herself have been entirely unaware; and, although this charge was unsub-
stantiated, it helped to make Lady Gordon the most unpopular of
Morvern's resident proprietors.[1] She died in 1881, having been responsible
for the eviction of close on 200 people, and the estate passed to her son,
Joseph Clement Gordon.

Patrick Sellar of Acharn and Ardtornish

The non-resident proprietors in mid-nineteenth-century Morvern were
mostly mere rentiers with little knowledge of farming; while the residents
generally managed at least part of their estates personally and knew a
good deal about sheep. Patrick Sellar was as professional a farmer as
any of the residents—he was indeed one of the most accomplished sheep-
masters of his day—but he visited his Morvern estate only occasionally,
administering it for the most part from Moray and Sutherland. Sellar
was already fifty-eight years old when he first bought property in
Morvern. This was in 1838, when the events in Sutherland which had
brought him notoriety were nearly a quarter of a century in the past;
those events were by no means forgotten, however, and he may well
have been the most widely hated man in the Highlands still.

Sellar, a Morayshire lawyer, had been employed as factor to the Marquis and Marchioness of Stafford (later Duke and Duchess of Sutherland)
from 1810 until 1819, when he was in his thirties. His employers had
concluded, on the advice of their Commissioner William Young, that it
would be advantageous to dispossess a good many of their tacksmen in
the north and east of Sutherland, "removing the people nearer to the
sea-shore, and putting the mountains under Cheviot sheep";[2] and it
had been Sellar's job to put this policy into effect, personally clearing
the smallholders from the inland pastures and making provision for
them on the coast. In some cases the people had resisted eviction and
force had been used to get them out, which meant that those who would
not leave their cottages were liable to have them pulled down about them,

[1] See the extracts from the writings of John MacDonald (who is not an entirely
reliable witness), pp. 213–22 below.
[2] Sellar, T. (1883), 48 (Patrick Sellar's 'Statement', 1825). Thomas Sellar's book,
although partial to his father, conveniently reprints all the available documents
concerning the Sutherland clearances of 1814; it is quoted here in preference to the
several originals.

the irreplaceable roof-timbers being valued, paid for and burned on the spot. One of the clearances carried out by Sellar in 1814 had been of a potential sheep-walk which he himself intended to farm as his employers' tenant; it was called Strathnaver, and it was here that an old infirm woman had died a few days after she was carried out of her son's house just as it was being set on fire. As a result of this incident and of others in which barns and crops had been destroyed, Sellar had been indicted in 1816 for murder and for crimes against property in Strathnaver. After a trial lasting for fifteen hours, Sellar had been found not guilty, in a verdict that the jury had reported (in accordance with Scottish practice) to be unanimous, the Judge afterwards expressing his agreement with the outcome.

Reading the report of Sellar's trial today with an open mind—which is not altogether easy in view of the attacks on its impartiality which have recently received renewed publicity—it seems incredible that a jury could have come to any other conclusion. The evidence offered by the Crown was weak and contradictory, and was supported by witnesses whose character was, in the two most important cases, suspect; the three referees who gave unambiguous written evidence of their high opinion of Sellar's integrity and humanity were distinguished men who could not have perjured themselves lightly; and there is no reason to suppose that the jury of fifteen men was packed on Sellar's behalf. It needs much better evidence than was offered then or later to make the beginning of a criminal case against Sellar; in its absence we must assume that the jury was right and that he was innocent.[1]

But of course that is not all there is to be said about the Strathnaver evictions. They were of their nature horribly unkind to the twenty-seven families concerned—about 150 people—and Sellar was intimately concerned with the ugliest aspects of them. They proved in the event to have been exceedingly ill-advised: "The name of the long, beautiful glen of Strathnaver will never be forgotten in the Highlands", wrote Dr Fraser Darling 140 years later. "The miseries which occurred there have been relived by subsequent generations of Highland folk who never knew Strathnaver nor had any connexion with it. The name became a symbol, and some of the hidden bitterness which may so easily flare up in Highland affairs today is referable to that time . . . "[2] If Strathnaver has become the symbol of all that was worst about the Highland clearances, Sellar has become the symbol of heartless greed in a Highland proprietor.[3]

---

[1] For the report of Sellar's trial, originally printed in 1816, see Sellar, T. (1883), [2]xi-lv. Recent attacks on Sellar and the clearances include Grimble, I. (1962) and Prebble, J. (1963), earnest followers of MacKenzie, A. (1883).

[2] Darling, F. F. (1955), 6.

[3] The absurdity of the Sellar folk-lore which persists in Scotland is indicated by the following introduction from the *Radio Times* to a Gaelic play broadcast in 1966: "At the Court of Justiciary in Inverness in April 1816 the notorious Patrick Sellar was charged with culpable homicide. The allegations were that Sellar, while acting as

Symbols are caricatures, and Sellar was more complicated than that. He was in many ways a good man. He was truthful, and honourable in his business affairs. He was a kind and agreeable friend, and he was accorded the complete devotion of his wife and nine children, not only for his lifetime but for theirs as well. He had a well-ordered mind, avoided humbug, and could express himself in clear, attractive prose. "I have known him intimately from his infancy", wrote one of the referees at his trial, "and he was for many years, while he resided in this country [Moray], my man of business. I always considered him a person of the strictest integrity and humanity, incapable of being even accessory to any cruel or oppressive action."[1] Thirty-five years later, shortly after Sellar's death, Benjamin Jowett wrote to his old pupil William Young Sellar: "I do not doubt that it is well with your father after his long and honourable life. . . . You need only a small portion of his energy and decision of character to give you success in life."[2]

The trouble with Sellar was that in him energy and decision of character were carried to excess. His ambition and his liking for efficiency led him to pursue success ruthlessly; he always lacked the ability to sympathise with the weaknesses of others, and he was supported by an egotistical certainty that whatever he did was right. "When [his son] William was six", wrote his daughter-in-law many years afterwards in a revealing story, "he was sent to Elgin Academy with his two brothers, Tom and Pat . . . and such progress had William made with his *studies*!—poor little mite!—that a year after, when he was only seven, he entered the Edinburgh Academy with his brothers. Mr Sellar, *père*, was a man of iron will, and was determined not only that his sons should have the best education, but that they should excell, and be at the head of their classes. This they were, and at the end of seven years, when he was fourteen, William was Gold Medallist and head of the school." Elsewhere, Eleanor Sellar spoke of her father-in-law's extreme dislike of being thwarted.[3]

Sellar tells us that, when he first went to Sutherland in 1809, he was "full of the belief that the growth of wool and sheep in the Highlands of Scotland was one of the most abominable and detestable things possible to be imagined. . .that the inroads then making on the ancient habits and manners of the children of the Gael were cruel and impolitic in the extreme".[4] What he saw when he got there himself—the

factor to the Countess of Sutherland, initiated and directed the clearing of whole tracts of the county of Sutherland and the burning of people out of their homes. Many of the victims of these evictions died as a result of shock, deprivation, and fatigue. At the trial Sellar was acquitted but the mystery remained. Was the verdict right according to the law of the time or was the trial conducted with a bland contempt for justice?. . .The scene is set in hell, with flashbacks to illustrate actual earthly events" (*Radio Times* (Scottish edition), 27 Jan. 1966, 23).

[1] Sellar, T. (1883), 2xlviii.   [2] Abbot, E. and Campbell, L. (1897), I, 222.
[3] Sellar, E. M. (1907), 25–6, 43.   [4] Sellar, T. (1883), 24.

land misused, the people incredibly poor—changed his mind entirely, and he became as convinced of the rightness of 'improvement' by clearance as he had previously been convinced of its wrongness. Believing, he acted; acting, he was impatient of any resistance to his efforts on behalf of the public good, and could not imagine that such resistance could be anything but wrong-headed or that it might be more than a temporary nuisance. Hence his ruthlessness, and hence too his otherwise inexplicable political error in clearing Strathnaver personally for his own use, for he could surely have arranged for someone else to carry out the evictions there if he had thought it worth while. (Even so it is amazing that he failed to see that, in the evictions he had carried out hitherto, his employers had protected themselves from the personal hatred of the people by using Sellar the factor as their instrument, while he as factor could disclaim responsibility for what he did as a disinterested servant carrying out instructions; and that in clearing personally a farm for his own use he was covered by neither sort of immunity.)

Undaunted by the trial and by the widespread hatred which followed him from then on, Sellar pursued exactly the same course as before; he always knew he was right. He continued to clear farms in Sutherland for his employers until 1819, and then retired from their service to devote himself to sheep-farming at Strathnaver, of which he remained tenant for the rest of his life. He succeeded so well at this during the 1820s and 1830s—a difficult time, it will be remembered, for Highland sheep-farmers—that within twenty years he was able to embark on the purchase of a substantial estate of his own; and the area he chose to buy it in was Morvern.

Sellar's first venture in Morvern was to buy the estate of Acharn from an unsuccessful non-resident proprietor, the father of a London solicitor; Sellar paid £11,250 for it in 1838, which was £4,400 less than his predecessor had paid thirteen years earlier. Acharn was the property north of Lochaline Estate, seven old farms totalling 6,816 acres grouped round Loch Arienas, and including half the fishing rights of the old estate of Kinlochaline. Sellar is said to have had a flock of sheep driven down from Sutherland to stock his new land; and to accommodate them he immediately evicted no fewer than forty-four families—about 230 people, more even than had been cleared from Strathnaver in 1814.[1] (It may be remarked here that neither at Acharn nor anywhere else in Morvern was eviction resisted physically by the people; all the authorities agree that no Morvern proprietor ever used force to implement the eviction notices as Sellar did in Sutherland or as the Skye proprietors were to do in the 1880s.) Next, Sellar bought the adjoining 4,794 acres of Clounlaid and Uladail from John Sinclair in 1841, paying £7,500 for the

---

[1] *Napier Commission evidence* (1884), 2288–90; see p. 220 below.

land together with the other half of the Kinlochaline fishings. It is not known who cleared the settlements of Clounlaid and Uladail, which together had probably reached a population exceeding 100; the people were already gone when Sellar took possession at Whitsun 1841 (which happened also to be the date of the Census enumeration), but it is possible that they were evicted on his instruction, as happened later at Ardtornish.[1]

So far Sellar had acquired a compact sheep-walk in the centre of the parish but it was no more than a simple farm, and it lacked accommodation suitable for a landowner and his family. He now proceeded to buy Ardtornish Estate from Gregorson's trustees, paying £11,100 in 1844 for its 9,965 acres, and requiring the few crofts which survived on it to be cleared by Gregorson before his departure.[2] This gave him Airds's pleasant mansion house (Plate 12), and the excellent arable land between Caolas and Ardtornish Point to add to his pasture. His own land in Morvern now totalled 21,575 acres and had cost him £29,850. In addition he rented grazings from his neighbours: the 1,203 acres of Unimore from Glenmorven, and Glensanda (6,637 acres) and Altachonaich (at this time 2,464 acres) from Kingairloch. The total area available for Sellar's flocks thus approached 32,000 acres, and was stocked in the 'fifties (the first period for which figures survive) with an average of 8,266 sheep, or 295 sheep per 1,000 acres.[3]

Now Sellar could bring his family to his new estate, and it became their practice to reside at Ardtornish House each year for the late summer and autumn. Sellar's children were the first representatives in Morvern of a new type of gentry: rich, cultured foreigners who had no professional interest in the land but who migrated to the West Highlands for lengthy holidays to walk and shoot and fish and relax in a country of insidious beauty utterly removed from their usual environment. Sellar's own beginnings had been entirely provincial but, with his accustomed energy and ambition, he had put his sons and daughters in reach of a wider world. His third son William, a favourite pupil of Jowett at Oxford, was a distinguished classical scholar who became Professor of Humanity in the University of Edinburgh; his youngest son, Alexander, was a member of parliament and Liberal-Unionist whip whose promising political career was cut short by an early death; his eldest daughter was the mother of Andrew Lang. In the 'fifties, after old Sellar's death, the children continued to spend happy summers at Ardtornish with their own young families, and on one occasion in 1853 Tennyson and Palgrave (who were friends of the William Sellars) came to stay for a few days.[4] They were as charmed with Ardtornish as their hosts could have wished,

---

[1] 'Disposition' of Clounlaid, 1841, *AP*; *Census*, 1841.
[2] *Napier Commission evidence* (1884), 2289–90.
[3] 'Ardtornish clipping journal', 1851–7, *AP*.   [4] Sellar, E. M. (1907), ch. iv.

even cancelling an intended visit to Skye so that they could stay a little longer; but it will be remembered that this was only nine years after John Gregorson had left the old tacksman's house on the Point. Times were changing quickly.

Sellar's Morvern estate had one serious disadvantage: it was split into two parts by the lands of Achranich, so that it was impossible to go directly from Ardtornish to Acharn or Clounlaid without crossing some-one else's property. This meant that Sellar was dependent on the good will of his neighbour for permission to move his flocks from one part of the estate to another for all the essential operations of the sheep-farmer's year. When Sellar bought Ardtornish in 1844, Achranich was owned by an entirely non-resident proprietor and presumably Sellar did not anticipate any difficulty in dealing with the Achranich manager, Peter MacNab. Just over a year later, however, Achranich was bought by a vigorous Englishman, Octavius Smith, who intended to reside in Morvern for half of each year, and who for strength of will and dislike of opposition was a match for Sellar himself. It may well be asked why Sellar let Achranich go to another purchaser in 1845—for if he could afford the rent of Unimore, Glensanda and Altachonaich, he could afford interest on the purchase price of Achranich, and it would have trans-formed his estate—but there seems to be no satisfactory answer; perhaps Smith was smarter or merely luckier, and out-bid Sellar or concluded the business before Sellar knew what was happening.

Predictably, Sellar and Smith quarrelled, even going to law before they could agree to live in amity as neighbours. Soon after their reconcilia-tion, in 1851, Sellar died at Elgin, his first home. His children kept the Morvern estate for a further nine years, appointing one of their number to act as managing trustee, before selling it to their neighbour, and now friend, Octavius Smith; in 1859–60 they obtained the excellent price of £39,500, almost £10,000 more than Sellar had paid for it. These events, following Smith's arrival in 1845, are dealt with in the next chapter.

Mrs Paterson of Lochaline

It will be recalled that when John Sinclair died in 1863 his heirs put Lochaline Estate up for sale, and that it was sold the following year for the very high price of £43,000. The purchaser was Mrs Campbell Paterson, a widow. Born Magdalene Hardie at Port Glasgow in about 1812, Mrs Paterson had been married to an Oban banker who was also factor of an estate in Mull, and who had in about 1848 become Argyll's tenant of Knock in Mull where he had farmed some 20,000 sheep.[1] Having paid £5 an acre for her new estate—when a hill farm such as Sellar's Ardtornish in 1859 went for under £2 an acre—Mrs Paterson was determined that

---

[1] Clerk, D. (1878), 69.

her fertile grazings should give her an adequate return. To this end she immediately set about evicting the small tenants whom Sinclair had allowed to remain, and replacing them with sheep. Mrs Paterson got possession of the estate at Whitsun 1864; notices were served on the smallholders of Achabeg and Knock in March 1865, and all the people were cleared off by Whitsun 1866—a total of at least twenty-eight families (plus two or three more from Achnaha and Achafors), or about 150 persons. Scarcely any compensation was paid, and no provision was made for the people's future; some of them settled in the village and found work on Ardtornish Estate, some migrated to Glasgow. How far Mrs Paterson profited by the exchange of crofters for sheep is not known precisely, because her farm and estate accounts have not survived, but the Valuation Rolls do give an indication of the annual cash value of the evictions. It may be calculated that the valued rent of Achabeg and Knock together was greater by £125 in 1870 than it had been in 1865, over and above the average rise in Morvern rents during the same period, and that £125 was ten per cent of the total valued rental of Lochaline Estate in 1865.[1]

This clearance was furiously resented in Morvern. Mrs Paterson was a stranger seeking advantage for herself at the expense of small tenants who had occupied their houses and their plots of ground for decades; furthermore she was doing it at a time when the population was already much reduced by emigration, and when public opinion generally was beginning to swing against 'improvement' if it involved eviction. She was attacked posthumously by the Napier Commission when it sat at Lochaline in 1883, during an angry examination of her nephew William Henderson Hardie, who was then managing trustee of Lochaline Estate:

"[*Lord Napier:*]...what was the object of this wholesale clearance of the people?—[*William Hardie:*] So far as I can understand it was a disadvantage to a sheep farm to have little bits of corn exposed where the sheep were all going round.

[*Napier:*] Did it ever suggest itself to the minds of the managers or proprietors at that time that a fence might have been put up?—[*Hardie:*] It might have been, but the buildings themselves were of so little value —none of those crofters' buildings were valued above £8 or £10.

[*Napier:*] The reason of their removal was that their presence was inconvenient to the neighbouring sheep farmer?—[*Hardie:*] Not only that, but they were not employing themselves in any occupation, such as fishing or that, to bring them in a livelihood.

[1] In the five years from 1865 to 1870 the valued rent of Achabeg rose from £169 to £264 (apart from Achnaha and Ardness), and of Knock from £83 to £144; the total valued rent of Morvern was £7,670 in 1865 and £8,591 in 1870; of Lochaline Estate, £1,213 and £1,477 (*VR* 1865, 1870).

[*Napier:*] They were removed from their little farms in order that they might obtain profitable employment for themselves?—[*Hardie:*] Those were not little farms, but crofts.

...[*Napier:*] As I understand your statement, the people were removed for the benefit of the sheep farm, and you may say for the benefit of the estate?—[*Hardie:*] And for the benefit of themselves.

[*Napier:*] But the people were not made the judges of their own benefit?—[*Hardie:*] They were not asked in the first place.

[*Napier:*] What I want to arrive at is this, the people were virtually and substantially removed for the benefit of the estate, in order that this sheep farm, or some other part of the estate, might be more profitably administered and held; in removing the people, did the proprietor, in consideration of their number and poverty, and the difficulty of obtaining other places, make them any allowance or gratuity?—[*Hardie:*] Not to my knowledge.

[*Napier:*] Do you know what became of them at all?—[*Hardie:*] Some of them removed to Glasgow and other centres of industry, and some of them removed to the village here.

[*Napier:*] You say the people were partly removed for their own benefit, in order that they might become more industrious, or have a profitable employment in the future, did the proprietor pursue these people with any care in order to assist them in their future amelioration? —[*Hardie:*] I am not aware.

...[*Mr Fraser-Mackintosh:*] You have given us a full and frank statement about the estate so far as you know it; have you ever heard the statement made with regard to property, 'I can do what I like with my own'?—[*Hardie:*] Yes, but I don't believe that.

[*Fraser-Mackintosh:*] Have you heard the other statement that property has its duties as well as its rights?—[*Hardie:*] Yes.

[*Fraser-Mackintosh:*] And which of these do you go upon?—[*Hardie:*] Property has its duties as well as its rights.

[*Fraser-Mackintosh:*] I may take it for granted in this case that the rights'of property were exercised when these people were put away?— [*Hardie:*] Yes.

[*Fraser-Mackintosh:*] Take the alternative now; what in the nature of duty was done by the estate for those people?—[*Hardie:*] I tell you I can give no information about it further than I have done.

[*Fraser-Mackintosh:*] Is there any use in beating about the bush; is it not the fact that those people were removed solely and entirely because they were in the way of sheep?—[*Hardie:*] Certainly not.

[*Fraser-Mackintosh:*] If not, what other reason was there?—[*Hardie:*] It would have entailed very considerable expenditure upon the proprietor to have built houses and put up fencing to have carried out any system of farming.

The new proprietors

[*Fraser-Mackintosh:*] That is what I say, the people were in the way. The proprietrix did not choose to spend that money, and therefore they must go and make room for the sheep; is that not so?—[*Hardie:*] I have given you all the facts I can.

...[*Fraser-Mackintosh:*] They said themselves they were happy and contented with their lot and made a living?—[*Hardie:*] They were always that, and yet periodically they were in great destitution, and every now and again, as Dr Macleod told me himself, subscriptions had to be got up to assist them.

[*Fraser-Mackintosh:*] And that being the case, the estate thought the best thing for them would be to deprive them of what they had?—[*Hardie:*] I cannot say what the proprietor then thought. I am merely giving you the information I have. I cannot state what the proprietor thought when I was not made aware of it.

...[*Fraser-Mackintosh:*] You stated you had some conversation with the late Dr Macleod, minister of the parish, in regard to the people?—[*Hardie:*] Yes.

[*Fraser-Mackintosh:*] How long is it since you have been resident here? —[*Hardie:*] Two years; but I have been acquainted with the district for a good many years.

[*Fraser-Mackintosh:*] Did Dr Macleod ever remonstrate or express any regret that the people generally in this parish have been removed?— [*Hardie:*] All ministers must take an interest in keeping their flocks together.

[*Fraser-Mackintosh:*] I am afraid the flocks you look after are not men?..."[1]

No doubt these were glib lawyers' victories over a small and stupid man, and Hardie was surely wondering how he had ever been fool enough to volunteer to give evidence. But really it was Mrs Paterson who was being examined, not her unhappy nephew, and she was roundly censured. If this now seems too facile a conclusion, it is because the examination stumbled over the central contradiction in the nineteenth-century approach to land-ownership: it was Mrs Paterson's duty as a patriarchal landlord to care for her dependants, but it was nevertheless her right as a capitalist to dispose of her property to advantage. We in the twentieth century have resolved the crux only by arranging for the State to confiscate some of the capitalists' wealth and to assume with it responsibility for those who used to be the landlords' dependants. We should not be too smug in condemning nineteenth-century individuals for failing to resolve it by themselves.

In fact, by lowering the density of the population and by building a number of substantial slated houses to replace the thatched, dry-stone

---

[1] *Napier Commission evidence* (1884), III, 2307–15.

cabins of Sinclair's time, Mrs Paterson and her trustees did raise the standard of living of those who remained on the estate. Apart from his own house and its steading, Sinclair's only slated buildings appear to have been Achnaha steading, Ardness, Keil farm-house and five or six houses in Lochaline village; the slated houses built or rebuilt between 1864 and 1888 by Mrs Paterson and her trustees, on the other hand, probably included Fiunary Cottage, Sandpit, Savary farm-house, Achnaha farm-house, the two 'Achabegs', Ardness Port House, Keil Smithy, Cuibheag and about a dozen houses in Lochaline.[1] Therefore the retribution which came when the estate was sold doubtless seemed undeserved to its owners. Mrs Paterson died in about 1880, and her trustees tried for several years to dispose of the property for something like the price she paid for it; but the market was against them, and they were eventually obliged to sell Lochaline Estate in 1888 for a mere £28,000, swallowing a capital loss of £15,000.

Other mid-century proprietors

The few other proprietors who held land in Morvern in the middle of the nineteenth century were as varied in their backgrounds as were those who have already been described. The MacLeans of Killundine, who like Sinclair lived on their property all the year round, were connections of Donald Campbell, the last tacksman. The Stewarts who had Glencripesdale came from Auch, and were related to Miss Stewart of Glenmorvern, but they did not reside in Morvern. Laudale belonged in 1850 to the trustee of the last owner, Dugald MacLachlan, and was farmed by tenants, as was Liddesdale, at that time the property of a Peebles man named Alexander. None of these proprietors, whose lands had been under sheep before they got them, did anything remarkable in the parish, and they were soon forgotten. The Smiths of Achranich, who were already in Morvern by this time, did a great deal, but their activities will be described in the next chapter.

Most of the Morvern proprietors of the mid-nineteenth century were non-resident—as usual, for at no time in its recorded history has more than a small fraction of the parish been administered by resident owners. Of the ten proprietors in 1850, only two (Sinclair of Lochaline and Maclean of Killundine) lived on their estates all the year round; one (Lady Gordon of Drinmin) resided for the greater part of the year; two (Sellar of Ardtornish and Smith of Achranich) came for lengthy holidays; while the rest came only briefly as visitors.

[1] These listings, which are tentative, are based on *Census*, 1861–91; *VR*; *Napier Commission evidence* (1884), III, 2292–3; *OS 1872*; and architectural style.

MORVERN IN 1850

Whatever the difficulties facing the mid-nineteenth-century proprietors, the situation of the ordinary people in Morvern was far worse. The population continued to increase until 1831, but emigration was already taking place on a large scale, keeping the rate of increase down. After 1831 the drain of emigration far exceeded the natural increase, and the population shrank for half a century, until by 1881 there were scarcely more than a third as many people in Morvern as had lived there in 1831. During the same period the average number of families that left the parish each year was nine, that is, an *annual* exodus of some forty-five people continued for fifty years.

Emigration by itself is demoralising enough—it is the young and active who leave first—but in addition the causes of emigration constantly impinged upon the lives of those who remained behind: wages low and hard to come by, a diet that was both meagre and monotonous (it consisted chiefly of potatoes) interrupted by periodic crop failures which led to famine, and the possibility of eviction a constant threat. Day labourers were paid 1s. 3d. in 1843 when they could find employment; fifty years earlier, in 1794, day labourers had got 1s.; and, since the cost of living was about the same in the 1840s as it had been in the 1790s, the mid-century wage-earners were in theory rather better off than their grandfathers had been. The trouble was that the new sheep farms needed far less work done than the available labour force could provide, so that few day-labourers could find steady employment, and the average standard of living appears to have declined during the first half of the century.[1]

The standard dropped catastrophically following crop failure. The corn harvest failed in 1836, and there was recurrent famine for the next two years. Some relief was afforded by the free distribution of meal by a charitable organisation, the Highland Relief Board, in which Norman MacLeod of St Columba's (the eldest son of the old minister of Morvern) played the most prominent part.[2] Bad as that time was, however, the potato famines of the late 1840s were far worse. Even in Morvern (which was better off than some parishes because of the excellence of its corn-lands) potatoes normally made up two-thirds of the people's diet, and the crop failed completely in 1846; by the New Year, 1847, it was estimated that what remained of the corn crop could support the rent-paying population for only two months more. Hastily reconstituted with Norman MacLeod as Secretary, the Highland Relief Board was sending out

---

[1] MacLeod, N. (1794), 266; MacLeod, J. (1843), 185–8, 193–5. Quantitative information about the standard of living, such as *AP* provides from 1850, is not available for the first half of the century.

[2] *Emigration (Scotland) report* (1841), pt 1, *passim* (reporting Norman MacLeod's three examinations before the Select Committee on Emigration); MacLeod, J. (1843), 194.

supplies of food as early as February 1847, when Morvern received twenty bolls each of oatmeal and wheatmeal. Supplies of meal continued to be sent for the rest of 1847 and for much of 1848 as well, but this time the recipients were required to perform some labour (provided that they were capable of it) in return for the food. It was hoped that this scheme would get some useful public works started (which it did), would avoid the demoralising effect of unearned charity (which it may have done) and would engender new habits of industry in the Highlanders (which it did not). In Morvern two major public works were undertaken under the supervision of the minister, John MacLeod (the younger brother of the Secretary of the Relief Board). First was a new pier for Lochaline opposite Caolas ferry which was begun early in 1847 and was completed by the Fishery Board in the following year, providing work for thirty-one families who were receiving aid on John Sinclair's estate; it is still in good order, though nowadays seldom used. The other public undertaking, of even greater potential importance to the society of the parish, was begun later in 1847 up at Bonnavoulin where there were forty-six families from Drimnin Estate on relief: it was a fine new road to replace the old statute-labour road along the Sound of Mull, and, although only the three miles from Bonnavoulin to the Killundine river were finished during the two years of the scheme, it was the first step towards the construction of the modern road system that the parish needed.[1] Some individual proprietors organised similar schemes on their estates; the great wall enclosing the area round Portabhata settlement in Drimnin was built at this time and paid for in relief supplies by Lady Gordon.[2]

The number of official paupers remained at about forty-five from the late-eighteenth century until the potato famines, but this was simply from lack of funds, not lack of need; as it was there was only enough money available to the Kirk Session in 1843 to give each pauper the ludicrous sum of three shillings a year. From 1845 poor relief was levied as a rate on the proprietors of the parish and was administered by a new Parochial Board, a committee of heritors whose Secretary was the minister, John MacLeod and whose first chairman, until his death in 1851, was Patrick Sellar. In the late 1840s and early 1850s both the number of authorised paupers in the parish and the funds allotted to them increased sharply; in 1849, eighty-five paupers received an average of £3 each, and in 1853, 106 paupers were allotted £5 each.[3]

[1] *Free Church destitution committee* (1847), 2nd statement, 12; *Highland relief board reports*, 1st report (1847), 41; 5th report (Aug. 1847), ²7, ²8–9; 10th report (Nov. 1848), ²21–2; report on the islands of Mull [etc.]...and on part of the parish of Morvern (Oct. 1849), 29; MacLeod, J. N. (1898), ch. x.
[2] Information from Miss Alice Horsman.
[3] *Minute books of the Parochial Board of Morvern*, 1845–51, etc., *ACOL*; *Poor board reports*, 1846–53; MacLeod, J. (1843), 193–4.

The clearances changed the distribution of the population in a radical way. A few small tenants were allowed to continue ón their holdings "from motives of compassion"—at Knock, Achabeg and Fernish, for instance—but most were dispossessed and became "the occupants of small allotments in wretched villages".[1] The largest of the villages was Lochaline; founded in about 1830, its population by 1841 was close on 200, and was over 300 by the middle of the century. In 1851 there was an average of more than seven persons living in each house, which were still in the main thatched cottages with one or two rooms, and even in 1861 there was an average of more than two persons living in every room. With such overcrowding and the extreme shortage of work, it is not surprising that Lochaline was a squalid slum with its inhabitants living in "penury and wretchedness".[2] There were also village-sized concentrations of people—little better off—at Knock (130 people in 1851), Auliston (115) and Bonnavoulin (76), and ten other communities of from thirty to sixty people. The import of manufactured goods for ordinary people had scarcely begun—they had no money to spare—and as late as 1851 there were still 23 craftsmen working in the clothing trades in Morvern: 9 tailors, 5 weavers, 5 shoemakers, 2 dressmakers, a draper and a dyer, besides a further 23 tradesmen engaged in building and manufacturing.[3]

John MacLeod, the "high priest" (he was over six and a half feet tall), lived at Fiunary Manse—altered and enlarged at about this time—and served the same two churches as his father had done before him, but the whole period of his ministry was overshadowed by the disappearance of the old order in the parish. He watched the depopulation of the country-side and the growth of the slum villages with dismay, yet he was no more able than were his contemporaries to see any solution other than emigration to Morvern's problems of overcrowding and poverty, for like almost everyone else he accepted the general principle of economic *laisser faire*. He expressed the ambivalence of his position plainly in giving evidence to the Select Committee on Emigration in 1841: "I consider it hard that a landlord should be prevented turning his land to the very best account, and that it is a very great hardship that those poor people should be placed in a situation in which they could not turn their time to any account."[4] "The conclusion, therefore," he wrote two years later, summing up his report on the parish, "is reluctantly but maturely come to, that every facility should be afforded to the poor in this and in other parishes similarly circumstanced, of acquiring, in other regions, the independence and comfort now unhappily denied them in their native country."[5] In spite of the love borne him by his parishioners

[1] MacLeod, J. (1843), 186.   [2] MacLeod, J. (1843), 186.   [3] *Census*, 1851.
[4] *Emigration (Scotland) report* (1841), pt 1, 102.
[5] MacLeod, J. (1843), 195.

and the admiration accorded his work by his contemporaries in the
Church, John MacLeod was a tragic figure, beset by increasing lone-
liness, torn between his understanding of the landlords' position and
his emotional involvement with the miseries of the people, "the sole
remaining link between the past and the present—the one man above
the rank of a peasant who remembered the old days and the traditions of
the people".[1] Of the 391 families in the parish in 1843, 370 were connected
with the established church, eight were Roman Catholic and two
episcopalian; the remaining eleven families were probably those who
came out with John Sinclair at the Disruption, and who were to worship
in the Free Church he built in Lochaline in about 1852.[2]

Education had improved considerably since the beginning of the
century, although isolation and poor communications still prevented
many children from getting to school. In the 'forties there were three
full-time parochial schools in Morvern (probably two in Lochaline and
the other at Bonnavoulin), and four other 'schools' for which people
in outlying districts employed itinerant teachers from time to time;
if all else failed even humble folk might maintain tutors, often themselves
mere children, such as those employed in 1851 by the shepherds at
Crosben and at Altachonaich who were aged fifteen and thirteen respectively. Schooling was necessarily distributed unevenly. All the children in Lochaline village went to school—when John Cameron took
over the General Assembly's school there in 1865 he had a weekly
attendance of up to ninety-two pupils, including grown men completing
their education in the winter months between spells of work away from
Morvern—and some of them went on to the University and the Training
College in Glasgow. But in 1843 there were 600 illiterates in a population of 1,575, including 252 children between the ages of six and fifteen;
and even in 1861, of the twelve children aged from five to fifteen in the
settlements of Durinemast, Ardantiobairt, Kinlochteacuis, Rahoy,
Glencripesdale and Camas Salach, not one went to school.[3] Until 1861,
when their status was improved by Act of Parliament, the schoolmasters
were ill-rewarded for their devotion: in 1841 the Morvern schoolmaster's
salary of £22. 10s. 0d. had to be divided between himself and two assistants, and he had nothing else but fees amounting to less than £5 a year,
a house and a small plot of land; he continued to combine his office with
that of postmaster.[4] The language spoken in the parish was still pre-
dominantly Gaelic; English was making headway as a second language,

[1] *Good words* (1882), 548 (from the obituary of John MacLeod by his nephew Donald
MacLeod).
[2] MacLeod, J. (1843), 191; *OS 1872 NB*; *King's memoirs*, p. 231 below.
[3] *Census*, 1841–61; MacLeod, J. (1843), 191–3; *Napier Commission evidence* (1884),
III, 2317–18; *MacKichan's memoirs*, pp. 241–2 below.
[4] *Emigration (Scotland) report* (1841), 104, 171.

however, and there were now a number of immigrants—proprietors, managers, shepherds and their families—who spoke nothing else.

By the middle of the century every large farm was fully committed to sheep. There were still a few groups of smallholders on the edges of the sheep walks (Knock had eighteen small tenants in 1851, Auliston twelve, Achabeg and Oronsay nine each, Fernish seven, and Barr and Larachbeg four each), but the great majority of people now hired themselves out when they could, and had no more than a potato patch to work for themselves. The sheep density in Morvern rose from an average of 150 per 1,000 acres in 1794 to double that number in 1843, with some proprietors taking their stocks up to as many as 500–600 per 1,000 acres by the 'sixties.[1] (This meant that some areas were certainly overgrazed, which was probably the cause of the reduction in the carrying capacity of the sheep farms that took place between the 1850s and 1880s.[2]) Intensive sheep-farming of this sort, with 800–900 sheep to the hirsel, required professional management; and of the fourteen managers and tenant-farmers who were more than crofters in 1851, most were Lowlanders, and only one (John MacInnes of Achafors) was a Morvern man; similarly, of the thirty-two shepherds working in Morvern at the same date, ten had been born in the parish, thirteen elsewhere in the Highlands, eight in the Lowlands and one in England.

There were a few communities of local people, however, which attempted for a while to compete with the large sheep-ranchers on their own terms. These were the small tenants who operated their combined holdings as 'club farms'. If the land was good enough they bought a flock of sheep for ownership in common between several sharers—usually six or eight in number—paying the wages of a shepherd and appointing one of their number to market the sheep and the wool on behalf of them all; there might also be individually-owned cattle, and there would certainly be areas of arable worked separately. Alternatively the club farmers might own cattle in common in addition to or instead of sheep. The system was an extension of the old runrig, cattle-raising township on a higher level of organisation. In the old days the cattle and sheep were grazed in common, but were always privately owned; the essence of club farming was some degree of common ownership.[3] The club farm in Morvern about which most is known was at Achadh nan Gamhna, where six tenants farmed between them 840 sheep, forty-eight cows and their followers and six horses on 2,265 acres of Achadh nan

---

[1] MacLeod, N. (1794), 270; MacLeod, J. (1843), 189; Ardtornish clipping journal, 1851–7, and Lochaline Estate conveyance papers, *AP*.
[2] See below, p. 105.
[3] See *Napier Commission report* (1884), 424–9 for a detailed description of the working of later club farms in the Highlands; some have survived up to recent times (Darling, F. F. (1955), 207–8).

Gamhna, Agh Choire and Unibeg, along the southern shore of Loch Arienas. This farm may have been organised as early as 1823–4 (when a club farm was started at Acharacle in Ardnamurchan); it came to an end when Sellar bought Acharn in 1838 and evicted the population.[1] About five years later the people who were moved by the Gordons from the Auliston area of Drimnin Estate to Oronsay Island formed themselves into a club farm of six members. The stock on this unpromising islet of 429 acres had to be mostly cattle, but these people achieved the remarkable feat of making it support a population of over fifty, dependent on approximately the same number of cows, over a period of twenty-five years (c. 1843–68).[2] Lastly there was a club farm on Lochaline Estate before its members were evicted by Mrs Paterson in 1866; this was probably Achabeg, where nine tenants each had a patch of arable in 1851 varying in size from eight to twenty acres and the only other householder was a shepherd. How much of the 1,242 acres of old Achabeg farm was allowed to them is not known, neither have any details of their stock survived except for the fact that they bought a bull from Achranich in 1852 for £6.[3]

Sheep and wool were overwhelmingly the chief exports from the parish in 1850. Cattle stocks were now relatively small (690 cows to 29,000 sheep in 1843, compared with 2,500 cattle to 14,000 sheep in 1794), and no other industry produced more than a trivial return; mining, quarrying for export and kelping were all given up, and although a good many oak trees were cut and barked for the tanneries—sixty-three people were engaged in stripping bark in June 1841—the annual return from this source was put by the minister at only £100.[4] The economics of an individual sheep-farm of this period will be examined in the next chapter, but some idea of the general increase in the productivity of the parish achieved between the mid-eighteenth and the mid-nineteenth century by the change from old Highland farming to sheep ranching may be had by following the successive increases in its rental values. From the 1730s to the 1750s the rentals of Argyll's two-thirds of Morvern totalled approximately £465. By the 1770s—that is before kelping had become a serious factor in the economy—Argyll's rents had more than doubled, to £974. During the Napoleonic Wars they rose half as much again, though here kelping rents and the general rise in prices will have affected the figure, which was rather more than £1,600. By 1853, well

---

[1] *MacKichan's memoirs*, pp. 235–6 below; the Acharacle club farm is described in *Napier Commission evidence* (1884), III, 2280–5.

[2] *Napier Commission evidence* (1884), III, 2301 ff.

[3] *Napier Commission evidence* (1884), III, 2307; *Census*, 1851; Journal, 19 May 1852, *AP*.

[4] MacLeod, J. (1843), 170–1, 189; *Census*, 1841; *MacKichan's memoirs*, pp. 240–1 below.

before the effects of the sheep boom were felt and in spite of the deflation of the immediately preceding years, the rental of what had been the Argyll properties in Morvern was put by the first of the realistic County valuations at about £3,382. Some of the increase, of course, must be attributed to the change in the value of money and to improvements in communications, but much the greater part of it resulted from changes in agricultural technique.[1]

It has already been said that a new era began with the introduction of regular steamer services to the Sound of Mull in the 1820s. Now the Morvern proprietors and their friends could come and go freely, no longer isolated in their remote province, and their livestock could be shipped out directly to its markets without the costly loss of time and quality that resulted from overland droving. From 1822 until 1855 Morvern was included in the Glasgow–Tobermory service; the best-known ship on the route was *Maid of Morvern*, a wooden paddle-steamer eighty-five feet long which operated from 1827 to about 1841. From 1855 to 1909 there was a twice-weekly service from Glasgow to Stornoway, with Lochaline as a port of call, on which two famous ships named *Clansman* worked: the first an iron paddle-steamer 185 feet long from 1855 to 1869, the second a screw-steamer with rakish schooner bow, 211 feet long, from 1870 until 1909.[2] There was no pier at Lochaline until 1848, but in that year the pier begun during the potato famine was completed, and was occasionally used by steamers. Unfortunately, although it was well placed for the ferry across the mouth of Loch Aline, the water swirls past it at five knots at half tide and is too shallow for ships at low water; consequently the scheduled steamers continued to pull up off the mouth of the Loch, passengers and freight being passed between ship and shore in small boats. Other ships called from time to time in addition to the scheduled services: a large paddle-steamer that called annually at Lochaline to take two or three thousand sheep directly to Liverpool around 1870, a passenger steamer hired for an excursion, a brigantine from Woodbridge that anchored at the head of Loch Aline in the late 'sixties, and any number of small sailing ships that traded casually up and down the coast throughout the century, selling goods and carrying freight.[3]

[1] *Napier Commission report* (1884), 390–1; Mull and Morvern rentals for 1744, 1750 and 1754, and *Book of Mull and Morvern tacks*, vols. '0' and '4', *ICP*; *VR* 1855 (but it is clear from the Achranich ledgers that this valuation had actually been made as early as 1853, although the Rolls do not survive).

[2] Duckworth, C. L. D. and Langmuir, G. E. (1950), *passim*. There are fascinating descriptions of conditions on board *Clansman* (I) in Smith, A. (1865), 69–70, 417–23 and 479–94.

[3] *MacKichan's memoirs*, pp. 235, 236, 242–3 below; *Photographs (Gertrude Smith)*, 45, probably *c.* 1867; and numerous references in the Achranich and Ardtornish ledgers, *AP*.

Road building lagged far behind the steamer services, and it is the almost incredible fact that until the late 1850s there were not five continuous miles of road in the parish on which even a cart could be driven; Achadh nan Gamhna bridge was built in 1821—though it can have been of little use for the next forty years without roads on either side of it—and the principal streams crossing the statute-labour road were bridged shortly before 1843, but, apart from the three miles of the Highland Relief Board's road at Bonnavoulin, absolutely no other road works had been carried out during the first half of the nineteenth century.[1]

The chance of Treasury assistance, lost when the proprietors of Morvern and Kingairloch refused in 1813 to pay half the cost of the Morvern road proposed by the Commissioners for Highland Roads and Bridges, did not come again. The Commission ceased all new road construction in 1821, and the ball was back in the County's court, where it remained, unplayed, for the next thirty-five years. The County authorities did in fact have powers to make as well as to repair public roads through district committees, given them in a series of private Acts of Parliament of which the most recent was the Argyllshire Roads Act (1843). This defined Argyllshire's Tenth District as comprehending the parish of Morvern and the lands of Kingairloch, and empowered its heritors of £200 and over to act as Road Trustees in the disposition of an assessment of from 4*d*. to 8*d*. in the £1 of valued rent, subject to County approval. But it was not until 1857 that additional road-assessments were authorised and the construction of an entirely new network of modern roads linking the most populous parts of the parish with the Moidart road was begun, the road system which is essentially the one that is in use today.

Unfortunately the Minute Book of the Morvern Road Trustees which covered the building of the new roads is lost—the surviving second volume was opened in 1864—but it appears from extra assessments "for new roads" which were entered in the Achranich and Ardtornish ledgers that the main period of road construction was from 1857 to 1862, and from the surviving Minute Book that the roads completed by 1864 totalled 41¼ miles in length and were divided into four sections.[2] These four sections—the numbering of which may have corresponded with the order in which they were completed—were, first, from the Moidart Road at Inversanda via Kingairloch to Torr na Caber (the road junction at

[1] MacLeod, J. (1843), 190; Achadh nan Gamhna bridge has a dated inscription; Acharn bridge may have been built in 1850–1 (*MacKichan's memoirs*, p. 238 below).

[2] *Minute book of the Morvern Road Trustees 1864–90*, ACOL, *passim*; Achranich ledgers 1853–7, 1858–65, *AP*, *passim*. From 1853, when the Achranich ledgers become specific on the subject, the maximum assessment of 8*d*. in the £ was levied every year, plus extra assessments for new roads in 1857 (3*s*. in the £) and 1858 (4*s*. in the £) and supplementary assessments of 4*d*. in the £ from 1858 to 1862.

Achagavel); second, from Torr na Caber to Keil Church, with branches into Lochaline village; third, from Keil to Bonnavoulin, on the shore-ward side of the old statute-labour road; and fourth, from the head of Loch Sunart via Liddesdale to Torr na Caber. These were properly built and graded roads, with metalled carriageways nine feet wide, fully bridged, on which any normal wheeled vehicle of the period could travel with ease; at Lochaline House in Mrs Paterson's time, for instance, there were five farm carts, a landau, a brougham, a phaeton and a dog-cart.[1]

Supposing the cost per mile of these roads to have been of the same order as Fulton's estimate of 1811, and allowing for the bridges and for the few miles of road already built at Bonnavoulin, the total cost of the new roads was probably between £10,000 and £11,000. Since a total of £5,142 was paid towards their cost by the proprietors of Morvern and Kingairloch in normal and extra road assessments during the decade 1853–62 (the rest being provided out of county funds), the proprietors had to pay their half share in the end. (When the roads were first completed a toll was charged for their use, a gate being placed just north of the road-junction by the present doctor's house, but this was discontinued within a few years.[2]) Although the new roads greatly increased the comfort and convenience of the inhabitants of the parish, it is doubtful whether its society or economy would have developed differently had the Morvern Road been built in 1812; even good roads make access to Morvern by land less difficult rather than easy, and to the present day the main line of communications has continued to be the steamer route up the Sound of Mull.

Before the public-road building programme got under way, a private road of comparable quality was made to link Achranich to the Ardtornish ferry at Caolas; this fine road, 2½ miles long, was built jointly by Smith of Achranich and the Sellars of Ardtornish in 1853–5, the first of six important estate roads that were to be completed before the end of the century.[3]

The mails continued to reach Lochaline via Oban, Kerrera, Grass Point and Bailemeonach ferry until 1860; then, when the new roads were opened, via Fort William, the Corran ferry and Kingairloch. In the later period the post-runner set out on foot from Lochaline with the out-going mails on Mondays, Wednesdays and Fridays, and returned from Kingairloch on Tuesdays, Thursdays and Saturdays with the incoming post; another runner carried the mails between Lochaline and Drimnin.

[1] 'Statement of stock and inventory of articles on Lochaline Estate, November 1887', *AP*.
[2] *MacKichan's memoirs*, p. 238 below.
[3] Achranich ledger 1853–7, *AP*; *MacKichan's memoirs*, p. 240 below.

In 1860–1 (the time when the post route was changed, and also when the parish schoolmaster's position was much improved) the post office was incorporated in the Cameron Arms Inn, a small hotel built by John Cameron in about 1848 opposite the new pier at the mouth of Loch Aline, Cameron himself adding the office of postmaster to that of innkeeper. There was as yet no telegraph, and no daily post.[1]

[1] *Oban Times*, 9 Apr., 14 May 1881; *King's memoirs*, pp. 231–2 below; *MacKichan's memoirs*, p. 245 below; Cameron Arms papers, *AP*. John Cameron the innkeeper was not the same man as John Cameron the schoolmaster.

3

HOLIDAY HOME
1850–1870

THE ESTATE AS A CONSTRUCTIVE HOBBY

OCTAVIUS SMITH AND ACHRANICH

A very different sort of person now enters the story, a wealthy and original member of the English intellectual aristocracy, who had little in common with his fellow-proprietors in Morvern except, perhaps, strength of character. Octavius Smith's father, William Smith (1756–1835), after a successful career in wholesale grocery in London, became the first Unitarian to sit as a member of parliament, where he represented Sudbury, Camelford and (chiefly) Norwich for forty-six years, an abolitionist, an emancipator and an outstanding philanthropist in early-nineteenth-century radical politics. His ten children—none of whom lived for less than sixty-eight years, and whose *average* length of life was eighty-two—included Benjamin, also a distinguished politician and the father of Leigh Smith the explorer and of Madame Bodichon the bene-factress of Girton College; Frances, the mother of Florence Nightingale; and two unmarried daughters, Patty and Julia, who were favourites in intellectual society. Two other daughters married respectively G. T. Nicholson of Waverley Abbey and John Bonham Carter; and there were connections by marriage with the Verneys, the Lushingtons and the Cloughs.

William Smith, having been obliged to meet election expenses amount-ing to £40,000 (towards which he sold a notable collection of pictures), had nothing left for his children; his whole estate, which he bequeathed to his wife, came to no more than £5,000.[1] Octavius, who was born in 1796, the eighth child and fourth son of the family, became a distiller, with a factory and private house nearby at Thames Bank in Pimlico.[2] "Having in early life", wrote his friend Herbert Spencer, "been some-what recalcitrant under the ordinary educational drill, he was in later life distinguished not only by independence of thought but by marked inventiveness—a trait which stood him in good stead in the competition

---

[1] Principal probate registry; William Smith, 1835/389.
[2] The Smiths' private residence was later moved successively to Bedford Square and Prince's Gate.

which, as the proprietor of the largest distillery in England, he carried on with certain Scotch rivals."[1] Octavius married in about 1819 Jane Gaches Cooke, a woman whose remarkable amiability and unselfishness complemented her husband's outgoing energy, and they had eight children, all born before he became a landowner in Scotland.

Old William Smith had been appointed an original Parliamentary Commissioner for Highland Roads and Bridges in 1803, and his work for the Commission during the next thirty years caused him to travel to many remote districts in the Highlands; he may well have visited Morvern when the abortive Morvern Road was under discussion in 1810–13. Octavius accompanied his father on some of these journeys, and it was during their travels together that Octavius "fell so much under the glamour of the West Highlands that he purchased [in 1845, ten years after his father's death] the estate of Achranich, in Morvern".[2]

The glamour of the West Highlands: the phrase is John Buchan's (who had the story from Octavius Smith's youngest daughter), and it aptly introduces a factor, new in 1845, which was to have as great an influence on Morvern's development in the second half of the nineteenth century as sheep-ranching and deflation had had in the first. So far the new proprietors had come to Morvern for a home and a position in society, or for a profitable farm; no one before Octavius Smith bought land there for its glamour. In fact no one in the early nineteenth century, except for the MacLeods at the manse, seems to have found Morvern aesthetically rewarding. A travel-journalist wrote in 1824: "That part of Morvern which bounds the Sound of Mull is now as familiar as Cheapside; but very few indeed, if any, have explored the wilds of this barren region."[3] Neither, he implies, could they want to, for a trip by sea to the romantic castles celebrated in Scott's poems would be exploration enough.

But Octavius Smith and his successors were not so much interested in stimulating a gothic imagination as in the possibility of escaping occasionally from the anxiety and pace of their working lives in the industrial south; and for this purpose Morvern was ideally suited. As remote from their everyday affairs as any desert island yet not beyond the reach of an English industrialist with a long annual holiday, Morvern had not only the fresh-scented hills, fertile valleys and winding arms of the sea that make up most of the west coast of Scotland, but also a special quality of other-worldly isolation that set it apart from its neighbours and gave it a magic that increased as other districts became

[1] Spencer, H. (1904), I, 375.
[2] J[ohn] B[uchan], obituary of Gertrude Craig Sellar: *The Times*, 25 Nov. 1929.
[3] MacCulloch, J. (1824), II, 171.

more accessible. Tennyson, when he stayed on at Ardtornish instead of visiting Skye as he had intended, wrote:

"If he did not see Loch Coruisk
    He ought to be forgiven;
For though he miss'd a day in Skye,
    He spent a day in Heaven!"[1]

—and, joking or not, Tennyson was by no means the last nineteenth-century visitor to Ardtornish to describe it as heaven. More prosaically Herbert Spencer wrote in 1877: "Should anyone hereafter use the materials of a biographical kind which will be left behind me, he will probably find clear enough evidence that the most of the happiest days of my life have been spent at Ardtornish."[2] Since the middle of the nineteenth century, in fact, a good many different people appear to have found in Morvern the land of their private dreams. This capacity for satisfying a wide variety of spiritual needs, which became apparent when trunk railways abolished the old difficulties of travel from the south, became a factor in Morvern's development that was as real and influential as its agricultural productivity or its stock of game animals.

In 1845, then, when he was a successful industrialist of forty-nine, Octavius Smith bought Achranich Estate from its non-resident owner for £12,000. No records of the purchase, other than the actual minute of sale, have survived; likewise the farms accounts up to 1849, if any were kept, are now lost. In April 1850, however, a thirty-six-year-old Dumfriesshire man named David Corson was appointed manager in place of Peter MacNab, the man whom Smith had taken over with the estate. Corson immediately started an account book in the form of a Journal, to be followed by Ledgers from 1853, and, although his book-keeping like his spelling was at first very shaky, it has nearly all been preserved; taken with various other estate papers, the valuation rolls and the official Census enumerations, these books give us a fairly clear picture of Achranich in the mid-nineteenth century.

To summarise: Smith had bought the same Achranich Estate as had been mapped for MacDonald of Borrodale in 1815;[3] 8,803 acres, mainly of rough pasture but with a little wood, the highest hill (Caol Bheinn) rising to only 1,395 feet. But whereas in 1815 a population numbering 125–150 persons appears to have been arranged in groups chiefly engaged in working arable strips round the periphery of the sheep farm, by 1851 the population of the estate was down to sixty-seven people, and all communal organisation for subsistence agriculture had disappeared. The Achranich people in 1851 were in three groups. The regular employees

[1] Sellar, E. M. (1907), 56.   [2] Duncan, D. (1908), 191.
[3] *Achranich plan 1815*; see above, pp. 17–18.

of the estate (paid six-monthly) and their families were the most numerous: four families and seven single persons, twenty-eight people in all, living (except for two of the three shepherds) at Achranich itself. Next came four families and a single person, twenty-five people in all, whose chief income derived from day-labour on the estate; their houses, like those of the regular employees, were occupied rent-free, but were further from Achranich. Finally there were three crofting families, fourteen people in all, with holdings in three different parts of the estate for which they paid rent, whose members were also employed casually by the estate.

As a business enterprise Achranich Estate in the 'fifties was both small and unprofitable. The books are not immediately easy to interpret because of their division of the material into separate trading accounts for the 'farm' and the 'estate', a practice which began with the first ledger of 1853 and was continued for the rest of the century. Throughout Corson's time this division resulted in a 'profit' for the farm which was consistently unrealistic because capital investment in the farm was always charged to the estate, and a consequent 'loss' on the estate which was equally unrealistic. The Smiths also subsidised the estate side of the accounts by refraining from passing certain items, such as architects' fees, through the books, while scrupulously paying Corson for goods and services consumed by the family. The hidden subsidy was always relatively small, however, and provided that 'rent' (or interest on the capital value of the property) is added to the combined account—for it was not entered until after the end of the century—the books give a very fair total picture of the estate's finances.

Gross receipts from 1853 to 1859 averaged almost exactly £1,000 a year, representing a crude output of about £16 per head of the population. Setting only current expenditure against receipts, the 'farm' showed an average annual profit of £421 during the same period, but the deficit on the 'estate' (or capital investment) side converted this into a net loss averaging £431 a year. The real cost of the estate to Smith can then be arrived at by adding the average valued rental (which represented a charge of about three per cent on the market value of the property) to this annual loss: the average total for 1853–9 was £763.[1] It is possible that a proprietor whose only aim was to make the estate pay—and it will be seen that Octavius Smith was anything but this—could have eliminated the cash deficit by getting rid of the less productive members of the population and by avoiding inessential capital outlay; but it seems most unlikely that anyone could have made a return on the purchase price.

The estate was of course stocked chiefly with sheep: sales of sheep and wool accounted for sixty-eight per cent of the gross receipts. From 1854

[1] There is a more detailed analysis of the Achranich accounts on pp. 173–5 below.

to 1859 there was an average stock of 2,050 beasts, mostly Cheviots but including four to eight per cent of black-faced, representing the moderate density of 233 sheep per 1,000 acres.[1] The tedious and wasteful process of 'smearing'—whereby a mixture of tar and butter was rubbed into the roots of the fleece as a protection against maggot—was still normal practice, although some dipping was also carried on at least from 1857; even a skilled man took half an hour to smear a single sheep, and the process had the additional disadvantage of lowering the value of the wool. There is no evidence that any sheep were wintered away from the estate before the winter of 1858–9, when sixty-six hogs were put into the parks of Alexander Ferguson of Lochaline, and none were wintered away from Morvern until the 'sixties. The stock of cattle averaged fifty-seven head in winter during the same period, including both dairy and black cattle; it was a 'flying stock', whereby the beasts were traded in such a way that the summer stock was larger than the winter stock, rising probably to a maximum of about eighty-five head. The cattle brought in a further seventeen per cent of the gross receipts, the remaining fifteen per cent representing sales of dairy produce, corn, horses, pigs, etc. The extent of the land under cultivation by the estate, as opposed to the private plots of employees and crofters, is not known, but it was certainly not large; of the 341 bolls of meal used from 1855 to 1859, 276 (eighty-one per cent) were bought in from elsewhere.

The permanent employees of the estate were engaged on a six-monthly basis. In the 1850s they generally numbered ten: a manager, three shepherds, four farm workers, a dairy maid and a kitchen maid; there was no gamekeeper except for a lad employed until 1852 (when he was eighteen) at a farm-worker's wage. All these employees lived rent-free, and were allowed to cultivate patches of ground round their houses if they wished. Representative annual wages in the mid-'fifties (following a general increase of about twenty-five per cent at the beginning of the decade), including the value of housing and of other payments in kind, were: manager, £65; head shepherd, £24; ploughman, £15. 10s. 0d.; dairy maid, £8. 10s. 0d.

During the same period some five to ten day-labourers and tradesmen were employed by the estate (the number varied with the season), the working day being of ten hours and the full week of sixty hours; from 1854 they were paid fortnightly. With the exception of two labourers who were virtually permanent employees, these men were employed for only part of the year—on the average they worked for seventy-five per cent of the available days—and were paid from 1s. 6d. to 1s. 8d. per day

[1] Livestock figures in the Achranich ledgers of the 'fifties refer to the situation in December of each year, which will not have been quite the same as the clipping stock (the figure more usually found); the difference, however, was generally small.

for an adult labourer. Ordinary earnings might thus total £16–£17 a year; most of them lived off the estate and paid rent elsewhere. Tradesmen's rates were higher, going up to 3*s.* 6*d.* a day in the case of the blacksmith. In the early 'fifties the Achranich smith had been a regular estate employee at a wage which eventually reached £42 (including a house) but from 1854 James Cowan the Keil smith was employed by the day, working at Achranich eight or nine days in twelve, fuel and iron provided by the estate; and this arrangement was continued, at the same rate, until 1880.

The twenty to thirty building workers and tradesmen who by 1857 were working virtually the whole year round on the estate were technically in the employ of the superintendent of masons, from 1854 a Perthshire man named Peter Haggart; he lived on the estate and acted as contractor for building works, drawing the men's wages fortnightly from the manager. Similarly Charles MacKichan the joiner, who started to come to the estate in 1853 and who resided permanently from 1856, acted as a joinery contractor, drawing wages fortnightly for himself and one or two assistants.

Achranich, then, was by no means a grand estate. With no 'mansion house'—there was simply an old farm house at Achranich which the proprietor shared with the manager and his family and with several farm workers (Plate 14*a*)—and with no shooting and fishing to speak of, Octavius Smith brought his family up for the first time in the autumn of 1846 to what probably seemed to them a glorified country cottage. It was at any rate a magnificent playground for the younger children. The eldest son of the family, Frederic, the playmate of his cousin Florence Nightingale, had died eight years before on Sir George Grey's expedition of exploration to Western Australia; and the second son, Valentine, who was twenty-one in 1846, appears to have made an unsuitable marriage at the age of fifteen and to have been estranged at this time from the rest of the family; but the other six children spent half their time in Morvern, and for them it became in every way a second home. There were two more boys, Gerard (aged nineteen in 1846) and Willie (eighteen), then four girls: Flora (twelve), Rosalind and Edith (about ten and eight respectively), and Gertrude, then a baby of two. They were encouraged to range widely over the property in an annual visit that generally lasted from late July to mid-December. Writing of the 1850s, Eleanor Sellar said of the Smith girls: "In those days schoolroom life in a London home was necessarily constrained and colourless, and the change to the freedom of their Highland home was pure joy to creatures so simple and active. They scoured the hills and valleys on their ponies, attended by Kitty Carson [*sic*], the manager's daughter, as a sort of female groom [she was two years younger than Gertrude],—a quaint arrangement, but characteristic of their father's unconventional ways. The boys cleaned their own guns, and did a hundred things for themselves which would now [1907] be done for them; but how happy they were, and the days never seemed to be long enough for all the delightful things that had to be done in them."[1]

There were visitors, too, and—after 1850—much social intercourse with the Sellars of Ardtornish. The game books, although one-sided because of the exclusion of women from all shooting and most fishing throughout the nineteenth century, probably give a fairly complete record of the Smith's male guests, and they show the visiting to have been on a modest scale in the 'fifties; indeed it could hardly have been otherwise, for the old farm-house at Achranich had only fourteen rooms in all at this time, and was occupied in any case by the Smiths, and by the Corsons and their rapidly-increasing family, a total of about fifteen persons in the late 'fifties even supposing that the seven farm workers who normally lived in the farm-house were boarded out in the neighbouring cottages. The sporting guests averaged five a year from 1853 to 1859 (not counting members of the immediate family or the Sellars), half of them being related to the Smiths either directly or by marriage.

In the early years shooting was a minor activity. No game book was kept before 1853; in that year only thirty-four grouse were killed, twenty-one in 1854 and none at all in 1855. Bags increased from 1856, but the annual average remained under 150 birds over the next five years. It is doubtful indeed whether really large bags of grouse were possible so long as the estate was fully stocked with sheep and cattle; Smith did the best he could by paying the shepherds a regular addition to their wages "for proticking the Game" from 1853 (when the post of gamekeeper was discontinued). Red deer were even less common; in 1843 they had paid "only occasional visits" to Morvern, and they remained a very rare sight until well into the 'sixties, none being killed on the estate until 1868. Roe deer were relatively frequent in the old woodlands and new plantations, and the Smiths sometimes organised roe drives in the Dubh Dhoire–Claggan area north of Achranich; a roe was killed in this way in 1857, and three more in 1859.

Fishing was of greater potential interest to Octavius Smith, but at first he came upon a hindrance to his favourite sport which was painfully frustrating. The River Aline—as the *Gearr Abhuinn*, or 'short river', was called from 1856—runs from Loch Arienas to Loch Aline; it is a very fair salmon river and remarkably good for trout. Smith had bought one bank of the Aline and, since the title to his estate specified that it was "with fishing", he was doubtless looking forward to fishing it. He soon discovered, however, that, owing to a complicated process of

[1] Sellar, E. M. (1907), 45–6.

conveyancing going back to 1768, all rights to fishing the River Aline were by this time the exclusive possession of the owner of Acharn and Clounlaid: his neighbour Patrick Sellar of Ardtornish.[1] Sellar, not the man to give up his rights easily, prohibited Smith from fishing the Aline, even from the Achranich bank, which was infuriating as being plainly against natural justice. However, Smith as the owner of Achranich was in a position to retaliate. Sellar's estate, it will be remembered, was divided into two parts, based on Ardtornish and Acharn respectively, with Smith's estate between them. The efficient operation of a large sheep farm such as Sellar's required the fairly frequent movement of flocks from one part of the property to another as the sheep were gathered for lambing, clipping, smearing and so forth; and Smith could make things very difficult for Sellar by hindering these movements. In 1848, therefore, he denied Sellar's right of way across Achranich Estate, facing him with the alternatives of a difficult droving route all the way round by Altachonaich, or of an equally difficult ferry route across Loch Aline. Sellar and Smith being "both men accustomed to have their own way, and very much disliking to be thwarted...a modern Montague and Capulet drama was enacted".[2] For the next two years Achranich and Ardtornish were not on speaking terms.

Awkward as Sellar was being about the fishing, there can be no doubt that he was legally in the right; he did own all the fishing rights concerned, and Smith could not really justify his denial of an established right of way. Eventually, therefore, Sellar took Smith to court, but before the case came to judgment more moderate councils prevailed. At the instance of a distinguished lawyer, the two men met "on the hill" between their estates and agreed to a settlement. In October 1850 they signed a lengthy 'Agreement', the most important provisions of which were that Sellar's rights of way across Achranich were defined and confirmed, and that he promised to sell half his fishing rights to Smith for £400.[3] Honours were even: Smith got what he wanted, and he could never have expected to get it for nothing; Sellar gave up what he could not decently keep, and was well paid for doing so. Eleanor Sellar wrote years later: "I remember Gertrude, Mr Smith's youngest daughter, telling me how the new peace was inaugurated by her mother, her three sisters, and herself, then a child of eight [actually six], lunching at Ardtornish. Mr Sellar set her beside himself and called her his little lady. ...The goings to and fro between the two places were as perpetual as they had been strictly forbidden the year before!"[4]

[1] See pp. 134–6, 139, 145–6 below, for an explanation of how this came about.
[2] Sellar, E. M. (1907), 43.
[3] The Sellar–Smith Agreement of 1850 is summarised in greater detail on pp. 179–80 below.
[4] Sellar, E. M. (1907), 43, 44.

When the Achranich fishing books were begun in 1853, the catches were mostly of trout; indeed there were several records in 1856 of what must have been the irritating spectacle of the Sellars catching more and heavier salmon than the Smiths. However, catches of salmon were shortly to improve, possibly helped by the salmon pass that was cut round the Uileann falls in 1855, reaching thirty fish killed in 1863 and fifty-two in 1864.

One of the fishermen was Herbert Spencer the philosopher, who in 1851 had been drawn into what became a close friendship with Octavius Smith by their common interest in economic *laisser faire*. He visited Achranich for the first time in 1856, and was delighted with the warmth and unconventionality of the family in their "temporary" quarters—by which was meant the old farm-house, which had actually been in use by the Smiths for the past ten years, and was not to be superseded by the new mansion house, then just begun, for a further ten. Writing home on 16 August, a fortnight after his arrival, Spencer said: "I am enjoying myself much here—so much so that I think scarcely at all about myself or my ailments. The days slip by very quickly—so much so that there generally seems no time for anything. Fishing, and rambling, and boating, and bathing, form the staple occupations; varied, occasionally, with making artificial flies and mending fishing rods. My friends are delightful people—extremely kind and considerate, cultivated and amusing." The visit was a success from every point of view, and Spencer was invited to extend it to six weeks. "During my stay", he wrote later, "there were picnics on the Table of Lorne (a flat-topped mountain visible from Oban) and at the Ullin waterfalls; ascents of Ben Yahten and Shean, whence there are fine views of Rum and Skye; drives to the village, to Ardtornish, to Glen Dhu, &c.; a boating excursion round to Loch Linnhe, with a picnic on its rocky, wood-clothed shore; a sketching trip to Killoonden Castle; and many days on the banks of the River Aline, or Aline water, and on Loch Arienas, during which I justified my heresy [his belief that there is no particular virtue in 'local flies'] by catching great numbers of sea trout."[1] It may be remarked that some of the activities mentioned by Spencer are for the hardy and active; the water around Morvern does not seem warm for bathing at any time of year; while Beinn Iadain (1,873 feet), Sithean na Raplaich (1,806 feet) and the Table of Lorn (*c.* 1,500 feet) were not easy of access from Achranich in the 'fifties, even with the aid of ponies.

The unconventionality of the Smiths' life at Achranich, which attracted others besides Spencer, derived from the character of Octavius Smith. He was, Eleanor Sellar wrote, "a very clever original man, overflowing with energy, and could scarcely believe in anything being well

[1] Spencer, H. (1904), I, 490, 491.

done unless he saw it done or did it himself. Dearly did he pay for this characteristic, for when the new house was building, of which he watched every detail, a charge of gunpowder used for blasting not having gone off as quickly as he expected, he went too near, and it exploded, damaging his eye. It was equally characteristic that when he was taken into the house,—and by this time it was dusk,—he blew out the candle that his wife might not see his wounded face. When I saw him, a glass eye had restored his appearance and scarcely marred his good looks, and his one eye saw more than most people's two...One day, I remember, they had decided to go to Mull, and though it was so stormy that any one else would have given up the expedition, Mr Smith would not be beaten, but made all his party wear life-belts! Another day...we sailed over to Mull, taking our luncheon with us; and because there was a notice, 'Trespassers will be prosecuted,' Mr Smith insisted on our taking our picnic in a nasty marshy field [i.e. the one with the notice] as a protest against what he considered 'over-legislation'!"[1]

In approaching the improvement of the estate to which he and his family were becoming increasingly devoted, Octavius Smith moved without undue haste; perhaps he felt that agricultural reform is best taken at an agricultural, not an industrial, pace; perhaps that at a cost of about £750 a year Achranich was already quite expensive enough—for, the estate having been turned over to sheep before he bought it, further improvement was likely to cost him more, not less, money. The appointment of Corson as manager in 1850 was in itself a reform, and it was symptomatic of Smith's approach that one of Corson's earliest purchases for the farm was a copy of "Johnstons Agricultril Chemestery".[2] But the sheep farm was working well and needed little physical change. Sheep drains were cut, for instance, on a small scale throughout the 'fifties, but no really large drainage works were undertaken until 1860, when the sheep boom justified them economically. What Smith did do in the 'fifties was to make a start on the remarkable series of estate buildings that was to be carried on by him and by his son until the end of the century, and which remain as an enduring monument to their proprietorship.

The Smiths' building in Morvern was carried out in four main phases of which the first, the reconstruction of the nucleus of the estate at Achranich, is of immediate concern. The first building of this group was a large barn and byre set by the Rannoch near the old farmhouse of Achranich (Plate 2a), and including rooms at the ends for the Smiths' servants and for bachelor farm-workers. Built c. 1851—like

[1] Sellar, E. M. (1907), 44–5, 46.
[2] Journal, 11 Oct. 1850, *AP*. The book which Corson bought for 5s. was Johnson, C. W., *Agricultural chemistry for young farmers*, London [1843].

several of the early buildings it is dated—it is a massive, functional building, but with a flavour of gothic in its decorative use of projecting roof-timbers, in the triplets of lancet-windows high on its gable-ends and in the pointed clerestory lights, that marked a turning-point in the architecture of the district: nothing so sophisticated or so foreign had been seen in Morvern before. The barn was followed in 1852–3 by a boat-house at the head of Loch Aline (Plate 2*b*, later superseded, as it could not be used for any but the smallest boats except at high tide), again with gothic lancets; and in 1856 by the beginning of work on a new mansion house on the rising ground over the Rannoch, north-west of Achranich steading. In the event this house—originally called Achranich New House, but renamed Ardtornish Tower—was to take ten years to complete, not because it was especially large (it had about thirty-five rooms in all) but because in most years work was carried on only in the summer and autumn when Octavius Smith was there to oversee it him-self, and because building was interrupted altogether for four years (1860–3) when Smith bought Ardtornish Estate and turned his attention to the improvement and repair of Ardtornish House. Its design, how-ever, is likely to have been fixed by 1856, and in fact the italianate-gothic approach that had been hinted at in the earlier buildings was now fully developed (Plate 5). The new house was cruciform, with steeply-pitched gables, heavy dormer-braces and patterned stonework; its most engaging feature was a romanesque clock-tower, which stood off to one side like a campanile. The architect (or architects) of these early build-ings cannot be identified, for their fees were not passed through the books of the estate, but there is a possibility that the mansion house was an early work of Alexander Ross of Inverness; Ross, who will appear again as the designer of the second Ardtornish Tower many years later, suc-ceeded to his father's architectural business in 1853, and there were strong stylistic links between the first mansion house and the second.[1]

Table 2. *Achranich and Ardtornish estate building: Phase I*

Description	Probable date	Evidence for date
Achranich barn and byre, with workmen's and servants' rooms (Plate 2*a*)	1850–2	Building dated "1851"
Achranich old boat-house (Plate 2*b*)	1852–3	Building dated "1853"; *MacKichan's memoirs*
Achranich New House, later called Ardtornish Tower (I) (Plate 5)	1856–9, 1864–6 (demolished 1884)	Ledgers; *MacKichan's memoirs*

[1] See below, p. 101.

If Smith did not rush into new schemes for re-organising his farm and his estate, he moved with at least as much care in his dealings with the people who lived on his land. There were, for instance, four crofting families still living on the estate in the early 1850s, and it is instructive to follow the details of their lives as they appear in the census enumerations and the estate account books.

Allan MacLachlan lived at Dubh Dhoire, probably in the house that stood up the 'Fiddler's burn' at M.R. 702487. In 1841 he had described himself as a hand-loom weaver, but by 1850, when he was about fifty years old,[1] he was a crofting labourer with a wife and seven children. They ended the year 1850 owing over £2 in rent, but from November 1850 to December 1851 Allan and the three eldest children earned just over £30, which cleared the arrears, paid the current year's rent (another £2) and left them with £26 to spend; of this they took £15-worth of oatmeal, etc., from the estate, £10 in cash, and left themselves £1 in credit. Their rates of pay at this time were: Allan, 1s. 5d. a day; John (allegedly aged twenty, but probably in fact fifteen), 1s. 4d.; Mary (allegedly seventeen, really thirteen), 8d., and Barbara (eleven), 4d.–6d. In 1852 Allan decided to emigrate—there is no suggestion that he was evicted—and in August the family sold their crops of barley and potatoes (£7. 10s. 0d.) and their furniture and tools (£3. 14s. 6d.) to the estate, and bought passages to Australia (£8. 10s. 0d.) for all of them and new clothes (£2). Having settled their rent and supplies against their earnings so far, they were left with a credit balance of £2. 7s. 6d., which they took in supplies and cash; and to this Octavius Smith added a present of £2. The family presumably sailed soon afterwards, but their subsequent career in Australia does not appear to be recorded.[2] The house at Dubh Dhoire was not re-occupied.

Alexander MacPherson, a married but childless crofter of forty-two, owed the estate no less than £11. 2s. 5d. at the end of 1850. He appears to have occupied his croft (which may have been on the site of the new mansion house at Achranich) right through the 'forties for, although he himself was not enumerated in the Census of 1841, his parents and wife were occupying the house at that date. It may be that the potato famines had prevented him from paying his rather stiff rent of £4 and that Smith, who had first come to reside on his new estate in the autumn

---

[1] MacLachlan's age was given as thirty-five in the Census of 1841 but as fifty-two in that of 1851. Such extreme vagueness, or untruthfulness, about ages is a common feature of the Census returns at this period; two of MacLachlan's children had their ages 'increased' in this way in 1851, probably because they were being paid for casual labour by the estate at rates higher than their real ages justified. Sometimes there were other motives for making a change: Anne MacMaster of Uileann was twenty in 1841, but only twenty-six—and still unmarried—ten years later.

[2] Information from the Mitchell Library, Sydney, N.S.W.

of 1846 at the very moment when the potato crops were failing most disastrously, had not pressed him. MacPherson earned £11. 7s. 5d. in 1851, but he was clearly not making ends meet, and in November his rent was reduced from £4 to £2. 10s. 0d. a year. Even at the lower rent he made only minimal progress towards repayment, and in May 1852 he left the estate. The debt was never repaid, and was written off the books. Again the croft was not re-occupied.

Donald Cameron, who in 1850 was a widower of rather over fifty, had also occupied his croft all through the 1840s, at Samhnach beside the lime-kiln at the foot of the 'Fossil burn'. With the help of his son Peter (then aged eighteen) and daughter Mary (twenty-four), who were both employed casually by the estate, he had managed better than MacPherson, and ended the year 1850 owing nothing; but in 1851, even with the children's help, he could not meet his rent of £2. 10s. 0d., and in December owed £1. 17s. 5d. The response of the estate was to cancel his rent altogether from the beginning of 1852; from then on, although he was still described as a crofter, he was in fact one of the day-labourers of the estate, figuring on the fortnightly pay sheet when it was started in 1854 at his usual rate of 1s. 10d. a day. For a while he was able to build up a credit balance, which reached £2. 13s. 2d. by the end of 1853, but thereafter his earnings fell off—probably as the result of infirmity—and he died in September 1855 with only £1 to cover his funeral expenses (coffin, 14s. 7¾d.; two bottles of whiskey, 5s.; biscuits, 1s.) and 10s. over. The house at Samhnach was still roofed in 1872, but it is not known who, if anyone, occupied it after Cameron's death.

Hugh Cameron, called 'Crosag' after his birthplace near Arienas settlement,[1] was not a crofter in 1850, but a 'wood-keeper' or 'wood-forester' employed by the estate at £7 a year with a cottage rent-free; he was then thirty-four years old, with a wife and family of four (to be increased to eight during the 'fifties). At the end of 1851, however, he exchanged this employment for a croft at a rent of 30s. a year; its location is unknown, but it was in the Achranich area, possibly near the new boat-houses where there was a house at M.R. 700467. From the beginning of 1852 he worked most of the time as a day-labourer for the estate, earning £21 at 1s. 6d. a day in that year (representing work on ninety per cent of the available days), and over £16 in 1853, when his rate was increased to 1s. 8d. a day. Even after paying his rent this left him with considerably more than he had got as a full-time employee, but his position was to be improved yet further. In 1854, when the fortnightly payment of the estate day-labourers was re-organised, Hugh Crosag headed the

---

[1] He was almost certainly the son born to Hugh Cameron, 'residenter' of Arienas, on 11 Feb. 1816; the Parochial Register of Births (*RGO*) actually enters this child as "Eun", but such mistakes were not uncommon and there are no other likely candidates.

list at the top rate of 2*s.* a day. Working virtually full-time he personally earned £29 in that year, which left him with £27. 10*s.* 0*d.* rent paid; even the head shepherd got only £24 including the value of payments in kind. Cameron was able to continue earning at the same rate throughout the 'fifties, never working less than ninety-two per cent of the available days, and actually getting a further increase when his rent was cancelled in 1857, so that in 1858 and 1859 he had £29 clear. Indeed, apart from the manager and from some of the skilled building-tradesmen (who did not live rent-free), Hugh Cameron was the highest-paid employee of the estate at this time; and, although in later years his earnings decreased relatively as other wages rose, he was never laid off right up to the time of his death in 1883, a striking example of security of employment in the case of a labourer who was valued by his employers.

The treatment accorded to these crofters indicates both imagination and flexibility in Octavius Smith's handling of the people on his estate, and suggests a reason for his uniformly good relations with the inhabitants of Morvern. Smith could so easily have swept all the crofters away, as Sellar had done, but instead he chose to treat each case individually, and with considerable generosity. It was an exercise in empirical philanthropy of which old William Smith would have approved, and it was to be followed by many more acts of benevolence by Octavius Smith and others of his family. In spite of his being a foreign proprietor—or in one way, perhaps, even because of his extreme foreign-ness, for at least he was not another in the depressing procession of Lowland Scots who exploited the Highlands—Smith was remembered, not as an oppressor, but as an unusually kind landlord who found work for people whenever he could, the only one of the Morvern proprietors no longer alive who received any praise in the evidence given to the Napier Commission in 1883.[1]

ACHRANICH BECOMES ARDTORNISH

Rosalind, the Smiths' second daughter, fell ill and died in 1853, to be followed by her sister Edith in 1855; then Gerard, the third son, was killed in a railway accident, probably in the early summer of 1858.[2] Gerard appears to have been particularly close to his father—they had been up at Achranich shooting together in March of the same year—and this second death by misadventure of a favourite son, coming so soon after the deaths of the two girls, must have been a serious blow to Octavius Smith. There was no family visit to Achranich in 1858; but in the following year Smith resumed the personal direction and improvement of the estate with renewed vigour, negotiating during the

[1] See below, pp. 218–21.   [2] Sellar, E. M. (1907), 45.

autumn with the heirs of Patrick Sellar for the purchase of Ardtornish Estate.

Since Sellar's death in 1851 his Morvern properties had been adminis-tered by one of his sons (first J. A. Sellar and later P. P. Sellar) acting as managing trustee through a farm-manager at Ardtornish, and it has been seen how various members of the Sellar family came to spend their holidays at Ardtornish House and were on friendly terms with their neighbours the Smiths. Ardtornish was a larger and a better sheep farm than Achranich. Discounting the rented hirsels of Glensanda and Altachonaich (in which Octavius Smith was not interested), but includ-ing the 1,203 acres of rented land at Unimore which was included in the hirsel of Unibeg and which Smith wanted to keep on, the total area of the two parts of Ardtornish was 22,778 acres, which was stocked in the mid-'fifties with an average of 6,605 sheep; this was more than three times the size of the Achranich sheep-stock, and it was grazed at the density of 289 sheep per 1,000 acres compared with Achranich's 233.[1] (The Ardtor-nish cattle were of very minor importance, averaging only eighteen head at the same period.[2])

But it was not only as a good sheep farm that Ardtornish was attrac-tive to the owner of Achranich. In addition it would give him a pleasant house to live in while his new one was being completed; it included the wild and beautiful coast from Ardtornish Bay to Eignaig; it would give him complete control of the fishing in the Aline, and the fishing in Loch Arienas as well; and would generally increase his privacy by enlarging the area available for recreation, and make of the two properties a new estate that would be greater than the sum of its parts. It could not be cheap—Achranich had cost Smith only 27*s.* an acre in 1845, but now with the sheep boom getting under way even hill-farms could cost 40*s.* or more—and on 12 September 1859 Smith agreed to buy Ardtornish from Sellar's heirs for £39,500, or 36*s.* an acre. That the price was a fair one is suggested by the County's official valuation of the property, which in 1858–9 had been raised to £1,165 per annum; at the usual rate of about three per cent this gave a price very close to what Smith paid. He took possession at Whitsun 1860.

Ardtornish Estate, as Octavius Smith immediately decided to call his whole combined property of Achranich, Ardtornish and Acharn, was something on an entirely new scale, being much the largest coherent estate that had ever been farmed by a single proprietor in Morvern. Smith had previously owned less than 9,000 acres, now he owned more than 30,000; the turnover of Achranich in the 'fifties had averaged £1,450 a year, that of Ardtornish in the 'sixties was to average £4,210;

[1] Ardtornish clipping journal 1851–7, *AP.*
[2] P. P. Sellar to Walter Elliot, 23 Aug. 1884, *AP.*

his regular employees had numbered ten, now they numbered thirty. The whole thing, in fact, was three times as large as it had been.

The economic position was also considerably improved. The crude output per head of the population of the estate (156 people in 1861 and about 150 in 1871) was, at £28 per annum, seventy-five per cent greater than that of Achranich in the 'fifties; the whole enterprise, moreover, taking 'farm' and 'estate' accounts together, showed an average trading surplus from 1861 to 1869 of £682 a year. Although this profit was more than offset by the valued 'rent' of the property, which averaged £1,728 a year during the same period, the proprietor was getting a good deal for himself out of the difference (or real deficit) of £1,046 a year: the completion of his new house, improvements to Ardtornish House and its maintenance, gamekeepers' and gardeners' wages, etc. It would appear that if the estate had been let during the 'sixties to a rent-paying tenant he could have operated at a modest profit while carrying out at least essential maintenance work on the estate, although capital re-investment on the scale in which Octavius Smith actually engaged (rebuilding cottages, roads, walls, drains, etc.) would not have been possible.

The sheep economy was even more absolute than before; over eighty per cent of the gross income of the estate came from sales of sheep and wool. The increased profits derived not only from the larger scale of the business but also from the greatly increased prices of sheep and (especially) wool, and from the technical innovation of dipping, rather than smearing, most of the sheep as a protection against maggot, which made it possible to produce a larger proportion of the more desirable 'white' wool. Table 3 gives decennial averages of the prices generally obtained for Scottish sheep and wool from 1840 to 1899.

The message of these prices—and especially of the huge margin of white Cheviot over laid (or smeared) black-face wool—did not escape Smith and his manager. Cheviot sheep continued to make up ninety per cent or more of the Ardtornish stock until the 'eighties, when their relative unsuitability to hill grazings, compared with black-face, began to tell against them as the prices and the profit margins fell. The estate produced only laid wool up to 1862, but in 1863 thirty-five per cent of the wool sold was white; by 1868 the percentage of white wool sold had risen to eighty-six, and in 1871 no laid wool was sold at all. The smearing of a few sheep continued for several years longer, but was completely abandoned during the 'eighties.

The Sellars' employees were taken over with the estate and, although a few of them moved away during the early 'sixties, the majority stayed on permanently at Ardtornish. Among them were the head shepherd at Ardtornish, William Nichol, a Northumberland man aged thirty-six in 1860, who had the responsible job of going to buy Cheviot tups from

Table 3. *Prices of Scottish sheep and wool, 1840–1899*

| | Sheep | | Wool per stone (24 lb.) | | | |
	Cheviot	Black-face	Cheviot laid	Cheviot white	Black-face laid	Black-face white
1840–9	17s. 11d.	12s. 0d.	14s. 0d.	—	7s. 0d.	—
1850–9	20s. 3d.	14s. 9d.	17s. 5d.	—	9s. 11d.	—
1860–9	24s. 5d.	17s. 11d.	25s. 3d.	36s. 4d.	13s. 3d.	—
1870–9	29s. 11d.	22s. 5d.	22s. 6d.	32s. 3d.	11s. 11d.	—
1880–9	28s. 2d.	22s. 7d.	16s. 10d.	26s. 9d.	8s. 0d.	12s. 4d.
1890–9	22s. 11d.	19s. 7d.	13s. 8d.	21s. 11d.	7s. 8d.	10s. 11d.

Notes: Based on figures given in *THASS*, 5th series, xxxiii (Edinburgh, 1921), 313–16. The price of sheep was first obtained for each year by averaging the three average annual prices of wethers, ewes and lambs respectively, and an average was then obtained for each decade. The price of wool, similarly, was first obtained for each year by averaging the maximum and minimum prices for each year, and an average was then obtained for each decade.

'Laid' means smeared; 'white' means not smeared, only dipped.

There was no trade in white Cheviot wool before 1860, or in white black-face wool before 1880.

time to time at Hawick, not far from his own country; Thomas Dalgleish, thirty-eight, the Ardtornish gamekeeper, whose son George was later to become underkeeper and give his name to the stretch of the River Aline by Craigendarroch; and Sam Henry, twenty-seven, a Dumfriesshire shepherd who worked at Crosben, and whose grandson of the same name was to become factor of the estate seventy years later. Corson continued as manager with his salary doubled from £50 to £100 a year, now busier than ever; in 1861, for instance, besides administering the daily affairs of the estate and keeping the books, he journeyed to Oban on estate business in May and June; to the Inverness and Fort William markets in July; to the Salen (Mull) market in October; and to Strontian to arrange for the wintering of the hogs in December. Most of the employees' wages and emoluments remained the same in the 'sixties as they had been at Achranich in the mid-'fifties, and the daily rates for labourers remained unchanged until the early 'seventies. The Ardtornish shepherds, however, had been paid rather more than those of Achranich; Nichol, for instance, got £22 in cash in 1860, plus grass for three cows and a quantity of meal, while MacMaster, the Achranich head shepherd, got only £16 in cash plus a similar quantity of meal; and the Achranich shepherds' wages were raised the following year to comparable levels. The keeper occupied a position of new importance, and was paid £30 in cash plus allowances in meal and coal, and other perquisites.

Improvements to the fabric of the estate made during the 'sixties included new steadings at Crosben (1863), new dykes (both stone and turf), a wire sheep fence erected on the march with Lochaline Estate (1869), and almost 200 miles of new sheep drains (mostly cut in 1860 and 1863). The estate roads were enlarged and extended (at Achadh nan Gamhna, for instance, in 1863), and the estate acted for the Morvern Road Trustees in organising the construction of some of the new County roads in the early 'sixties.

But the most important improvement of this period was the construction of six new shepherds' cottages between 1857 and 1866, constituting the second phase of the estate building carried out by the Smiths. Six cottages may not seem much, but they began the great series of Achranich and Ardtornish employees' houses which was to extend to thirty fine new dwellings by the end of the century. Hitherto the majority of the estate employees had lived in the usual thatched, dry-stone cabins of one or two rooms into which households of five or six persons were somehow fitted, dirty, damp and cramped. Some of the luckier ones had slated, lime-built cottages with chimneys, which were a good deal more comfortable although still very small. The inadequacy even of estate-built housing—in this case the Bonnavoulin terrace built by the proprietor of Glenmorvern in about 1840—was made all too plain in evidence given to the Napier Commission as late as 1883:

"[*Lord Napier:*] What sort of houses are they? Are they all slated houses?—[*Alexander MacDonald of Bonnavoulin:*] They are slated houses. ... [They] are reasonably large, but there is only one room.

[*Napier:*] Do you mean that there is a kitchen and one room, or only one room, which is a kitchen and everything else?—[*MacDonald:*] There is only one apartment.

[*Napier:*] Is the apartment divided by the beds being put across the middle?—[*MacDonald:*] The arrangement of the beds, or how they are placed, is left to ourselves, but they are generally placed along the wall. ...

[*Napier:*] Is there any loft above?—[*MacDonald:*] Yes.

[*Napier:*] Do people sleep in the loft?—[*MacDonald:*] Yes, a bed can be placed in the loft, but we have to use the loft as a barn. It was intended for that. ...

[*Napier:*] About what size is this one room?—[*MacDonald:*] The houses are from 12 feet to 14 feet each way."[1]

The average number of persons per household at Bonnavoulin from 1851 to 1891 was 5·6, so that each person had an average of only thirty square feet of living space.

Octavius Smith's new cottages, the first of which was the head

---

[1] *Napier Commission evidence* (1884), III, 2298.

shepherd's house and byre at Uileann, built in 1857–8 before the purchase of Ardtornish, were conceived from the start on an entirely different scale: they were substantial slated houses, mostly of two storeys, containing a kitchen–living-room, scullery and pantry (or similar arrangement) downstairs and generally three bedrooms above. They had double the accommodation even of the better cottages that they supplanted. At Old Ardtornish, where one end of an existing double cottage was rebuilt by Smith for William Nichol in about 1862, the other half of the original building was left standing for use as a milk-house and store, and a direct comparison of the old and new houses can be made (Plate 6b). The old cottage was a good one for its period; dating perhaps from around 1840, it is a slated, lime-and-rubble building with two rooms and a closet, and chimneys at each end; its area, measured according to the Scottish Development Department's current 'Rules' for assessing the size of houses, is 385 square feet.[1] Smith's new cottage, on the other hand, has six rooms (sitting-room, kitchen and pantry, with three bedrooms upstairs), and measures 911 square feet. This is a size that would be acceptable in a new house built today; the average number of persons living in agricultural workers' houses in Morvern in the second half of the nineteenth century was 5·5, and the areas laid down in 1956 by the Scottish Development Department for new three-bedroomed cottages for five and six people were 890 and 960 square feet respectively.[2]

Table 4. *Achranich and Ardtornish estate building: Phase II*

Description	Probable date	Evidence for date
Uileann shepherd's cottage and byre (Plate 3a)	1857–8	Ledgers: building dated (?) "1857"
Durinemast shepherd's cottage (Plate 3b)	1861–2	Ledgers: building dated "1861"
Inninmore shepherd's cottage (Plate 6a)	1862	Ledgers
Old Ardtornish shepherd's cottage (Plate 6b)	(?) 1862–3	Ledgers
Eignaig shepherd's cottage (Plate 7a)	1864	Ledgers
Clounlaid shepherd's cottage	1866	Ledgers: building dated "1866"

The designer of the first group of cottages is again unknown. But they do not appear to be the work of a professional architect, being singularly free

---

[1] The Rules require the total internal area of a house to be measured, including partition walls but excluding staircases (*Scottish housing handbook*, pt 3, 'House design' (HMSO, Edin. 1956), 25–6). No allowance is made here for the possibility of using the space above the roof joists of the older house.

[2] *Scottish housing handbook*, pt 3, 'House design' (HMSO, Edin. 1956), 23.

of the architectural clichés of the time, and it may be that Peter Haggart, the estate superintendent of masons, was chiefly responsible for them. They are solid, unsophistocated buildings, showing thick walls to suggest snug interiors, but enlivened by recessed façades, contrived arrangements of building stones and wide-hanging eaves; lacking the refinement of Barham's later cottages, but fitting naturally into the landscape.

The Smith family moved across from Achranich farm-house to Ardtornish House as soon as it belonged to them, spending the seasons of 1860 to 1865 inclusive at their new home. At last, in 1866, the new house at Achranich—henceforth called Ardtornish Tower—was finished, and the family moved back from Ardtornish House on 11 October. Although the proprietor was once again based at Achranich, Ardtornish House was by no means abandoned, and the family moved freely between it and the Tower until the 'eighties.

Apart from these removals, the Smiths' family life in Morvern continued much as before, with a visit of five or six months in each year, from July to December; Mr and Mrs Smith always came, together with Flora and Gertrude, usually Willie (now with his wife, Harriet) and, from 1859, Octavius's heir Valentine who, although he never stayed for long, appears to have patched up his differences with the family at least to this extent. A notable—and for us invaluable—family activity at this time was photography. From 1864 or 1865 until the mid-'seventies Gertrude Smith—or Gertrude Craig Sellar as she became in 1870—took an admirable series of landscapes, architectural studies and portraits at Ardtornish, of which some ninety have survived. (There are also ten more Ardtornish photographs taken in 1867 by "S.S.", who may have been Gertrude's friend Sophie Strutt, the elder daughter of Lord Belper.) While these hundred pictures hardly compare with the superlative work being done at the same time by the great mid-Victorian photographers, they are nevertheless of considerable merit, artistic as well as technical, and are also remarkable as being the work of a girl in her twenties using the difficult wet-collodion process (Plates 5, 8, 9, 14*a* and 16).[1]

The number of sporting guests in the 'sixties (other than members of the family) increased to an average of eleven a year, of whom four were relations, and there were also as a rule one or two guests who did not shoot or fish, such as the Arthur Cloughs and Mrs Gaskell.[2] In general

---

[1] No copies of these photographs (the locations of which are given in the Bibliography, pp. 253–4 below) are dated, but most of them can be placed within a year or two from internal evidence. It is just possible, although improbable, that Gertrude Smith used one of the early dry-plate processes rather than wet collodion.

[2] The Cloughs stayed for three weeks in Aug.–Sept. 1860 (Game book, 26–7 Aug. 1860, *AP*; A. H. Clough to C. E. Norton, 11 Oct. 1860, *Correspondence*, II (1957), 578). The date of Mrs Gaskell's visit is uncertain, but it may have been later in 1860 (E. C. Gaskell to G. Behrens, *Letters* (1966), 784).

the emphasis on sport was rather heavier than it had been. Soon after the purchase of Ardtornish, Octavius Smith cleared the sheep off about a tenth of his 30,000 acres, a roughly rectangular patch of some 3,060 acres behind Achranich stretching from Dubh Dhoire south-eastwards to Srath Shuardail, in order to improve the grouse shooting.[1] Bags of grouse rose steadily, exceeding 300 birds in each of the years 1867 and 1868; and seventeen roe deer were shot between 1861 and 1869. Perhaps more significant, in view of future developments, were the sightings of red deer, of which the first was recorded in 1864: "Saw a splendid Stag on Larch Wood at Arienas."[2] Exactly why red deer, which in the 1840s had been only occasional visitors to the parish, should now have been re-colonising Morvern is not clear. It can hardly have been the result of taking the sheep off Achranich, the first area to be cleared for sport in Morvern, because the deer appear to have spread down through the White Glen; the answer may be that there was less poaching for food now that the human population was smaller and more concentrated. Whatever the reason, sightings of deer in the area Clounlaid–Crosben–Uladail increased rapidly in frequency during the next few years, until eventually a hind was shot in the Uladail area in October 1868; and in the following year, although there was still no attempt at stalking, two stags were killed near Claggan.

Fish, too, were pursued with enthusiasm and ingenuity. On 9 October 1860 Herbert Spencer caught a seven-pound salmon "with a fly of his own making", but the next day he "fished the river with a magnet, caught nothing, fish wouldn't rise";[3] a few weeks earlier Willie Smith had caught a six-pounder on the Aline at 5.0 a.m.; Alfred Bonham Carter caught a nine-pound and an eighteen-pound salmon on the same day in 1863 and put both of them back; and in 1868 Willie *speared* five grilse in a pool below Uileann falls. Apart from the year 1862, when there were "no Fish caught except a Salmon 8 lbs by Papa out of season!", the 'sixties saw an annual average of twenty-five salmon and 327 sea-trout taken at Ardtornish. But perhaps the best idea of the outlook of the sportsmen of the period is given by an entry in the game book for 19 October 1866 written by Hugh Bonham Carter:

"[Weather:] strong south wind with squally showers and heavy cloud. [River:] low but rising, water discoloured.

---

[1] The precise date of the clearance of the sheep off Achranich is not established by surviving documents; it certainly took place in the 1860s and probably earlier in the decade rather than later. Walter Elliot, giving evidence in 1884, said that it happened as soon as Smith bought Ardtornish, but Elliot was not reliable about events that had taken place long before he came to the estate (*Case for Thomas Valentine Smith Esq.*, *24 January 1885*, 31, *AP*); no herding books survive for this period, and the game books and shepherds' pay-sheets are inconclusive.

[2] Game book, 5 Nov. 1864, *AP*.   [3] Game book, 9 Oct. 1860, *AP*.

"First flood after the long drought, the consequence of previous 24 hours rain. River still quite low, but water discolored. Hooked a fish in the edge of the stream, close to the island in the Big Pool, & lost him after 5 or 6 minutes play. Hooked *the* large fish [a twenty-pound salmon], off the point of the island, in the stream a little below the greentopped rock. He sulked steadily at first, but on being well stoned, by little Crosheck [Hugh Cameron's son], ran fiercely down the pool & jumped, twice, then came back & sulked in the stream. I then got him into the weedy bay, where I crossed the creek, wading. It being impossible to land him there, after playing him ¾ an hour more, we drove him, with stones into the creek, & recrossing it at the flat stone, I brought him to the net, & Dalgliesh [the gamekeeper] landed him on the island after 1¼ hours play

"—Hooked the next fish [an eight-pound salmon], in the bottom of the Washing Pool, close to the top of the island—he ran instantly *down* the small stream, on the East side of the island, under the trees, where I expected, he would have entangled my line; getting clear by some miracle of the boughs & stems, he rushed thro' the bridge, & I down the river after him, to a small pool below the sawpit—After a little rest, he then took me, wading, down the stream to 70 yards below the Plantation, where the left bank being clear of trees, I got out & killed him, after the most exciting run I ever had. In short it was the best days sport in my life."[1]

The growing importance of sport is also indicated by the position of Thomas Dalgleish, the gamekeeper, whose wages averaged £54 a year in the mid-'sixties, including payments in kind, compared with the £48 of the head shepherd. The Dalgleishes moved from Old Ardtornish to the head of the loch in about 1868, where they occupied the new keeper's house in the grounds of Ardtornish Tower;[2] and in that year George Dalgleish, then aged only thirteen, was appointed under-keeper at a wage of £16 a year. 'Vermin money' was not yet paid, but Dalgleish was at first able to supplement his already high income by taking the estate's rabbit-trapping contract for £10 a year, and selling the bag which was worth £30–£40. (From 1867 the estate employed a trapper directly and raised Dalgleish's cash wage by a further £10 a year, financing the increased wage from the profits of the rabbit-trapping and gaining the benefit of the time Dalgleish had previously spent trapping.) Game money continued to be paid to the shepherds; from 1860 the regular payment was changed to a piece-rate of 6*d*. per bird shot on the hirsel, and from 1869 5*s*. per stag was paid as well.

[1] Game book, 19 Oct. 1866, *AP*. Bonham Carter's twenty-pounder was caught just south of Achadh nan Gamhna bridge; the location of the second run is uncertain, but he probably hooked the fish just north of Achadh nan Gamhna bridge and may not have killed it until he was approaching George's bridge.
[2] The date of their removal is uncertain; see below, p. 91.

But, even more than Achranich had done, Ardtornish offered the Smiths something better than holidays with shooting and fishing. More than an escape, more than sport, more than land and profitable flocks, Ardtornish was 150 people, a community in precarious equilibrium with enough to eat for the moment but without wealth enough to forget the threat of hunger. Seeing that they were needed, the family responded eagerly. Help could be given directly to the needy, a boll of meal here, half a ton of coal there; "the poor of this locality", the local paper reported when the Smiths returned to London at the beginning of 1868, "and of other adjoining landed properties, will feel the absence of Mrs Smith, as she regularly and personally visited them, and supplied them with many necessaries of life."[1] The account books record many such gifts of supplies made by Mrs Smith and Flora over the next ten years—the need of the poor was so great that there was little danger of hurting anyone's pride by a direct approach—but there were also less obvious ways of helping the community.

Provision was made for the schooling of children living around the head of Loch Aline who were too young to walk to school in Lochaline village. Duncan Cowan taught at Achranich at the estate's expense in 1860, and a little later (probably from 1861 to 1877) the disused kitchen of Achranich farm-house was used as a 'side-school' for infants by the Morvern School Trustees. "Mrs Smith," the *Oban Times* went on, "whose kind-hearted qualities cannot be fairly expressed, has, during her stay here [in 1867], been busily engaged in supplying the children of this locality with school materials and other valuable and useful gifts; and her frequent visitations to the school encouraged and pleased the children very much."[2]

Quite as important as good works and educational assistance were the social functions which the proprietors initiated and took part in. First among them was the great annual Ball that was held at Achranich early in October—it evolved during the 1850s from a lesser harvest-home festival—to which all the people on the estate, and those associated with it from the village and elsewhere, were invited. Octavius Smith's hospitality (all paid for out of his private account) was magnificent: there were fiddlers and pipers, plenty of whiskey, and huge quantities of food and drink to which everyone sat down at two distinct meals during the night.[3] At the Ball of 1867 dancing began after tea "and was continued until morning dawn"; Corson the manager was master of ceremonies, and beside Mr and Mrs Smith, Willie, Flora and Gertrude, the function was attended by their friends the Strutts, Miss Julia

---

[1] *Oban Times*, 18 Jan. 1868.   [2] *Oban Times*, 18 Jan. 1868.
[3] *Oban Times*, 5 Oct. 1867, 22 Oct. 1870, etc. There was also a 'barn ball' at Ardtornish on 22 Sept. 1859, to which the Smiths were invited (Game book, 1859, *AP*).

Tollemache and Mr MacNichol of Garmony, Mull. In 1870, at the last Estate Ball that Octavius Smith was to attend, there were two hundred guests, and when Mr and Mrs Smith retired early—at 1.0 a.m.—from the 'ballroom' in the great barn there were speeches and they were cheered over and over again. On another occasion, in 1866, Smith chartered the Hutcheson paddle-steamer *Pioneer* and took all the employees of the estate and their families on a trip round Mull to Staffa and Iona, a jolly outing which ended with "three ringing cheers" for Mr Smith and "a Volley from the old Cannon on the look-out hill [Torr na Fhaire], by old Murdoch the Ferry-man".[1]

The occasionally sycophantic terms in which the Smiths' benevolence was described by contemporaries no doubt concealed the views of some members of the community who resented the very existence of large landowners no matter how good their intentions or how lavish their contribution to the wealth of the district, for the animosity towards the Morvern landlords which flared up in the 'eighties had been smouldering for at least half a century. But this is not to say that the gratitude so expressed was generally insincere, and it is worth noting that the glowing description of the steamer outing was written in old age by an Ardtornish employee who had been prominent in the agitation against the Morvern landlords in the 1880s.

[1] *MacKichan's memoirs*, pp. 242–3 below. MacKichan places this event in September 1865, but the *Oban Times* for 5 Oct. 1867 makes it clear that in fact it took place in 1866.

4

RICH MAN'S CASTLE
1870–1900

THE ESTATE AS A MACHINE FOR SPORT

THE 'SEVENTIES: A CHANGE OF DIRECTION

Several events affecting Morvern occurred about the year 1870 which were part cause, part effect, of a change of direction in the development of the parish, a change which was to alter its social and economic balance yet further by the end of the century. First, in 1869, Mrs Stewart and her fellow-trustees of Glencripesdale put their sheep farm of some 13,500 acres up for sale; the detached farm of Beach went in that year to Robert MacFie of Airds, but the remainder was sold in 1871 to members of the Newton family, Warwickshire people with wealth deriving from property in Birmingham, who later the same year bought the adjacent sheep farms of Laudale and Liddesdale and called the whole 23,500-acre result Glencripesdale Estate. Glencripesdale was not as large as Ardtornish, but it was of the same order of size, and it was conceived—even more than Ardtornish had been in 1860—as a recreational estate, with sport uppermost in the proprietors' minds. Secondly, at Ardtornish itself (which dominated the life of the parish for the rest of the century and which must remain our chief subject) a stag was stalked and killed for the first time on 20 August 1870; and six months later, on 27 February 1871, Octavius Smith died in London, the estate passing to his eldest surviving son, Valentine. Finally, the average price of white Cheviot wool dropped from its record price of 50s. 6d. a stone in 1864 to a low of 25s. 6d. in 1870.[1] Wool prices were to recover some of their former buoyancy during the rest of the decade, but the writing was on the wall: it said "Made in Australia". The industry of the emigrants abroad was going to be no easier to bear than had been their idleness at home.

Highland agriculture, like that of the rest of Great Britain, was to suffer severe depression by the end of the nineteenth century. In the 'seventies, however, it was unaffected by the slump in wheat prices which ruined the English and impoverished the Lowland farmers; and, while imports of Australian merino wool, unchecked by any tariff, reduced one source of the Highland sheep-farmer's income, prices for sheep

---

[1] *THASS*, 5th series, xxxiii (Edinburgh, 1921), 316.

(unaffected as yet by the import of frozen carcasses) continued to rise and thus offset some of the loss on wool. The increased emphasis on sport at the two largest Morvern estates during this period, therefore, was at first not so much a reaction to the agricultural situation as the satisfaction of a new desire. Valentine Smith wanted more stags stalked each year than were available at Ardtornish in 1870; and as he was already a rich man, he could afford to make this possible.

Octavius Smith, who had inherited no wealth from his father, died worth close on £400,000; he left most of his money to his wife and younger children, while Valentine as eldest son got the means of making more money—the distillery business—and also Ardtornish Estate, which enabled him to spend some of it.[1] Valentine Smith was forty-five years old at the time of his succession, a small man, moody and with-drawn; with his father's brains and energy and ambition but lacking the effervescent enthusiasm that had been so attractive in Octavius; sharing, too, his father's philanthropic liberality but without the personal charm that was needed to raise his giving above the level of institutionalised charity. Perhaps he was unhappy. He had married, at the age of fifteen, a woman of thirty-three, from whom he later parted. Now he was living with another woman (whom he eventually married when his wife died in 1900), but it was a situation that would never be accepted by the society of his time, a furtive liaison that everybody knew about and nobody acknowledged. It is unlikely that Lydia, his first wife, ever visited Ardtornish, or that Annie, his mistress, did so openly before their marriage. But the whole pathetic affair was surrounded by such a fog of euphemism and secrecy that many unconnected details of Valentine's life and character are now lost.[2]

[1] Principal probate registry; Octavius Henry Smith, 1871/352; copy probate dated 12 May 1871 in *SRO*. Octavius Smith bequeathed to his wife his personal posses-sions, £5,000, and an income of £8,000 a year from the distillery and his leasehold coal-mines; half of his coal-mine shares to Valentine and half to William; the income on £50,000 to William, on £70,000 to Flora, and on £130,000 to Gertrude (who was now married and likely to produce an heir); and the residue of the estate, valued at under £300,000 in all (not counting Ardtornish), to Valentine. By a dis-position of 27 Feb. 1867 Octavius had technically given Ardtornish Estate (then valued at £70,000) to his wife, who on his death passed it at once to Valentine (*RSA* 1871: 92, 93).

[2] Such information as there is comes from personal recollections, and from a diary kept by Valentine Smith in 1900 (the year of his first wife's death and of his marriage to his former mistress) in *AP*; there are also a number of letters written by Smith in *AP*, most of them addressed to his manager Walter Elliot, but includ-ing none of a personal sort. There was a great burning of family papers at Ardtornish on the death of Gertrude Craig Sellar at the end of 1929 (when the estate was about to be sold out of the family), in which all personal documents concerning the Smiths and the Sellars were destroyed, and which Valentine Smith's diary of 1900 survived probably because the book in which it was written resembles the gamekeeper's journals of the period.

We do know, though, that he was a keen and successful shot who was not much interested in fishing. Eighteen-seventy was a comparatively late date for the beginning of stalking at Ardtornish—Scrope's *Art of deer-stalking* had appeared in 1838, forests elsewhere were regularly let by the early 'sixties, and Alexander Craig Sellar, who maintained a close friendship with the Smiths, had been stalking at Rhifail in Strathnaver since 1865[1]—but it is likely that there were simply not enough stags in Morvern until that date to make stalking worth while. As it was, only seven stags were killed in 1870, six in 1871 and five in 1872. The gradual return of the deer was soon accelerated, however, by the clearance for their accommodation of a series of grazings by Valentine Smith. It has already been mentioned that Octavius Smith cleared the sheep off about 3,000 acres of land behind Achranich soon after 1860, chiefly in order to improve the grouse shooting; now Valentine enlarged this area by clearing the adjacent hirsels of Claggan (about 1,330 acres, 1873), Tearnait (3,600 acres, 1874) and Inninmore (3,200 acres, 1880), finally protecting this new forest of some 11,200 acres by putting up a sheep fence from Uileann to Eignaig in 1882–3.[2] Bags quickly increased: the first five years' stalking (1870–4) yielded an average of seven stags a year; the second five years (1875–9), seventeen stags a year; and the third five years (1880–4), twenty-five stags a year (Plate 16). Stalking was not confined to the forest—Acharn–Crosben and Clounlaid–Uladail were regularly stalked—but about three-quarters of the stags were killed on ground that had been cleared (seventy-two per cent, for instance, in 1880–4).

Besides clearing sheep to make a deer forest, Smith encouraged the preservation of all game on the estate by the payment from 1872 of 'vermin money'; the rate, which remained unchanged for the rest of the century, was 6*d.* each for birds' heads and eggs (mostly hoodie crows, but including a few 'gledes' or hawks), £1 for each vixen, 10*s.* for each dog fox and 5*s.* for each fox cub. In 1872–9 the annual totals of vermin claimed for averaged 118 heads, 38 eggs, 3·0 vixens, 2·1 dog foxes and 9·4 fox cubs.[3] Most of the money was earned by the keepers, but occasionally shepherds, who also benefited professionally by this attack on predators, were able to put in a claim.

But social life at Ardtornish was not yet dominated by sport—or, indeed, by Valentine Smith. In June 1870 his youngest sister Gertrude

---

[1] Scrope, W. (1838); *Stirling Maxwell Committee report* (1922), 3–5; Rhifail game book, 1864–70, *AP.*

[2] Uileann hirsel appears to have had its regular stock of sheep removed in about 1885, but the area continued to be used until after 1900 for pasturing hogs after wintering, and for gathering. See Map 9.

[3] Totals of vermin killed did not alter much over the next twenty years; equivalent annual averages for 1893–8 were 101 heads, 63 eggs, 2·0 vixens, 1·2 dog foxes and 10·7 fox cubs.

was married in London to Alexander Craig Sellar, the youngest son of Patrick Sellar, and the Craig Sellars now took over Ardtornish House (where each of them had lived at different times when they were younger) as their own holiday home, having it rent-free from the estate but paying the taxes. From 1871 to 1877 Mrs Smith came every year to the Tower (she died in 1878), and Flora continued to visit Morvern for some years longer, living at first with her mother at the Tower and later with the Craig Sellars at Ardtornish House. All of them stayed for longer holidays than did the owner himself, whose practice was to come up for no more than three or four weeks a year, from late August to late September, when he got what shooting and stalking he could before hurrying back to his business and his mistress in London.

The life at Ardtornish of the Craig Sellars, Mrs Smith, Flora and their friends in 1872 and 1873 is engagingly described in the diary of two sisters, Gertrude and Conny Astley, who came to stay as the guests of Gertrude Craig Sellar.[1] The Astley sisters, who were respectively five and seven years younger than Mrs Craig Sellar, were the daughters of the late F. D. P. Astley of Felfoot and Dukinfield, and were at this time co-proprietors with their brother and another sister of Arisaig Estate. In 1881, following the death of her brother, Gertrude became sole proprietor of Arisaig, and two years later was married to Arthur William Nicholson, a great-nephew of Octavius Smith; Conny never married. These spirited girls had already visited the Smiths in Morvern in 1869, when they had fished Loch Arienas and the Aline—the only women to appear in an active role in any of the Ardtornish game books of the nineteenth century—and had caught between them seven sea-trout (including a three-pounder) and a six-and-a-half-pound salmon.

The sisters' journey from Edinburgh to Ardtornish in the autumn of 1872, before the days of the railway to Oban, was an astonishing adventure. Gertrude Astley was then twenty-three years old, and Conny twenty-one. Their train was late at Greenock on the evening of Thursday 3 October, which caused them to miss the *Clansman*, the Hutcheson steamer that plied a regular weekly service from Glasgow to Stornoway, calling at Lochaline on Fridays (outward) and Tuesdays (return). Discovering that another steamer, Martin Orme's *Talisman*, was due to leave for Oban and Mull later that night, they got themselves on board. At Oban the next morning, however, a storm was blowing down the Sound and no boat could be found to take them across to Morvern. Neither would the *Talisman* stop before it got to Quinish on the north-west coast of Mull. The girls decided to stay on board nevertheless, persuading the Captain to run in close to Ardtornish Point and fly a

[1] The parts of the diary which refer to Ardtornish are transcribed on pp. 188–212 below.

signal, hoping that their hosts at Ardtornish House would notice it and put off for them in a boat. The signal was seen and its meaning correctly guessed—there was as yet no telegraph into Morvern, but the Craig Sellars were worried by their guests' non-arrival and were watching for developments—but unfortunately no boat could be got off in time, and the *Talisman* proceeded up the Sound with its unwilling passengers. At Tobermory a small boat came out to the ship, and the Captain did after all stop to let them go ashore; but they were still a long way from Ardtornish. Undaunted, the girls looked again for help, and this time persuaded two boatmen to set off with them at 6.0 p.m. in an open boat to sail the fifteen miles back down the Sound. It was a difficult, stormy passage, the bitter wind chilling and frightening them, but they reached Ardtornish pier at last after dark, stiff with cold but safe and in good spirits, to be welcomed with relief by their friends at the House.[1]

This episode scarcely accords with our conventional belief in the incapability of well-bred Victorian girls, but it fits in well with the energy and enthusiasm with which people at Ardtornish approached their diversions at this time. Gertrude Craig Sellar, for example, who was then nursing her first baby, would go for long, fast walks dressed (for there was no alternative) in the heavy, unpractical clothes of the 'seventies, including full-length skirts and several petticoats. One day after lunch the Craig Sellars and the Astley girls were rowed the seven miles across the Sound to Salen in Mull, then walked by road to Torosay in the hope of seeing their friends the Guthries, and—finding them out—back to Craignure, where they took the steamer to Loch Aline and walked home in time to change for dinner: a total of sixteen or seventeen miles walking in the afternoon.[2] Again, when they were all staying at Ardtornish Tower (the family moved freely between the two houses), Gertrude Craig Sellar started for Eignaig with Gertrude and Conny Astley, this time together with a manservant and a pony; they were to walk fourteen miles altogether, mostly on a rough hill path. It started to pour with rain, soaking the women's clumsy dresses, but they persevered and reached the cottage with time for a hurried meal as puddles of water spread round their feet. "After partially drying their pocket handkerchiefs, gloves, etc. they retrace their steps G[ertrude] & C[onny] feeling as if their petticoats were lined with lead"—and this on a track which climbs abruptly seven hundred feet up from Loch Linnhe.[3] On other occasions women as well as men cut down trees, sailed John Sellar's schooner up the Sound and clambered up the rough cliffs at Garbh Shlios; and in September 1873 the Astley sisters reached Ardtornish from Moidart after

[1] *Astley diary*, 3 and 4 Oct. 1872; and 'Chapters of a future story' (not transcribed).
[2] *Astley diary*, 10 Oct. 1872.   [3] *Astley diary*, 28 Oct. 1872.

a journey which ranked in complication and enterprise only after their amazing voyage from Greenock of the year before.[1]

The Sabbath was not taken very seriously. There was no shooting or fishing on Sundays, but walks were freely undertaken, and sometimes games as well; on a Sunday in 1873 Gertrude and Conny Astley "break the Sabbath by playing croquet with M[r] J Sellar & M[r] Rutson". The only Sunday on which anyone was recorded as having been to church was immediately following a social visit to the Manse, when Gertrude Astley wrote: "M[r] T Sellar, Miss T[ollemache] and G[ertrude] go to Kirk. They are supported under their sufferings by feeling that they are keeping up the character of the family." On the other hand the party at Ardtornish House ended a wet Sunday by singing hymns before going to bed.[2]

Enthusiasm for the scenery was frequently and lyrically expressed. "Never did Ardtornish"—wrote Conny Astley in a particularly gaudy passage—"better deserve J R's emphatic name of 'that Heaven' than on this lovely morning. L. Aline may truly be said to have *given itself up* to reproducing the glory of the hills & woods, seeming with a wonderful & subtle appreciation to give back each delicate shade of beauty, from the faintest mist of blue smoke to the hues of a bit of rainbow nestling in the hollow of a hill."[3] Equally evocative was the romance of "the Monarch of the Morvern Hills"; here are Alex Craig Sellar ('Friend-in-law') and Conny Astley ('Jetsam') stag-watching on an October evening in 1873 near Craigendarroch: "...Suddenly a deep & awful sound is heard proceeding from the flat sort of Strath which stretches between them & the stag. It sends a thrill of excitement through them & the 6 pt[er] suddenly pauses & listens. They creep a little further forward & behold the Big Stag!...F-in-law & J gasp & murmur ecstatically 'What horns! What music!' For a full hour & ½ they lie on the hill enjoying the exciting spectacle of this despot surrounded by his wives challenging all comers, chasing the foolhardy youngsters who ventured to come between the wind & his nobility. ...Twilight was rapidly turning to darkness when Friend-in-law & Jetsam arose—stiff—somewhat damp about the knees & elbows, but edified & exultant!—F-in-law remarked to Jetsam when he bade her good night in the evening 'We feel that today we have not lived in vain.'"[4]

It will be apparent that the Astley diary, despite the triviality of much that its authors recorded—partly, indeed, because of that very triviality—gives us a vivid and intimate glimpse of the life led by

[1] *Astley diary*, 16 and 18 Oct. 1872; 8 and 23 Sept., 8 and 11 Oct. 1873.
[2] *Astley diary*, 13 Oct. 1872, 7 Sept. and 5 Oct. 1873.
[3] *Astley diary*, 14 Oct. 1873, additional entry.
[4] *Astley diary*, 3 Oct. 1873, and additional entry of the same day.

the owners of a Highland estate in the 'seventies, a document to place alongside the tale of Phineas Finn's doings at Loughlinter. The account books can tell us what the owners had to pay for their pleasures, but this diary shows us, as nothing less personal can do, what those pleasures were, what the proprietors actually got out of owning their sporting estate. The life that the sisters described so disarmingly was one of unproductive ease, led by a tiny class of mutually-acquainted gentry—the majority of the men and women they name can be identified in the memoirs and reference books of the period—who might make little contribution to the life of the district in return, but who were generally kindly, civilised and philanthropic.

Valentine Smith himself is noticeably absent from the diary. Although he was certainly resident at the Tower when Gertrude and Conny Astley were staying at Ardtornish House from 5 to 9 September 1873, they do not mention him at all, and he took no part in the outings and other activities which were shared by parties from both houses; similarly, while a large party from Ardtornish went annually to the Argyllshire Ball at Oban in the 'seventies, Valentine Smith (although usually in residence at the time) never went with them.[1] This is not to say that he was a recluse—later on, especially after he had built his yacht, he often went on expeditions with his guests—but he was not much interested in country pursuits unless he could carry a gun, and he seems to have had little time for his brother and sisters.

Dobhran, a 320-ton steam yacht, was built for him at Port Glasgow in 1875–6 at cost of about £20,000,[2] and Valentine used her frequently, both for stalking the forest from the Loch Linnhe shore and for the sake of the new mobility in the district that she offered him and his friends. *Dobhran* was almost lost one morning at the end of August 1877 when running at full speed on a southerly course off Applecross on the Inner Sound of Skye; the owner and seven guests were on board, and a crew of twenty-one. "Mr. Smith and the captain had gone below to consult the charts before entering Loch Carron", wrote Herbert Spencer, who was on board, "leaving the vessel in the charge of the mate, with directions respecting his course. But the mate, thinking he could make a short cut, quickly put an end to our cruise. . . . The vessel struck [a reef] and heeled over to about 45° forthwith, and her stern began to sink. We all got into the boats safely in about five minutes. . . . We hung around for some time to see what would happen: some of the sailors fearing that the vessel, which was continuing to blow off steam, would explode, . . . and others fearing that she would slip off the rock and go down. Spite of all

---

[1] *Oban Times*, 6 Sept. 1873, 13 Sept. 1879, etc.
[2] *Lloyd's yacht register* (1878), *s.v.* 'Dobhran'; Spencer, H. (1904), II, 307. Built by Cunliffe and Dunlop, *Dobhran* measured 193 feet overall, and was fitted with a 100-H.P. two-cylinder steam engine.

protests, Mr. Smith, with the daring characteristic of the family, insisted on going on board again to get the ship's papers and other valuables; and presently returned, bringing, among other things, a quantity of wraps for the ladies."[1] *Dobhran* was floated off by the insurers ten days later and sent back to Port Glasgow for repair, after which she remained in service until the end of the century; nobody says what happened to the mate.

An extract from Herbert Spencer's diary for 1879 gives an idea of the uses to which the yacht was put, and of the range of activites undertaken by Valentine Smith and his friends: "[Tuesday] 12th [August 1879]. Left [Oban] at 7 by Skye-boat; Loch Aline at 8½; and Ardtornish [Tower] at 9½; afternoon, netting in Loch Arienas and picnic with the ladies there. 13th. Revising, walking, and drive to old Ardtornish in afternoon. 14th. In the yacht Dobhran up Loch Sunart to Strontian; back by 9 o'clock. 15th. Started at 8 in the Dobhran to Staffa; fine day; explored cave; back by 6½. 16th [and 17th]. Walking, revising and reading. ...18th. Started in Dobhran up Loch Linnhe; saw two stags stalked and shot by V. Smith [at Inninmore, with a left and a right]; on to Loch Corrie and Loch Leven; back at 8. 19th. Fishing on Loch Arienas; 14 sea-trout and 12 loch-trout in 5 hours. 20th. Revising, reading, and walking. 21st. Fishing on Loch Arienas; no sport. 22nd. Revising, walking, and playing lawn tennis. 23rd. Excursion in the Dobhran to Loch-na-Kiel, in Mull. In the sound saw a whale about 50 ft. long (which accompanied us for a mile or more). 24th. Revising, billiards, and walking; went to Old Ardtornish in the afternoon. 25th. Fishing from 11 to 5 in river; 6 sea trout—one 5 lb. one 2 lbs.; missed 4 salmon. 26th. Fishing in river 11 to 5; got 2 salmon—one 7 lb., one 6 lb.; and lost a third. 27th. Revising and walking. 28th. Fishing from 11 to 3; 3 sea trout—one of 2 lbs. 29th. Revising and walking; afternoon, to Acharn with the ladies. 30th. Revising and walking. 31st. Revising and walking to Old Ardtornish in afternoon. *Sept.* 1st. Revising, very wet; in all day. 2nd. Ditto. 3rd. Ditto; packing up. 4th. Left for Oban by the Plover at 2; Oban at 4..."[2]

There was little mention in all this of the work-people of the estate. The keepers, of course, were in constant touch with the gentry, as were those estate workers who acted as house servants or as gillies while the family was in residence: Gillean MacLean, for instance, a ship's carpenter by trade who came to work at the estate in the summer of 1872 when he was twenty-eight years old, and who served the Craig Sellars for several seasons at Ardtornish House in the intervals of working for the estate as a tradesman at daily rates.[3] But the personal contact between owners and people appears to have decreased during the 'seventies: Flora

[1] Spencer, H. (1904), II, 307–8.
[2] Spencer, H. (1904), II, 328; *Oban Times*, 30 Aug. 1879.
[3] MacLean later became prominent in the land-league agitation of the 'eighties, and left the estate by 1891.

continued her charitable visiting in the village at least until 1883,[1] but estate functions which had been shared by everybody, such as the proprietor's ball, were discontinued after the death of Octavius Smith; while Valentine Smith's annual visits to the estate were so short that there was little time available for him to develop a personal relationship with his employees, a task for which he was in any case ill suited by his appearance of misanthropy. The status of the people was consequently reduced and they became more truly (as they were described in the account books) 'farm servants'. Neither was much effort made at this time by the people themselves either at Ardtornish or elsewhere in Morvern to organise their own social functions; there were shinty matches at the 'old' New Year, but none of the concerts, soirées and cottage balls that were such a feature of the 'eighties and 'nineties.[2]

Nevertheless the effect of the proprietor's practical generosity was soon felt. From 1874, for instance, Valentine Smith made annual *ex gratia* payments of from £1 to £3 to five (later eight) regular day-labourers of the estate who were not accommodated in estate cottages, to cover their rent in Lochaline village, an act that was imaginative as well as liberal. More importantly he stepped up the rate of estate building, the third phase of which—lasting from the late 1860s until 1882—included amongst other things no fewer than seventeen new workers' cottages, so that by the early 'eighties most of the estate employees were living in commodious, modern houses that would have been a credit to any 'model village'.

The old superintendent of masons, Peter Haggart, was retired in 1870, and was succeeded by an Englishman of thirty-four named Samuel Barham. The 'contract' system of estate building was discontinued at the same time, the building tradesmen thenceforth working at Barham's direction—he was called 'master of works'—and being paid fortnightly by the estate at daily rates. Barham himself never received more than accommodation and expenses from the estate, his salary or fees coming from another source; possibly he had started as an employee of the Smiths' distillery business in London and was still carried on the company's books.[3] The authorship of the earliest buildings of the third

---

[1] *Oban Times*, 1 Dec. 1883.

[2] Negative evidence from the *Oban Times*, convincing in view of the triviality of much of the local news that was printed.

[3] The Smiths' business records have disappeared. The Thames Bank Distillery Company did not survive the First World War, and its records are not now traceable. The Bow Brewery, which Valentine Smith acquired in 1869, remained in the family (as Smith, Garrett & Co.) until 1927, when it was bought by Taylor Walker, subsequently Ind Coope, subsequently Allied Breweries; most of Taylor Walker's business records (including those of Smith, Garrett) were destroyed by German bombing in 1941, but Ind Coope (East Anglia) Ltd. hold seven leases and other deeds dating from 1869 to 1897 to which Valentine Smith was a signatory (information from Keith Parkhurst, Esq., of Flowers Breweries, and the Historical MSS. Commission).

phase is uncertain—that is, of the keeper's cottage in the grounds of Ardtornish Tower, Craigendarroch double cottage and Rose cottage— but, although the keeper's cottage probably and Craigendarroch possibly were built by Haggart, their design resembles that of the later buildings known to be Barham's as much as that of Haggart's earlier shepherds' cottages (Plate 7*b*); it is possible that Barham was their architect, sending plans (now lost) to Haggart. These three cottages were also the last of the estate buildings to be constructed of lime and rubble; from the Achranich coach-house of 1871–2 onwards (which was also the first building of which Barham's signed and dated plans survive), all were built of concrete.[1]

Barham followed the coach house with Castle cottage (Plate 10*a*, another double, where he himself was to live, with Hugh 'Crosag' as his neighbour), a gardener's cottage at Achranich, a terrace of six houses at Larachbeg (Plate 10*b*, chiefly for building tradesmen and day labourers), Caolas Ferry House and its stables (Plate 11*b*), and a double cottage at Ardtornish Bay. Together with Claggan school (Plate 11*a*), and the new manager's house which replaced old Achranich farm-house in 1880 (Plate 14*b*), these cottages of the 'seventies mark the high point of Ardtornish—and indeed of Morvern—architecture. The shepherd's cottages built in Haggart's time had had a solid, unsophisticated charm, but Barham's houses, while being equally at home in their environment, were conspicuous for an elegance of design that was refreshing without being either pretentious or condescending.[2] Each one differing from the last—but obviously all of common parentage—these delightful buildings with their high gables and decorated barge-boards were intentionally picturesque, carefully sited where their beauties could be appreciated, but never sacrificing convenience to appearances.

The cottages, which were estimated to cost about £200 each,[3] mostly contained the standard estate accommodation of three bedrooms and three other rooms, although there were minor variations; the two end houses at Larachbeg, for instance, were rather larger than the rest, having four bedrooms each, while the middle four cottages of the terrace lacked pantries. Beginning with the gardener's cottage of 1874, some of them had water-closets indoors, a remarkable luxury for workmen's houses of the period.

---

[1] This was a very early use of concrete construction; indeed the Achranich coach-house may well be the first concrete building in Scotland.

[2] It is possible that the designs of the Ardtornish cottages were influenced or even inspired by examples shown in the architects' pattern-books of the period. But although some of the Ardtornish motifs (recessed porches, italianate eaves, decorated barge-boards) are found in designs published in the early nineteenth century, they had quickly become part of the British architectural vernacular, and it is unlikely that Haggart and Barham were directly following published patterns.

[3] Elliot's statement to the Napier Commission, see p. 181 below.

Table 5. *Achranich and Ardtornish estate building: Phase III*

Description	Probable date	Evidence for date
Keeper's cottage, Achranich (Plate 7 b)	(?) 1868	*Photographs (Gertrude Smith)*, 31; *MacKichan's memoirs*
Craigendarroch, double cottage (blacksmith and underkeeper)	1870–1	Ledgers; *Census*, 1871; *OS 1872*
Rose cottage (joiner)	1871–2	Ledgers; *OS 1872*
Coach-house range, Achranich	1871–2	Plans signed "SB" and dated; building dated "1871"; ledgers
Castle cottage, double cottage (master of works and coachman) (Plate 10 a)	1873	Ledgers; *Astley diary* 1 Oct. 1873
Gardener's cottage and boiler-house, Achranich	1874	Plans signed "SB" and dated
Larachbeg, terrace of six houses (building tradesmen and labourers) (Plate 10 b)	1875	Plans signed "SB" and dated; ledgers
Claggan school-house (Plate 11 a)	1877–8	Plans signed "SB" and dated; ledgers
Ferry house and stables, Caolas (Plate 11 b)	1879	Plans signed "SB" and dated; ledgers
Bay Cottage, double cottage (gardener and trapper)	1879	Ledgers
Manager's house, Achranich (Plate 14 b)	1880	Plans signed "SB" and dated
Smith's shop and piggeries, Achranich	1881	Plans signed "SB" and dated
Crosben, shepherd's cottage	(?) 1881–2	Plan of bridge to cottage signed "SB" and dated 1881; *Census*, 1881

The signs of change in the economy of the estate in the 'seventies are harder to read because the surviving account books are incomplete after 1874, but the effect of falling prices was already evident in the middle of the decade, with the gross income of the estate decreasing as Corson hung onto an increasing stockpile of wool year after year in the vain hope that the market would improve. From 1861 to 1869, gross receipts from wool had averaged £1,938 a year, but from 1870 to 1879 they were down to an average of £1,096 a year, the most depressing period being the end of the 'seventies, when wool sales grossed as follows: 1875, £1,702; 1876, £1,705; 1877, £130; 1878, £9; and 1879, £34.

Estate expenditure nevertheless continued to rise. In addition to the building works that have already been mentioned, two major estate roads were built in 1872–3 (Achranich–Tearnait and Acharn–Crosben), which totalled over five miles in length and cost something like £1,500; and there was no pause in the usual round of dyking, draining, etc., fifty-one miles of sheep drains being cut and cleaned, for example, in 1878. In addition the employees of the estate received substantial wage increases in the early 'seventies, mostly of the order of twenty per cent. In making these increases the estate was responding not to any rise in productivity (which had actually occurred ten years earlier) but to a national trend of rising wages, as it was obliged to do if it was to compete in the labour market.[1] Although the cost of living rose at the same time, the improvement of estate housing made during the same period meant that many of the estate's employees did experience a net increase in their real wages. The total number of employees during the 'seventies was just over fifty, about twenty-six being on six-month engagements and an average of twenty-seven being paid fortnightly at daily rates. Of the regulars, there were seventeen shepherds (reduced during the decade to fourteen, as the grazings were cleared for deer); two keepers and a trapper; one or two gardeners; from five to seven farm workers (cowmen, ploughman, etc.); and a manager. Casual female labour—mostly the wives and daughters of employees—was taken on in addition for hay-making, reaping, gardening and so forth as required, but mechanisation was soon to reduce the women's pay-sheet; the estate first used a mowing machine in about 1875, and bought a Wood's combined mowing-machine in 1878.

The total population of the estate, 150 in 1871, was down to 132 by 1881, chiefly as a result of reductions at the Old Ardtornish end, some of them temporary; but by the later date the estate also provided for at least fifty other people living outside its boundaries—non-resident day-labourers and their families—and its population in both categories was actually to increase during the 'eighties.

The years around 1880 were more patently a time of change even than before. Old Mrs Smith died in 1878; and about four years later Gertrude Craig Sellar quarrelled with her brother—the details have not survived—and gave up Ardtornish House, not to return to the estate until Valentine died in 1906.[2] At Whitsun 1880 David Corson, now aged sixty-four, retired to Appin after twenty-nine years' service as estate manager, and was succeeded by Walter Elliot, a Selkirk man of only twenty-eight. Elliot was 'a better class of man' than Corson—meaning that he could spell and had the manners of a gentleman—and he was put in at a high salary (£400 in 1890, where Corson had never got more than £160), probably in the hope that he would mend the estate's fortunes. By this

---

[1] See p. 177 below, for a summary of Ardtornish wages, and the notes to the summary which compare estate wages with national trends.

[2] John Buchan (*The Times*, 25 Nov. 1929) says that Gertrude Craig Sellar did not return to Ardtornish after 1881, but in fact she and her husband attended the Argyllshire Ball in Oban in 1882 (*Oban Times*, 16 Sept. 1882). The breach between the Craig Sellars and Valentine Smith was not complete, for Alexander Craig Sellar, and later their son Gerard, continued to stalk at Ardtornish with Valentine between 1882 and 1906.

time, however, they were past mending, and it may be doubted whether Smith benefited by the change from Corson's local knowledge and practical wisdom. Elliot moved at once into the fine new manager's house at Achranich with his young wife, and all their children were born there.

There were changes elsewhere in Morvern, too. Mrs Paterson, proprietrix of Lochaline Estate, died in 1880, leaving her property in the hands of trustees; and she was followed in 1881 by another widow notorious for past evictions, Lady Gordon of Drimnin, whose estate passed to her son, J. C. Gordon, now aged forty-three. Then in May 1882 Dr John MacLeod, 'the high priest of Morvern' and 'father of the Scottish church', died at Fiunary at the age of eighty-one. More than a hundred years before, his father Norman MacLeod had come from Skye to bring peace to the rebellious inhabitants of Morvern. During that century the society of the parish had been fundamentally changed as most of its members were dispersed around the world and the remainder changed their ways of living. But, even as the body of John MacLeod was carried to Keil churchyard, events were taking place in Skye that were to provoke the last, dying struggle of the old Morvern.

THE POOR MAN AT THE GATE

By 1881 the population of Morvern was down to only thirty-eight per cent of the maximum reached in 1831. Although a few other West Highland parishes (Small Isles parish, for instance, and one parish each in Upper and Lower Lorne, Kintyre and Islay) had experienced comparable reductions by the same date, Morvern was the extreme example of mid-nineteenth-century depopulation in a coherent, relatively fertile area that was without any particular natural disadvantages.[1] Its immediate neighbours were still much nearer their earlier maxima— Ardnamurchan in 1881 had sixty-eight per cent of its maximum population, Ardgour fifty-one per cent, Lismore and Appin eighty per cent, Mull fifty-two per cent—and local people believed that Morvern's relative emptiness resulted directly from the great evictions of 1824–68. This belief probably had some justification, but its corollary—that the inhabitants of the parish would have been prosperous and contented in 1881 if there had been no evictions—was of course absurd. Famine and emigration would have come in any case, as we have seen, and the overcrowding and poverty that was experienced in crofting parishes that were unaffected by clearances or eviction in the mid-nineteenth century discredited the myth of the Morvern that might have been. This was

[1] Figures from Darling, F. F. (1955), 85–8.

not always clear at the time, however, especially to dispossessed and émigré Highlanders, and there was a tendency to blame, not only the evicting landlords, but also the people who had tamely allowed themselves to be forced out; certainly there was admiration in Morvern for the crofters of Skye who were now forcibly resisting any further encroachment upon their meagre holdings.

Discontent gathered head in Skye in 1881 when evictions were threatened there, but it was not until the spring of 1882 that actual assaults upon sheriff-officers who were trying to serve eviction-orders or summonses for non-payment of rent provoked the authorities into powerful retaliation: a gunboat sent to the island in February 1882 and a force of fifty Glasgow policemen in April, followed by the arrest and imprisonment of a number of crofters. Intimately concerned with these disturbances was the development in Scotland of a 'land-league' movement, influenced initially by the Irish Land League but soon acquiring a character of its own. Deriving from the association in Glasgow in 1881 of a number of professional men of radical sympathies, the Highland Land League was essentially a pressure group working for the reform by legal means of the existing land laws, with the object of restoring land to dispossessed Highlanders and of enabling them to work it in adequate security. Branches were soon active in Edinburgh and London, and a year or two later locally in the Highlands as well.[1]

Morvern's involvement in the land-league agitation was due initially to the efforts of a Morvern man, John MacDonald, whose family had once worked a holding on Drimnin Estate, and who was now living in Glasgow where he was a clothier's shop-assistant. MacDonald's stories of what happened to his own people at Drimnin and of the evictions elsewhere in Morvern are in some respects self-contradictory and cannot be entirely true, but the general purport of his tale was never denied and must be accorded some weight.[2] The most likely course of events was this: MacDonald's family was one of those which were moved across the estate from Auliston to Oronsay Island in the early 1840s, two or three years before John's birth in 1847. His father, a member of the Oronsay

---

[1] Crowley, D. W. (1956), *passim*. The *North British Daily Mail* and the *Oban Times* both carried full reports on the disturbances in Skye.

[2] The chief source for MacDonald's biography is the transcript of his evidence to the Napier Commission (*Napier Commission evidence* (1884), III, 2301–6); see also his writings transcribed on pp. 213–22 below. The clear and specific details he gives of his birth on Drimnin Estate in about 1847 and of his family's subsequent removal to Oronsay are not corroborated by contemporary documents: his birth was not recorded in the Parochial Register and his family was not enumerated in the Censuses of 1851 or 1861 either in Oronsay or anywhere else in Morvern. This is negative evidence, however; and, while MacDonald's controversial writings certainly abound with exaggerations and evasions, he answered the Commissioners' questions in public, in Morvern, in the hearing of people who knew what had really happened.

club farm, died when the children were still young, leaving the family in some distress—Mrs MacDonald had to give up both land and cows—and in 1864 they moved to Glasgow, when John was seventeen. Here he kept in close touch with affairs in his old home, going there for his holidays and supporting the Ardnamurchan, Morvern and Sunart Association of Glasgow (of which he eventually became Secretary).[1] In this way he learned that, about four years after he had left Oronsay, some of the remaining members of the club farm there were evicted by Lady Gordon (owing no rent, and without compensation for the land they had reclaimed or the houses they had built) because she had been persuaded by one of her tenant-farmers, who coveted Oronsay, that the club-farmers had been stealing his sheep. Whatever the rights and wrongs of this affair, MacDonald used it as his chief example in a long letter which he wrote to the *North British Daily Mail* and the *Oban Times* in May 1882 to show how grasping landlords 'improved' people off their land altogether, naming Lady Gordon and suggesting that her son, now the proprietor of Drimnin, should make restitution to the evicted club-farmers "as he is now in a manner reaping the benefit of their toil".[2] Nine months later MacDonald followed this up with an even longer and more inflammatory letter to the *Oban Times* in which he gave a tendentious account of the Lochaline Estate eviction of 1866, and went on to attack Valentine Smith for having turned part of Ardtornish Estate into a deer forest, which "is of no use to any one unless that it affords a few months sport to Mr Smith and *his party* during the shooting season. Mr Smith does not let the shooting so that he receives no revenue whatever from the greater part of his estate. Will any sane man assert that this sort of policy has been productive of good to the people or the State? when good land (better there is not in the district) has been laid waste for the pleasure of one single individual, and those whom he may delight to honour."[3] Radical stuff indeed, and with the power to sting for all the inconsequence of its argument and inaccuracy of its facts.

Within a couple of months (in May 1883) the "working men resident in the vicinity of Lochaline" met to choose delegates and prepare evidence for the Royal Commission which had just been appointed to enquire into the condition of the Highland crofters;[4] and it is scarcely a surprise to learn that one of the delegates chosen to meet the Commissioners when they sat in Lochaline in August was John MacDonald of Glasgow, or that the people's formal statements were written by him. That fine summer day when a chartered steamer brought Lord Napier and his fellow-Commissioners across from Tobermory to their meeting

[1] *North British Daily Mail*, 22 April 1882.
[2] *North British Daily Mail*, 2 May 1882, pp. 213–15 below.
[3] *Oban Times*, 3 Mar. 1883, pp. 215–17 below.   [4] *Oban Times*, 19 May 1883.

in the crowded Free Church at Lochaline brought a phase of Morvern's history to an end. The old grievances were voiced in public at last by men who had nursed them for years, and stories of the evictions were told in dialogues that were sometimes as funny as their subjects were sad. Now it all came out; but, as one of the Commissioners said, "you are complaining of what happened forty years ago; what do you wish today?"; and the sixty-seven-year-old witness answered, "I would like to be the way I was before, if it were possible; that is, I should like to have a croft and my cows back again as before."[1]

MacDonald himself, who was probably aware of the new political doctrines of the time (although there was no left-wing organisation in Glasgow until 1884), urged a programme on the Commissioners that was pure socialism: he asked that the old croft lands and traditional township grazings should be taken away from their present owners by the State, and leased by the State to the dispossessed crofters at low rents. Failing State ownership, which he was realistic enough to see was unlikely to be achieved, he wanted the landlords to be forced to lease these lands to the old crofters at controlled rents.[2] It is obvious to us that no government of the 1880s, however radical, would have contemplated legislation to deprive owners of rights in land which they had purchased perfectly legally between twenty and sixty years before. In the 'eighties, however, with socialism nascent in the cities, with civil disorder in Skye and near-rebellion in Ireland, during the parliamentary struggle for electoral reform and Home Rule which included "the most dramatic thirteen months in English party history",[3] really radical reform of the land laws, even to the extent of interfering with existing estates, may well have seemed possible.

Agitation continued, and even increased, after the Commissioners had gone away to make their report. The *Oban Times*, now under new management with a lively twenty-one-year-old editor who was an outspoken and practical supporter of the crofters' cause, threw its weight behind the movement with weekly encouragement. In July 1882 this paper promoted the formation of local branches of the Land League under the name of the Highland Land Law Reform Association (H.L.L.R.A.), with the object "by constitutional means and irrespective of party politics, to effect such changes in the Land Laws as shall prevent the waste of large tracts of productive lands in the north".[4] At first the movement made little headway, but in 1884 an event of major importance for the Scottish counties, and for the Highlands in particular, gave it life: this was the passage of the third Reform Bill.

[1] *Napier Commission evidence* (1884), iii, 2286.
[2] See below, p. 221.
[3] Ensor, R. C. K. (1936), 99, referring to the period June 1885 to July 1886.
[4] *Oban Times*, 1 July 1882.

Hitherto ordinary Highlanders had simply not been represented in parliament. Prior to 1832 the franchise was limited to forty-shilling proprietors 'of old extent', and owners of property did not qualify for registration as electors unless they possessed huge tracts of land, perhaps half the size of Morvern; and in practice the great heritors (in Argyllshire the Duke of Argyll) had absolute control of the county elections.[1] The first Reform Bill of 1832, while it was an advance of the old system, did not yet take suffrage very far; in the Scottish counties votes were restricted to owners of properties of a net rental value of £10 a year and to certain classes of tenants, which in Morvern meant those paying an annual rent of £50.[2] Although no registers of electors for Argyllshire for any year before 1889 have been preserved, it is possible to calculate from the Valuation Rolls (cited in the Act as the relevant authority) how many people were entitled from 1855 onwards to be put on the Register.[3] Thus the number of persons qualified to vote in Morvern in 1860–1 under the provisions of the 1832 Act was about twenty-two, which was seven per cent of the adult male population at that date. The second Reform Bill of 1867–8, although it granted household suffrage in the burghs, made little difference to the franchise in the Scottish counties;[4] votes were now allowed to £5 owners and £14 tenants, but there were so few even of these lesser men that in 1870–1 and 1880–1 there were still only twenty-eight and twenty-seven persons respectively qualified to vote in Morvern, or twelve per cent of the adult male populations at the same dates. It was the Enfranchisement Act of 1884 that really made a difference in the Scottish counties, for it extended the suffrage to all householders, both tenants and owners of whatever value, specifically including those who occupied houses "by virtue of office, service or employment".[5] This brought in both crofters and estate employees, with the result that the number of electors actually on the Register for Morvern in 1890–1 was 140, or sixty per cent of the adult male population. Although the parliamentary polling place for Morvern remained at Lochdonhead in Mull until 1894 (when it was removed to Lochaline), the ordinary people could now have a hand in choosing their own representative for parliament, and in choosing him, thanks to the secret ballot which had been introduced in 1872, uninfluenced by the wishes of the proprietors or their agents.[6]

[1] Wilkie, T. (1895), 323–37.
[2] Representation of the people (Scotland) Act 1832; 2 & 3 Will. IV c. 65.
[3] Following surviving Registers, certain classes of owners and tenants (heirs, trustees and shooting tenants) are excluded from the calculations. The fact that a person was qualified to vote does not of course prove that he was put on the Register; the figures given for 1860, 1870 and 1880 are therefore maxima.
[4] Representation of the people (Scotland) Act 1868; 31 & 32 Vic. c. 48.
[5] Representation of the people Act 1884; 48 Vic. c. 3.
[6] Register of electors for Argyllshire, Parish of Morvern, 1890, 1894, etc., *ACOL*.

The point was quickly taken by the land-league reformers. So far the crofters had been unable to protect themselves except by illegal resistance; now their elected representatives would be able to speak for them in Westminster and even—who knew?—carry through the legal reinstatement that they sought. The early months of 1884 saw an increase in the number of newspaper attacks on the landlords, such as the following from a Morvern correspondent of the *Oban Times*: "The landlords pauperised the people by clearing them off the land. They were far seeing enough to foresee the consequences. To save themselves, and cast to the people a sorry sop in lieu of the land taken from them, they got the parochial relief Act extended to the Highland parishes...",[1] and more in the same style. Meetings were held up and down the west coast during the summer, and branches of the H.L.L.R.A. were formed in nearly every district. In July 1884 an open air meeting was held at Lochaline, when a hundred people were addressed by the Reverend Donald MacCallum, who had been John MacLeod's assistant in Morvern in 1880–2, and who was one of the very few presbyterian ministers who actively supported the crofters. "We who have taken an interest in the question of land reform", wrote the Morvern correspondent of the *Oban Times*, "are greatly indebted to the Rev. Mr. MacCallum for his disinterested devotion to the cause, and we can assure him, that his time could not be spent to better purpose than in stirring up the people of Morven, for whom we know he has a great regard, to their duties and responsibilities. The people of our district being without any land, and almost entirely dependent on day labour for their support, are in particular dependent on the ruling class of landlords and factors, and have hitherto been, very naturally, afraid to take a leading part in anything which might be supposed to be against the wishes of their masters, although this fear may have been altogether groundless."[2] At a second open air meeting a month later a resolution was passed to form a Morvern branch of the H.L.L.R.A. "We cannot refrain", the correspondent remarked on this occasion, "from expressing the pleasure it gives us to see the men of Morven asserting themselves in defence of their just rights, without having the fear of either landlord or factor before their eyes. This slavish fear of the powers that be has done more than anything else we know to unman and degenerate the character of the people. Let them be ready to suffer for the cause, if need be...of suffering humanity."[3] Officers were elected in November (John MacDonald of Glasgow, President; John MacKenzie, Lochaline, Vice-President; Malcolm MacLachlan, Kinlochaline, Secretary; and Donald MacKichan, Achranich, Treasurer), when a relatively

---

[1] *Oban Times*, 5 Apr. 1884.
[2] *Oban Times*, 2 Aug. 1884.   [3] *Oban Times*, 23 Aug. 1884.

sober programme was adopted: the Association "did not countenance any very extreme views. ...Their object was reform, not spoliation. They wished...to keep the agitation within proper and legitimate bounds."[1]

For the next two years the Morvern branch of the Association met monthly (generally in the Cameron Arms hotel, the School Board refusing permission for school premises to be used) under chairmen such as Archibald Graham, the innkeeper; Gillean MacLean, the Ardtornish joiner who had served the Craig Sellars at Ardtornish House; and Alexander Cameron, a mason's labourer resident in the village but working at Ardtornish, who later became Valentine Smith's lodge-keeper.[2] Occasionally there were visiting speakers such as John Mac-Pherson 'the Glendale Martyr', who addressed a mass meeting on Torr na Fhaire in August 1885, urging "agitation in a constitutional manner".[3] In the same year the movement was stimulated by another favourable event: at a general election, the first to be held since the introduction of the householder franchise in the Scottish counties, a 'crofter' candidate for Argyllshire was sponsored by the H.L.L.R.A.; this was Donald MacFarlane, a Caithness man who had previously sat as member of parliament for Co. Carlow, and he was elected in December, raising the hopeful enthusiasm of the reformers to a new pitch. It was indeed something of a revolution in the County's politics. From 1868 until 1885 the seat had been held, quite in the old style, by sons of the Duke of Argyll (the Marquis of Lorne from 1868 to 1878, and Lord Colin Campbell from 1878 to 1885), both sitting as Liberals. In 1885 Lord Colin Campbell withdrew, and MacFarlane, standing as a 'Liberal crofter', polled 3,336 votes to 2,852 for an Independent and 665 for a straight Liberal, sixty-seven per cent of the electorate voting.[4]

Euphoria was short-lived, however. Another general election followed only a few months later, and this time a Tory landlord, Malcolm of Poltalloch, stood alone against MacFarlane and beat him in July 1886 by 3,658 votes to 3,054, the poll again being sixty-seven per cent.[5] What caused even keener disappointment amongst the reformers were the provisions of the Crofters Holdings Act, the result of the report of the Napier Commission, which passed through parliament that spring and summer.[6] In fact the bill gave them all that they could reasonably have hoped for—it guaranteed security of tenure, fair rents and compensation

[1] *Oban Times*, 8 Nov. 1884.
[2] *Oban Times*, 23 Aug. 1884; 8 Aug. 1885; 17 Apr. 1886; and *passim*. Gillean MacLean later became President of the Morvern branch of the Association.
[3] *Oban Times*, 8 Aug. 1885.   [4] Wilkie, T. (1895), 51.
[5] Wilkie, T. (1895), 51. MacFarlane eventually got back in 1892, beating Malcolm by only 3,666 votes to 3,586, with 73 per cent of the electorate voting.
[6] Crofters holdings (Scotland) Act 1886; 49 & 50 Vic. c. 29.

for improvements, to all existing crofters—but of course it did nothing towards satisfying their unreasonable but nonetheless fervent longings to put back the ex-crofters into holdings taken from the landowners. The reformers termed it "a sham", "a meagre measure", "a poor compromise", and called for further action,[1] but at the same time they began to see that there was no real chance of breaking into the great estates for the sake of the crofters; and the realisation eventually killed the land-league movement. Association meetings continued to be held, but with decreasing frequency. In Morvern the last ordinary meeting of the Land League (as the H.L.L.R.A. was now re-named) took place in August 1889; and the Morvern branch finally died, split by faction, in 1892.[2] Even the publication in 1895 of the report of the 'Deer-forest Commission', which actually recommended the creation of new small-holdings in the Highlands, failed to revive the movement. The land in Morvern recommended by this later Commission for conversion into new and extended crofters' holdings included 7,477 acres of Ardtornish Estate (the Knock group of farms and Clounlaid), 1,731 acres of Killundine, 1,130 acres of Glenmorvern, 1,345 acres of Drimnin and 5,794 acres of Glen-cripesdale;[3] but by this time the social and economic situation was not the same as it had been in the 'eighties, and the people may also have felt that the report would never really be acted upon—as indeed it never was.

The reaction of the Morvern landlords to the land-league agitation was to sit tight and say nothing, which from their point of view was undoubtedly sensible. They took only a small part in the hearing of the Napier Commission in Lochaline in 1883—Hardie of Lochaline Estate, whose savage cross-examination has already been quoted, was the only proprietor to offer himself for general questioning—and they ignored the insults of the *Oban Times*. It might be thought that Valentine Smith, as the greatest proprietor and the owner of the only extensive deer-forest in the district, was in an especially vulnerable position, but in fact, since he was also easily the largest employer of day-labour in Morvern, this was far from being the case. By the early 'eighties Ardtornish Estate was supporting an average of over forty day-labourers, nearly all of them Morvern men, in addition to its regular employees. Then in 1884, when the land-league ferment was at its height, the initiation of what was to be the fourth and final phase of the Smiths' estate building programme completely altered the balance of labour in the parish.

Finding that Ardtornish Tower (which had been completed by his father in 1866) was infected by dry rot, and wanting a much larger

[1] *Oban Times*, 13 Mar. and 17 Apr. 1886.
[2] *Oban Times*, 24 Aug. 1889, 22 Mar. 1890 and 5 Nov. 1892.
[3] Royal Commission (Highlands and Islands) 1892; *Report* (1895), 17, 20, 21, and Appendix, map sheets XLIV, LII.

house in any case, Valentine Smith demolished the building in 1884, preserving only the separate clock tower which had given the house its name, and commissioned an entirely new house from the architect-antiquary of Inverness, Alexander Ross.[1] Ross's new Ardtornish Tower, which was built with little alteration from one of three pencil sketches which he produced for Smith, had clear stylistic links with the earlier house—the cruciform plan, the drawing-room looking out over the same view through a similar iron pillared veranda, the carriage tunnel leading through to the courtyard—but it lacked both the conviction and the charm of its predecessor. The massing of its blocks and turrets in a truncated cross, with the original clock tower, re-roofed, rising behind them, did have a certain grandeur; but the detailed design of walls, roofs and lights was generally clumsy and unconvincing, and resulted in a house that was not so much grand as grandiose, an irrelevant impersona-tion of a French château of uncertain age (Plate 13).

Smith was determined that Ardtornish Tower should be very large—it was to have about seventy-five rooms, some of them of considerable size[2]—and that no expense should be spared on the quality of its con-struction. The work was begun in 1884 by contractors—a Tobermory builder and an Oban joiner—but soon after the start Smith decided that the house had better be built by the estate; he therefore payed the con-tractors off and put his own master of works, Samuel Barham, in charge early in 1885.[3] The labour force employed by the estate rose steadily, exceeding 100 on daily rates by the end of 1885, and reaching a peak of 160 in the summer of 1888. Plans for 'barracks' which were built at Achranich in 1884 and 1885 show that about fifty of these workmen came from outside the Loch Aline area (and probably from outside Morvern); but the rest were Morvern men.[4] Numbers dropped again when the main constructional work on the house was finished, and by the end of 1889, some six months before it was to be ready for occupation, an average of sixty to seventy day-labourers was still employed. Even at this rate Valentine Smith was offering as much work as the day-labour force available in the area could regularly supply, and the scale of the

[1] Alexander Ross, LL.D. (1834–1925), succeeded to his father's architectural business in Inverness in 1853 when he was nineteen years old, and later designed numerous large buildings throughout Scotland; he specialised in the restoration of castles (Ross, A. M. (1932), 112–13).
[2] The precise number depends on the definition of 'room'. The figure of about 75 included bathrooms, pantries, boot-rooms, etc., but not passages, cupboards and cellars. The numbers of rooms submitted with applications for fuel allocations were 52 in 1919 and 69 in 1940; but if every room-like space is included the number comes out to about 150.
[3] *MacKichan's memoirs*, p. 244 below; Men's time and pay books, *AP*.
[4] Ross's first plan for a workmen's barracks was dated 12 Feb. 1884 and provided for 21 beds in 3 rooms; a further plan, dated 1885, shows a larger building with 30 beds in 6 rooms, *AP*.

estate building works that followed the completion of the Tower ensured that it was not reduced any further in Valentine Smith's time. In this way, ironically, the workmen of Lochaline entered a period of full employment—which was in fact to prove permanent—at the very time when their agitation against the landlords was most urgent; and the building of Smith's pompous castle, itself a gross symbol of landlordism, was responsible for ending the endemic unemployment that was the main underlying cause of the people's discontent, and thus for helping to bring the land-league movement to an end.[1]

During the building of the new house, Valentine Smith bought Lochaline Estate. The trustees of the late Mrs Paterson had been anxious to sell the property since her death in 1880, but land prices were tumbling and a buyers' market in Highland estates was becoming ever more firmly established. In spite of this the trustees continued to hope that they could get back the £43,500 that Mrs Paterson had paid for the estate in 1864, and perhaps a bit more. They were to be disappointed; failing for seven years to find another purchaser, they finally accepted Valentine Smith's more realistic bid of £28,000 for the estate less stock in November 1887. "Tell me what you think of the purchase", wrote Smith to his manager on 11 November. "Is it really a much lower price than they expected to be obliged to take—if so they were laughing at me the whole time when they were asking £60,000—£50,000—& £40,000—Were there ever any other buyers at all in the market?..."[2]

Smith was pleased enough with his bargain when it was made—his letters to Elliot show him enjoying the details of the negotiations—but it may be doubted whether Lochaline Estate was a good buy from his point of view even at £28,000. It was certainly a fine sheep farm, but Smith knew well enough by this date that Highland farming did not pay, and in fact the intensification of the agricultural depression during the next few years brought the value of the Lochaline portion of his estate down to about £17,500 by 1906,[3] representing a greater percentage drop in nineteen years than Mrs Paterson's trustees had suffered after twenty-four. Furthermore Smith's whole estate was run at a loss quite apart from capital depreciation, and in general more property meant a

[1] A romantic travel-journalist (and keen propagandist of Highland folklore) made a spirited attack in the 1920s on Ardtornish Tower and what she imagined it stood for: "After the aggressively alien intrusion of the pretentious 'mansion house', it is infinite relief to turn to the retrospect of the native simplicity of Kinlochaline Castle. The severe restraint of its dignified tower, seen across the water, is a standing rebuke to the flaunting vulgarity of the modern pile opposing it, and the glaring contrast well typifies the gulf that eternally separates the plutocratic *parvenu* from the humblest inhabitant who really belongs to the country, and is truly, therefore, of a 'county' family" (Donaldson, M. E. M. (n.d. [1926]), 323).
[2] Valentine Smith to Walter Elliot, 11 Nov. 1887, *AP*.
[3] Calculated from George Malcolm's valuation (see pp. 183–5 below).

greater deficit; as he wrote at the time, "every house bought means a considerable outlay to put it into a decent state".[1] Finally, Lochaline Estate was no use for sport; it was unsuitable for conversion into a deer forest, nurtured few grouse and had no salmon river. On the other hand, possession of Lochaline Estate did give Smith control of the social and economic core of the district rounded off Ardtornish into a property that might be the envy of any London magnate; and—perhaps most importantly for Smith—freed him from the threat of undesirable neighbours. For Valentine Smith became even more withdrawn in his old age than he had been before: he abhorred strangers, fiercely forbade trespassing on the estate, and suffered constantly from the neurotic fear that his privacy was in danger of violation by tourists and holiday makers. Lochaline Estate gave him additional protection from the outside world.

The remainder of the fourth phase of Ardtornish estate building was somewhat miscellaneous, connecting the Achranich area with Lochaline

Table 6. *Achranich and Ardtornish estate building: Phase IV*

Description	Probable date	Evidence for date
Ardtornish Tower (II) (Plate 13)	1884–91	Plans signed "Ross" and dated; ledgers; *MacKichan's memoirs*
Kinlochaline Bridge	1888	Plan signed "Ross" and dated
Kinlochaline Castle (restoration)	1890	Donaldson, M.E.M. (n.d.)
Lochaline Farm byre	1890	Plan signed "SB" and dated
Lodge House	1890–1	*VR*; *Census*, 1891
Acharn, head shepherd's house (later converted to a double cottage)	1892	Unsigned, dated plans
Rannoch (or Riverside) double cottage (steward and ploughman)	1894–5	Unsigned, dated plans; *VR*
Lochaline piermaster's house and post office (Plate 15b)	1898–9	Unsigned, dated plans; *Oban Times*, 22 July 1899
Kinlochaline, double cottage (labourers)	1899	Unsigned, dated plans
Claggan cottage (underkeeper)	1902–3	*VR*

The estate also built several houses in Lochaline village between 1890 and 1910 of which plans do not survive; they included a terrace of five houses in the high street (c. 1899 by Samuel Barham) and two or three others.

village and filling in a few gaps elsewhere. First came Alexander Ross's Kinlochaline Bridge (1888) and restoration of Kinlochaline Castle (1890), which was joined by a new road along the shore of Loch Aline to a Lodge at the entrance to the village, completed in 1891. A new byre was built

---

[1] Valentine Smith to Walter Elliot, 12 Jan. 1888, *AP*.

at Lochaline Farm in 1890, the last building of which plans signed by Barham survive, and it was followed by a further seven estate workers' houses built between 1892 and 1903, only two of them on what had been Lochaline Estate. The remaining buildings were a combined pier-master's house and post office at Lochaline pier (1899, Plate 15 b), and a small number of houses in the village. These later buildings—Acharn and the Lochaline pier house are probably the best of them—were a good deal more massive, even ponderous, in design than Barham's cottages of the 1870s had been, and it is possible that they were the work of another architect; there is no other evidence that this was the case, however, and it is perhaps more likely that Barham, who remained master of works at Ardtornish until 1906, changed his architectural style as he grew older, influenced (perhaps) by Ross.

Smith's Morvern property, now that Lochaline Estate was added to it, was of a formidable size, totalling just under 39,000 acres. The owner himself thought it was 10,000 acres larger still, an expensive if gratifying belief, for it had caused him in 1885 to fight a legal action against the County Valuation Officer to achieve a reduction in his rates which he could have got simply by having the area of the estate measured from the recently published Ordnance maps.[1] The eventual maximum area was 41,000 acres, reached when Altachonaich was purchased in 1900. The deer forest, still about 11,200 acres in 1888, was increased to about 14,500 acres in 1898 (Smith thought it was 20,000 acres), when the Clounlaid grazings were cleared of sheep. The population of the estate in 1891 was 420, including 140 people living in Lochaline village not quite all of whom were Valentine Smith's tenants. With the total number of employees now about a hundred and the average family-size still over four persons, the estate continued to support the great majority of its inhabitants directly, even allowing for bachelor labourers.

In the early 'nineties there were normally fifteen shepherds—a largish number for the average stock of 9,476 sheep at the same period, or one shepherd to only 632 sheep—two gamekeepers and three watchers, six ploughmen or farm labourers, five farm girls (dairy-maids, etc.), a trapper, a forester, a smith, a joiner, a coachman, a steward (Fiunary) and a manager (Ardtornish); a total of thirty-eight regular employees in addition to the sixty or seventy tradesmen and labourers on daily rates who were engaged on estate building work. Money wages had not changed much since the 'seventies, although real wages were increased in some cases (especially those of the shepherds) by increased opportunities of selling 'croft produce' to the estate.

The most peculiar appointment was that of Alexander Cameron as Lodge keeper in 1891. Cameron, a mason's labourer then aged fifty-seven,

---

[1] See pp. 181–3 below.

had been cleared off Knock by Mrs Paterson in 1866 and had been working at Ardtornish as a day-labourer since 1869. When the land-league agitation began in Morvern, Cameron was amongst its leaders, giving evidence to the Napier Commission for the ex-crofters in 1883 and becoming a pillar of the H.L.L.R.A. To make him guardian of the Lodge may have been Smith's way of heaping coals of fire; and the irony of the situation was made more exquisite by the publication of the following attack in the *Oban Times* for 4 July 1891: "From time im-memorial there has been a public right-of-way along the foreshore [of Loch Aline], but the present proprietor has now appropriated this road, and constructed a private one, at the entrance of which a lodge has been erected for the purpose of excluding all except the few visitors to the estate. However strangers and visitors may regard such exclusive dealing it is exceedingly aggravating and humiliating to those born and brought up in the district to be hunted like hares if they but dare exercise their right to the foreshore."

There were changes in the pattern of farming: an increase of sheep density resulting from the addition of the Lochaline grazings, the gra-dual supercession of Cheviot by black-face sheep stocks, and an increase in the emphasis on cattle. In the early 'eighties, before the acquisition of Lochaline Estate, the Ardtornish stock had averaged 5,340 sheep, of which about 500 had been black-face and the rest Cheviots, at an average density of 262 sheep per 1,000 acres. The arrangement of the grazings had of course been changed by the clearances for deer, but this figure did in fact represent a reduction in their sheep-carrying capacity, the average stock on the Ardtornish hirsels in the 'eighties being about fifteen per cent less than it had been in the 1850s, probably as the result of over-grazing, although the precise mechanism of the process is uncertain.[1] Something similar had probably happened at Lochaline Estate, but its grazings were initially much richer, and when the farm was taken over in 1888 its black-face stock numbered 4,500 sheep at a density of 526 sheep per 1,000 acres. When the estates were combined, the stock in the early 'nineties averaged 9,476 sheep (4,873 Cheviots and 4,603 black-face) at an average density of 328 sheep per 1,000 acres. Black-face soon proved the more profitable stock—the price margin between Cheviot and black-face wool was now much less that it had been, and black-face sheep were hardier and cheaper than Cheviots—and it was therefore Cheviots that were discarded when Clounlaid was cleared in 1898; five years later the remaining Cheviots began to be sold, the last batch going in 1906.

[1] The hirsels for which comparative figures can be established were Achadh nan Gamhna, Clounlaid–Uladail, Crosben–Durinemast and Unibeg–Unimore, where the total stock was reduced from an average of 3,962 sheep in 1853–7 to one of 3,367 sheep in 1881–4 (Ardtornish clipping journal 1851–7, Ardtornish herd books 1880–4, *AP*). Concerning overgrazing see Darling, F. F. (1955), 167–9.

For a few years around the end of the century the centre of interest on Ardtornish farm swung from sheep to cattle, both because of the gloomy state of the sheep and wool markets and because Valentine Smith developed an enthusiasm for breeding prize 'Highlanders'. The Ardtornish fold of West Highland cattle was established in about 1889 and made an immediate impact on the Scottish shows, becoming indeed (in the words of a paper read to the Highland and Agricultural Society in 1900) "the most remarkable prize-winning herd of the past ten years".[1] The new byre at Lochaline farm was built in 1890 to house the sixty breeding cows that were the heart of the herd (though they were only a minority amongst the four-hundred-odd cattle of all sorts that the estate kept during the 'nineties). The prize herd was kept up until Valentine Smith's death and, although it was gradually run down thereafter, survivors remained on the estate until 1933.

But the prime function of the estate at the end of the nineteenth century had little to do with farming: it was the provision of recreation —chiefly in the forms of sport—for Valentine Smith and his guests. Bags rose to new levels. Taking the 'nineties alone, 1,268 grouse were killed in 1891, 248 pheasants in 1895, 50 stags and 50 hinds in both 1895 and 1899, 52 salmon and 843 sea trout in 1893. These huge totals were due not to larger numbers of guns or rods, or to better marksmanship— the sporting guests at Ardtornish were no more numerous in the 'nineties than they had been twenty years earlier and they scored just as many misses—but to the more efficient preservation of game and fish by a larger staff of keepers and watchers, to the clearance of sheep in favour of grouse-moor and deer-forest, and to the artificial rearing and introduction of animals to be shot. Records of introductions are incomplete for this period, but English stags were let out into the forest in October 1888, and deer were hand-fed at Eignaig at least from the late 'nineties; similarly, over a hundred English grouse were turned out at Keil, Achafors, Achranich and Ardtornish in 1897. All the pheasants had to be raised in the estate hatcheries, pheasants not being native to Morvern; the numbers thus introduced eventually became enormous, 2,609 birds being released in 1914, with a return of approximately two pheasants shot for every three turned out. The artificiality of these arrangements, indeed, is perhaps their most noticeable feature today, when a chancy rough shoot over the stubble is a commoner form of sport than an organised pheasant drive. There was something both ludicrous and sinister in the expensive rearing of thousands of exotic birds so that they might

[1] James Cameron, 'Famous Highland bulls and cows', *THASS*, 5th series, XII (Edin. 1900), 182. The nucleus of Smith's herd may have been the Highland cattle he bought with Lochaline Estate in 1888, which probably derived from Sinclair's fine herd of Highlanders (see below, p. 227; and cf. p. 183).

be driven carefully over the waiting guns, repetitious and unheroic performances that were to be grimly parodied a few years later on the Western Front. At the time, however, the pursuit was considered to be not only 'sporting', but one in which the very birds might be expected to join with enthusiasm. The attitude was well caught in a reproachful note written some years later in the Ardtornish game book: "Fifty birds were again put down in the Clock Tower Wood; but they could not be brought over the guns. They hide in the rhododendrons, and run out into the heather at the back."[1]

The social life at Ardtornish in the 'nineties lacked a diarist, but much of the style and spirit of the time was carried into the twentieth century by Valentine Smith's nephew and successor, Gerard Craig Sellar, who happened to meet John Buchan in South Africa when they were both members of Milner's 'kindergarten' in 1902. The Buchans stayed regularly at Ardtornish both before and after the First World War, and Lady Tweedsmuir recalled many years later: "Ardtornish House is tall and ugly on the outside, but inside was beautifully furnished and full of lovely objects. The contrast between the ordered comfort of the house and the wild mountain scenery outside was very piquant, and John delighted always in his return in the evening after a hard day's stalking in rough weather to its peaceful charm and pleasant conversation. Life at Ardtornish had a style and form of its own. A member of the younger generation said to me recently, opening her eyes wide, 'Is it true that you dressed for dinner every night?' And I replied, 'Not only did we do this, but when we returned to the house with muddy boots and shoes we took them off in the hall, rather than soil the beautiful pale green carpet on the stairs.' This life can never come again, but I cannot forbear to linger a little on the recollection of its charm. Some of the stalking and fishing is reflected in John's books, and he became noticeably more carefree and happy when we boarded the boat at Oban to take us to Gerard's little kingdom."[2] It will be recalled that Ardtornish Tower appears briefly in the fifth chapter of John Buchan's *Mr Standfast* (1919); and that some of the best of the stalking and fishing to which Lady Tweedsmuir refers is reflected in *John MacNab* (1925, dedicated to Gerard Craig Sellar's sister Rosalind Maitland).

It was a gracious life, but it was also a very expensive one. Valentine Smith's thirty-nine thousand acres and his hundred employees, the vast new house and the other estate works, and the production of thousands of live targets for the guns—these things all cost a lot of money, and were not to be financed by a falling market in sheep and wool and by a prize herd of Highland cattle that was unprofitable however decorative. Even

[1] Gerard Craig Sellar's notes for 1925–6 in Game book 1925–36, *AP*.
[2] Tweedsmuir, S. (1947), 101–2.

the trading deficit of the estate in the 'nineties was up to an average of £4,100 a year; and to this had to be added interest on its capital value (now down to about £1,500 a year, but still a perceptible sum[1]), architects' fees, the cost of all imported building materials and furnishings, the cost of staffing and provisioning Ardtornish Tower, of running the steam-yacht and the other boats, of the carriages, horses and coachmen, and most of the direct costs of the stalking, shooting and fishing—none of these items were charged against the estate, all were paid for by the proprietor. The real cost of Ardtornish Estate to Valentine Smith at the end of the nineteenth century may be put at anything from £6,000 to £8,000 a year, depending on how the various charges are allocated; but it was in any case a huge sum—well over £50,000 a year in modern terms—and of inestimable value as a subsidy to the district. As the *Oban Times*—no friend of the landlords—very handsomely put it in 1899: "It is to the credit of the proprietor of Ardtornish that the officials and labourers on his estate are probably the best housed and the best paid in all Argyllshire."[2] But even more important than excellent housing and good wages, Valentine Smith's money brought full employment and security in old age to about half the inhabitants of the parish.

Valentine Smith died on board his new 500-ton steam-yacht *Rannoch* (*Dobhran* had been sold in 1900) on 8 August 1906, in Gourock Bay. He was eighty-one years old and he left property to the gross value of almost two million pounds, Ardtornish Estate being valued at £52,000. Of the net personalty of £1,838,000, estate, legacy and succession duties took £250,000, bequests and gifts of property another £31,000, while annuities tied up about £333,000. The residuary legatee was his sister, Gertrude Craig Sellar, who thus inherited property valued at about £1,214,000, with more to come as the annuities fell in, and including Ardtornish Estate, her childhood home. The bequests included £1,000 to the Ardtornish manager, Walter Elliot (who died only a few months later, sitting at table at Achranich); and there was an annuity of £50 for Samuel Barham, master of works and designer of picturesque cottages.[3]

[1] This is three per cent of Malcolm's probate valuation of 1906; the official County valuation now lagged far behind tumbling property values, and still stood at £3,000.
[2] *Oban Times*, 22 July 1899.
[3] *The Times*, 21 Sept. 1906; *Glasgow Herald*, 21 Sept. 1906; *Oban Times*, 29 Sept. 1906. The larger figures are to the nearest thousand pounds.

A NEW EQUILIBRIUM:
MORVERN AT THE END OF THE
NINETEENTH CENTURY

A native of Morvern, returning home in the middle of the nineteenth century after an absence of fifty years, would have noticed many changes in the parish: a new pattern of land-holding under an entirely different set of proprietors, the disappearance of township agriculture beneath omnipresent sheep, the majority of the people huddled in squalid villages on the edges of the sheep-walks, steamers on the Sound bringing the outside world within reach. The changes which took place between the middle and the end of the century, on the other hand, were less obvious, and a native returning after fifty years in 1900 would have found many of the same families in possession of their estates, the hills still largely covered with sheep and the Sound of Mull steamers still forming the chief link between Morvern and the south; nevertheless there was during the later period an improvement in the condition of the people that was as important and as revolutionary as anything that had happened before.

Although the methods of sheep-farming changed little in Morvern during the second half of the nineteenth century, the days of its prosperity were over by 1900 as a result of the import of cheap antipodean wool (from the 1870s) and mutton (from the 1880s). Proprietors continued to farm, however, because there was no alternative that would not have been equally unprofitable, and also perhaps—though this is hard to prove—because of the hardship that their employees would have suffered if they had stopped. The number of crofters and small-tenant farmers was reduced from seventy-seven in 1851 to twenty-six in 1891, due chiefly to eviction on Drimnin and Lochaline Estates; but the total area of the large sheep farms actually became somewhat less during the same period owing to the clearance of some of the least fertile grazings for deer-forest. The use for deer of such poor land as the Garbh Shlios area of Ardtornish was entirely justified at the time the sheep were cleared, and by the end of the century it made even better economic sense; it is moreover extremely doubtful whether even the more fertile grazings of Clounlaid (which were cleared for deer-forest in 1898) could have been worked successfully as smallholdings as the Deer-forest Commissioners proposed in 1895.[1]

The only other change in land usage resulted from plantations of wood, but the areas affected were not large. Small plantations had been

[1] Royal Commission (Highlands and Islands) 1892; *Report* (1895), 21, and Appendix, map sheet LII.

made on Lochaline, Ardtornish and Achranich Estates in the period 1840–60, but more sizeable woods were planted on Ardtornish Estate between 1860 and the end of the century, chiefly on the west side of Loch Aline from Larachbeg to the Lodge, and on the east side from Achranich to Old Ardtornish; all these plantations together totalled about 600 acres, and there was also plantation on a smaller scale in the Drimnin, Glencripesdale and Laudale areas.

Communications were considerably improved although, as far as the movement of people and goods was concerned, the change was one of degree rather than of kind (Map 8). The steamer service was enhanced in 1881 when the Callander and Oban Railway (in which the Smiths of Ardtornish had a financial interest) was completed; the Sound of Mull ferry and mail service was begun in April that year, superseding after twenty-one years the twice-weekly service by post-runner between Lochaline and Kingairloch.[1] The first ship on the route was the old paddle-steamer *Pioneer* (built in 1844), which berthed at Tobermory and ran daily to Oban and back with calls each way at Salen (Mull), Lochaline and Craignure; she was succeeded in about 1894 by the *Carabinier*, another paddle-steamer, which was in turn replaced in 1908 by the *Lochinvar*, the diminutive and much-loved motor-vessel which continued on the route until 1961.[2] In 1883, two years after the beginning of the ferry service, Mrs Paterson's trustees completed a new steamer pier and access road south-west of Lochaline village at a cost of £3,700, obviating the need for the clumsy ferrying to and fro between ship and shore which had hitherto been the usual practice.[3]

Two more public roads were built after the main system was completed in the early 1860s. These were the Achadh nan Gahmna–Rahoy road (seven miles) started privately by Mrs Stewart of Glencripesdale in 1867, and taken over by the Road Trustees in 1871; and the Drimnin–Doirlinn road (also seven miles long), built in about 1880; both were built as minor roads with seven-foot carriageways.[4] All the public roads in Morvern were handed over to the County, and the parochial Road Trustees disbanded, when the County Councils Act came into force in 1890.[5]

More important, perhaps, was the establishment of two new informa-

[1] Hector Currie, who had been post runner for forty-four years (twenty-three years with the packet between Mull and Lochaline, and twenty-one years between Kingairloch and Lochaline), was presented with a purse by the people of the district when he retired; *Oban Times*, 9 Apr. and 14 May 1881.
[2] Duckworth, C. L. D., and Langmuir, G. E. (1950), *passim*. The *Lochinvar*, renamed *Anzio*, foundered with all hands in the North Sea in 1966.
[3] *The Lochaline Pier Order 1881* (in *AP*); *Oban Times*, 3 Nov. 1883; *Napier Commission evidence* (1884), III, 2307.
[4] *Minute book of the Morvern Road Trustees 1864–90*, 4 June 1867; 12 Sept. 1871; accounts 1883–4; *ACOL*.
[5] *Minute book of the Morvern Road Trustees 1864–90*, 6 May 1890; *ACOL*.

tion services. First was a local newspaper, the *Oban Times*, founded by an Oban printer in 1861 as *The Oban Monthly Pictorial Magazine*, and converted into a weekly newspaper in 1866. For its first sixteen years as a weekly the *Oban Times* tended to be stodgy and uncontroversial, but in 1882 it was bought by Duncan Cameron (owner of the Waverley Pen company) who put in his son—also Duncan Cameron—as editor at the age of twenty-one; from then on the paper's spirited radicalism enlivened local politics.[1] The other information service was the telegraph, which reached Lochaline in 1876 and was carried on to Drimnin in 1898. The Post Office had originally intended to extend the telegraph line from the head of Loch Sunart to Lochaline in 1872, by the direct route now followed by A 884, but T. H. G. Newton, one of the family which had just bought Glencripesdale, Laudale and Liddesdale, refused to allow the line to be built over Newton property unless it was taken round in a great loop by Glencripesdale and Drimnin. This the Post Office refused to do, and negotiations dragged on for four years, the interests of the other Morvern landowners being represented by Valentine Smith of Ardtornish and his brother-in-law Alexander Craig Sellar. Newton was eventually persuaded to withdraw his objection, but by this time the Post Office would only build the line provided that the proprietors of the district would guarantee charges of £150 a year for seven years; this they unwillingly did, the Ardtornish manager collecting the subsidy. In 1883 the Post Office required a further guarantee of £62 a year for seven years more (later extended into the 'nineties); Smith was furious but was obliged to pay up, the actual receipts from telegraph charges being only about £40 a year.[2]

But the most important of all the changes which took place in Morvern between 1850 and 1900 concerned the condition of the people. Not only was the standard of living higher at the end of the century than it had been in 1850, but nobody was now threatened by arbitrary eviction, famine or serious unemployment. These tremendous gains, which resulted partly from legislation but chiefly from the willingness of wealthy proprietors to subsidise their estates, could not have been made had there not also been a painful reduction of the population; there were less than half as many people living in Morvern in 1901 as there had been in 1851, and sadness at the loss of their kinsfolk soured some of the pleasure that people took in their prosperity.

The last known eviction in Morvern was the minor clearance made by Lady Gordon at Oronsay in 1868. Individual notices to quit were

[1] Duncan Cameron junior (1861–1954) stood for parliament as Land League candidate for Inverness-shire in 1885, but withdrew in favour of Charles Fraser-Mackintosh. He was not related to Dr Charles Cameron, proprietor of the *North British Daily Mail*.

[2] *Telegraph papers, AP; Oban Times*, 15 Oct. 1898.

certainly served after that date—for instance on Duncan Cameron, ex-police-constable of Lochaline, who was required to leave one of Valentine Smith's houses in the village in 1889—but they were not necessarily more than a legal form.[1] There is also a curious photograph of unknown provenance (the original of which is now destroyed) which was reproduced in the *Radio Times* in 1954 with the caption: "An eviction in the Lochaline district of North Argyll—from a photograph taken in the 'eighties."[2] It shows a group of people leaving a house under the eyes of a policeman and another man who might be a Sheriff Officer; but the people, who are dressed in their Sunday best, have no luggage with them, and it seems likely that the picture shows something other than an eviction. It is at any rate almost incredible that there should have been an otherwise unrecorded eviction of the bad old sort as late as the 1880s, the decade of the land-league agitation, the Napier Commission and the Crofters Holdings Act.

The actual distribution of the people at the end of the century was not much altered; the crofting communities of Auliston, Achabeg, Knock and Camas Salach were gone, but otherwise people lived in the same areas as they had done in 1850 but in smaller numbers (Map 6). A particularly beneficial change was the conversion of Lochaline village (chiefly by Mrs Paterson and her trustees, and Valentine Smith) from a dismal slum of largely unemployed cottars into a relatively prosperous and well-housed centre of day labour (Plate 15a). In 1851 the population of the village had been 309, with seven persons living in each house; in 1891 it was down to 147, with only three persons per house, which were themselves better buildings. Housing was generally much improved. There were now relatively few of the old thatched, dry-stone cabins, and those that remained were having their walls pointed and their interiors plastered or panelled. Comfortable slated cottages containing from four to six rooms and varying degrees of plumbing were to be found all over the parish, those of Ardtornish Estate being outstandingly good. A clear indication of the progress made in Morvern's housing is to be found in the increase in the average number of rooms per house from 2·7 in 1861 to 3·8 in 1891; and the average number of persons living in each room fell between the same dates from 2·1 to 1·3.

The standard of living of employed labourers rose between the 1870s and the 1890s, not because of any significant increase in money wages but because of the improvements in housing and because of a small reduction in commodity prices over the same period; on the base of 1853–7 = 100, the Ardtornish labourers' real wages index was 124 in

---

[1] Agreement to remove, Duncan Cameron to T. V. Smith, 2 Apr. 1889; *AP.*
[2] *Radio Times*, 10 Dec. 1954; the original photograph was deliberately destroyed when the *Picture Post* Library was taken over by BBC Publications.

1873–7, and 142 in 1893–7, which accorded very closely with trends elsewhere.[1] What mattered far more than this increase in the standard of living of employed persons, however, was the fact of full employment in the parish as a whole; from the mid-1880s onwards, virtually every family had a wage-earner, and scarcely anybody was starving—probably for the first time in Morvern's history. In the 1850s there had been more than a hundred paupers on relief in the parish, or seven per cent of the population, and this percentage remained unchanged in 1878, when there were still sixty-seven paupers; but by the end of the century the number of paupers was down to twenty two, or three per cent of the population, of whom no more than eight were under the age of sixty-five.[2] There was also more money in circulation, with the result that people depended less on home industries than they had done; they grew less food round their cottages, burned cheap sea-coal rather than labour-wasting peats, and bought clothing and implements that had been made in the industrial south, not in the parish—all signs of economic strength, however much the disappearance of the old skills might be regretted.

This situation was directly due to the landlords of the 'eighties and 'nineties—especially Valentine Smith of Ardtornish—who not only improved the housing on their estates, but who prevented the effects of the agricultural depression from reaching their dependants by defraying the losses on their properties and thus maintaining full employment. Far from being parasites sucking the lifeblood from a dying culture (as Highland propagandists would sometimes have us see them), Morvern's proprietors at the end of the nineteenth century were making a vital contribution to the welfare of the parish, which was analogous to that made nowadays by the State: they alone provided the equivalents of the farming subsidies, pensions, sickness benefits, film units, travelling libraries and so forth with which Highland society is sustained today.

Predictably, the great estates became more than ever the centres of real power in their districts. With few crofters and independent small farmers left, the large landowners were in complete control of the economies of their properties, and also to a great extent of the individuals who peopled them. In addition they controlled *de facto* the two most important instruments of local government, the School Board and the Parochial Board, both being committees of heritors until the last years of the century; even after 1895, when the Parochial Board became a Parish Council elected by all the rate payers, the landowners continued to dominate it, Valentine Smith's representative remaining Chairman. A resident proprietor such as J. C. Gordon of Drimnin might exercise his

---

[1] See the wages summary on p. 177 below.
[2] *Poor board reports*, 1853; *Return relating to parochial boards (Scotland)*, 1879; *Fourth annual report of the local government board for Scotland*, 1899.

power personally, directing the affairs and entertainments of his people and sitting personally on the local committees; a non-resident such as Valentine Smith might delegate these duties to his manager. Walter Elliot, the manager at Ardtornish, was a man of substance in the 'nineties: paid ten times as much as an estate labourer (Corson had been paid only twice the labourers' wage in the 'fifties) Elliot controlled the employment of all who worked for the estate, and thereby the living and welfare of over half the total population of the parish; he was besides the leader in all the social activities in the area, and served as a Justice of the Peace, a member of the School Board and chairman of the Parochial Board. The ultimate responsibility, of course, remained with Smith, for Elliot was still an employee who must carry out his master's wishes if he was to keep his position.[1]

This immense power—too much, we would say today, for any individual not answerable for his conduct—might easily have been abused; in fact it was exercised with paternalistic care and generosity. Besides providing work and housing, the proprietors of the 'nineties, in collaboration with the ministers of the two churches, actively promoted the social life of the parish. Mr and Mrs Gordon of Drimnin, Mr and Mrs Hay (tenants of Mungasdail) and Elliot at Ardtornish each organised several functions every year in the 'nineties for the people on their properties, including dances, social evenings, concerts and lectures; and there were also occasional dances and soirées given by the Morrises of Killundine and by the MacEwans, shooting tenants of Drimnin cottage. The ministers (now the Rev. D. MacFarlane of the established church and the more radical Rev. A. MacDiarmid of the Free Church) were assiduous in promoting the temporal as well as the spiritual welfare of their flocks, and they co-operated with the landowners in arranging numerous outings, teas and school treats; while Miss MacKenzie, the mistress of Claggan School, presented an ambitious annual entertainment by her pupils, usually including a pantomime. The response was enthusiastic, the functions always being well attended, not on Ardtornish Estate alone as in Octavius Smith's time, but all over the parish.[2]

What is perhaps more surprising is that a kindly feeling towards the landlords grew up at the same time, a genuine sense of gratitude for what they were doing for their people. After all, it was not long since the growth and collapse of the land-league movement in Morvern, and there is besides a universal tendency to envy and resent great possessions,

[1] Valentine Smith wrote crossly in his diary on 12 October 1900: "Elliot & wife returned to Ardtornish after being away 8 days—without asking permission"; and on 28 November of the same year "Elliot to leave   Notice [given] 10 weeks before". Smith relented, however, and crossed the later entry out (Valentine Smith, Diary for 1900, *AP*).

[2] Dozens of these events were reported in the *Oban Times* during the 1890s.

however philanthropic their owners may be. Nevertheless there were, for instance, stories of Valentine Smith knocking down parts of his new mansion house in order to provide Morvern people with the work of building them up again, and of his inventing light work especially for old people who would otherwise have been unemployed, stories which are very likely apocryphal, but which were believed and which are still told.[1] And when the Morvern correspondent of the *Oban Times* wrote in July 1899 "Mr. T. Valentine Smith arrived at Ardtornish last week, and, to the delight of everybody, seems to be in better health than when he last visited Morvern", it was remarkable not only as referring to a difficult and unapproachable old man, but also as a complete reversal of the attitude expressed in similar circumstances ten years earlier.[2]

This is not to suggest that the people of Morvern had become vacant lackeys of the proprietors, eager to touch their forelocks in return for bread. On the contrary, there is every indication that their relative prosperity brought with it renewed cultural vigour and independence of mind, more constructive than the dull misery of the mid-century and the frustrated anger of the 'eighties because people were now prepared to accept their world as it was, yet were determined to make the best they could of it. Cottagers welcomed their cousins coming on holiday at the time of the Glasgow Fair, together with a few tourists who now began to come even to Morvern; the crofters of Drimnin sailed their fishing boats in the races at Tobermory (and won); and 'balls' were held at the New Year in such unlikely places as the remote cottages of Achagavel, Torraneidhinn and Durinemast.[3] The landowners did not entirely lack critics, the folk who had left in despair were still remembered, but in 1900 the mood was one of hope. The bad old days—still too well-remembered to have become the good old days—were past; surely they would never return?

RETROSPECT; AND AFTERWARDS

Looking back over the whole of the nineteenth century, social and economic change in Morvern can be seen as part of one large pattern. The basic economic fact affecting the parish—and indeed the whole of the West Highlands—was its infertility relative to farm lands elsewhere that had less rain and more sun. So long as the landowners were prepared to accept small financial rewards from their properties, as they were until 1745, and so long as the working population would live in earth-floored cabins and eat porridge and potatoes, as they would until the

[1] Information from 'North Argyll' and others.
[2] *Oban Times*, 22 July 1899.
[3] *Oban Times*, 25 Jan. 1896; 23 Jan., 30 Jan., 6 Feb. 1897; 22 July 1899.

early nineteenth century, the society of the parish could survive in the traditional form that was allied to the marginal agriculture of runrig and cattle-raising; but when first one and then the other interest began to ask for rewards comparable with those obtainable from richer lands elsewhere, the old ways were bound to change. The mechanism that effected the change was the introduction of sheep, which gave a demonstrably higher yield per acre than the old agriculture; and there developed from 1750 until 1880 an increasingly ruthless struggle to overcome the natural disadvantages of the country by means of sheep-farming.

This struggle for increased productivity took place in two stages. During the first, from about 1750 to about 1820, Highlanders of the landowning class introduced sheep-ranching on top of the old runrig-cattle economy, and allowed both to proceed together. The people, retaining much of their traditional culture and isolated from the rest of the nation by poor communications and a separate language, accepted the situation, and dealt with their surplus population (which became increasingly burdensome during this period) by means of voluntary emigration. The turn of the century was thus a time of relative stability and equilibrium. Around 1820, however, the economic inefficiency of this arrangement, combined with a national agricultural depression and the personal failure of the sixth Duke of Argyll, caused the landlords of Highland origin to sell out to new men from the south, and the struggle entered its second stage, which was characterised both by eviction and by a massive increase in the rate of voluntary emigration. The new farmers proposed to increase the efficiency of Highland sheep-farming by pursuing it to the exclusion of the traditional agriculture, and to this end most of the smallholders were deprived of land during the next fifty years. The increasing population was thus met head on by decreasing resources, whereupon a catastrophic collapse of the traditional society was precipitated by a series of evictions (1824–68), by the crop failures of the 1830s and 1840s, and by the continuing flow of emigrants leaving to seek a higher standard of living elsewhere.

How far were the landlords to blame? Not very much, it seems, as far as the larger aspects of these events were concerned. In the first place, the attempt to increase the efficiency of their operations was essential if the agriculture of the region was not to slip back into primitive subsistence farming, and a regression of this sort was not a genuine alternative in the climate of opinion of the mid-nineteenth century. Secondly, the continuing growth of the population, combined with a standard of living that was not rising commensurately with standards elsewhere, put smallholders in a position that was intolerable quite apart from the consequences of crop failure and eviction. As was to be seen in districts where crofting agriculture continued throughout the nineteenth century, the actual alternative to the re-organisation imposed by sheep-farmers was chronic depression; and it is arguable that the drastic surgery of the clearances was preferable to the wasting of the population by poverty for a further fifty years, that the belief of the evicting landlords that they were acting for the greatest good of the greatest number was in fact justified. It is not the policy of the clearances, then, that merits criticism so much as the methods that were used to carry it out, which sometimes involved a casual cruelty, a mindless disregard for the dignity of the people who were evicted that cannot be excused.

With the completion of the Morvern clearances in 1868, sheep-farm-ing in the parish reached the peak of its efficiency, but the success of the improvements was not to endure for long. Falls in the prices of sheep and wool, accompanied by a deterioration of the grazings, caused in about 1880 an economic collapse from which the district never recovered; once modern communications brought wool and mutton from sunnier, drier lands to British markets, farming in the Highlands was found to be impossible without subsidy. In Morvern the subsidy came initially from wealthy proprietors who were prepared to pay for the pleasure of owning a Highland estate, and whose bounty—to their great credit—sometimes went far beyond the minimum necessary to secure their own comfort and convenience. At the same time, following social unrest in the 1880s when it was hoped that a return to crofting might be imposed and paid for by the State, the people eventually awoke from their dreams of the past and accepted with laudable spirit the fact of their integration (as pensioners although they were hardly aware of it) into the society and economy of a modern industrial state. Again the turn of the century saw a period of relative stability and equilibrium.

But historical processes are not halted by the ends of centuries and, although the subject of this book is the transformation of Morvern be-tween 1800 and 1900, it may be added that the period of equilibrium around 1900 was to prove as evanescent as had been that of a hundred years before. Although the subsidy of the district was maintained without pause (until the First World War by the landlords and after-wards increasingly by the State) the population of the parish continued to decline. During the thirty years from 1881 to 1911 the population went down from 819 to 694, a total reduction of only fifteen per cent or a net wastage of 4·1 persons a year; but during the next twenty years, from 1911 to 1931, it was reduced by a further thirty-four per cent, at a net wastage of 10·4 persons per year from 1911 to 1921 and of 13·0 per-sons per year from 1921 to 1931. Thus in the 1920s, when the rate of natural increase was very small, some two-and-a-half per cent of the population was emigrating from the parish every year, not so far short of the 3·2 per cent which was the average annual exodus from Morvern in the years of its greatest population decline, 1831–51.[1] Once again the emigrants were leaving in response to a standard of living that was rising faster outside the Highlands than at home, and the result was a marked deterioration in the social coherence of the parish. Today half the population (422 in 1961) lives in Lochaline village, many of the people there being immigrant workers of the Lochaline sand mine and their families; the remainder are scattered widely over the rest of Morvern —their average density is about one-and-a-half persons to the square mile—dependent not so much on their neighbours as on the lifelines of the post and grocery vans. Sheep-farming continues, but huge tracts of former farmland are now occupied by Forestry Commission plantations or are abandoned altogether.

Although the Forestry Commission is now the greatest landowner in Morvern, other large estates are still privately owned. Drimnin was not sold out of the Gordon family until 1943 and is carried on by its present owner much as before, and there are sizeable portions of the Newtons' Glencripesdale owned as private estates based on Rahoy and Laudale. Ardtornish Estate, reduced by the sale of the Fiunary area to the Forestry Commission in 1930 but with the later addition of Beach, remains at over 30,000 acres much the largest area in private hands.

It will be remembered that when Valentine Smith died in 1906 he left Ardtornish Estate and a great deal of money to his youngest sister Gertrude Craig Sellar, who was then aged sixty-two. Mrs Craig Sellar, returning to Morvern after an absence of a quarter of a century, was horrified by the monstrous growth of Ardtornish Tower at the head of Loch Aline, but she found that Ardtornish House was now derelict and uninhabitable, and on grounds of sentiment—for she had been happy there—she ordered its demolition. Her son Gerard was associated with her in the management of the estate from the beginning, and in 1909, when he was thirty-eight, she handed it over to him entirely. They lived on together at the Tower, Gerard remaining unmarried, until the early winter of 1929 when they died within a few weeks of each other; Gerard was then aged fifty-eight and his mother, the widow of Patrick Sellar's youngest son and the last surviving child of Octavius Smith, was eighty-five.[2] The estate was sold within the year to its present owners, who have maintained it ever since without fundamental change.

[1] For nineteenth-century figures, see pp. 122–3 below; later statistics from the historical table in *Census 1961, Scotland*: County Report, Vol. I, pt 7 (Argyll), 26.
[2] Willie had died in 1899, and Flora in 1919.

APPENDIXES

APPENDIX A

MORVERN STATISTICS, RENTALS, ETC.

I. EARLY STATISTICAL SURVEYS, 1755–1843

(1) *Extract from Webster's census, 1755* (Kyd, J. G. (1952), 34).

Morven...

Papists	6
Protestants	1,217
Total	1,223
Fighting Men	244$\frac{3}{5}$

(2) *Extract from OSA, 1794* (MacLeod, N. (1794), 270–1).

Sheep (of the South Country breed)	14,000
Black cattle	2,500
Breeding mares	100
Working horses	150
Number of souls in 1755	1,223
Number in 1793	1,764
Families	384
Males	914
Females	850
Under 10	501
From 10 to 20	473
20 to 50	586
50 to 70	149
70 to 80	43
Above 80	12
Annual average of births for the last 5 years	35
Annual average of marriages, ditto	9
Weavers, male	24
Weavers, female	10
Taylors	15
Blacksmiths	2
Shoemaker	1
Broguemakers	4
Joiners	3
Wheelwrights	2
Cowans [dykers, etc.]	8
Boatcarpenters	2
Gardener	1
Coopers	2

Millers	3
Retailers of spirits	12
Mills	3
Dramhouses	12
Real rent, Sterling	L. 2,200
Valued rent, ditto	L. 256: 19: 11

(3) *Extract from NSA, 1843* (MacLeod, J. (1843), 187, 189).

The yearly average of births for the last seven years	40
Marriages	7
There is no register of deaths kept	
Population of the parish by the census of 1831	2,036
The average number of persons under 15	685
betwixt 15 and 30	438
30 and 50	495
50 and 70	368
upwards of 70	50
Number of proprietors of the yearly value of	
L. 50 and upwards	11
of unmarried men, bachelors, and widowers	
upwards of 50	54
[of unmarried] women upwards of 50	156
of families	391
Average number of children in each family	5⅓ nearly
Number of insane, fatuous, deaf, dumb, &c.	5
Number of arable acres	4,054
pasture	78,246
wood	3,069

Produce.—

29,000 sheep at 2s. 6d. per head	L. 3,625	0	0
690 cows at L. 2 per head	1,380	0	0
Sowing of 512 bolls oats, 3½ returns, L. 1 per boll	1,792	0	0
Planting of 1,290 barrels potatoes, 15 returns, at 2s. 6d. per barrel	2,418	15	0
16,000 stones of hay, at 8d. per stone	533	6	8
Produce of woods per annum	100	0	0
Fisheries, say	25	0	0
Miscellaneous produce	100	0	0
	9,974	1	8

II. THE NATIONAL CENSUS, 1801–1901

Population, emigration and housing in nineteenth-century Morvern

	1801	1811	1821	1831	1841	1851	1861	1871	1881	1891	1901
Total population of Morvern	2083	1883	1995	2137	1786	1589	1220	967	819	818	730
Estimated total of emigrants in each decade	458	140	127	606	416	552	395	263	107	189	
Persons per family (total population)	5·7	5·8	5·8	5·1	5·2	—	4·9	4·8	4·2	4·3	4·2
Persons per house (total population)	5·9	6·0	5·8	5·1	5·5	5·7	5·8	6·1	4·9	4·9	5·1
Agricultural workers: persons per house	—	—	—	—	5·4	5·5	5·4	5·7	5·0	5·7	—
Lochaline village: persons per house	—	—	—	—	5·2	7·0	7·5	7·6	4·1	2·9	—
Rooms per house (except large houses)	—	—	—	—	—	—	2·7	3·6	3·6	3·8	—
Persons per room (except large houses)	—	—	—	—	—	—	2·1	1·7	1·4	1·3	—

SOURCES. *Census of Great Britain*, 1801–31; *Census of Scotland*, 1841–1901; *Census of Scotland*, 1841–91, enumeration schedules, *RGO*.

TOTAL POPULATION. The enumerations for 1841 to 1891 (all that are available for study) have been recounted. For 1861, 1871, 1881 and 1891 they agree with the published figures (less ships), but in 1841 and 1851 the population of Achagavel, Liddesdale, Glasbhil and Achleek was included with that of the parish of Strontian (to which these people were attached *quoad sacra*). Some attempt appears to have been made to get these additional people into the published figure for 1841, but in 1851 they were left out altogether; they are included here. It seems likely that the published figures for 1801 to 1831 are similarly defective, but for these years no enumeration schedules have survived, and it is only possible to repeat them. No boundary changes took place during the nineteenth century, and it must be emphasised that Liddesdale, etc., were always part of the parliamentary parish of Morvern.

Estimated total of emigrants in each decade. Two figures are used here: the intercensal change; and the estimated natural increase of ten years calculated at the rate of 13 per thousand per annum on the average population of the decade. The rate of increase is based on figures given in Kyd, J. G. (1952), *passim*.

Agricultural workers and *Lochaline village: persons per house.* From the enumeration schedules. In the first line large houses (20 or more rooms) and the houses in Lochaline village, together with their occupants, are excluded.

123

Rooms per house and *Persons per room* (except large houses). From the enumeration schedules; 'windowed rooms' were counted only from 1861. Houses of 20 or more rooms, and their occupants, are excluded.

III. ARGYLL ESTATE RENTALS, 1754, 1807

(1) *Extract from 'Sett & Rentall Mull and Morvern for 1754', ICP.*

Morvern as Sett By the Proprietor and pay[ll] Crop 1754, Cefs at five shill[s] The peny Land included

P[enny] L[and]			Ster[l]		
			£	s.	d.
Beoch	5	Ewen M[c]Fie	19	5	–
Achagavill	4	Lieu[tt] Colin Campbell	15	13	4
		Sett by the present Duke			
Laudell & Camisallich	7	John Campbell of Ardslignish	35	15	–
		Sett by the present Duke for			
		£2 above Rent 1753			
Aulastin & Portavaty &	8	Allan M[c]Lean of Drimnin	20	–	–
Polchoren		Sett by the present Duke			
Baar	10	Duncan Campbell	31	–	–
		Sett by the present Duke			
		for £– 15fh above Rent 1753			
Ardtorinish	5	Donald Campbell of Airds	37	–	–
		Sett by the present Duke for			
		£1. 5 above Rent 1753			
Savary	5	Sett to Small Tennants	21	5	–
Miln Thereof		Donald M[c]Kenzie	6	–	–
Ferinish	8	Sett to Small Tennants	25	–	–
Kenlochteagus	5½	Colin Campbell	21	7	6
		Sett by the present Duke for			
		£3 above Rent 1753			
Innimore [Unimore]	4	M[rs] Jean Cameron	11	–	–
Glencreipidell	5	Dugald M[c]Lauchlane	19	5	–
		N: The peny of Camusalloch			
		usualy Sett upon this farm			
		is now Sett upon Laudell and			
		the Rent thereof £6. 5			
		deducted from this farm			
Finnary	5	M[r] Alex[r] M[c]Tavish	15	15	–
Mungisdell & Drimchagag	8	John Beaton	23	–	–
		Sett for £3 above Rent 1753			
Miln thereof		Donald M[c]Eachern	4	16	–
Changehouse of Ferinish	–	Ronald M[c]Donald	1	1	–
Laggan & Sallachan	10	John Campbell	42	10	–
		Sett for £3 above Rent 1753			
Killindin	5	Alex[r] Campbell	19	–	–
		Sett in Tack by the present			
		Duke for £0. 5fh above			
		Rent 1753			
Rahoy & Ardintipirt	7½	Arch[d] Campbell & Hugh	31	–	–
		M[c]Lauchlane			
		Sett by the present Duke			

	P[enny] L[and]		Ster[l]
			£ s. d.
Kilcolumkill	3	Lauchlan McLauchlan & John Cameron	7 15 –
Ternat	3	Donald Campbell of Airds Sett by the present Duke for £: 15fh above Rent 1753	15 – –
Lidisdell & penygown	6	Lieu^{tt} Colin Campbell Sett in Tack by the present Duke	41 10 –

Ballance unaffected of the Bifhop and Ministers Tiends of Morvern after paying the incumbent £58. 18. 10⅔ in full of Stipends, Communion Elements Effeiring to his Graces property in Morvern and Gleib Rent is £ . 6. 11⅓ Gleib Rent as presently Sett 1. 10

	1 16 11¼
	465 14 9¼

(2) *Proposed schemes of rents for Rahoy and Laudale, 1807.*

Extracts from 'Instructions to Chamberlains, 1804–1811', ICP, pp. 75, 77, 80. In his "Report of the Chamberlain of Mull" of October 1807, James Maxwell produced a "Scheme of Rents proposed to be laid upon the following Farms; on the supposition that each of them is to be let to a Tenant who will reside upon it and derive his only means of subsistence from the produce of the Land" (p. 74). The new rent proposed for Rahoy, adopted in 1809, remained in force until the Glencripesdale group of properties was sold by Argyll in 1821; that proposed for Laudale may have been adopted in 1810, but there is no record of it in the Tack Book, and a much lower rent was allowed when a new tack was set in 1813 (see below, pp. 161–2, 163).

[RAHOY: proposed rent]

	£ s.
Rahoy out of Lease at Whitsunday 1810—	
35 Tydie Cows/keeping the Stotts till 3 y^{rs} old at £3 5	113 15
12 Tons of Kelp at 50/-	30 –
	£143 15
Present Rent	95 –
Augmentation	£ 48 15

To lay out £100 in improvements and to uphold the Wood fences when the Woods are cutt. The Deduction for want Grafs when that happens to be ascertained by Skillful persons mutually chosen—

Appendix A

[RAHOY: estimated return]

Rahoy

		£	s
32 head of black Cattle—one half three year old Stotts—			
the other half shott heifers & old Cows at £6		192	–
12 Tons of Kelp at £8	£96 –		
Deduct for Making	36	60	–
		252	–
Rent		143	15
Remains for the Tenant		£108	5

[LAUDALE: proposed rent]

Laudil out of Lease at Whitsunday 1811—

		£	s
2200 Sheep at 2/-		220	–
25 Tydie Cows/keeping the Stots till 3 y^r old at £3 5		81	5
10 Tons of Kelp at 50/-		25	–
		£326	5
Present Rent		81	–
Augmentation		245	5

To lay out £150 in improvements without any Claim for repayment and to be under the same Obligation as to Woods as the Tenants of Rahoy—

[LAUDALE: estimated return]

Laudil

		£	s
25 Score of Sheep half Wedders & half old Ewes at £12		300	–
300 Stone of Wool at 7/6		112	10
22 head of black Cattle, half three year old Stotts half			
shot heifers & old Cows at £6		132	–
10 Tons kelp at £8	£80		
Deduct for making	30	50	–
		£594	10
Rent		245	5
Remains for the Tenant		£269	5

IV. COUNTY VALUATION ROLL, 1802

Extract from the Valuation Roll for the County of Argyll, 1802; MS. at ACOL.

The Roll for 1802 is closely based on the first comprehensive Roll for the County, that of 1751 (also in MS. at *ACOL*), the valuations for each property being taken over unaltered from the earlier document. Comparison of these valuations with the actual rents charged for some of the properties by Argyll in 1754 (see the preceding section of this appendix) will show how unrealistic they were even then; and by 1802 the mid-century rents had themselves been increased by factors of from four to eight.

Parish of Morvern

Merklands/ Penny Lands	Names of Proprietors	Names of Lands	Valuation Sterling [£ s. d.]		
5	John Duke of Argyll	Beach	8	10	4
4		Auchaghavil	4	1	7
6		Laudill	11	–	5
8		Aulastin Portvait, and Polcharran	8	3	8
8		Mungastil Drumchraigag and Mill	8	5	8
10		Barr	11	19	10
5		Ardtorinish	13	2	1
5		Savarie and Acre	9	5	8
8		Ferinish & Carnocalloch	8	16	11
5½		Kenlochteacus	7	8	10
4		Inimore [Unimore]	4	11	10
6		Glencribisdil & Camusalloch	8	13	9
5		Finnary	6	7	6
5		Laggan	8	6	4
5		Killindrine	6	15	3
5		Sallachan	3	15	7
7½		Rahoy & Ardintibbirt	10	6	5
3		Kilcolmkill	2	10	2
3		Ternait and Eignaig	6	5	3
6		Liddisdale	16	0	5
		Quarter Teinds of Morvern	2	14	3
6	Charles McLean	Drimnin	7	10	–
6		Achalinan	7	19	6
1	James Forbes of Kingerloch	Isle of Carna	2	19	3
5		Altachonich	2	14	1
5	John Duke of Argyll	Auchabeg & Arncfs	4	3	4
4		Knock & Gualachelish	5	11	1
2	Duncan McLachlan	Achaforse	2	4	5
5	John McLean Inverscaddle	Achnagawn	4	6	8
4		Agorie	2	6	8
2		Inibeg [Unibeg]	2	15	6
½		Derinamart	1	16	8

Appendix A

Parish of Morvern

Merklands/ Peny Lands	Names of Proprietors	Names of Lands	Valuation Sterling [£ s. d.]		
1		Aryinnis	2	6	8
1		Crosphein & Muckeroch	2	15	6
5	Duncan McLachlan	Clelet and Corvain	4	11	8
1	John McLean	Auchacharn	1	15	7
5	John Duke of Argyll	Achnaha	4	11	8
5	John McDonald Borrodle	Aucharonich	5	11	1
5	Duncan MacLachlan	Ulladill	7	10	–
5	Do and Borrodle	Strone and Ullin	5	11	1
2½	Duncan McLachlan	Achatyvickrousklan	2	5	10
	Do and Inverscadle	Salmon Fishing of Kenlochalen	2	–	–
	Duncan MacLachlane	Kenlochaline	6	11	11
			£256	19	11

V. THE PRINCIPAL EVICTIONS, 1824–1868

Notes to page 129

It is emphasised that the known total of 150 families evicted is unlikely to be quite complete, but also that unrecorded evictions of this period were probably no more than a small fraction of the known total.

The total numbers of families known to have been evicted by the various proprietors are as follows:

Patrick Sellar	48
The Gordons	34 (+ 3 re-evicted)
Mrs Paterson	28
Miss Stewart	25
John Sinclair	at least 15

The principal evictions in nineteenth-century Morvern

Date	Estate	Proprietor	Places cleared	No. of families evicted	References
1824	Glenmorvern	Miss C. Stewart	Mungasdail Unimore Barr (part)	25	*Nap. Com. ev.* 2288.
1838	Acharn	P. Sellar	Whole estate	44	*Nap. Com. ev.* 2288–90.
(?) c. 1840	Lochaline	J. Sinclair	Clounlaid–Uladail	?	*Census,* 1841.
(?) c. 1840	Drimnin	Sir C. Gordon	Achleanan	7	*Drimnin plan 1836; Oban Times,* 20. xii. 84.
c. 1843	Drimnin	Sir C. Gordon	Carraig Auliston (part)	c. 6 (to Oronsay)	*Nap. Com. ev.* 2288–9, 2301, 2304, 2321–2.
1844	Ardtornish	P. Sellar	Ardtornish	4	*Nap. Com. ev.* 2288–90.
1841–51	Lochaline	J. Sinclair	Keil	7	*Nap. Com. ev.* 2293; *Census,* 1841, 1851.
1851–61	Lochaline	J. Sinclair	Savary	8	*Census,* 1851, 1861.
1855	Drimnin	Lady Gordon	Auliston	21	*Oban Times,* 20. xii. 84; *Census,* 1851, 1861.
1866	Lochaline	Mrs M. Paterson	Achabag Knock Achnaha Achafors	28	*Nap. Com. ev.* 2288; *Oban Times,* 10. ii.83, 20. xii. 84; *Census,* 1861, 1871.
c. 1868	Drimnin	Lady Gordon	Oronsay	3	*Nap. Com. ev.* 2288–9, 2301, 2304, 2321–2; *Census,* 1861, 1871.

APPENDIX B

NINETEENTH-CENTURY MORVERN
PROPERTIES

Introduction

BOUNDARIES. See Map 10 which is intended to show the boundaries of *c.* 1825; sources are given in the descriptions. Marches on high ground were often ill-defined, and have always been liable to varying interpretation; but estate boundaries, often confirmed in the later nineteenth century, are more reliable than the old divisions between farms.

AREAS. Acreages are given from an early source when one is available (converted to Imperial measure), and from measurements made from the Ordnance map according to the boundaries of *c.* 1825 (see above). The OS areas do not include fresh-water lochs or the inter-tidal zone.

DATES OF OCCUPATION. No dates before 1755 are given for the occupation of particular settlements because *Roy's Scotland 1747–1755* was the first map that was sufficiently accurate to enable individual settlements to be identified.

POPULATION. The two figures separated by an oblique stroke are respectively the number of occupied houses, and the number of people resident in these houses, at a particular date.

OWNERSHIP AND CONVEYANCES. The ownership of the properties that were not included in nineteenth-century Ardtornish (groups V–XI) is dealt with in slightly less detail than that of the first four groups.

REFERENCES GIVEN IN 'DESCRIPTIONS'. (See Bibliography for full references.)

[a] *Argyll estate plans 1770*
[b] *Argyll farms plan 1819 (and copy)*
[c] *Census 1841–91*
[d] *Drimnin plan 1836*
[e] *Clounlaid plan 1833, Uladail plan 1833*
[f] *Sellar's plan (fishings) 1848*
[g] *Sellar's plan (roads) 1848*
[h] *Acharn plan 1815*
[i] Cregeen, E. R. (1963)
[j] *Ainslie's Scotland 1789*
[k] *Knock plans 1788, 1815*
[l] *Langlands' Argyll 1801*
[m] *Achranich plan 1815*
[n] Macphail, J. R. N. (1914)
[o] *OS 1872, OS 1872 NB*
[p] *Air photographs 1946*

q   *AP*
r   *Roy's Scotland 1747–1755*
s   Scott, J. F. (1956)
t   *Thomson's atlas 1824*
u   *ICP*
v   *VR*
w   *APS*
x   *OPS* ii. pt 1, 188–93
y   *RSA*
z   author's personal observation
OS Ordnance Survey

I. ARDTORNISH ESTATE

DESCRIPTION. Composed of Ardtornish, Eignaig and Tearnait; 9,965 acres (OS). See Map 10.

ARDTORNISH (Ardtorinish, 1380[x]; Ardthoranis, 1390[x]; Ardtorinche, 1451[x]; Ardtornys, 1461[x]; Ardtorreneish, 1674[n]; Ardtornish, 1755[r]).

BOUNDARIES: see Map 10[a,b,m].

AREAS: 1770: 5,662 acres (98 arable, 5,510 pasture, 56 wood)[a]. OS: 5,735 acres.

SETTLEMENTS:

Ardtornish Castle: 692426; outlines of 4 buildings to the E and SE of the castle, and of 1 building to its N[z]; probably associated with the occupation of the castle, and abandoned by the late 17th cent.

Ardtornish: (1) 691443; outline of 1 building[z], but other traces (several houses in 1755[r]) obliterated by 19th-cent. planting; occupied by 1755[r], farm centre moved to (2) by 1770[a], site (1) abandoned *c.* 1850[t,c].

(2) 693433; mansion house built 1755–70[r,a], demolished 1907[q]; steading late-18th cent.; cottage at 691435 rebuilt *c.* 1862, occupied until 1959, now intermittently occupied.

Camas Gorm: remains of a house marked in 1872 at 775424[o], but no traces found[z] and the map may have been in error.

Caolas (Caolis, 1801[l]): 683447; outline of cottage immediately S of Ferry House[q,z]; Ferry House and stables (now Ferry cottage) built 1879[q]; occupied by 1770[a], and continuously since then.

Garbh Shlios (Garlies, 1841[c]; Guerelas, 1872[q]; also known as *MacKinnon's Bay*): 754412; remains of 1 house, no arable[z]; occupied by 1841, abandoned by 1851[c].

Inninbeg: (1) 698433; remains of 2 buildings[o,z]; 1 house occupied 1851[c], and probably earlier, until 1879 when cottages at (2) were built. (2) 695434; double cottage built 1879[q]; occupied until 1964, and intermittently since then.

Inninmore: 727418; remains of 5 houses[s,z]; occupied by 1770[a], *See p. ix* 2 houses in 1841[c], 1 in 1851[c]; present cottage built 1862[q], abandoned

1939[v]. The outlines of 5–6 further buildings at 724419 probably derive from a much earlier settlement abandoned before 1755[z,r].

Rubha an t-Sasunnaich: 710423; remains of 2 houses, no arable[z]; intermittent occupation connected with quarrying, probably *c.* 1830.

Samhnach (Saunichan, 1841[c]; Saunich, 1848[r]): 695459; remains of 1 house and razed remains of at least 2 other buildings 100 yds SSE[o,z]; 2 houses occupied 1841, 1 in 1851, abandoned by 1861[c]. (See also *Samhnach*, Achranich.)

SHIELINGS: (1) probably 705447, 800 ft a.s.l., the destination of an old track leading up from Ardtornish Castle via the two Ardtornish sites.
(2) possibly 700436, 600 ft a.s.l., where there is a stock wall by the stream.

No remains of shieling structures at either site.

POPULATION: 1779, –/55[1]; 1841, 12/74; 1851, 7/37; 1861, 6/29; 1871, 5/39; 1881, 4/21; 1891, 5/29[c].

EIGNAIG (Egnaig, 1770[a]; Eignaig, 1820[y]).

BOUNDARIES: See Map 10[a,b].

AREAS: 1770: 466 acres (38 arable, 428 pasture)[a]. OS: 467 acres.

SETTLEMENT: 794439; no certain early remains (Scott's ruins were those N of Allt na Criche[s]), but settlement was on site of present cottage[a] (which was built in 1864[q]); occupied by 1770[a], abandoned *c.* 1935[v], re-occupied intermittently 1963.

POPULATION: 1841, 2/16; 1851, 1/7; 1861, 1/12; 1871, 1/5; 1881, 1/6; 1891, 1/6[c].

TEARNAIT (Ternaid, 1674[n]; Ternill, 1755[r]; Ternet, 1770[a]; Ternate, 1819[b]; Tearnait, 1872[o]).

BOUNDARIES: See Map 10[a,b,m].

AREAS: 1770: 3,118 acres (53 arable, 3,065 pasture and loch)[a]. OS: 3,763 acres.

SETTLEMENTS:
Doire Dharaich: 763477; remains of 2 houses[o,z]; probably occupied by 1770[a]; probably abandoned by 1841, certainly by 1851[c]; possibly connected with the 18th-cent. copper mines (see p. 171 below).

Leacraithnaich: 739470, on the Tearnait bank of the march burn; outlines of at least 2 houses[o,z]; period of early occupation uncertain, but abandoned by 1872[o], and probably several decades earlier.

See p. vii *Tearnait:* 745474; outlines of at least 3 houses, with parks, etc.[z]; walled arable area at 747474, and outlines of (?) earlier buildings to the N at 747475; remains of a house at 744473[o,z]; house at 742472, occupied in

1872°, later reroofed as a sporting bothy; occupied by 1744^r, last house abandoned *c.* 1874^q.

POPULATION: 1779, –/12^1; 1841, 2/12; 1851, 1/3; 1861, 1/7; 1871, 1/9; 1881, 0^c.

Summary of ownership

Argyll property through the eighteenth century. Tearnait and Eignaig were let separately from Ardtornish until 1754, but in that year Donald Campbell of Airds, Argyll's factor, was given the tack of all three at a total rent of £52. Airds was succeeded as tacksman by Angus Gregorson in 1773 (£105, raised to £150 in 1801), and Angus Gregorson by his son John in 1813. Put up for sale in 1819, the property was bought by the tacksman John Gregorson for £9,000. Bought from Gregorson by Sellar in 1844 for £11,100, who farmed it together with Acharn–Clounlaid and rented property. Sellar's complete estate bought from his heirs in 1860 by O. H. Smith for £39,500, Smith naming the combined estate 'Ardtornish'. Inherited by T. V. Smith, 1871; by Mrs A. C. Sellar, 1906; transferred to G. C. Sellar (her son), 1909. Bought by the present owner (Mrs O. H. Smith, no relation of the nineteenth-cent. owners) in 1930.

To Sellar's Ardtornish, Acharn and Clounlaid and Smith's Achranich were added Lochaline Estate (1888); Altachonaich (1900); and Beach (1936). Most of the Lochaline section and part of Acharn were sold to the Forestry Commission in 1930; the coastal strip from Lochaline village to the Savary river was repurchased for Ardtornish in 1955. For details of the properties other than Ardtornish itself, see Sections II, III, IV, VIII and IX below.

Conveyances

1701 "Estate of Argyll, including the lands of Ardtornish and others" resigned by and newly enfeoffed to John Marquis of Lorne, heir to the Duke of Argyll, 30 Dec. 1701; Ch. Res. G.S., 10 May 1702 ('Inventory' of title deeds, 9 Feb. 1820, *AP*; *Inventory 1872*, 7).

1754 Set to Donald Campbell of Airds, rent £37 (Ardtornish) and £15 (Tearnait [and Eignaig]) ("Sett and rental of Mull and Morvern 1754", *ICP*).

1773 Set to Angus Gregorson, rent £105; lease extended, same rent, 1785; lease extended, rent increased to £150, 1801; lease transferred to John Gregorson, same rent, 1813 (*Book of Mull and Morvern tacks*, vol. '0', 21, 58, 245; *ibid.*, vol. '4', 68, *ICP*).

1819 John Gregorson 'of Acharn', 'of Ardtornish', buys Ardtornish Estate from the trustees of the Duke of Argyll; disp. dated 3 and 10 Nov. 1819; price £9,000; Ch. Res. Conf. G.S., 2 Jun. 1820 ("Disposition", *AP*; *Inventory 1872*, 7; *RSA* 1820: 3209).

1844   Patrick Sellar of Acharn buys Ardtornish, Eignaig and Tearnait from the trustees of John Gregorson; disp. dated 14 May 1844; price £11,100 ("Disposition", *AP*; *Inventory 1872*, 8; *RSA* 1844: 575).

1860   Octavius Henry Smith of Achranich buys the same, together with Acharn and Clounlaid, from the trustees of Patrick Sellar, 5–8 May 1860; price £39,500 (Receipt, *AP*; *Inventory 1872*, 16; *RSA* 1860: 1739; *GRS* 3082.181).

1871   Disposition and settlement by O. H. Smith in favour of Jane Gaches Smith dated 27 Feb. 1867 (*RSA* 1871: 92). Disposition by J. G. Smith in favour of Thomas Valentine Smith dated 3 April 1871 (*RSA* 1871: 93).

II. KINLOCHALINE ESTATE

Summary of early ownership

In 1730 Angus MacLean of Kinlochaline sold the "lands of Kinlochallan" to Sir Alexander Murray of Stanhope, the proprietor of the Strontian and Lurga mines. The Sasine specified the individual properties of Kinlochaline, Dubh Dhoire, Clais Bhreac, Sron, Achnatavishruskline, Achranich, Srath Shuardail, Uladail, Torr a'Chall and Achnaha (spellings modernised). In practice there were four main groups of properties:

The Knock group: Achabeg, Achnaha and Knock (but not including Keil, which was Argyll's property).

The Kinlochaline group: Achafors and Kinlochaline.

The Clounlaid group: Clounlaid and Uladail.

The Achranich group: Achranich, Claggan, Dubh Dhoire and (probably) Uileann.

The Lurga mine soon failed, and Murray got rid of his Morvern properties. In the Valuation Roll of 1751 all these lands (except Kinlochaline farm) are listed as belonging to the proprietor of the Acharn group of properties, Allan Cameron of Glendessary, although it was not until 1767 that a formal Disposition of them was made to him. When the Disposition did come, it was to sell them to Cameron and to Allan MacLean of Drimnin jointly; and in 1768 Cameron and MacLean agreed to divide Kinlochaline Estate equally between them. Cameron took the Knock and Kinlochaline groups of properties to add to his existing estate of Acharn, while MacLean took the eastern half, the Clounlaid and Achranich groups. Cameron and MacLean also agreed to divide 'the fishings of Kinlochaline' equally between them; this applied to the fishing station at Kinlochaline, and to the Aline River, which Cameron could now fish from the west bank and MacLean from the east.

Cameron's properties were disposed of by his trustees (in bankruptcy) in 1776. The Knock group went to Campbell of Ardslignish. Kinlochaline went to MacLean of Drimnin, but without a half share of the fishings of Kinlochaline, presumably because MacLean had already got a half share of them with Clounlaid–Achranich. Cameron's share of the fishings of Kinlochaline was therefore attached to his Acharn group of properties, which went to MacLean of Inverscaddle. The subsequent histories of these groups of properties will be found in the individual summaries; Kinlochaline in the present section of this appendix, Acharn in section III and Knock in section IV.

The properties of MacLean of Drimnin were also disposed of as a result of the bankruptcy of their owner, in 1798–1800. In an action against the trustees of Charles MacLean of Drimnin, the Kinlochaline and Clounlaid groups, together with MacLean's half of the fishing of Kinlochaline, were adjudged to belong to MacLachlan of Callart. The Achranich group, without the share of the fishings, went to MacDonald of Borrodale. Their subsequent histories will be traced in the individual summaries in this section, but it is worth mentioning now that the Kinlochaline and Clounlaid groups with the half share of fishings remained together until 1841, when John Sinclair (who was then their owner) sold the Clounlaid group together with the share of fishings.

Thus, in 1841, half 'the fishings of Kinlochaline' was attached to the property of Acharn, and the other half was attached to the property of Clounlaid; while the Kinlochaline and Achranich groups of properties, which each had a considerable length of the bank of the Aline River, had no fishing rights at all.

The fishing station at Kinlochaline, part of 'the fishings of Kinlochaline'. The station consisted of a corf house placed at the south end of the small island in the Aline opposite Rose cottage, and the fisherman's house (which was approximately on the site of Castle cottage), together with the bank and shore between them to an average distance of 40 yards in from the water. (Boundaries determined in 'Fence award' dated 7 June 1873, *AP*; further details in the Sellar–Smith agreement of 1850, *AP*, and *MacKichan's memoirs*; the fisherman's house shown in *Photographs (Gertrude Smith)*, 46. No trace of the corf house now remains.)

The fishing station, in common with the rest of the fishings of Kinlochaline, was owned jointly by separate proprietors from 1767–8 until 1841, when the whole of the Kinlochaline fishings were reunited in the hands of Patrick Sellar.

A. THE KINLOCHALINE GROUP

DESCRIPTION. Composed of Achafors and Kinlochaline; 896 acres (OS). See Map 10.

ACHAFORS (Achefors, 1494[x]; Achaforse, 1751[v]; Achfors, 1755[r]; Auchforsis, 1781[y]; Achaforses, 1806[y]; Auchforse, 1817[y]; Achafors, 1872[o]).

Appendix B

BOUNDARIES: see Map 10[k,b]. Northern boundary uncertain.

AREAS: 1851: *c.* 30 acres arable, 317 acres heath[c]. OS: 518 acres.

SETTLEMENT: 687473[o]; all remains obliterated by forestry planting except sheepfold[z]; occupied by 1755[r], 2 houses in 1841[c], abandoned *c.* 1888[v].

POPULATION: 1841, 2/61; 1851, 2/14; 1861, 3/15; 1871, uncertain; 1881, 1/2; 1891, 0[c].

KINLOCHALINE (Achagalain, 1390[x]; Achkalen, 1496[x]; Kynloch, 1496[x]; Auchigawlen, 1557[x]; Kinloch, 1681[w]; Kenlochaillyn, 1755[r]; Kinlochaline, 1781[y]; Kinlochaline called Auchzallan, 1806[y]).

BOUNDARIES: see Map 10[k,b,o]. Southern boundary uncertain.

AREAS: 1851: *c.* 100 acres arable, 250 acres heath[c]. OS: 378 acres.

SETTLEMENTS: in 2 groups in the 18th cent., 693475 and 695478[r]; fields marked[z], and 3 ruins around southern site[o]; occupied by 1755[r]; 7 houses in 1841[c]; present double house built 1899[q], intermittently occupied since 1963. Fishing station and Castle cottage at 697475 (see above) were separately owned by the proprietor of half the fishings of Kinlochaline; present Castle cottages built *c.* 1873[q].

POPULATION: 1841, 7/31; 1851, 8/31; 1861, 7/25; 1871, uncertain; 1881, 5/24; 1891, 2/9[c] (Castle cottage included up to 1881).

Summary of later ownership

When Drimnin's estates were disposed of in bankruptcy in 1800, the Kinlochaline and Clounlaid groups of properties and half the fishings of Kinlochaline were awarded to Duncan MacLachlan of Callart for £6,462. In 1825 they were sold to Hugh MacQueen w.s. for £11,000, and by MacQueen later the same year to Patrick Grant for £16,000. Grant failed in 1836, when John Sinclair of Lochaline secured these properties for £10,010. Sinclair sold the Clounlaid group and the fishings to Sellar in 1841 for £7,500, but kept the Kinlochaline group as the north-east corner of Lochaline Estate with which it was sold in 1864 (see Section IV).

Conveyances

1730   Sir Alexander Murray of Stanhope acquires the lands of Kinlochaline from Angus MacLean of Kinlochaline (Inst. of Sasine dated 17 Dec. 1730, *AP*; *Inventory 1872*, 2).

1767   James Montgomery, Lord Advocate, acquires the lands in Peeblesshire, Ardnamurchan, Sunart, Kinlochaline and elsewhere belonging to Sir Alexander and Charles Murray of Stanhope, and sells them in the same month for £40,700 to James Riddell of

Ardnamurchan (11 and 15 Aug. 1767). Two months later Riddell sells the lands of Kinlochaline for £6,450 to Allan Cameron of Glendessary and Allan MacLean of Drimnin jointly, including the fishings; disp. dated 4 Nov. 1767 ("Disposition" of 17 December 1770, *AP*; *Inventory 1872*, 2).

1768   Allan Cameron and Allan MacLean agree to divide the lands and fishings of Kinlochaline equally between them, Cameron taking "Achnaha, Kenlachalin, Achlayvicrouslin" and half the fishings, and MacLean having "Achranich Ulladil and Strone" and the other half of the fishings; contract dated 3 Mar. 1768, registered 3 Feb. 1769 ("Extract Registered Contract", *AP*; *Inventory 1872*, 2).

(For the subsequent history of the Knock group of properties, see Section IV.)

1776   Half the fishings of Kinlochaline sold by Allan Cameron's trustees with the estate of Acharn to MacLean of Inverscaddle; for details and subsequent history see Section III below.

1776   Allan MacLean of Drimnin buys the Kinlochaline group of properties from the trustees in bankruptcy of Allan Cameron, without fishings; disp. dated 4 July 1776 ("Disposition" missing in 1872; details from "Extract Instrument of Sasine" dated 20 July 1776; *Inventory 1872*, 13).

1800   At the bankrupt sale of the properties of Charles MacLean (who had inherited from his father Allan MacLean in 1792), the Kinlochaline and Clounlaid groups, with MacLean's share of the Kinlochaline fishings, are sold to Duncan MacLachlan of Callart for £6,462; disp. and conv. dated 27 Feb. 1800 ("Disposition and Conveyance", *AP*; *Inventory 1872*, 13; Ch. Sale and Conf. by Argyll, 1803, *RSA* 1817: 2755).

1825   Hugh MacQueen buys the same from Duncan MacLachlan; disp. dated 28 Mar. 1825; price £11,000. MacQueen sells the same to Patrick Grant of Lakefield (perhaps acting as MacLachlan's agent rather than as an independent speculator); disp. dated 27 Oct. 1825; price £16,000 (second "Disposition", which refers to the first one, *AP*; *Inventory 1872*, 14; *RSA* 1825: 772).

1836   At the bankrupt sale of the properties of Patrick Grant, the same are bought by John Sinclair of Lochaline; decreet of sale dated 19 Jan. and 7 July 1836; price £10,010 ("Extract Decreet of Sale", *AP*; *Inventory 1872*, 14; Ch. Sale and Conf. by Argyll, 4 Nov. 1836; *RSA* 1837: 1088).

(For the subsequent history of the Kinlochaline group of properties, see Section IV. For the subsequent history of the Clounlaid group of properties, with half the fishings of Kinlochaline, see subsection B below.)

B. THE CLOUNLAID GROUP

DESCRIPTION. Composed of Clounlaid and Uladail, in which were included the old sites or properties of Achnatuasaig, Achtidonile, Doire Leathan, Muicrach and Sron; 4,794 acres (OS). See Map 10.

CLOUNLAID (Cleynlondre, Cormawin, 1494[x]; Clenlet, 1755[r]; Clilaid, Corrivaine, 1781[y]; Clolead, 1801[l]; Clenlie called Cervain, Clonhead and Carvun, Clenbed, 1806[y]; Clounlaid, 1872[o]).

BOUNDARIES: see Map 10[e].

AREAS: 1833: 3,338 acres[e]. OS: 3,386 acres.

SETTLEMENTS:

Achtidonile: a name in pre-18th-cent. deeds (Achintadownol, 1496[x]; Auchitadonill, 1681[w]); the only later reference appears to be a pencil note on the mounted copy of *Achranich plan 1815* in *AP* which places "Achtidonile" at about 735502. There is a cairn at this spot (which may be the result of Muicrach cultivation). Possibly a settlement before 1700.

Clounlaid: 754530; remains of 5 houses[s,o,z]; occupied by 1755[r], probably cleared *c.* 1840; present house built at 750523 in 1866[q], occupied until 1959, and since then intermittently[v].

Sron (Nasrone, 1390[x]; le Strone, 1496[x]; Strone, 1557[x]; Stron, 1755[r]; Sron, 1872[o]): 743505; outlines of 2 houses[o,z]; occupied by 1755[r], 1 house occupied by 2 women in 1841[c], abandoned by 1851[c]. (*Note:* the old settlement of *Achnatavishruskline*, 1,000 yds NE of Sron, was conveyed with Achranich (in spite of being within the Clounlaid boundary), and is dealt with in subsection c, below.)

POPULATION: 1841, 2/6; 1851, 1/9; 1861, 1/10; 1871, 1/5; 1881, 1/5; 1891, 1/5[c].

ULADAIL (Vlgadall, 1390[x]; Owladoll, 1496[x]; Vlladill, 1681[w]; Ulladill, 1755[r]; Ulladile, 1837[y]; Uamhdail, 1872[o]; Uladail (OS 1 in. 7th S)).

BOUNDARIES: see Map 10. The 'Derrilean dyke' (of which the remains are still visible) ran E from the Black Water along Allt Poll Doire to the march with Clounlaid at 731515, cutting Uladail in half; the northern half was originally called *Doire Leathan*, the southern *Uladail*.

AREAS: 1833: 1,429 acres[e]. OS: 1,408 acres.

SETTLEMENTS:

Achnatuaisaig: 708508; remains of 1 house[o,z], outlines of 2 more buildings 100 yds further E[z]; probably occupied in 1755[r] and 1833[e].

Doire Leathan: 717519; remains of 2 small houses[z]; period of occupation uncertain, but after 1755[r] and before 1841[c]. No arable seen, and the site may latterly have been a shieling.

Muicrach: 729504; remains of at least 3 houses and (?) kiln[s,z]; occupied by 1801[1], abandoned by 1841[c] (probably cleared *c.* 1840).

Uladail: 717506; remains of 12 houses[o,s,z]; Roy shows arable only on the meadow S of the houses[r] ("Dail Uladail"[e]), but by 1815 there was an extensive area of Uladail arable S of the river[m,z] ("Srath Uladail"[o]). Occupied by 1755[r], probably cleared *c.* 1840, 1 house occupied by 2 women in 1841[c], abandoned by 1851[c].

POPULATION: 1841, 1/2; 1851, 0[c].

Summary of later ownership

John Sinclair, who had acquired Kinlochaline and Clounlaid in 1836, sold the Clounlaid group, together with half the fishings of Kinlochaline, to Sellar in 1841 for £7,500. In 1860 Clounlaid was sold, with the rest of Sellar's Morvern properties, to Smith of Achranich. It still belongs to Ardtornish Estate.

Conveyances

1851   Patrick Sellar of Acharn buys the Clounlaid properties "and half of the Salmon Fishings and other Fishings belonging to the Estate of Kinlochaline" from John Sinclair of Lochaline; disp. dated 10 May 1841; price £7,500 ("Disposition", *AP*; *Inventory 1872*, 14; *RSA* 1841: 45).

1860   Octavius Henry Smith of Achranich buys the same, together with Ardtornish and Acharn, from the trustees of Patrick Sellar, 5–8 May 1860 (see Section I, *Conveyances*, above).

C. THE ACHRANICH GROUP

DESCRIPTION. Composed of Achranich, Claggan, Dubh Dhoire and Uileann, in which were included the old properties of Achnatavishrusk-line, Clais Bhreac, Srath Shuardail and Torr a'Chall, and the old settlements of Ath Buidhe and Samhnach; 8,803 acres (OS). See Map 10.

ACHRANICH (Achagranach, 1390[x]; Achranich with le Straithe, 1496[x]; Auchrannycht, 1557[x]; Archanych, 1541[x]; Auchransh, 1681[w]; Achranich, 1755[r]).

BOUNDARIES: see Map 10[m].

AREAS: 1815: 3,040 acres, inc. 165 acres arable[m]. OS: 3,027 acres.

SETTLEMENTS:

Achnatavishruskline (Achagtaeegeneruflang, 1390[x]; Achtowickruflick, 1496[x]; Auchlychtmatruflan, 1534[x]; Aquittiywitrufling, 1557[x]; Auch-tonnoch and Kousland, 1681[w]; Auchnatravishrasline, 1781[y]; Achtay-wickrusline, 1806[y]; Achnatavishruskline, 1833[y]; etc. 'f' read as 'f' in 14th-, 15th- and 16th-cent. versions):748512; outline of at least 1 building,

139

and other markings; occupied by 1755[r], probably abandoned by 1801[l]. (Position identified with name on copy of 1815 plan annotated by Sellar[m-in-q]; a part of the Achranich titles, though on land that was part of Clounlaid at least since the early 18th cent.; made over to the owner of Clounlaid in 1850 (see below, p. 142).)

Achranich: 704474; no early remains, but 9 houses in 1815[m]; occupied by 1755[r], and continuously since then. Old farm-house (? *c.* 1815) replaced in 1880[q]; barn, 1851[q]; coach house, 1871–2[q].

Samhnach: 693460; outline of 1 house beside road N of lime kiln, remains of 2 houses and a (?) grain kiln on the plateau above it[o,z]; all 3 houses occupied 1815[m], upper pair abandoned by 1841[c], lower house possibly abandoned in 1855[q], though still roofed in 1872[o]. Remains of another house at 700467, period of occupation uncertain. (See also *Samhnach*, Ardtornish.)

Srath Shuardail: 732458; remains of 2 buildings[m,o,z]; occupied by 1815[m], 1 house in 1841, 1851[c], abandoned *c.* 1857[q].

SHIELING: 723449, 675 ft a.s.l. ("Gortanderg")[m]. No remains found.

POPULATION: (Achranich alone): 1841, 6/32; (Achranich and Dubh Dhoire): 1851, 6/36; 1861, 4/48; 1871, 6/40; 1881, 7/37; 1891, 6/41[c].

CLAGGAN (Le Clasche, 1496[x], and Straclasch, 1681[w], may refer to Claggan; Claggan, 1801[l]).

BOUNDARIES: see Map 10[m].

AREAS: 1815: 1,455 acres, inc. 87 acres arable[m]. OS: 1,490 acres.

SETTLEMENTS:

Ath Buidhe: 718504; remains of 1 house[o,z]; no house in 1815[m], occupied 1841, 1851, abandoned by 1861[c].

Claggan: 700496; outlines of 2 houses SE of lip of sandpit[z] (out of 6 in 1815[m]); 2 further houses at *c.* 698489 in 1815[m], no trace now visible; main site occupied by 1755[r] and continuously since then; present school built to NW in 1877, and Claggan Cottage *c.* 1903[v].

Torr a'Chall (Torkail, 1781[y]; Rightorachaul, 1815[m]): 729487; remains of 1 house, and outlines of other buildings on a knoll to the S[z]; period of occupation uncertain, but after 1755[r], and probably abandoned by 1815[m].

SHIELINGS: (1) 704494, 275 ft a.s.l.[m] No remains. (2) 728494, 250 ft a.s.l. No remains.

POPULATION: 1841, 4/18; 1851, 3/14; 1861, 1/6; 1871, 1/9; 1881, 1/3; 1891, 1/3[c].

DUBH DHOIRE (Dubgaere, 1390[x]; Dowgree, 1496[x]; Dowderre, 1534[x]; Drongerie, 1681[w]; Dowgarie, 1781[y]; Dougouarie, 1801[l]; Douzen,

1806[y]; Dubhdhaoire, 1815[m]; Dowder, Dugharry, 1833[y]; Dubh Dhoire, 1872[o]).

BOUNDARIES: see Map 10[m].

AREAS: 1815: 1,569 acres, inc. 38 acres arable[m]. OS: 1,580 acres.

SETTLEMENTS:

Clais Bhreac (Claschebreke, 1496[x]; Clashbrack, 1681[w]; Clashbreck, 1781[y]; Claisvreck, 1815[m]): 729473; outline of 1 house (cut by road immediately W of bridge), and probably of another N of road[z]; period of occupation uncertain, not marked in 1755[r] or 1801[l]; 1815 plan shows 3 houses but suggests recent abandonment[m].

Dubh Dhoire: 702487; remains of 1 house[z] (in position shown in 1815[m]), *See p. vii* occupied by 1801[l], probably abandoned 1852[q]; outline of another house at 713482[z]. 1815 plan marks 2 further houses in field between Craigendarroch and Rose cottage (both probably built 1871–2[m,q]).

POPULATION: 1841, 4/20[c]; population afterwards inc. with *Achranich*, q.v.

UILEANN (Ulline, 1635[x]; Ullin, 1781[y]; Ulin, 1801[l]; Uileann, 1872[o]).

BOUNDARIES: see Map 10[m]. The area on the Kingairloch side of the parish boundary marked A was exchanged with Forbes of Kingairloch, perhaps *c.* 1850, for the area on the Morvern side of the boundary marked B' and B''[q].

AREAS: 1815: 2,355 acres, inc. 40 acres arable[m]. OS: 2,706 acres.

SETTLEMENT: 748506, spreading W to 744506; outlines of 3 buildings[z] (10 houses in 1815[m]); occupied by 1801[l] continuously until 1958, and intermittently since then; present combined cottage and byre built 1857–8[q].

SHIELINGS: (1) 786498, 900 ft a.s.l. ("Lubluaruch")[m]. No remains. (2) 754507, 350 ft a.s.l.[m]. No remains. (3) 750487, 600 ft a.s.l.[m]. No remains.

POPULATION: 1841, 3/13; 1851, 1/6; 1861, 1/5; 1871, 1/9; 1881, 1/7; 1891, 1/4[c].

Summary of later ownership

At the bankrupt sale of the property of Charles MacLean of Drimnin in 1799–1800, John MacDonald of Borrodale secured the Achranich group (without any of the Kinlochaline fishings) for £5,806; Uileann was included but, because of a legal technicality, had to be redisposed to MacDonald in 1802. Angus MacDonald, John's son and heir, sold the group to a solicitor acting as trustee for Charles Campbell for £11,000 in 1838; Graham (the solicitor) and Campbell sold it to O. H. Smith in 1845 for £12,000. When Smith bought Sellar's lands in 1860 he named the whole estate 'Ardtornish', and called the house which he had begun to build on Dubh Dhoire land in 1856 (but which was not completed until 1866) 'Ardtornish Tower'.

Conveyances

1800   John MacDonald of Borrodale buys "Claggan, Ullin, Auchranish and Dugharry" from the trustees of Charles MacLean of Drimnin, decreet of sale dated 26 June 1800; price £5,806. 9s. 0¾d., which was still mostly unpaid at Whitsunday 1804, and which was by then increased to £7,115. 13s. 7d. by interest charges from Martinmas 1799 ("Abstract decreet of sale", *AP*; *Inventory 1872*, 2; *GRS* 2332.23; "State of the price of Acharanich &c.", *AP*; *Inventory 1872*, 24).

1802   Disposition of Uileann by Charles Grant to John MacDonald, on account of a disposition of the same made to Grant's father by Allan MacLean in 1775 but never enfeoffed; disp. dated 28 June 1802; price nominal ("Disposition", *AP*; *Inventory 1872*, 3).

1826   John MacDonald wills the same to his son Angus; disp. dated 28 Oct. 1826 ("Disposition", *AP*; *Inventory 1872*, 3; *RSA* 1833: 332).

1838   Humphrey Graham w.s. acquires the same as trustee for Charles Campbell of Combie from Angus MacDonald; disp. dated 10 July 1838; price, £11,000 ("Disposition", *AP*; *Inventory 1872*, 3; *RSA* 1838: 1289).

1845   Octavius Henry Smith of Thames Bank buys the same from Humphrey Graham and Charles Campbell; term of sale Martinmas 1845; price £12,000 ("Minute of sale" dated 9–17 Oct. 1845, *AP*; *Inventory 1872*, 6; *RSA* 1846: 101).

1850   Achnatavishruskline, having been "for a long period possessed" by Patrick Sellar of Ardtornish, is "allowed, granted and confirmed" to him by Octavius Smith, as part of an agreement chiefly concerned with rights of way and fishing ("Agreement", *AP*; *GRS* 2515.182).

III. ACHARN ESTATE

DESCRIPTION. Composed of Achadh nan Gamhna, Acharn, Agh Choire, Arienas, Crosben, Durinemast, Larachbeg and Unibeg; 6,816 acres (OS). See Map 10.

ACHADH NAN GAMHNA (Achenagawyn, 1494[x]; Achngown, 1755[r]; Achnagaune, 1808[y]; Achnagauna, 1815[h]; Achadh nan Gamhna, 1872[o]).
BOUNDARIES: see Map 10[h].

AREAS: 1815: 544 acres[h]. OS: 614 acres.

SETTLEMENT: 689493; remains of 3 houses in 1872[o], now under forest; occupied by 1755[r], cleared 1838 (*Nap. Com. ev.* III. 2288).

POPULATION: 1841, 0[c]. Achadh nan Gamhna, [Agh Choire] and Unibeg operated as a club farm with 6 tenant families for some years before 1838 (*MacKichan's memoirs*).

ACHARN (Auchacharn, 1674[n]; Achcharne, 1755[r]; Achahurn, 1801[l]; Achacharn, 1808[y]; Acharn, 1815[h]).

BOUNDARIES: see Map 10[h].

AREAS: 1815: 985 acres[h]. OS: 954 acres.

SETTLEMENT: 700504, 698507; no early remains at first site, but outlines of 2 large houses at second[z]; occupied by 1755[r], and continuously until the present day; present house built 1892[q].

POPULATION: 1841, 1/8; 1851, 1/3; 1861, 1/7; 1871, 1/5; 1881, 1/6; 1891, 1/5[c].

AGH CHOIRE (Ycory, 1509[x]; Yaore, 1534[x]; Aquorie, 1806[y]; Aighcorrie, 1815[h]; Agh Choire, 1872[o]).

BOUNDARIES: see Map 10[h].

AREAS: 1815: 794 acres[h]. OS: 742 acres.

SETTLEMENT: no site known; none shown in 1755[r], no remains marked in 1872[o], practically the whole area now under forest.

POPULATION: 1841, 0[c].

ARIENAS (Areangus, 1494[x]; Arienas, 1755[r]; Arighinnis, 1815[h]; also locally known as *Crosag*).

BOUNDARIES: see Map 10[h].

AREAS: 1815: 912 acres[h]. OS: 889 acres.

SETTLEMENT: 687514; remains of 7 houses[o,s,z]; occupied by 1755[r], cleared 1838 (*Nap. Com. ev.* III, 2288), 1 house occupied 1841[c], abandoned by 1851[c].

POPULATION: 1841, 1/8; 1851, 0[c].

CROSBEN (Corosmedill, 1494[x]; Corryospich, 1755[r]; Coresmiddle, commonly called Corrosphune and Muckerack (see p. 147 below), 1806[y]; Corrospeine, 1808[y]; Corospine, 1815[y]; Crosben, 1872[o]).

BOUNDARIES: see Map 10[h,a,b]. The 1815 plan shows an area SE of Beinn Iadain as "claimed by Rahoy"; a compromise solution along the lines suggested by Argyll's plan of 1770 appears to have been reached[a,h]. The modern boundary from Meall a'Chaise to the Black Water runs further E than it did in the early 19th cent.

AREAS: 1815: 2,285 acres[h]. OS: 2,086 acres.

SETTLEMENTS:

(1) 719543; outlines of 8–9 houses, enclosures, grain-kiln, etc.[z]; occupied by 1755[r], probably cleared 1838.

(2) 719538; remains of house, probably built *c.* 1838, occupied by 1841[c], abandoned *c.* 1882.

(3) 720543; house built *c.* 1881–2[q], occupied until 1950, then abandoned.

POPULATION: 1841, 1/7; 1851, 1/12; 1861, 1/7; 1871, 1/10; 1881, 1/9; 1891, 1/11[c].

DURINEMAST (Dienemart, 1509[x]; Dernamart, 1534[x]; [Loch] Derrynamart, 1755[r]; Doirenamart, 1815[h]; Durinemast, 1872[o]).

BOUNDARIES: see Map 10[h].

AREAS: 1815: 587 acres[h]. OS: 602 acres.

SETTLEMENTS: 667523; remains of 5 houses[o,s,z]; no occupation marked in maps of 1755[r], 1801[l] or 1824[t], but two of the remains appear to be of early (pre-19th-cent.) houses; present cottage built 1861–2[q] at 670522, occupied until *c.* 1930, and intermittently since then[v].

POPULATION: 1841, 1/7; 1851, 1/8; 1861, 1/8; 1871, 1/9; 1881, 1/10; 1891, 1/8[c].

LARACHBEG (Larichbeg, 1815[h]; Larachbeg, 1872[o]).

BOUNDARIES: see Map 10[h]. Northern boundary uncertain.

AREAS: 1815: 19 acres[h]. OS appears to confirm this.

SETTLEMENT: 695484; 5 separate houses[o] replaced by terrace of 6 houses in 1875[q]; period of early occupation uncertain, not marked in maps of 1755[r], 1801[l] or 1824[t]; 4 crofters in 1851[c]; still occupied.

POPULATION: 1841, 5/22; 1851, 5/16, 1861, 4/17; 1871, uncertain; 1881, 6/31; 1891, 6/42[c].

UNIBEG (Hennyngbeg, 1494[x]; Unybeg, 1755[r]; Unnibeg, 1801[l]; Inibeg, 1806[y]; Unibeg, 1824[t]; Aonach Beag, 1872[o]).

BOUNDARIES: see Map 10[h]. Later extended W to Allt an Aoinidh Mhor (see p. 155 below).

AREAS: 1815: 828 acres[h]. OS: 909 acres.

SETTLEMENTS: (1) 665508; remains of 11 houses[s,o], now covered with forest; occupied by 1755[r], cleared 1838 (*Nap. Com. ev.* III, 2288).

(2) 679506; remains of 3 houses[s,o], now covered with forest; period of occupation uncertain, but presumably also cleared in 1838.

POPULATION: 1841, 0[c].

Summary of ownership

Cameron of Glendessary acquired Acharn from Argyll in 1703; Achadh
nan Gamhna, Arienas, Crosben and Unibeg from MacLean of Lochbuy in
1708; and Agh Choire (with Larachbeg) and Durinemast from MacLean
of Kingairloch in 1739. The whole of Glendessary's Morvern estate—
i.e. the Kinlochaline, Acharn and Knock groups of properties—was put
up for sale in bankruptcy in 1775–6, when it was bought for £8,720 by
Hugh MacLean w.s., acting on behalf of others. The Acharn group, with
half the fishings of Kinlochaline, was passed on by Hugh MacLean to
MacLean of Inverscaddle for £4,589. In 1808 Angus and John Gregorson
of Ardtornish bought Acharn Estate from Inverscaddle for £14,500,
and sold it in 1825 for £15,650 to William Fraser, a London solicitor
acting on behalf of his father Alexander Fraser; Fraser then sold it to
Sellar in 1838 for £11,250. In 1860 Acharn, together with the rest of
Sellar's Morvern properties, was sold by his trustees to Smith of Achranich,
and became part of Smith's Ardtornish Estate. Most of it still belongs to
Ardtornish, but parts of Achadh nan Gamhna, Agh Choire and Unibeg
were sold to the Forestry Commission when Ardtornish changed hands
in 1930.

Conveyances

1703   Allan Cameron buys Acharn from the Duke of Argyll; disp.
dated 21 Aug. 1703 ("Disposition", *AP*; *Inventory 1872*, 8).

1708   Allan Cameron acquires Achadh nan Gamhna, Arienas, Crosben
and Unibeg from Murdoch MacLean; disp. dated 29 June 1708
("Disposition", *AP*; *Inventory 1872*, 9).

1739   Allan Cameron buys Agh Choire and Durinemast from Lachlan
MacLean; disp. dated 11 Oct. 1739 ("Disposition", *AP*; *Inventory
1872*, 8).

1776   Hugh MacLean w.s. buys the Acharn, Kinlochaline and Knock
groups from the trustees of Cameron of Glendessary; disp.
dated 3 July 1776; price £8,720 ("Disposition", *AP*; *Inventory
1872*, 10).

1776   John MacLean buys the Acharn group of properties, together with
half the fishings of the estate of Kinlochaline, from Hugh
MacLean; disp. dated 4 July 1776; price £4,589 ("Disposition",
AP; *Inventory 1872*, 10).

1808   Angus and John Gregorson buy the same from John MacLean;
disp. dated 27 Feb. 1808; price £14,500 ("Disposition", *AP*;
Inventory 1872, 10; *RSA* 1808: 1883); this disposition did not
include the superiority of the property which John Gregorson
acquired in later years (see *Inventory 1872*, 11; *RSA* 1820: 3209,
etc.).

1825   William Fraser, solicitor of Lincoln's Inn, buys the same from John Gregorson; disp. dated 22 July 1825; price £15,650 ("Disposition", *AP*; *Inventory 1872*, 12; *RSA* 1826: 847).

1826   Alexander Fraser of Tavistock Square, London, acquires the same from William Fraser, his son; disp. dated 13 May 1826 ("Disposition', *AP*; *Inventory 1872*, 12; *RSA* 1826: 932).

1838   Patrick Sellar of Westfield buys the same from Alexander Fraser; disp. dated 11 May 1838; price £11,250 (original document missing from *AP*; date and other details from *Inventory 1872*, 12; price from "Notes on the lands and estate of Ardtornish...1938", 4, in *AP*, which was taken from the original document; *RSA* 1838: 1234).

1860   Octavius Henry Smith of Achranich buys the same, together with Ardtornish and Clounlaid, from the trustees of Patrick Sellar, 5–8 May 1860 (see Section I, *Conveyances*, above).

IV. LOCHALINE ESTATE

Summary of Sinclair's purchases

John Sinclair bought the Knock group of properties (A, below) in 1813; he added the Fiunary group in 1821 (B, below), and called the result 'Lochaline Estate'. In 1836 he added to it the Kinlochaline and Clounlaid groups of properties together with half the fishings of Kinlochaline Estate, but in 1841 he resold the Clounlaid group and the fishings to Sellar of Acharn (Section II, A and B, above). Eventually, therefore, Lochaline Estate consisted of the Knock, Fiunary and Kinlochaline groups of properties, without any of the Kinlochaline fishings; it was this estate which was sold to Mrs Paterson in 1864, and by her trustees to T. V. Smith to become part of Ardtornish Estate in 1888.

A. THE KNOCK GROUP

DESCRIPTION. Composed of Achabeg (with Ardness), Achnaha, Keil and Knock (with Lochaline village); 4,154 acres (OS). See Map 10.

ACHABEG (Achenbeg, 1494[x]; Achbeg, 1755[r]; Achabeg, 1788[k]).

BOUNDARIES: see Map 10[b,k]. The 1815 plan shows a boundary stopping short of the Agh Choire march.

AREA: 1,242 acres (OS).

SETTLEMENTS: *Achabeg:* 654454; outlines of 6 houses[z]; occupied by 1755[r] (when there were other houses at 656456[r]), 10 houses mid-19th cent.[c], cleared 1865; the 2 cottages called Achabeg at 648454 (actually in Achnaha) and 652454 probably both built by 1880 and occupied since then.

146

Ardness (Yecomys (?), 1494[x]; Arness, 1806[y]; Yrness, 1808[y]; Ardness, 1872[o]): 661450; remains of 1 house; Low Ardness or 'Port House', 664445, built on the site of a ruin in 1872–81[o,c]; period of occupation uncertain, but one house occupied in 1815[k], 4 in 1851[c], reduced to 2 by 1881[c]; abandoned by 1925[v].

SHIELINGS: 662469, 667477 ("Poulivaan"), 671478 ("Pouligou") and 677472, 750–900 ft a.s.l.[k,z]. These are probably the main sites of a common shieling area shared by Achabeg, Keil, Knock and (probably) Achafors between Lochan na Cille and Lag Mor on the S slopes of Beinn Bhan; three tracks (now partly under forestry plantation) led up to it from the site of Achabeg settlement, from Keil just E of the Keil/Achabeg march and from Knock settlement[o]. (The area may have been called 'Muckerack'. A deed of 1708 (disp., Murdoch MacLean to Allan Cameron, date 29 June 1708; *Inventory 1872*, 9) refers to "Arnes and Achabegg with the shealling of Muckerack"; Cnoc Carach is immediately to the W of the area, and the name could be *Magh Carach*. By a scribal error the name 'Muckerack' became attached in later deeds to Crosben.)

POPULATION: 1841, 11/67; 1851, 14/75; 1861, 12/63; 1871, 1/6; 1881, 2/9; 1891, 4/28[c].

ACHNAHA (Achagnaha, 1390[x]; Achnaha, 1496[x]; Auchnohay, 1557[x]; Auchnahag, 1681[w]; Achnacha, 1755[r]; Aucholia called Auchanorlia, 1806[y]; Achantra, 1872[o]).

BOUNDARIES: see Map 10[k,b].

AREA: OS: 1,280 acres.

SETTLEMENTS:

Achnaha: 644456; outline of 1 house and other markings[p,z]; probably a subsidiary group of houses at about 649457[r], no remains found; the farm house was a ruin in 1872[o], and was rebuilt *c.* 1889 as a double cottage (since reconverted into a single house); steading probably built by Sinclair, mid-19th cent., still in use; occupied by 1755[r], and continuously until 1960 except for the period *c.* 1865–89[v]; now occupied intermittently. 12–13 houses in 1788 and 1815[k].

Dounanlui: 648483; 2 houses on 1788 plan, but marked as a shieling in 1815[k]; now under forest.

SHIELINGS: (1) 653490, 750 ft a.s.l.; named "Arishelanach" in 1815[k]; traces of at least 4 circular structures[z].

(2) 'Dounanlui', 400 ft a.s.l. (see *Settlements*, above), used as a shieling in 1815[k].

POPULATION: 1841, 5/22; 1851, 2/13; 1861, 2/16; 1871, 0; 1881, 1/5; 1891, 2/10[c].

KEIL (Killcollumbkill, 1674[n]; Kill, 1755[r]; Keel, 1770[a]; Keil, 1788[k]; Kiel, 1808[y]).

BOUNDARIES: see Map 10[a,k,b].

AREAS: 1770: 384 acres (arable, 137; pasture, 242; churchyard, 5)[a]. OS: 550 acres.

SETTLEMENT: 667454; remains of 3 houses[o], and outlines of others[p], now covered by forest; other sites are Sinclair's mid-19th-cent. farm buildings (670453); and Cuibheag (669448), built on the site of a ruin *c.* 1872[o,c]. Culchille (a name which appears in old titles, and as an occupied house in 1881[c]) appears to have been associated with Keil, but the most likely site is Ardness Port House in Achabeg. Occupied by 1755[r], and continuously since then; main clearance 1841–51[c].

SHIELINGS: see Achabeg, *Shielings*.

POPULATION: 1779, –/51[1]; 1841, 10/70;[1]851, 3/22;[1]861, 2/15; 1871, 2/15; 1881, 2/8; 1891, 2/14[c].

KNOCK (Knock, 1755[r]; Tighacnoic, 1872[o]).

BOUNDARIES: see Map 10[k,b].

AREA: 1,082 acres (OS).

SETTLEMENTS:

Cul a'Chaolais (Kowilkelis, 1494[x]; Coulcheillis, Coulkyles, Guilechelish, 1806[y]; Chulie Kyles, 1848[f]): location uncertain, but perhaps 681457, where there were remains of buildings and a dyke running down to low-water mark[o,p]; in any case the area lay between Knock and the Allt Achadh Forsa[f,q]. No record of occupation.

Knock: 675454, extending SW; markings of many early works[p]; occupied by 1755[r], and continuously since then, except for a few years before 1912, when the present house replaced the old farm house[v]; cleared 1865.

Lochaline village: 678447, and vicinity; founded *c.* 1830 (see p. 32 above); population: 1841, 37/191; 1851, 42/309; 1861, 31/231; 1871, 29/220; 1881, 44/182; 1891, 50/147[c].

POPULATION (Knock): 1841, 25/109; 1851, 23/130; 1861, 22/104; 1871, 4/15; 1881, 2/8; 1891, 4/21[c].

SHIELINGS: see Achabeg, *Shielings*.

Summary of ownership

In 1776 the Morvern estates of Cameron of Glendessary were put up for sale in bankruptcy (see Section II, introductory summary, above). The Knock group—which did not then include Keil, Argyll's property—went to Campbell of Ardslignish for £2,019. Campbell in turn went bankrupt, and the three farms of Knock, Achnaha and Achabeg were sold to the Duke of Argyll, the owner of Keil, in 1786 for £2,800. Knock was set to Dugald MacTavish and his sons in 1793 for a rent of £62 (*Book of Mull and Morvern tacks*, vol. '2', 254; *ibid.*, vol. '3', which probably gives the rents for Achnaha and Achabeg, is temporarily missing from *ICP*). In 1806 Argyll sold the whole group for £9,500 to MacDonald of Glenaladale, and MacDonald sold it to John Sinclair in 1813 for £10,000.

The whole of Sinclair's Lochaline Estate (the Knock, Fiunary and Kinlochaline groups of properties) was sold to Mrs Paterson in 1864 for £43,500; and was bought in 1888 from her trustees by T. V. Smith of Ardtornish for £28,000. When Mrs Hugh Smith bought Ardtornish Estate from Smith's heirs in 1930, nearly the whole of what had been Lochaline Estate was sold to the Forestry Commission, and, although the coastal strip from Lochaline village to the Savary River was repurchased for Ardtornish in 1955, the greater part of Sinclair's Lochaline Estate is now a part of Fiunary Forest.

Conveyances

1776 John Campbell of Ardslignish buys Knock, Achnaha and Achabeg from Hugh MacLean w.s., who had purchased them on his behalf from the trustees of Allan Cameron of Glendessary; disp. dated 4 July 1776; price £2,019. 7s. 5d. ("Disposition", *AP*; *Inventory 1872*, [2]1).

1786 The Duke of Argyll buys the same from the trustees of Campbell of Ardslignish; disp. dated 15 July 1790, but referring to the sale of 20 Dec. 1786; price £2,800 ("Disposition", *AP*; *Inventory 1872*, [2]1).

1806 Alexander MacDonald of Glenaladale buys the same, together with Keil, from Argyll; disp. dated 1 Aug. 1808, but referring to the sale of 19 and 22 Dec. 1806; price £9,500 ("Disposition", *AP*; *Inventory 1872*, [2]2; *RSA* 1808: 1882).

1813 John Sinclair, merchant, of Tobermory, buys the same from Alexander MacDonald; feu charter dated 8 July 1813; price £10,000 ("Feu Charter", *AP*; *Inventory 1872*, [2]2; *RSA* 1814: 2375).

1864 Magdalene Hardie, relict of Campbell Paterson, buys the same, together with the Fiunary and Kinlochaline groups of properties, from the trustees of John Sinclair; disp. dated 7 May 1864; price £43,500 ("Disposition" now missing from *AP*; details from *Inventory 1872*, [2]5; price from "Notes on the lands and estate of Ardtornish...1938", 7, in *AP*, which was taken from the original document; *RSA* 1864: 1224).

Appendix B

1888 Thomas Valentine Smith of Ardtornish buys the same from the trustees of Mrs Paterson; term of entry 3 Jan. 1888; price £28,000 ("Minute of sale", *AP*; *RSA* 1888: 1340).

(For the subsequent history of the Lochaline properties, see Section I above.)

B. THE FIUNARY GROUP

DESCRIPTION. Composed of Fiunary (with the Glebe) and Savary (with Savary Mill); 3,502 + 58 acres (OS). See Map 10.

FIUNARY (Fynhorra, Fynthora, 1545[x]; Finnarie, 1674[n]; Funiry, 1755[r]; Fewnary, 1770[a]; Funary, 1789[j]; Finnarie, 1872[o]; Fiunary[os] 1 [in.]).

BOUNDARIES: see Map 10[a].

AREAS: Fiunary without the Glebe: 1770: 1,122 acres (275 arable, 847 pasture)[a]. OS: 1,434 acres. Glebe: 1770 and OS: 58 acres, mostly pasture.

SETTLEMENTS: (1) 617468; Manse (built 1779, rebuilt *c.* 1860) and steading on site of main settlement; outline of at least one early house at 617469[z]; 19th-cent. cottages at 618469, 618465; occupied by 1755[r] and continuously to present day.

(2) 622467; Lochaline House and steading; built 1821–5, demolished 1910 (house) and 1914 (steading)[q].

SHIELING: 628501, 925 ft a.s.l.; outlines of 17 structures (10 ft circles and 11 ft × 7 ft rectangles); remains of one larger house (17 ft × 11 ft); track leads up from behind Lochaline House and traceable most of the way through plantations; some of the structures are on the Salachan side of the march burn.

POPULATION: 1779, –/28[1]; 1841, 9/55; 1851, 6/49; 1861, 6/53; 1871, 5/31; 1881, 4/25; 1891, 5/27.

SAVARY (Savarie, 1674[n]; Savory, 1755[r]; Savarick, 1789[j]; Savary, 1801[1]).

BOUNDARIES: see Map 10[a,k].

AREAS: 1770: 1,887 acres (339 arable, 1,548 pasture)[a]. OS: 2,068 acres.

SETTLEMENTS: (1) 639463; remains of 5 houses[o,p], now covered by forest; occupied by 1755[r], probably abandoned by 1861[c].

(2) 640459; remains of mill and 2 other buildings[z]; 6 houses inc. mill in 1872[o]; occupied by 1755[r], abandoned by 1890[v].

(3) 635461; steading inc. 2 dwellings, built 1871–81, still occupied.

SHIELING: 642510; 1,225 ft a.s.l.; outlines of 7 structures, similar to those at Fiunary shieling[z]; track leads up from between settlements

(1) and (2), the first part now rebuilt as a forestry road, traceable nearly all the way.

POPULATION: 1779, –/83[1]; 1841, 13/59; 1851, 5/36; 1861, 3/18; 1871, 1/3; 1881, 3/22; 1891, 3/16[c].

Summary of ownership

Argyll property throughout the eighteenth century. Fiunary was leased to Jean Cameron before 1750, then for four years to small tenants, and from 1754 to the minister to add to his Glebe; Savary was set to small tenants continuously from before the Rebellion, the Mill being the subject of a separate tack. In 1819 both farms were put up for sale together with the Killundine group. In 1821 John Sinclair bought the Fiunary group for £7,500 a price which included the feudal superiority of Killundine Estate; the Killundine properties were sold simultaneously to another buyer (see Section V).

(For the later history of the estate, see the Knock group, A above, *Summary of ownership* and *Conveyances.*)

Conveyances

1753   Fiunary leased to Alexander MacTavish, Minister of Morvern, during his incumbency, rent £15. 15s. 0d. ("Sett and rental of Mull and Morvern 1754", *ICP*); this tack was not recorded in the *Tack Books*, but was transferred to Norman MacLeod when he succeeded MacTavish in 1775.

1754   Savary set to small tenants, rent £21. 5s. 0d. ("Sett and rental of Mull and Morvern 1754"); Mill leased for £6 (*ibid.*). Reset to 6 small tenants, rent £49, 1774; Mill £9, 1774 (*Book of Mull and Morvern tacks*, vol. '0', 24–5, *ICP*).

1821   Donald Campbell, residing at Killundine, and John Sinclair, merchant in Tobermory, purchase the whole of the Fiunary and Killundine groups of properties from the trustees of the Duke of Argyll for £15,000; Campbell to have possession of the Killundine group, and Sinclair to have possession of the Fiunary group and superiority of the whole, paying £7,500 each; disp. dated 4, 12 May, 2 June 1821 ("Disposition", *AP*; *Inventory 1872*, [2]2–3; *RSA* 1821: 106).

V. KILLUNDINE ESTATE

DESCRIPTION. Composed of Killundine, Lagan and Salachan; 4,422 acres (OS). See Map 10[a,b].

KILLUNDINE (Kilintein, 1674[n]; Dungaul, 1755[r]; Killundin, 1770[a]; Dounagal, 1789[j]; Killundine, 1801[l]).

Appendix B

AREAS: 1770: 1,487 acres (281 arable, 1,181 pasture, 25 wood)[a]. OS: 1,741 acres.

SETTLEMENTS:

Gleann nan Iomairean (Glen Immeren): 603503: outlines and remains of at least 10 houses, arable enclosure[z]; occupied by 1770[a], probably abandoned by 1819[b]; a (?) later house at 601503.

Killundine: 586494: on the site of Killundine House (built 1871–2[o], demolished 1950s); no early remains; occupied by 1755[r], and (steading) continuously to present day.

SHIELING: 600505, 475 ft a.s.l., and towards Gleann nan Iomairean settlement; traces of circular structures, including a massive one 14 ft in diameter[z].

POPULATION: 1799, –/43[l]; 1841, 5/40; 1851, 6/35; 1861, 4/25; 1871, uncertain; 1881, 6/26; 1891, 7/44[c].

LAGAN (Laggan, 1674[n]; Lagan, 1770[a]).

AREAS: 1770: 1,148 acres (250 arable, 898 pasture)[a]. OS: 896 acres.

SETTLEMENT: 595481; outlines of 6–8 houses[z]; occupied by 1755[r], 1 house occupied mid-19th cent., probably abandoned by 1871[c].

POPULATION: 1779, –/36[l]; 1841, 1/12; 1851, 1/8; 1861, 1/9; 1871, uncertain; 1881, 0[c].

SALACHAN (Sallachan, 1674[n]; Sallochan, 1770[a]; Salachan, 1872[o]).

AREAS: 1770: 1,914 acres (168 arable, 1746, pasture)[a]. OS: 1,785 acres.

SETTLEMENT: 613474; ruins of *c.* 7 houses[o,z] and of 2 more further W at 608475[o], all now under forest; both sites occupied by 1755[r], W site abandoned by 1841, E site occupied until *c.* 1900[o,c].

SHIELING probably shared with Fiunary, q.v.

POPULATION: 1779, –/37[l]; 1841, 1/7; 1851, 2/7; 1861, 1/4; 1871, uncertain; 1881, 1/6; 1891, 1/11[c].

Summary of ownership

Argyll property throughout the eighteenth century; all three farms were let separately—generally to small tenants—until 1754. In that year Salachan and Lagan were leased together to John Campbell at a rent of £42. 10s. 0d., and Killundine to Alexander Campbell for £19 ("Sett and rental of Mull and Morvern 1754", *ICP*). The former pair went to Donald MacLachlan in 1773 for £93, while Alexander Campbell's rent was increased to £38 from the same date (*Book of Mull and Morvern tacks*, vol. '0', 28–9, *ICP*). In 1792 the arrangement of the leases was changed: Hugh Campbell had Killundine with Lagan for £93. 8s. 1d. (raised in

1802 to £160), while Salachan was let separately to Donald MacLachlan for £42 (*ibid.*, 117, 181, 251).

Put up for sale with the Fiunary group in 1819, Killundine Estate was sold in 1821 for £7,500 to Donald Campbell, the tacksman then residing at Killundine; Campbell immediately passed the property on to Dr John MacLean of Ardow ("Disposition" of Fiunary, *AP*; *Inventory 1872*, [2]2-3; *RSA* 1821: 55). Lieutenant-Colonel Charles Cheape, residing at St Andrews, bought the property from MacLean's widow in 1859 (*RSA* 1859: 1316); and the Cheapes retained it until 1895, when it went to their relations the Morrises. Bought by the state just before the Second World War, the Salachan end was eventually planted with trees by the Forestry Commission, while the Killundine end was farmed by the Department of Agriculture; the Department's farm has now been sold back into private ownership.

VI. GLENMORVERN ESTATE

DESCRIPTION. 'Glenmorvern' was the name adopted for a new estate made up of 5 of Argyll's farms sold as a single lot in 1824; they were Ardantiobairt (previously attached to Rahoy), Barr, Fernish (Achnasaul), Mungasdail (with Druim Cracaig) and Unimore; 9,510 acres (OS). See Map 10[a,b].

ARDANTIOBAIRT (Ardintibert, 1674[n]; Ardnatipirt, 1801[1]; Ardantiobairt, 1872[o]).

AREAS: 1770: 292 acres (52 arable, 236 pasture, 4 wood)[a]. OS: 288 acres.

SETTLEMENT: 644550; remains of 3 houses[o,s] now under forest; occupied by 1755[r], probably abandoned by 1851[c] and cottage built at 649544 (called Ardantiobairt although outside the old boundaries); later cottage occupied until *c.* 1950, now rebuilt for intermittent occupation.

POPULATION: 1841, 3/7; 1851, 2/11; 1861, 2/8; 1871, 3/21; 1881, uncertain; 1891, 1/7[c]. Figures for 1851, 1861 and 1871 include houses at the head of Loch Teacuis.

BARR (Barre, 1534[x]; Barr, 1674[n]).

AREAS: 1770: 3,767 acres (274 arable, 3,310 pasture, 183 wood)[a]. OS: 4,224 acres.

SETTLEMENTS:
   Baile Geamhraidh: 622558; remains of 8 houses[o,s] now under forest; occupied by 1770[a], abandoned by 1872[o].
   Barr: 617560; remains of 4 houses[o,s] now under forest; occupied by 1755[r], Barr house occupied until *c.* 1930[v].

Eilean nan Eildean (or *Friel Island*): 610583; remains of 1 house[z], occupied by a fisherman 1871–81[c].

Gleannaguda: (1) 612578; outlines of two houses and an enclosure[z]; dates of occupation unknown, but before 1841[c].

(2) 610579; remains of house and byre, and of another house at 609579[z]; 1 house occupied in 1841 and in 1871–81[c], but period of occupation otherwise uncertain.

Torraneidhinn: 623565; extending to 624564 (*Cnocandubh*); remains of 9 houses including a mid-19th-cent. cottage[o,s,z]; occupied by 1872[o], not finally abandoned until *c.* 1950.

SHIELING: 601549, 750 ft a.s.l. (*Coire Buidhe*); remains of turf dykes.

POPULATION: 1779, –/72[1]; 1841, 8/48; 1851, 5/35; 1861, 7/29; 1871, 7/34; 1881, 8/39; 1891, 5/26[c].

FERNISH (Fereneish, 1674[n]; Ferinish, 1755[r]; Feornish, 1770[a]; Fairnish, 1789[j]; Fernish, 1801[l]).

AREAS: 1770: 2,171 acres (409 arable, 1,762 pasture)[a]. OS: 2,336 acres.

SETTLEMENTS:

Carnacailliche: 583506; remains of 7 houses[o,z]; occupied by 1841[c], abandoned shortly after 1945[v].

Fernish (later called *Achnasaul*): 572516; 7 houses and a ruin in 1872[o], now only late-19th-cent. farm buildings; remains of 3 houses at 573513[o,z]; occupied by 1755[r] (main site) and continuously since then.

Glenmorvern: 567515; proprietor's house built by 1841[c].

Rhemore: 573505; 7 small buildings in 1872[o], some of which are incorporated in the present farm buildings; probably occupied by 1824[t], and continuously since then.

SHIELINGS: 601521, 1,000 ft a.s.l., and 594523, 850 ft a.s.l.; outlines of 4–6 circular structures at each site[z].

POPULATION: 1779, –/88[1]; 1841, 13/65; 1851, 12/48; 1861, 14/81; 1871, 11/59; 1881, 12/49; 1891, 9/29[c].

MUNGASDAIL (Mungastill, 1674[n]; Mungcastle, 1755[r]; Mangastel, 1789[j]; Mungustil, 1801[l]; Mungasdail, 1872[o]).

AREAS: 1770, 1,736 acres (246 arable, 1,490 pasture)[a]. OS: 1,459 acres.

SETTLEMENTS:

Bonnavoulin: 560537; no early remains; the neighbourhood of Mungasdail Mill occupied by 1755[r]; terrace of 10 one-roomed houses built *c.* 1840, and altered to present form after 1883.

Druim Cracaig (Drumchragaig, 1674[n]; Druim na Cracaig, 1872[o]): probably 567523, near the late-18th-cent. Fernish church, although this was inside the Fernish march of 1819; Roy placed a settlement here in 1755, calling it "Killindine" in the finished version of his map (it was unnamed in the draft)[r]; the same settlement named "Drimchragaig" in 1801[1]; leased in the 18th cent. as part of Mungasdail, before 1750 with a change-house which was then transferred to Fernish Ferry (probably Rhemore)[u]; occupied by 1755[r], probably until the mid-19th cent.; no houses in 1872[o].

Mungasdail: 567537[a]; on the site of the present farm, although Roy shows the settlement further to the NW, near the church of Killintag at 564538[r], and associated with the neighbourhood of Mungasdail Mill; occupied by 1755[r], and continuously to the present day; probably cleared in the 1820s. No early remains[z].

Mungasdail Mill: 559538; on the Drimnin side of the Amhainn Mhungasdail; remains of mill-house and kiln[z]; occupied by 1744[u], a ruin by 1882[Drimnin papers].

SHIELINGS: 578542 (650 ft a.s.l.), outlines of 4 circular structures, and a stock wall; 583539 (800 ft a.s.l.), outlines of at least 6 circular structures[z].

POPULATION: 1779, –/85[1].

Bonnavoulin: 1841, 12/58; 1851, 8/76; 1861, 13/64; 1871, 8/55; 1881, 9/32; 1891, 12/52 (usually including the Mill)[c].

Mungasdail: 1841, 1/12; 1851, 2/14; 1861, 1/8; 1871, 1/6; 1881, 2/10; 1891, 1/14[c].

UNIMORE (Janenmoir, 1674[n]; Unymor, 1755[r]; Innimore, 1770[a]; Unnimore, 1801[1]; Iniemore, 1819[a]; Unimore, 1824[t]; Aonachmor, 1872[o]).

AREAS: 1770: 1,607 acres (139 arable, 1,468 pasture and loch)[a]. This includes an area to the W of the Allt a'Bhioda which—according to the survey of 1815[h]—belonged to Unibeg. At the end of the nineteenth century all the land between the Unimore/Unibeg march of 1815 and the Allt an Aoinidh Mhor was added to Unibeg. OS: 1,203 acres.

SETTLEMENT: 656519; remains of 21 houses, enclosures[o,s], now mostly covered by forest; occupied by 1755[r] and until c. 1841[c], main clearance 1824.

POPULATION: 1779, –/45[1]; 1841, 2/10; 1851, 0[c].

Summary of ownership

Argyll property throughout the eighteenth century. Fernish was let to small tenants at least until 1804 (rents: 1754, £25; 1774, £61. 1s. 0d.; 1785, £67. 1s. 0d), as were Unimore throughout the period (without a written lease) and probably Barr after 1792 ("Rental of Mull and

Morvern", 1744, etc.; *Book of Mull and Morvern tacks*, vols. '0' and '4', *ICP*). Druim Cracaig and Mungasdail were let separately before 1750, but after that year they were united and leased to John Beaton and his descendants until 1824, the rents being £21. 9s. 0d. (1750, including the Mill), £23 (1754, without the Mill), £60 (1773) and £90 (1813) ("Sett of Morvern 1750", etc.; *Book of Mull and Morvern tacks*, vol. '0', 22, 66, 258, vol. '4', 109, *ICP*). Barr was let to Duncan Campbell from 1754 for £31 (raised to £80 in 1773), but the lease was not renewed in 1792 ("Sett and rental of Mull and Morvern 1754"; *Book of Mull and Morvern tacks*, vol. '0', 26, *ICP*).

Put up as a single lot by Argyll in 1819, Glenmorvern was sold to Miss Christina Stewart, then residing at Abercromby Place, Edinburgh, early in 1824 (*RSA* 1824: 461). The estate remained in the same family until Miss Mary Stewart Beattie disposed of it in 1898–9 to Mrs Marion Higgins Urmston. The Urmstons kept it until the mid-1930s, when it was sold to the Forestry Commission, the present owners, Mrs I. H. Pilkington becoming feuar proprietrix of Glenmorvern cottage and policies (36 acres).

VII. DRIMNIN ESTATE

DESCRIPTION. Composed of Achleanan, Auliston, Drimnin, Druimbuidhe, Glasdrum, Oronsay Island, Poll Luachrain, Portabhata and Sornagan; 5,606 acres (OS). See Map 10[a,d].

ACHLEANAN (Auchillenen, 1528[x]; Auchleynane, 1559[x]; Achlianan, 1755[r]; Achalean, 1801[1]; Achalianan, 1836[d]; Achleanan, 1872[o]).

AREAS: 1836: 1,331 acres[d]. OS: 1,427 acres.

SETTLEMENTS: 561544; on the site of present farm buildings, with another group of houses further NW at 557546[d] (about 13 buildings in all[d]); occupied by 1755[r], and continuously to the present day. Cleared c. 1840.

POPULATION: 1841, 5/30; 1851, 4/22; 1861, 3/16; 1871, 1/4; 1881, 1/4; 1891, 1/7[c].

AULISTON (Anlastill, 1494[x]; Hawlastill 1674[n]; Auliston, 1755[r]).

AREAS: 1770: 989 acres (194 arable, 795 pasture)[a]. 1836: 975 acres[d]. OS: 909 acres.

SETTLEMENTS:
Auliston: 549571; remains of 31 houses, (?) grain-kiln, enclosures, etc.[o,s,z], about 25 buildings in 1836[d]; occupied by 1755[r], cleared 1855.
Auliston Point: 546577; remains of 10 houses[o,s,z]; dates of early occupation unknown, not marked on plans of 1770 or 1836[a,d].

Carraig: 553578; remains of 10 houses[o,s,z] (9–10 buildings in 1836[d]); date of early occupation unknown, not marked 1770[a], cleared *c.* 1843; remains of another house at 557572[o,z].

POPULATION: 1779, –/58[1]; 1841, 21/109; 1851, 22/115; 1861, 0[c].

DRIMNIN (Druma, Drummyn, 1528[x]; Drummyne, 1534[x]; Drummy-nane, 1559[x]; Drummin, 1755[r]; Drimnin 1789[j]).

AREAS: 1836: 624 acres[d]. OS: 614 acres.

SETTLEMENTS:
Drimnin: 554551; around the site of Drimnin House (rebuilt *c.* 1850); no early remains here, but remains of two early houses at 547552[z]; occupied by 1755[r] and continuously to the present day.
Drimnin Crofts: centred on 546565; remains of 7 houses[o,z] (9 buildings in 1836[d]); occupied by 1836[d], abandoned by 1872[o].

POPULATION: 1841, 7/32; 1851, 8/26; 1861, uncertain (12/58 with Glasdrum); 1871, 5/31; 1881, 6/28; 1891, 6/30.

DRUIMBUIDHE (Drumbuy, 1755[r]; Drimbuy, 1801[1]; Drumby, 1824[t]; Druimbuidhe, 1872[o]).

AREAS: 1836: 440 acres[d]. OS: 403 acres.

SETTLEMENTS:
Doirlinn: 607586; 1 house (which was an inn 1841–72[c,o], a private house in 1881 and empty in 1891[c]), and remains of another[z]; occupied by 1801[1], intermittently occupied since 1881.
Druimbuidhe: 601581; outlines of 2 houses each at 600580 and 602582[z]; 7 buildings in 1836[d], 5 houses in 1851[c]; occupied by 1801[t] and until the mid-1950s; intermittently since then. Remains of 1 house at 593578[z].

POPULATION: 1841, 4/24; 1851, 6/33; 1861, 3/13; 1871, 4/18; 1881, 2/10; 1891, 1/7.

GLASDRUM (Glasdrum, 1836[d]; Glasdrim, 1841[c]).

AREAS: 1836: 110 acres[d]. OS: 102 acres.

SETTLEMENTS: a line of dwellings running from Glasdrum Crofts centred on 553543 SE to Drimnin Cottage (*Achnacriche*) at 559539; *c.* 14 buildings in 1836[d]; NW cottages remain; SE end also called *Bonnavoulin*[d] as is the settlement on the Mungasdail side of the march; SE end occupied by 1755[r], NW end by 1836[d]; the crofts abandoned in the 1950s.

POPULATION: 1841, 8/43; 1851, 4/19; 1861, uncertain (see Drimnin); 1871, 5/27; 1881, 6/25; 1891, 5/14[c].

Appendix B

ORONSAY ISLAND (Oronsa, 1755[r]; Orosa, 1789[j]; Oransay, 1801[l]; Ormsaig, 1835[y]; Oronsay, 1836[d]).

AREAS: 1836: 458 acres (East Oronsay 224, West Oronsay 234)[d]. OS: 429 acres.

SETTLEMENTS: remains of 19 houses, mostly in the centre and E end of the island[o,s,z]; 9 buildings in 1836[d]; occupied by 1801[l], partially cleared *c.* 1868, remaining houses abandoned 1871–81[c].

POPULATION: 1841, 9/42; 1851, 11/54; 1861, 6/31; 1871, 3/17; 1881, 0[c].

POLL LUACHRAIN (Polchoren, 1750[u]; Polcharan, 1808[y]; Pollacher, 1836[d]; Poll Luachrain, 1872[o]).

AREAS: 1770: 141 acres (all wood)[a]. 1836: 282 acres[d]. OS: 243 acres.

SETTLEMENT: 594572; remains of 2 houses[o,z], and an area of arable[d]; a shieling in the 18th cent.[u], and later woodland; period of occupation uncertain, but houses unoccupied in 1836[d]. Outline of another house nearby (though technically in Sornagan) at 593573[z].

POPULATION: 1841, 0[c].

PORTABHATA (Portavate, 1674[n]; Portavata, 1750[u]; Portvaid, 1755[r]; Port-au-Battre, 1836[d]; Portabhata, 1872[o]).

AREAS: 1770: 550 acres (154 arable, 396 pasture)[a]. 1836: 728 acres[d]. OS: 634 acres.

SETTLEMENTS:
Portabhata: 573573; remains of 11 houses[o,s,z] and (?) kiln (11 buildings in 1836[d]); occupied by 1755[r], abandoned by 1871[c].
Sruthain: 566578; remains of 4 houses[o,s,z] (2 buildings in 1836[d]); occupied by 1836[d], abandoned by 1872[o].

POPULATION: 1779, –/16[l]; 1841, 5/21; 1851, 0; 1861, 2/4; 1871, 0[c].

SORNAGAN (Sornagan, 1801[l]).

AREAS: 1836: 878 acres[d]. OS: 845 acres.

SETTLEMENT: 583578; remains of 4 houses[o,s,z] (3 buildings in 1836[d]); occupied by 1801[l], abandoned by 1851[c].

POPULATION: 1841, 2/7; 1851, 0[c].

Summary of ownership

Probably in the sixteenth century, and certainly by the middle of the seventeenth, the lands that were eventually to be united as Drimnin Estate were divided into two main parts. One part, consisting of Auliston and Portabhata, was associated with the Tennandry of Aros; together with most of the rest of Morvern, it belonged to MacLean of Duart until the 1670s, when it was taken by Argyll. The remaining Drimnin lands were associated in the sixteenth century with the Free Barony of Coll, and became the estate of MacLean of Drimnin from the mid-sixteenth to the late-eighteenth century.

Auliston and Portabhata were leased by Argyll to separate tenants before 1750; they were then united and set to MacLean of Drimnin together with "the sheilling of Pulcherine or Polcharan formerly a pendicle of...Mungastill", at rents of £18 (1750), £20 (1754) and £51. 10s. 0d. (1769) ("Sett and rental of Mull and Morvern", 1744, 1750, 1754; *Book of Mull and Morvern Tacks*, vol. '0', 1, *ICP*). This group was then let (1788) to small tenants without tacks (Cregeen, E. R. (1964), 142).

The Drimnin lands apart from the Auliston group were held by MacLean of Drimnin until 1797–8—they were not forfeited after the Rebellion despite Drimnin's prominent part in it—when they were sold in bankruptcy (*RSA* 1797: 1014, 1015). At the bankrupt sale of 1800 the Drimnin group was secured by Alexander MacDonald of Glenaladale (*RSA* 1803: 1436); and Glenaladale's trustees sold it to John MacLean of Boreray in 1817 or 1818 (*RSA* 1818: 2941). At about the same time Boreray bought Auliston, Portabhata and Poll Luachrain from Argyll (*RSA* 1817: 2768), so completing the nineteenth- and twentieth-century Drimnin Estate.

In 1835 Sir Charles Gordon bought Drimnin from the trustees of MacLean of Boreray (*RSA* 1835: 762), and the estate remained the property of the Gordon family until it was bought by Miss Alice Horsman, the present owner, in 1943.

VIII. GLENCRIPESDALE ESTATE

DESCRIPTION. Composed of Beach (detached), Beinniadain, Glencripesdale, Kinlochteacuis and Rahoy; 13,504 acres (OS). See Map 10[a,b].

BEACH (Beach, 1674[n]; Veach, 1755[r]; Beioch, 1770[a]; Beaoch, 1801[l]).

AREAS: 1770: 2,645 acres (119 arable, 2,526 pasture)[a]. OS: 3,213 acres.

SETTLEMENT: 766534; outlines of 6 houses, and a (?) kiln[s,z]; occupied *See p. vii* by 1755[r], and continuously since then.

POPULATION: 1779, –/11[l]; 1841, 3/18; 1851, 1/5; 1861, 1/10; 1871, 2/9; 1881, 1/6; 1891, 1/8[c].

BEINNIADAIN (Ben Yattan, 1755[r]; Bainaiton, 1770[a]; Ben-ea tan, 1801[l]; Beneaton, 1819[b]; Beinniadain, 1872[o]).

AREAS: 1770: 833 acres (20 arable, 813 pasture)[a]. OS: 646 acres.

SETTLEMENT: 695547; remains of 4 houses[o,s,z]; perhaps originally a shieling of Rahoy, but the substantial houses, the marks of cultivation, and the 1770 plan make it certain that it was at one time a permanent settlement in spite of its isolation and altitude (925 ft a.s.l.); occupied by 1770, abandoned by 1841[a,c].

POPULATION: 1841, 0[c].

GLENCRIPESDALE (Glencribastill, 1674[n]; Glen Cribsdale, 1755[r]; Glencripisdale, 1770[a]; Glengrebisdale, 1789[j]; Glencribisdale, 1801[l]; Glencrispisdale, 1819[b]; Glencripesdale, 1872[o]).

AREAS: 1770: 4,581 acres (70 arable, 4,255 pasture, 256 wood)[a]. OS: 4,621 acres.

SETTLEMENT: 662593; remains of 2 early buildings[s], probably those at 681593; the Newtons' concrete mansion house at 662590 (built *c.* 1878, became derelict during World War II, demolished 1963); two 19th-cent. farm-houses; occupied by 1755[r], and more or less continuously since then.

SHIELING: probably 697582, 550 ft a.s.l. ('Airigh Anndail')[p], now under forestry plantation.

POPULATION: 1779, –/22[l]; 1841, 5/29; 1851, 5/23; 1861, 2/12; 1871, 4/16; 1881, 1/6; 1891, 3/11[c].

KINLOCHTEACUIS (Kenloch, 1674[n]; Kenlochteachgus, 1755[r]; Kinlochtegus, 1770[a]; Kanlochteaus, 1801[l]; Kanlochteacus, 1819[b]; Kinlochteacuis, 1872[o]).

AREAS: 1770: 2,610 acres (195 arable, 2,415 pasture)[a]. OS: 2,899 acres.

SETTLEMENTS:

Innbhir Mor: 651556; remains of 4 houses and (?) fank to the W[o,z]; period of occupation unknown, but abandoned by 1872[o] (this is probably the "tenement...called Invine, more" mentioned by Forbes of Culloden in 1737; *Napier Commission report* (1884), 391).

Kinloch: 657550; the 19th-cent. farm-house is on the site of the settlement originally known as *Kinlochteacuis*[r,a]; early remains uncertain; occupied by 1755[r], and continuously since then; there were also houses, now gone, at *Achadhcoirbte* by the S side of the bridge at 658548[o].

Kinlochteacuis: the 19th-cent. settlement of this name was at 653544[o], on the site of the school-house of 1878–9; 3 occupied houses and 4 ruins in 1872[o] of which outlines of 2 are still visible[z]; there was a subsidiary settlement at 651543 (remains of 3 houses[o,z]), possibly called *Baile Brucaiche*[o]; the late-19th-cent. cottage now called *Kinlochteacuis* is at 656545; dates of early occupation uncertain.

POPULATION: 1779, –/26[l]; 1841, 8/35; 1851, 7/31; 1861, 4/19; 1871, 4/31; 1881, 5/41; 1891, 3/21[c]. The Kinlochteacuis houses at 653544 were probably included with the enumeration of Ardantiobairt, q.v.

RAHOY (Rahway, 1674[n]; Rahoy, 1755[r]; Raho, 1789[j]).

AREAS: 1770: 2,238 acres (6 arable, 1,758 pasture, 474 wood)[a]. OS: 2,125 acres.

SETTLEMENTS:

Archalnacrick: the name is associated with Rahoy in the rental of 1674[n]; no known remains, but the Allt Coire na Criche enters Loch Teacuis at 629567.

Caol Charna: 623580; remains of a house associated with arable, and of another at 626584[o, z]; probably occupied in 1770[a].

Camas Glas (Camusglass, 1674[n]): 647586; remains of 2 houses, occupied in 1872[o], abandoned by 1891[c], now under forest[o, z]; remains of another building at 642587[z], period of occupation unknown.

Carnliath: 645560; remains of 4 houses (2 rebuilt)[o, s, z], and of 2 further houses at 644562[o, z]; period of early occupation uncertain, but both sites occupied in 1872[o], and intermittently since.

Rahoy: 639564; no early remains; occupied by 1755[r], and continuously since then; present house mostly mid-19th cent.

SHIELING: 643569, 650–750 ft a.s.l.; circular structures and walled gulleys, etc., in the crags SE of Am Biod and on the slopes immediately below.

POPULATION: 1779, $-/55$[l]; 1841, 6/29; 1851, 5/30; 1861, 5/34; 1871, 2/12; 1881, 4/18; 1891, 2/10[c].

Summary of ownership

Argyll property throughout the eighteenth century. In 1754 Beach was let to Ewen MacFie for £19. 5s. 0d. and Glencripesdale to Dugald MacLachlan for the same amount. These two properties were set together in 1775 to Duncan Campbell of Glenure for £50 (Glencripesdale itself having previously been let with Camas Salach, which was transferred in 1754 to Laudale). Glencripesdale and Beach were reset to Dugald Gregorson in 1781 (£90), and in 1800 to James Gregorson (£130) ("Sett and Rental of Mull and Morvern 1744", etc.; *Book of Mull and Morvern tacks*, vol. '0', 154, vol. '2', 113, vol. '4', 91, *ICP*). Rahoy, together with Ardantiobairt (later to become part of Glenmorvern Estate) and Beinniadain, was set to Archibald Campbell and Hugh MacLachlan in 1754 for a rent of £31, to Archibald Campbell alone in 1772 (£70), and to Robert MacLachlan in 1791 (£95, raised in 1809 to £145) ("Sett and rental of Mull and Morvern 1754"; *Book of Mull and Morvern tacks*, vol. '0', 18, 125, vol. '4', 19, 53, *ICP*). Kinlochteacuis was set to Colin Campbell in 1754 (£21. 7s. 6d.), to Dugald MacLachlan, the sub-tacksman of Tearnait, in 1773 (£53. 5s. 4d.) and to Ewn

MacLachlan in 1792 (£95) ("Sett and rental of Mull and Morvern 1754"; *Book of Mull and Morvern tacks*, vol. '0', 24, 109).

The whole estate was bought from Argyll in 1821 by Donald Stewart residing at Auch, who was probably a connection of Miss Christina Stewart of Glenmorvern (*RSA* 1821: 107). It passed to his son John Stewart in 1828 (*RSA* 1828: 1229), and then to John's brother Alexander in 1834 (*RSA* 1834: 504). The estate remained in the hands of Alexander Stewart (and eventually of his trustees) until Beach was sold to Robert MacFie of Airds in 1869 (*RSA* 1869: 402), and all the rest to the Rev. William Newton, the Rev. Horace Newton and J. H. G. Newton in 1871 (*RSA* 1871: 39). Later in the same year the Newtons bought Laudale and Liddesdale Estates (*RSA* 1871: 295, 395), and called the whole 23,500-acre result 'Glencripesdale Estate'. All these properties remained in the hands of various members of the Newton family until after the First World War when they were sold to various purchasers, the Rahoy group going out of the family last. The Newtons' estate is nowadays in three parts: Laudale–Liddesdale (except for Camas Salach), Mr T. Abel Smith; Glencripesdale–Camas Salach, the Forestry Commission; and Rahoy–Kinlochteacuis, Mr A. Colville. Beach stayed in the MacFie family until it was bought for Ardtornish Estate (to which it still belongs) in 1936.

IX. LAUDALE ESTATE

DESCRIPTION. Composed of Camas Salach, Laudale and Lurga; 7,284 acres (OS). See Map 10[a, b].

CAMAS SALACH (Ramishallich, 1674[n]; Camisallich, 1674[n]; Polochan, 1755[r]; Camisalloch, 1770[a]; Camusalach, 1801[l]; Camusaloch, 1819[b]; Camas Salach, 1872[o]).

AREAS: 1770: 1,079 acres (28 arable, 724 pasture, 327 wood)[a]. OS: 1,229 acres.

SETTLEMENT: 684612; remains of 6 houses[o, s, z]; occupied by 1755[r], abandoned by 1891[c].

POPULATION: 1841, 5/37; 1851, 5/21; 1861, 4/16; 1871, 2/12; 1881, 1/6; 1891, 0[c].

LAUDALE (Laldie, 1494[x]; Lawdill, 1674[n]; Laudale, 1755[r]; Laudell, 1770[a]; Glenladale, 1789[j]; Laudile, 1824[t]).

AREAS: 1770: 5,274 acres (38 arable, 4,630 pasture, 606 wood)[a]. OS: 5,549 acres.

SETTLEMENTS:

Camas na h-Airdhe: 730607; remains of 2–3 houses[o, s]; period of occupation uncertain, but probably after 1770[a]; abandoned by 1872[o].

Laudale: (1) (*'Glenlaudale'*) 741604; remains of 6 houses[o, s, z]; occupied by 1755[r], two of the houses occupied until World War II.

(2) 749598; includes mansion house, farm buildings, etc.; occupied by 1801[l], and continuously since then.

Note: Ainslie's map of 1789[j] shows a settlement at 'Ardrenish', i.e. *Aird Earnaich, c.* 708627, but there is no other evidence of such a settlement, and Ainslie may have been mistaken.

POPULATION: 1779, —/34[l] (probably including Camas Salach); 1841, 6/58; 1851, 5/35; 1861, 3/19; 1871, 3/21; 1881, 2/24; 1891, 2/21[c].

LURGA (Lowrubuie, 1770[a]; Lurgvoy, 1819[b]; Lurgroy, 1824[t]; Lurga, 1841[c]).

AREAS: 1770: 381 acres (all pasture)[a]. OS: 506 acres.

SETTLEMENT: 735553; remains of 5 houses, 1 of them associated with the lead mine at 733554[z]; occupied in the 1730s when the mine was open; abandoned by 1755[r]; re-occupied by 1770[a], abandoned in 1911[v].

POPULATION: 1841, 1/5; 1851, 1/4; 1861, 1/3; 1871, 1/8; 1881, 1/3; 1891, 1/3[c].

Summary of ownership

Argyll property throughout the eighteenth century. Camas Salach, having previously been set with Glencripesdale, was transferred to Laudale in 1754, when the two properties were leased to Campbell of Ardslignish for £35. 15s. 0d. Lurga was not mentioned and may still have been attached to the lease of the lead mine, but it was added when the properties were reset to Ardslignish in 1773 with the rent increased to £80. Transferred to Lieut. Archibald Campbell in 1792 (£80. 8s. 4d.), and to Ewn MacLachlan, tacksman of Kinlochteacuis, in 1813, who thenceforth paid the combined rent of £200 ("Sett and rental of Mull and Morvern 1754"; *Book of Mull and Morvern tacks*, vol. '0', 23, 191, vol. '4', 115, *ICP*).

In 1825 the estate was bought by Dugald MacLachlan of Laudale and Killiemore (Mull), probably related both to Ewn MacLachlan, the last tacksman, and to Duncan MacLachlan of Callart, who sold Clounlaid in the same year (*RSA* 1831: 144). In 1851 it was acquired from Dugald MacLachlan's trustee by John Johnston residing at Hunterheck near Moffat (*RSA* 1851: 63), passing in 1864 jointly to Johnston's sons James (Hunterheck), John (Laudale) and William (a merchant in Liverpool) (*RSA* 1864: 1229). The Newtons of Glencripesdale bought Laudale from the Johnstons in 1871; see Section VIII, *Summary of ownership*, for its subsequent history.

Appendix B

X. LIDDESDALE ESTATE

DESCRIPTION. Composed of Achagavel and Liddesdale (divided from 1807 to 1826 into West and East Liddesdale); 7,508 acres (OS). See Map 10[a,b].

ACHAGAVEL (Auchagavill, 1674[n]; Achagaville, 1755[r]; Achigavill, 1770[a]; Achagavil, 1819[b]; Achagavel, 1872[o]).

AREAS: 1770: 1,660 acres (75 arable, 1,585 pasture)[a]. OS: 2,010 acres.

SETTLEMENT: 763560; remains of 4 houses[o,s,z], and a 19th-cent. cottage; occupied by 1755[r], and continuously to the present day.

POPULATION: 1779, $-/32$[1]; 1841, 3/16; 1851, 2/9; 1861, 1/4; 1871, 1/5; 1881, 1/9; 1891, 1/6[c].

LIDDESDALE (Ledistill, 1541[x]; Lidistill, 1674[n]; Leidisdale, 1755[r]; Lidisdale, 1770[a]; Liedgesdale, 1789[J]; Liddesdale, 1872[o]).

BOUNDARIES: From 1807 to 1826 "the lands of Liddisdale, Penny-gowan and Auchgavel" were divided into West Liddesdale and East Liddesdale, by a march dyke near a "rivulet called Aulnakuvie" (*Book of Mull and Morvern tacks*, vol. '3', 329, 334, vol. '4', 59, *ICP*). The dyke is probably the one which runs from just E of Liddesdale settlement, by Allt na h-Airbhe, southwards to Taobh Dubh (785569), making East Liddesdale slightly the larger of the two parts. The "Pennygowan" area is unidentified.

AREAS: 1770: 5,013 acres (4,735 pasture, 278 wood). OS: 5,498 acres.

SETTLEMENTS:

Achleek: 794601; remains of 3 houses[o,s,z]; occupied by 1801[1], and continuously since then; remains of another house at 807597.

Liddesdale: 778597; remains of 3 houses, including the Mining Company's store, built *c.* 1737 and later converted into the tacksman's house (see p. 168)[o,s,z]; occupied by 1755[r] and continuously since then; part of the settlement known as *Glasbhil* (probably *Glac Sabhail*)[c].

Loch-head: 833603; remains of 2–3 houses[o,s,z]; period of occupation uncertain, but abandoned by 1872[o].

POPULATION: 1779, $-/53$[1]; 1841, 10/59; 1851, 6/33; 1861, 6/31; 1871, 5/17; 1881, 4/16; 1891, 7/33[c].

Summary of ownership

Argyll property throughout the eighteenth century. Leased to Lieutenant Colin Campbell (who succedeed Alexander MacLachlan as tacksman of the whole property) in 1754 at £41. 10*s*. 0*d*. Reset in 1772–3 to Allan and Hugh MacDougall (£120). In 1807 the property was divided, West

Liddesdale being leased to John Campbell for £160 and East Liddesdale to Allan and Hugh MacDougall for £180, making the very high aggregate rent of £340—almost double the average, acre for acre, of the rest of Argyll's Morvern rents at this time ("Sett and rental of Mull and Morvern 1754"; *Book of Mull and Morvern tacks*, vol. '0', 19, 329, 334, vol. '4', 59, *ICP*).

Bought by John Gregorson of Ardtornish by 1826 (*RSA* 1826: 825, but the disposition may have taken place a year or two earlier), and sold by Gregorson's trustee to James Alexander of Easter Happrew in 1840 (*RSA* 1840: 1633). Alexander's daughters inherited the estate in 1860 (*RSA* 1863: 814), and passed it to Charles Alexander, tenant of Liddesdale, in 1863 (*RSA* 1863: 985). Charles Alexander sold it to Robert Tennant of Scarcroft Lodge near Leeds in 1864 (*RSA* 1864: 1394), who in turn sold it to John Scott of Rodono in 1866 (*RSA* 1866: 739). The Newtons of Glencripesdale bought Liddesdale from Scott's widow in 1871; see Section VIII, *Summary of ownership*, for its subsequent history.

XI. KINGAIRLOCH PROPERTIES IN MORVERN

DESCRIPTION. Two properties in Morvern belonged to the owner of Kingairloch Estate for the greater part of the nineteenth century: Altachonaich and Carna Island. Total area in Morvern 2,918 acres (OS). See Map 10[o],[a],[q].

ALTACHONAICH (Auldconnych, 1509[x]; Aldachonnycht, 1534[x]; Aldchonnich, 1755[r]; Aultaconnuch, 1801[l]; Altaconnich, 1824[t]; Altachonaich, 1872[o]).

AREAS: 2,464 acres in the parish (OS), of which an eastern portion of 410 acres was not sold to Ardtornish in 1900.

SETTLEMENTS:

(1) 754513; remains of 2 houses, outlines of 3 more[z]; occupied by 1755[r] and until 1851[c], abandoned by 1861[c].

(2) 748507; cottage built between 1861 and 1871[c], occupied until the early 1950s.[v]

POPULATION: 1841, 1/7; 1851, 3/16; 1861, 0; 1871, 1/8; 1881, 1/9; 1891, 1/4[c].

CARNA ISLAND (Carna, 1509[x]; Carnish 1801[l]).

AREA: 454 acres (OS).

SETTLEMENTS:

Achadhlic: 615581; remains of 3 houses[o,z]; periods of occupation unknown, but abandoned by 1872[o].

Appendix B

Dailechreagain: 624587 and 626590; remains of *c.* 20 houses[o,s]; occupied by 1755[r], and continuously since then.

POPULATION: 1841, 11/60; 1851, 7/35; 1861, 5/24; 1871, 2/9; 1881, 2/6; 1891, 2/10[c].

Summary of ownership

Both Altachonaich and Carna were attached to Kingairloch by the early sixteenth century (*OPS*, II, 1 (1954), 191–2). In 1751 Altachonaich appears in the Valuation Roll as the property of Lachlan MacLean of Kingairloch, Carna then being wadsetted to Mrs Jean Cameron (probably the sister of Glendessary who was Argyll's tenant in the mid-eighteenth century of Unimore and other farms). James Forbes of Kingairloch is recorded as possessing both properties in the Valuation Roll of 1802, and they remained the Forbes's property until they were sold separately in the late 1870s. Altachonaich went then to James Duncan of Benmore; in 1887 it passed to John Bell Sheriff of Kingairloch, who sold the greater part of it to T. V. Smith of Ardtornish in 1900. Carna was sold to John J. Dalgleish by 1879, who sold it in turn to the Newtons of Glencripesdale in 1881–2; it passed to the family of the present owner, Miss Hewer (a grand-daughter of Canon Horace Newton of Glencripesdale), in the early 1920s.

APPENDIX C

REMAINS OF THE HISTORIC PERIOD IN MORVERN

I. CASTLES

ARDTORNISH CASTLE. 692426; 14th-cent. tower house, lower walls only; outlines of 4 buildings to E of Castle (2 of them large), and of another large structure to its N; much decayed by the 1860s, pointed in 1873; a major restoration programme by Ross and Macbeth of Inverness projected for 1891–2, but not executed; further repaired with the addition of a spurious window in the S wall in 1910 and 1914–15 (*Photographs* (*Gertrude Smith*); *Astley diary*, 4 Oct. 1873; MacGibbon, D. and Ross, T. (1887–92), iii (1889), 122–4; Ross and Macbeth's 'Sketch for restoring Ardtornish Castle 1892', dated Jan. 1891, *AP*; *Photographs* (*Sinclair*); Account sheets, 1910, 1914, 1915, *AP*).

KINLOCHALINE CASTLE. 697476; 15th-cent. tower house; extensively damaged by the 1860s, with huge vertical gashes in the masonry of the E and W walls; restored, probably by Ross and Macbeth, with internal wooden floors, much new stonework and a good deal of imagination, in 1890; the tall roof-ridge of the restoration lowered in the 1920s (*Photographs* (*Gertrude Smith*); MacGibbon, D. and Ross, T. (1887–92), iii (1889), 168–70; *Photographs* (*Sinclair*); Donaldson, M. E. M. ([1926]), 313–17, and plate facing p. 311; undated plans, *AP*).

GLENSANDA CASTLE (Caisteal na Gruagaich, Nagair, en-Coer, Mearnaig; in Ardgour parish, but included to complete the list of castles in the Morvern peninsula). 824468; 15th-cent. tower house; unrestored beyond minimal pointing, and with walls almost up to full height in some places (MacGibbon, D. and Ross, T. (1887–92), iii (1889), 170–2).

KILLUNDINE CASTLE (Caisteal nan Con, Castle of Dogs). 584487; a sizeable quadrilateral building, with one gable standing, probably 15th or 16th cent.; unrestored; supposedly a hunting lodge connected with the Castle of Aros (across the Sound at 563450) (MacGibbon, D. and Ross, T. (1887–92), iii (1889), 447).

DRIMNIN CASTLE. 547550; site only, the castle having been demolished in 1838 by Sir Charles Gordon to make way for his private R.C. chapel, itself now derelict (MacLeod, J. (1843), 184; *OS 1872*; *OS 1872 NB*).

Appendix C

II. CHURCHES

KEIL (Cill Choluimchille). 672452; part of the porch and chancel of a pre-Reformation church; 12 grave slabs (removed in 1914 to the interior of the present parish church) and a cross. The present parish church was built in 1898, north of the medieval ruin, on the site of a former parish church dating from 1799, which itself replaced a yet earlier parish church on the same site (MacLeod, N. (1794), 271–2; MacLeod, J. (1843), 191; *OPS* II, pt 1 (1854), 188–9; reports, plans and factorial accounts, *AP*). The church in Lochaline at 678450 was built as a Free Church in 1896 on the site of Sinclair's Free Church of *c.* 1852; it now belongs to the Church of Scotland.

KILLINTAG. 564538; ruin of a church, in use until 1780, graveyard still in use; named 'Cill Dhonnaig' in *OS 1872* (which gives the name 'Cill Leuntaig' to the graveyard at Killundine, 579498), but the name Killintag is established by *OPS* and by *Morvern map 1865* (*Argyll estate plans 1770*; *OPS* II, pt 1 (1854), 189 and map; report in *AP*).

FERNISH. 567523; ruin of a church, built 1780 and in use until the present Fernish church was built in 1892 at 564523 (MacLeod, J. (1843), 191; *OPS* II, pt 1 (1854), 189; *OS 1872*).

III. OTHER LARGE BUILDINGS

AIRIGH SHAMHRAIDH. 843495; in Ardgour parish, but included as the only example in the peninsula of an early proprietor's house; ruins of 2 large two-story buildings, enclosure and many other remains; called 'Aryhaurie or Kingairloch' in *Roy's Scotland 1747–55*, and appears then to have been the dwelling of MacLean of Kingairloch.

LIDDESDALE. 779597; ruin of a large two-story building; probably built in the 1730s as a store for the Morvern Mining Company (Murray, Sir A. (1740), "A plan of Loch Sunart &ct"). This is probably the 'Slated Store house' at Liddesdale converted into a dwelling house for the tacksman, Lieut. Colin Campbell, in 1752–4 ('Instructions to the Factor for Mull and Morvern', 1752, 1753, 1754, *ICP*).

ARDTORNISH HOUSE. 693433; house of about 22 rooms built 1755–70; dismantled 1896, demolished 1907; steading at 693434, built after 1770, still in use (*Roy's Scotland 1747–55*; Cregeen, E.R. (1964), xviii; *Argyll estate plans 1770*; *Census* (for rooms); Half-yearly settlement book, *AP*; *Oban Times*, 5 Aug. 1899; *MacKichan's memoirs*, v.p. 244; Reports and valuations, 1906–7, *AP*; *Photographs* (*Gertrude Smith*) and (*Arisaig*)). Plate 12.

LOCHALINE HOUSE. 622467; house of about 20 rooms, built 1821–5, *See p. vii*
altered and enlarged 1870s, dismantled 1899, demolished 1910, walls
still standing (*King's memoirs, passim*; *Census*; *Oban Times*, 5 Aug.
1899; *MacKichan's memoirs*, v.p. 245; Reports and valuations, 1888,
1906–7, *AP*). Plate 4.

IV. SETTLEMENTS AND SHIELINGS

SETTLEMENTS. All the known settlement sites in Morvern (there are
about 110 in all, of which more than half are abandoned) are detailed in
Appendix B above. The largest deserted settlement (31 houses) is
Auliston at 549571 (Plate 1); the most easily accessible is Uladail beside
the main road at 717506; the most remote is Beinniadain, 925 ft a.s.l.
at 695547. The remains of a number of settlements have recently been
obliterated by Forestry Commission planting.

SHIELINGS. Similarly, all the known shieling sites (numbering 25,
including doubtful cases) are detailed in Appendix B. There are several
examples with clear remains of huts and pens, of which the Fiunary
shieling in Coire Bhorradail at 628501 is the most remarkable; but some
sites (such as those on Achranich Estate), although they are known from
early maps to have been shielings, have left no traces on the ground. The
Morvern shielings ranged in altitude from 250 ft a.s.l. (Claggan) to
1,225 ft a.s.l. (Savary), and in distance from the settlement from ½ to
2½ miles; several were reached by clearly defined tracks which can still
be traced.

V. AGRICULTURE AND INDUSTRY

ARABLE LAND. Large areas of disused arable—approaching 5,000 acres
in all, including outfield and taking all periods together—are to be found
all over the parish. Strips are often visible; there are well-preserved
examples on various types of ground at Torr a'Chall (729487) which are
unlikely to have been touched for 150 years.

DYKES. Very varied. The dry-stone dykes in the SE quarter of the
parish are generally older, more crudely made and in worse repair than
those in the NW. There is a superb dyke, still in perfect order, on the
march between Mungasdail and Fernish farms. Galloway dykes are rare.
There are many early turf dykes, notable examples being found between
Old Ardtornish and Miodar Bay.

WOODS. Some of the preserved woods of the late 18th and early 19th
cents. are still standing (e.g. in the Rahoy area), but mid-19th-cent.
planting, cropping, gales and—above all—the Forestry Commission
have altered the pattern.

KILNS, ETC. There are *lime kilns* on either side of Loch Aline, that at Samhnach being in use as late as 1933–6. Remains of *circular kilns*, probably used for drying corn, are found at Auliston, Beach, Crosben, Muicrach, Samhnach (Achranich) and Portabhata; and there is the ruin of a large *corn kiln* at Mugasdail Mill. No *kelp kilns* have been found. There is a *smithy* at Bonnavoulin, recently abandoned, but Keil smithy which stood at 669453 was demolished in 1911 (*AP*).

MILLS. CORN MILLS. Acharn: no remains; precise position unknown; ceased working before 1841 (*Census*, 1841; *MacKichan's memoirs*). Mungasdail: 559538; ruin of mill building and of adjacent kiln, and trace of 150-yard lead; ceased working between 1872 and 1881 (*OS 1782*; *Census*, 1881). Savary: 640459; outlines of buildings, and trace of 250-yard lead with sluices; ceased working between 1881 and 1891 (*Census*). The positions of the leads at Mungasdail and Savary suggest that both mills had overshot wheels; there are no remains of wheels or mill-stones at either site. Presumably there was once a mill on the Allt a' Mhuilinn (Killundine), but no site is known. SAW MILLS. Fiunary: private mill with dam, wooden lead-trough and 12 ft overshot wheel at Lochaline steading (623467), of which only the dam survives (plan dated 1905, *AP*). Achranich: there was a mill in use in the late 19th cent. just NW of the old bridge over the Rannoch, but there is now no trace of it (plan in *AP*).

FISH-TRAPS. There are tidal fish-traps built of stone at Inninmore (726417); Inninbeg (694433); Killundine (584487); Bonnavoulin (559534); and Oronsay Island (601586). The examples at Inninmore and Inninbeg are simple semicircles abutting on H.W.M.S.; that at Inninbeg has a radius of 60 yards and is centred on a small stream of fresh water. The Killundine trap is a straighter line of boulders cutting off the little bay to the E of Killundine Castle. At Bonnavoulin there are two pairs of substantial walls making two box-like traps against two reefs, one outside the other. The trap at Oronsay makes use of the considerable tidal flow into and out of the large eastern inlet, and consists of a massive double wall at the neck (possibly used with one-way entrances as a corf) with a lagoon inside them contained by a further wall 110 yards further back. All these traps are in a ruinous condition (having been breached, tradition says, following the passage of the Salmon Fisheries (Scotland) Act, 1868, which forbade the use of 'fixed engines' for fishing).

MINES. COAL: carboniferous sandstones containing thin seams of coal are exposed at various points round Loch Aline and in Inninmore Bay; there were attempts to work them opencast in the 18th cent., and three levels were cut, probably in the early 19th cent., NW of Inninmore settlement at 725419 (now flooded), but without economic success (MacLeod, N. (1794), 276; 'Report of the Mineral and Coal Appearances in the lands of Inveraray, Morvine and Mull...taken by William MᶜCall 14 July–2 Aug.1775', *ICP*; MacLeod, J.(1843), 169; Phemister, J.(1960), 81). COPPER: pegmatites containing copper sulphates were mined and *See p. vii* smelted in the 18th cent. beside the Allt an Doire Dharaich at 765478 where spoil heaps and a water-filled shaft are visible, and slag is found; this mine appears to have been in use at the time of Roy's survey 1747–55, but it had been given up by 1794 (*Roy's Scotland 1747–55*; MacLeod, N. (1794), no mention; MacLeod, J. (1843), 170). LEAD: barytes and quartz, containing galena and zinc-blende, were mined and smelted in the 18th and 19th cents. at 733554 in Lurga, the vein being worked opencast and by level; one of the two main levels is still accessible for 20 yards, but otherwise the workings are blocked by water; dam, lead, washing floor, hearths and smithy are traceable; originally opened in association with the Strontian mines in the early 1730s, and closed about 10 years later; re-opened in 1803, when about 6 tons of lead were obtained in 6 years by the Strontian company; a lead-miner lived at Liddesdale in 1841, and may have been working at Lurga (Murray, Sir A. (1740), "A plan of Loch Sunart &ct"; MacLeod, N. (1794), 276; 'Queries & Answers regarding the Morvern Mines July 1809', *ICP*; *Census*, 1841; MacLeod, J. (1843), 170; Wilson, G. V. (1921), 90–1).

QUARRIES. Sections of limestone and sandstone are easily accessible on both sides of Loch Aline, and have been quarried there for centuries. Stone was exported for the construction of Eilean Musdile light-house, Lismore, in 1833, and limestone for burning was quarried at Allt na Samhnachain as recently as 1933–6 (MacLeod, N. (1794), 276; MacLeod, J. (1843), 170–1).

VI. COMMUNICATIONS

ROADS AND TRACKS. PUBLIC ROADS: the statute-labour road along the Sound of Mull ran further inland than B849 from Savary to Mungasdail, and this section can still be followed for most of its length. Traces of other public roads antedating the new construction of the mid-19th cent. are few and slight, but there are short sections of the original White Glen road to be seen beside A884 between Uladail and Muicrach and on a straight line from Muicrach to Sron (where the proposed new White Glen road is to take the same short cut); and of the Arienas ford–Achadh nan Gamhna road (696506 to 691501). Opposite Uileann there is a half-mile loop of what is probably the original road, reconstructed around 1860, and then abandoned shortly before the First World War in favour of a lower route when the roads were widened for motor traffic; this lower road is itself shortly to be superseded by new construction. OTHER ROADS: the road made in the 1730s from Liddesdale to Lurga by the Morvern Mining Company can be followed easily from Achagavel to Lurga; and the road from Lurga to Acharn is also traceable, at its southern end further to the east than the present Crosben road which was built in 1872-3. Two sections of the Achranich road can also be followed: from Craigendarroch to Claggan, and from Acharn to Ath Buidhe. TRACKS: there are numerous footpaths and pony tracks, some of them certainly very old; good examples run from Fernish to Barr, from Miodar Bay to Ardtornish and from Kinloch to Glencripesdale. Some of the old shieling tracks running NE from the Sound of Mull are now covered by Forestry plantation, but very plain examples may still be seen in the vicinity of Cnoc Carach/Lochan na Cille in Achabeg, and north of Old Ardtornish. BRIDGES AND FORDS: the Achadh nan Gamhna bridge is dated 1821, and there is a bridge of about the same date taking the statute-labour road across the Salachan burn at 615471; these appear to be only early bridges in the parish apart from a few small ones on pony-tracks. Entries to fords can be seen at 696506 and 697478 (west bank).

PIERS, ETC. There is a massive disused pier at Fiunary (618465), and two jetties are just traceable near Drimnin Mains at 545556. It seems likely that there was an earlier pier at Lochaline (679446) which was superseded by the present pier of 1847-8, and which was linked by ferry with the large disused pier at Bailemeonach in Mull (660424); there is a natural inlet but no pier at the Rhemore ferry (569506). There is a pair of concrete pillars for leading lights at the Lodge on the W shore of Loch Aline, set up by Valentine Smith for bringing *Dobhran* in at night.

APPENDIX D

ARDTORNISH PAPERS:
SUMMARIES AND EXTRACTS

I. ACHRANICH AND ARDTORNISH ACCOUNTS:
SUMMARIES

Notes to Achranich and Ardtornish accounts 1853–1874 (overleaf)

General. Analysed from the 'balance sheets' (actually trading accounts) in Corson's ledgers (*AP*), made up annually to 31 December. All figures are to the nearest pound. Accounts are for Achranich alone from 1853 to 1859; in 1860 the account was for Achranich alone up to Whitsun, with the addition of Ardtornish after that date; and from 1861 to 1874 for the combined estate of Achranich–Ardtornish.

Receipts: sheep and cattle. The figure covers beasts only; dairy products and meat are included under 'sundries'.

Payments: wages. Shepherds', manager's and farmservants' wages only; day-labourers' wages are included under 'works'.

Payments: works. Repairs and improvements of all kinds, including new construction; workmen's wages included.

Trading surplus, deficit and balance. These figures are a summary of those under *Receipts* and *Payments*; the *balance* also represents the annual cash turnover of the estate.

Valued rent. From the Valuation Rolls; it represents an interest charge of about 3 per cent on the value of the property.

Adjusted surplus, deficit and balance. These are the trading figures with the incorporation of the *Valued rent*.

SUMMARY OF ACHRANICH AND ARDTORNISH ACCOUNTS 1853–74

Year	Receipts				Payments					Trading surplus or deficit	Trading balance	Valued rent	Adjusted surplus or deficit	Adjusted balance
	Wool and skins	Sheep	Cattle	Sundries	Wages	Sheep	Cattle	Works	Sundries					
1853	314	518	63	75	178	15	57	374	218	+ 128	970	317	− 189	1159
1854	318	290	259	118	185	17	129	499	304	− 149	1134	317	− 466	1451
1855	224	278	190	144	186	16	100	581	421	− 468	1304	317	− 785	1621
1856	247	339	234	112	197	136	80	919	273	− 673	1605	317	− 990	1922
1857	355	355	168	129	204	51	89	968	357	− 662	1669	317	− 979	1986
1858	380	387	184	291	211	10	57	1358	344	− 788	1980	317	− 1105	2297
1859	433	401	118	119	184	0	76	840	378	− 407	1478	420	− 827	1898
1860	385	2123	161	98	405	40	280	1222	1031	− 210	2977	1002	− 1212	3979
1861	1468	1412	423	112	593	59	270	1224	1273	− 4	3419	1585	− 1589	5004
1862	3446	1793	485	124	576	38	273	1332	1334	+ 2195	5848	1585	+ 610	5848
1863	1992	1546	430	174	581	60	291	1507	1298	+ 405	4142	1585	− 1180	5322
1864	253	1857	562	187	578	25	219	1224	1405	− 592	3451	1800	− 2392	5251
1865	3632	857	382	193	566	68	313	1137	1072	+ 1908	5064	1800	+ 108	5064
1866	191	1991	261	127	563	102	142	863	1195	− 295	2865	1800	− 2095	4665
1867	166	1305	533	173	557	51	189	1065	1295	− 980	3157	1800	− 2780	4957
1868	3788	679	416	226	585	24	180	1047	1379	+ 1894	5109	1800	+ 94	5109
1869	2510	1826	312	191	581	43	80	1124	1400	+ 1611	4839	1800	− 189	5028
1870	279	1724	252	268	650	120	101	1186	1314	− 848	3371	1800	− 2648	5171
1871	2710	1819	248	291	653	246	166	1147	1304	+ 1552	5068	1800	− 248	5316
1872	635	2162	430	268	689	51	175	1227	1783	− 430	3925	1800	− 2230	5725
1873	1939	1697	304	344	701	275	165	1175	2043	− 75	4359	1800	− 1875	6159
1874	1815	1528	317	363	636	2	201	1077	1905	+ 202	4023	2200	− 1998	6021

ACHRANICH AND ARDTORNISH ACCOUNTS 1853–74

THREE-YEAR AVERAGES OF ADJUSTED SURPLUSES AND

DEFICITS (NEAREST £)

Appendix D

SUMMARY OF ARDTORNISH ACCOUNTS 1891–1907

YEAR	TRADING DEFICIT	VALUED RENT ÷ 2	ADJUSTED DEFICIT
1891–2	2569	1534	4103
1892–3	3821	1491	5312
1893–4	3931	1448	5379
1894–5	3021	1448	4469
1895–6	4205	1448	5653
1896–7	1307	1448	2755
1897–8	5698	1448	7146
1898–9	5370	1445	6815
1899–1900	4982	1455	6437
1900–1	6079	1503	7582
1901–2	5379	1502	6881
1902–3	4660	1497	6157
1903–4	4712	1500	6212
1904–5	4706	1504	6210
1905–6	3599	1505	5104
1906–7	6392	1506	7898

Notes

Trading deficit. From the entries for 'T. V. Smith Capital Account' in Elliot's ledgers (*AP*), made up to 31 May each year. No trading account for this period has survived. Figures are to the nearest pound.

Valued rent. From the Valuation Rolls, divided by 2 because the Assessor's figure represents about 6 per cent of the value of the property at this period (p. 184 n. 4 below).

II. SUMMARY OF ACHRANICH AND ARDTORNISH ANNUAL WAGES

	1853–7	1863–7	1873–7	1893–7
Money wages (nearest £)				
Manager	50	100	160	400
Head keeper	—	30	60	65
Head shepherd	16	27	32	32
Labourer (maximum)	29	29	35	35
Wages in kind (nearest £)				
Manager	15	15	15	20
Head keeper	—	24	16	14
Head shepherd	8	21	23	39
Labourer	0	2	5	9
Total wages (nearest £)				
Manager	65	115	175	420
Head keeper	—	54	76	79
Head shepherd	24	48	55	71
Labourer (maximum)	29	31	40	44
Wage disparity (managerial total wages as factors of labourer's total wages)				
Manager	2·2	3·7	4·4	9·5
Head keeper	—	1·7	1·9	1·8
Head shepherd	0·8	1·5	1·4	1·6
Estate commodities index	100	101	112	108
Labourer's real wages index	100	106	124	142

Notes

Money wages. From Journals (*AP*). The labourer's (maximum) wage is based on the highest rate paid to a day-labourer, assuming that he works 90–95 per cent of the available days (cf. p. 70 above).

Wages in kind. From Journals (*AP*), *VR*, etc. Includes rent at the accepted valuations of the period (generally speaking, 22 years' purchase); allowances of meal and coal at current estate selling prices; cows' grass at £2. 10s. 0d.; and game money and vermin money as actually paid during the periods concerned.

Estate commodities index. Derived from the estate's selling prices for an imagined 'weekly ration' consisting of 8¾ lb meal, 3½ pts skim milk, ½ lb butter, ½ lb ordinary cheese and ½ lb mutton or beef. Potatoes are not included because the wage-earners normally grew their own; neither is coal, which was not normally purchased by estate employees until the 'seventies.

Labourer's real wages index. Derived from the sum of *money wages* adjusted according to the estate commodities index and *wages in kind* unaltered. (For comparison, the following indexes have been calculated from figures given in Wood, G. H. (1909): *UK real wages* (all trades, unchanged grade): 1853–7, 100; 1863–7, 109; 1873–7, 124; 1892–7, 150. *Scottish agricultural real wages* (money wages adjusted by Ardtornish commodity prices): 1855, 100; 1866, 95; 1874–7, 126; 1896, 140.)

III. SUMMARY OF ACHRANICH AND
ARDTORNISH GAME AND FISHING BOOKS

Year	Black-game and grouse	Pheasants	Roe	Stags	Hinds	Salmon	Sea-trout
1853	56	0	0	0	0	4	235
1854	21	0	0	0	0	2	28
1855	—	—	—	—	—	—	—
1856	204	0	0	0	0	9	45
1857	207	0	1	0	0	9	41
1858	—	—	—	—	—	—	—
1859	157	0	3	0	0	7	244
1860	114	0	3	0	0	14	253
1861	177	0	2	0	0	19	430
1862	—	—	—	—	—	—	—
1863	57	0	0	0	0	30	206
1864	189	0	2	0	0	52	444
1865	135	0	2	0	0	29	369
1866	238	0	4	0	0	14	289
1867	344	0	2	0	0	17	257
1868	404	0	5	0	1	22	314
1869	[210]	—	—	2	0	20	305
1870	[400]	—	—	7	0	35	164
1871	[414]	—	—	6	0	—	—
1872	[316]	—	—	5	0	34	203
1873	363	0	2	6	0	58	410
1874	[331]	—	4	10	0	55	257
1875	[300]	—	1	13	0	27	298
1876	277	1	1	16	0	22	351
1877	173	0	0	15	0	12	412
1878	155	5	0	18	0	14	374
1879	89	5	2	22	3	28	348
1880	256	28	3	25	3	5	176
1881	—	—	—	27	11	—	—
1882	—	—	—	24	25	—	—
1883	407	10	7	27	17	40	441
1884	500	7	—	23	—	—	—
1885	542	27	—	23	—	—	—
1886	519	9	0	21	4	30	782
1887	514	75	0	25	25	—	—
1888	619	16	0	25	31	22	615
1889	951	68	0	27	26	2	459
1890	1042	80	0	30	39	25	556
1891	1268	145	0	39	41	29	400
1892	512	112	3	35	50	34	759
1893	674	139	9	33	39	13	843
1894	258	0	1	39	48	41	497
1895	434	248	3	50	50	31	359
1896	574	116	0	38	37	52	600
1897	516	237	2	42	43	35	515
1898	—	—	—	—	—	17	815

(continued on p. 179)

Year	Black-game and grouse	Pheasants	Roe	Stags	Hinds	Salmon	Sea-trout
1899	379	187	7	50	50	42	292
1900	400	14	0	30	40	16	636
1901	334	330	0	40	40	17	540
1902	276	200	0	50	39	45	630
1903	303	400	2	40	30	26	409
1904	484	364	0	40	32	40	484
1905	430	377	0	36	31	9	441
1906	263	61	0	27	31	16	303
1907	309	199	0	45	26	13	603
1908	549	348	0	40	29	17	436
1909	478	760	0	40	56	9	255
1910	517	958	0	48	60	12	544
1911	459	1011	0	51	57	18	511
1912	321	1017	5	46	70	9	445
1913	312	1112	0	50	12	6	182
1914	260	1568	0	41	57	8	255

Notes

Sources: Game and fishing books, 1853–80; Gamekeeper's journals, 1883, 1887–1905; Game book, 1907–15; Stalking journal, 1870–84; all *AP*. Summary of Ardtornish fishing records, 1861–1932, made in 1934, *AP*.

Lacunae in the records are indicated by dashes. There was probably no shooting or fishing in 1858.

Black-game and grouse: the bracketed figures for 1869–72 and 1874–5 are calculated from the game-money paid to the shepherds in those years (Journals, *AP*), and refer to *total birds* killed; the number of black-game and grouse may have been 10 to 20 per cent less.

Salmon and sea-trout: figures refer to fish caught by the rod only; fish were also netted occasionally before 1888 and regularly thereafter until 1921.

IV. SELLAR–SMITH AGREEMENT, 1850

Summary of 'Agreement between Patrick Sellar...and Octavius Henry Smith', signed 23 Sep., 9 Oct. 1850; AP.

The main points of the agreement (which extended to thirty-four foolscap pages, with additions in Sellar's hand) were as follows:

I. Defines the 4 rights of way claimed by Sellar: (1) Ardtornish to Tearnait via Srath Shuardail; (2) Tearnait to Acharn via Uladail ford; (3) Acharn to Dubh Dhoire via Claggan; (4) Dubh Dhoire to Tearnait via Clais Bhreac.

1. Smith agrees to confirm and allow these rights of way; agrees to build a bridge at the Uladail ford, Sellar contributing £20; in return for which Smith may angle on Loch Arienas for 12 days a year.

2. Sellar agrees to renounce the fourth right of way, and parts of the second and third, when the road from Achranich to Caolas is completed.

3. Sellar and Smith agree to complete the road already begun by Smith from Achranich to Caolas.

4. Smith agrees to attempt to persuade the Road Trustees to accept the Dubh Dhoire–Claggan road as a public road in place of the Larachbeg–Claggan road. [He failed.]

5. Sellar agrees to allow Smith right of way across Tearnait to Glensanda, and across Clounlaid from the Uileann ford to the public road.

6. Defines procedure for marking roads, and for adjustments.

II. 1. Sellar agrees that Smith may have fishing rights on the E banks of the Aline, White Water and Loch Aline, Sellar to retain those on the W banks, the Fishing Station and Loch Arienas.

2. Both agree to limit all fishing in these waters to rod alone.

3. Sellar excepts the Kinlochaline Fishing Station tack from II. 2, but agrees to end the tack as soon as legally possible.

III. Sellar binds himself to dispose of the fishings to Smith as in II. 1, and Smith binds himself to pay Sellar £400.

IV. Sellar is to have the legal, as he already has the actual, possession of Achnatavishruskline.

V and VI. Procedure for arbitration; and penalties.

The agreement is illustrated by *Sellar's plan (roads) 1848* and *Sellar's plan (fishings) 1848.*

V. EVIDENCE OF WALTER ELLIOT, 1883, 1885

(1) *Extract from 'Statement [1883] by Walter Elliot, Esq., Manager for T. V. Smith, Esq. of Ardtornish'; Napier Commission report* (1884), Appendix A, LXXXIV, 378–9.

Ardtornish Estate, including Achranich and Acharn, all as possessed by T. V. Smith, Esq., extends to about 40,000 acres,[1] and is entered in the valuation roll as of the annual value of £2200. Three-fourths of the estate is under sheep, and the remaining one-fourth is under deer and black cattle.

There are really no crofters on the estate, Murray, who pays £8 of rent, being a road contractor.[2] There have been no crofters on this estate for

---

[1] The estate actually extended to only 30,378 acres at this time (see p. 103 and Appendix B above).

[2] This was William Murray, who had moved to Larachbeg from Knock in the 'sixties and who was given one of the end houses of Larachbeg terrace when it was completed in 1876 (*Census; VR*).

many years. It was all under sheep when purchased by the late Mr Sellar,[1] from whose representatives it passed to the late Mr Smith.

The family are resident on the estate for six months in the year.[2]

We employ from thirty-five to forty men all the year round: they are paid fortnightly. Labourers' wages run from 17*s.* to 18*s.* per week of 60 hours; blacksmith, joiners, and foremen from 20*s.* to 27*s.* Some of these have houses and potato ground, the others walk from the village of Lochaline. These men do not include gamekeepers, gardeners, shepherds, and farm servants. Our women workers get 1*s.* 3*d.* per day, summer and winter.

We supply those on the estate with milk at half the price it would cost them in town. They seldom cut peats, but get the best household coal at present laid down at their door for 15*s.* per ton.

For the last twenty years Mr Smith and his father have been spending from £2000 to £3000 a year more than the return from the estate.[3] His shepherds' and workmen's houses, to the number of twenty-two,[4] are all recently built, and have each cost over £200.

The estate has also been improved by planting, fencing, draining, liming, and road-making. New mansion-house, manager's house, and offices have also been built.

Mr Smith has built all his houses of concrete,[5] which, with the aid of a foreman, enabled him to employ the native population to a greater extent. . . .

(2) *Extracts from Walter Elliot's evidence in 'Case for Thomas Valentine Smith, Esquire, of Ardtornish, Argyllshire; for the opinion of the Judges under the Lands Valuation Acts'; printed Case, 29–33 (AP).* (Evidence of 5 May 1885.)

Examined.—I am manager for Mr. Smith, the appellant in this case. I have been so for four years. The property is mostly under sheep. A portion of it has been cleared for [deer] forest. There is practically no wintering for sheep on the estate. The acreage I understand to be about 40,000 acres,[6] exclusive of Inniemore [Unimore]. The figures as to

---

[1] Untrue; Sellar cleared 44 families from Acharn and another 4 from Ardtornish (see p. 129 above).

[2] No individual members of the family (with the possible exception of Flora Smith) were resident for anything like six months in the year at this period; but they and their guests came and went from July to December.

[3] This claim is certainly unjustified as far as the first ten of "the last twenty years" were concerned. From 1863 to 1872 the estate produced an average trading surplus (though this was converted into a deficit when 'rent' was added). There is reason to suppose, however, that there was a trading deficit on the scale indicated by Elliot in the 1880s; by the 'nineties the average deficit had reached almost £5,000 a year. When pressed in 1885, Elliot qualified his original assertion (*Case*, 33).

[4] Actually twenty-three since 1857.

[5] Concrete construction was not used until 1871; the first ten cottages were built of lime and rubble.

[6] The same mistake as before; see p. 180 n. 1.

stocking do include Inniemore, for which £75 of rent is paid by Mr. Smith. We have twelve shepherds on the estate.[1] In July 1884, 5488 sheep were clipped. From 1st July 1883 to 1st July 1884, 846 deaths occurred among the stock. That was a little less than the average of the previous four years. The last two years we have wintered all the hoggs. In 1883, the number of hoggs wintered off the farm was 1400, and the amount paid for wintering was £565: 15: 7, including freight and carriage. The stock is composed of 5000 Cheviots and 500 blackfaced sheep. We keep some cows and cattle on the farm as well. There are 14 dairy cows and calves, and a few crosses. The calves get cows' milk. The cows are principally for the use of the estate in summer. I think there are only about 10 crosses. The stirks are one or two year old, and they are the offspring of the cows we keep. Besides that there is a stock of black cattle on the estate, mostly on the sheep farm and partly on the ground cleared for forest. That is a flying stock. It consists of 40 stirks bought in; 40 two-year old stots kept all the year round, and 40 three-year old bullocks for the summer grazing, and sold off in October. There are thus 80 of the black stock in winter and 120 in summer. There are no breeding cows on the estate. I have given you the stock applicable to the period previous to last September. The place could not of itself keep all this stock which I have mentioned, and we supplement its capabilities by supplying feeding stuffs. These feeding stuffs cost us £259 odds, the winter previous to this. With regard to farm horses we generally keep about 8 of them. There are also 3 carriage-horses during the autumn season. These are fed to some extent by hay and oats grown on the farm. We buy the oats and maize, which are also used for feeding horses, and the oats and maize thus employed cost about £180. There is a portion of the ground cleared for forest. That portion carried 1650 sheep before it was cleared. We graze about 60 cattle every year on it now. They are not included in the numbers already given; . . .

Cross.—. . . I don't know what number of deer we have in the forest. There may be 200 or 300. The deer are not confined to the forest; part of it is fenced, but not fenced as for deer. The deer may go over the estate. There is a good part of the estate which we never get any deer on. We kill about twenty stags and twenty hinds in the year. . . . Occasionally the sheep get into the forest. We cannot keep them out. We aim at keeping the sheep out as much as possible, for we do not wish them to go into the forest. . . . Some of the arable ground has been drained. There is a small limekiln on the estate, but we generally buy our lime. The arable land is included in the rental. I think that we have only sixty acres or thereabouts of arable. . . . In 1883 I stated [in evidence before the Valua-

---

[1] No doubt correct, but the absence of most of the account books of the early 'eighties makes this and other figures in the report impossible to check.

tion Committee] that we had twelve Highland cows and followers. We have given them up and substituted nothing. . . . It may be that using oil-cake and other feeding stuffs improves the land; but that is a very gradual and slow process. We have only carried on the process for two years. . . .

Re-examined.—. . . The total expense of drainage has only been about £200. That has been spent on the ground that we cultivate.

Re-cross.—Nothing has been spent on sheep drains before the present year. We clear those that are already there, and put in a few more. It may be the case that Mr. Corson cut a few drains.[1] I have only spoken with reference to the period up to September last year [1884], but it is only since that time that we have done any sheep draining. I have been trying for some time to get men to do that sort of work, but I have only succeeded this last winter.

By the Bench.—The clipping account of sheep on the farm gives a total of 5500, without the cleared land. In 1881 the clipping account was 5690. In 1882, 5118; in 1883, 5322; and in 1884, 5488. These are the actual numbers clipped.

VI. REPORTS AND VALUATIONS, 1906, 1907

(1) *Extracts from 'Report and valuation by George Malcolm, Invergarry, Licensed Valuator, of the Estate of Ardtornish', dated 15 December 1906.*

In accordance with instructions from Messrs Finlay and Wilson, s.s.c., Edinburgh, Agents for the Executors of the late Thomas Valentine Smith of Ardtornish, I have visited the various parts of the Estate and beg to report as follows:

. . . The family residence is of modern construction, and is a most substantial, handsome and commodious house. It is amply provided with the usual offices and accessories. The kitchen garden and hothouses and greenhouses, which are not of large extent, are near the Mansion House, as are also the factor's house, the Home Farm buildings, and the workshops for the various Estate tradesmen. There is also a small saw-mill, driven by water power, which is used only for Estate purposes.[2] Here and in the neighbourhood are also a number of cottages for the various estate departmental servants and the workmen employed under them.

The whole of these buildings from the Mansion House downwards are at present in a condition of first rate repair.

The private policies surrounding the Mansion House are not extensive, but are very carefully and tastefully kept, and are well protected by suitable fences.

[1] Corson had in fact cut a great many sheep drains. See above, pp. 74, 92.
[2] There are undated plans in *AP* of the Achranich water wheel, which was placed against the north bank of the Rannoch, about 10 yards west of Achranich Bridge; no trace of it now remains.

On the South-western portion of the Estate, *videlicet,* Loch Aline, the house of that name and certain farm buildings are not at present in good repair. This portion of the Estate has been in the proprietor's natural possession, and it has not been necessary to repair or rebuild certain houses and offices which have not been let to tenants.[1]

On the Estate there is a large extent of iron and wire fences of a useful and substantial description, and so far as I observed, all these are in very good repair. ...

Ardtornish Estate is chiefly occupied as sheep farms, but about twenty thousand acres are set apart as deer forest.[2] A copy of the Rental of the Estate as extracted from the Argyllshire Valuation Roll for the year 1905–6 is hereto annexed. It will be seen that the first entry in the Rental is "Lands Ardtornish, Achrannich, Acharn and Fumary Farms £1481." These farms are in the natural occupation of the proprietor of the Estate. They are believed by me not to be capable of carrying more than 7,500 sheep, with certain number of cattle; and I have been informed that at the date of the late proprietor's death, the total number of sheep on these farms was only about 6,500.[3] The stock is all black-faced. Any highland landlord would in these times think himself fortunate if he obtained a rent at the rate of two shillings per sheep on the carrying capacity of a farm with black-faced stock. In very many cases the rate is much less, but taking it at two shillings for 7,500 sheep, the amount of

rent would be		£750	0	0
And if the grazing rate or rent for the following cattle be added, say 20 dairy cows at £7	£140			
130 grazing cattle at £2	260	400	0	0
The total rent would be		£1150	0	0

The Reporter, while feeling bound to state the foregoing as his view of the amount at which the proper rent of these farms at current rates should be, has however adopted the rent appearing in the Valuation Roll in arriving at the Valuation stated below, seeing that the late proprietor appears to have aquiesced in the latter amount of rent.[4]

There are seven small Feus on the Estate at Lochaline village of the

---

[1] Lochaline House was 'dismantled' in 1899, but it had probably not been occupied since 1888; it was demolished in 1910 (see p. 169 above).

[2] Actually 14,500 acres.

[3] The sheep stock at 31 May 1906 totalled 6,841 beasts, including 203 Cheviot ewes (annual balance sheet in Ledger, *AP*).

[4] If the Valuator's estimate of the real rent of the farm is accepted, the total rental value is reduced to £2,691. 8s. 6d. (compared with £3,011. 15s. 0d. in the Valuation Roll), and the final valuation to approximately £46,300. In either case the rental is almost 6 per cent of the value.

total annual value of £10. 13*s.* 6*d.* Particulars of these are appended hereto. Owing to its somewhat inaccessible situation, I am of opinion that the Estate has at present no prospective feuing value. Practically the only access to the Estate from Oban and the South is by a steamer plying between Oban and Tobermory, which calls at Loch Aline Pier every week day when weather permits, but there are occasions, not infrequent, when the steamer cannot "take" the pier owing to stormy weather, and passengers for Ardtornish are carried past to Tobermory or Oban as the case may be.

The following is an Abstract of the Rental of the Estate as appended hereto—

(1)	Farms	£1656	17	0
(2)	Houses	385	18	0
(3)	Shootings and Fishings	915	0	0
(4)	Hotel	14	0	0
(5)	Pier	40	0	0
(6)	Feus	10	13	6
		£3022	8	6

...And subject to the Public and Parochial Burdens and other usual deductions aftermentioned, I estimate the selling value of Ardtornish Estate as at eighth August last [1906] at Fifty two thousand, and two pounds and thirteen shillings and sixpence (£52,002. 13*s.* 6*d.*)...

(2) *Extracts from 'Memorandum of Visit to Ardtornish, 19th to 23rd December, 1907'. Unsigned, but made for Gerard Craig Sellar by Mr Murray of MacAndrew Wright and Murray, his Edinburgh solicitors, who were taking over from Valentine Smith's solicitors, Finlay and Wilson of Edinburgh.*

...

Properties: Acreage about 50,000.[1]

...

Mansion House: Ardtornish Tower, built by Mr Valentine Smith about 15 years ago on site of former house built by Mr Octavius Smith and demolished by Mr Valentine Smith on account of dry rot.

...

Accounts: Estate financed from London by remittances as required to credit of an account in the name of Factor with National Bank, Oban.[2]

---

[1] A pencil note by Gerard Craig amends this figure to 55,000 acres, which is even more wildly wrong; the true figure was 41,000 acres.

[2] This method of finance had been practised ever since Corson was appointed manager of Achranich in 1850. The factor (as the manager was now called) at the time of Murray's visit was Jonah Davidson, who had been appointed following the death

Appendix D

After crediting sales of stock and wool—only sources of revenue—the annual cost of running the estate is said to be between £4000 and £5000. The accounts are kept by the Factor and submitted for audit (so-called) annually to the Secretary (Mr Walker)[1] in London. No regular annual Estate Account is at present made up....

Home Farm Buildings [Achranich]: Excellent, but site inconvenient. Silo offensive. Congestion of departments—stables, Clerk of Works, etc. Suggestion to remove farm buildings to a suitable site up the River [Rannoch],[2] retaining stables (with developments) and Clerk of Works' offices. Coachman's house some distance from stables.

Acharn Buildings: Shepherd's house and extra rooms now being converted into second cottage. Suitable sheep farm offices, fanks, dipper, etc.

Old Ardtornish: Farm buildings need repair but are fairly good and suitable. Old house just been pulled down for sentimental reasons.[3]

Fiunary, Savary, and Loch Aline all have small steadings. Fiunary being the largest, but none of them are in good repair or in comparison with rest of estate buildings. This property was acquired about 10 [actually 20] years ago by Mr Valentine Smith. Suggestion to form new steading in centre of three farms and work all (low ground and hill) together. At present all the low ground is worked by Overseer (Mulvie) and the hill ground by shepherds under Factor direct. The arable land is of good quality and capability. Did not see hill. Large stock of polled Angus and a few Highlanders. Fiunary House has been allowed to fall into disrepair and is to be pulled down.[4]

The whole Estate except one small farm—rent £90—at Loch Aline Village is in proprietor's hands and farmed and managed by Factor. ... Loch Aline Pier, where steamers touch, belongs to Estate—pier dues of 2*d.* a head being charged.

Estate Servants, of whom there are about 100, receive houses free, good wages, and probable pension.[5]

of Elliot at Achranich earlier in the same year; Davidson proving "not suited to his post", he was sacked at Whitsun 1908 and was succeeded by James MacKenzie, probably the ablest of all the Ardtornish managers.

[1] R. W. M. Walker had been Valentine Smith's business secretary in London.
[2] Craig Sellar commented in a pencil note, "When considering site the water question is a difficult one." The buildings were not in fact moved.
[3] The sentimental reasons are nowhere explained, but the chief one was probably Gertrude Craig Sellar's distress, on returning to Ardtornish after twenty-five years' absence, at finding the beautiful old house, in which she had spent the happiest years of her girlhood and early married life, dismantled and derelict. Left to himself Gerard Craig Sellar would probably have preserved it, and indeed towards the end of his life he was considering a scheme to build a new house on the site. The demolition of this fine building, the only surviving eighteenth-century 'mansion house' in the parish, was a great loss to Morvern. See pp. 168, 244.
[4] I.e. Lochaline House, demolished in 1910. See pp. 169, 245.
[5] This figure includes day-labourers as well as those employed on a regular basis.

Game: Achranich and that portion of Ardtornish south [actually south-east] of an imaginary line drawn from Old Ardtornish farm buildings to Ardtornish Tower house is deer forest and cleared of sheep. Between said line and the sea [i.e. Loch Aline] is grouse ground and sheep grazing. Acharn is under sheep with some deer. The north side lands are grouse moors with sheep grazing. There are strips of the usual West Highland coverts.

About 40 stags, 150–200 brace of grouse (very bad lately—used to be about 500 brace), with a fair winter bag of the usual kind.

The sea-trout fishing in Loch Arienas and the River is magnificent, and although under the mark lately the salmon fishing in the River is good. . . .

Gardens: Small and not well situated for sun. May be demolished and new garden formed more suitable to the place.

Anchorage for yacht about 300 yards from house. The tonnage of the yacht is 550 and there is a bar at the mouth of Loch Aline which cannot be crossed at low water or half tide. Proposal to deepen channel. . . .

APPENDIX E

DIARIES, MEMOIRS, ETC.

I. EXTRACTS FROM THE ASTLEY DIARY, 1872, 1873

[The following extracts describe the visits made in 1872 and 1873 to
Ardtornish by Gertrude Susan Astley (1849–1920) and her sister
Constance Charlotte Astley (1851–1935) as the guests of their friend
Gertrude Craig Sellar. The diarists refer to themselves in the third
person, first as 'G' and 'C', and later as 'F' and 'J' (for the nick-
names 'Flotsam' and 'Jetsam'); the name 'Gertrude' in full refers to
Mrs Craig Sellar, and 'F-in-law' or 'Friend in-law' to her husband
Alexander Craig Sellar.

The chronology of the sisters' visits was as follows: they arrived at
Ardtornish on Friday 4 October 1872, stayed there for 5 weeks and 4 days,
and left on Tuesday 12 November; the next year they arrived at Oban
for the Argyllshire Gathering on Wednesday 3 September, proceeded to
Ardtornish 2 days later, and left for the north on Tuesday 9 September
after a stay of 4 days; they then returned to Ardtornish on 23 September
1873, stayed for 3 weeks and 3 days, and left on Friday 17 October.

The sisters' '1ˢᵗ Journal' consists of lined quarto sheets quired into
a leather-bound book of blank paper, and the text is supplemented by
numerous drawings and photographs. Most of it was written out by
Gertrude, but Conny wrote a few passages and contributed most of the
illustrations. The '1ˢᵗ Journal' was given by Gertrude's daughter, the
See p. vii late Carlotta Astley Nicholson, to Mrs John Lipscomb; Gertrude's and
Conny's later diaries remain at Arisaig House. See also pp. 84–7 above.]

1872

[Edinburgh, Thursday] 3ʳᵈ [October 1872] They spend the morning in
laying in provisions for G & C's journey & at 2.15 pm the two latter start
for Greenock having been safely seen into the train by Miss Courtenay.
They are half an hour late at Greenock and on enquiring for their portmanteau it is nowhere to be found. They confide their troubles to the
Station Master who promises to make due search for it; & then hurry
through Greenock, an ancient mariner carrying their bundles of wraps,
their sole remaining possession. Arrived at the pier an awful shock
awaits them. The steamer is "awa" 20 minutes ago.[1] What is to be

---

[1] This was *Clansman* (II) (see above, p. 53), which at this time left Glasgow on Thursdays for Stornoway, calling at Lochaline on Fridays (outward) and Tuesdays
(return).

done. their one fixed idea is to reach Ardtornish some time the next day if humanly possible. In despair G pathetically appeals to a grey headed & respectable looking individual who happens to be near & he assures her that the steamer Talisman will leave Greenock sometime that night & reach Oban 12 hours after she starts.[1] They determine to embark in her & see what happens & pass the intervening hours very comfortably roasting apples before the waiting room fire. The waiting room is presided over by a being whose voice resembles as C says an asthmatic heron's. At last the steamer comes in & they go on board & find to their great relief that there are no other ladies so that they will have the cabin to themselves. After a miscellaneous meal they examine the state of their finances & discover that they possess exactly £4-10-6½. Therefore says G we must be prudent & not indulge in any unnecessary expense. C only grunts & remarks that she means to get to Ardtornish tomorrow. At 12 pm the Talisman starts & G turns in meaning to sleep all the way round the Mull [of Kintyre] if possible. C is more romantic & remains on deck star gazing.

[Friday] 4th [October 1872] A bitterly cold morning; the prospect is not cheering. The Talisman does not, will not & cannot call at any place between Oban & Queenish a place in Mull many miles north of Ardtornish.[2] At Oban things look still more dreary. It is blowing a gale down the Sound & no boat could get to Loch Aline A smack is starting for Mull with letters but she does not look inviting & as they find that even if they go in her to Mull they will not be able to get across that night, they determine to remain in the Talisman. They persuade the captain to fly a signal & keep close to the shore as they pass Loch Aline & are a little comforted by hearing that a boat is coming off to the steamer from Tobermory in which boat if all else fails the benighted pair may be landed at Tobermory. They receive an immense amount of advice & sympathy from a compassionate fellow passenger but G is unable to spend the awful moment of passing Loch Aline on deck & retires below. C betakes herself to the bridge; there is the Bay, the cliffs, the woods, the house! The signal is waved; not a human being in sight. C wildly thinks of asking them to ring the dinner bell and to request all steerage passengers to utter a simultaneous shout.—The signal is hauled down & hope is extinct.[3] C hurries below & finds the callous & unfeeling G in the arms of Morpheus. NB. G says this is a base libel.—Tobermory

[1] *Talisman* was a small screw-steamer built for Martin Orme in 1871; from May 1872 she ran weekly from Glasgow to Barra and back via Oban, Quinish, etc., leaving on Thursdays (Duckworth, C. L. D. and Langmuir, G. E. (1950), 174, 226).

[2] Quinish, north-west of Dervaig in Mull.

[3] At Ardtornish the signal was seen and understood, but the Craig Sellars—having thought that the girls would now come via Corran since they were not on the *Clansman*—were not ready for it and could not get a boat out in time ('Chapters of a Future Story', probably by Julia Tollemache, attached to the diary).

is reached about 5.30, the boat comes off & on the way to the shore G. as a last despairing hope asks if there is any possibility of getting to Loch Aline that night. Oh unlooked for joy, they are told there is no difficulty & two men are pointed out on whom their fate depends. They land & humbly ask if the said men who are leaning against the parapet looking sea-ward Can they & will they take them? No answer, after a pause they repeat the question; the only response is a grunt. At last with a deep sigh the men turn round & silently & mournfully prepare their boat. At 6 o'clock G & C again trust themselves to the stormy ocean, in an open boat, with 2 unknown boatmen & a brown sail. Never did shipwrecked mariner trust himself more gladly to a life boat. They could not for joy wish the seats less hard or the wind less bitter, for were they not on the way to Ardtornish. They approach the long wished for haven, the mast does not break, the boat does not upset as C fully expects it will, & though the wind almost deserts them they at last reach the harbour, they land. yes—they actually stand on the land of Ardtornish—They are received at the Pier by the never to-be-sufficiently praised Gillyan who was just starting in search of them.[1] It was very dark & they were stiff with cold but joy gives them wings. C speeds on in front rushes to the dining room window & peers in. There sit Gertrude, her husband, Miss Tollemach & Mr Rutson.[2] One tap at the window—cold & hunger, loss & disappointment, the tempestuous Mull & the dreary Sound fade like a dream, for are they not at Ardtornish?

[Saturday] 5th [October 1872] G & C cannot at first believe that they have not to start off some where & try & catch something but gradually the pleasant truth is impressed upon them that they have only to rest & be thankful. Poor Gertrude S is kept indoors with a shocking cold, Mr Sellar is out deer stalking[3] but the others walk over the hill to Ardtornish Tower. They find Mrs Smith & Flora[4] wonderfully well & having related all their adventures they return home by the road.

[Sunday] 6th [October 1872] The whole party drive over to Ardtornish Tower to lunch. Home in the evening, which turns very stormy.

[1] Gillean MacLean, aged 28, was attached to the Craig Sellars as a servant while they were in residence, and worked the rest of the year as an estate joiner; see above, pp. 88, 99.

[2] Julia Tollemache (also called 'Douce'), who was married in May 1873 to C. S. Roundell, M.P., was a friend of Gertrude Craig Sellar; she appears in photographs taken at Ardtornish Tower in 1867. Mr Rutson is unidentified.

[3] Without success; the last stag of the season was killed on 29 September (Game Books, *AP*).

[4] Octavius Smith's widow, and his eldest daughter. Although there was good deal of movement between the two houses, Mrs Smith and Flora generally stayed at Ardtornish Tower, while the Craig Sellars had Ardtornish House.

[Monday] 7th [October 1872] Drive to Acharn from which place Mr S. Miss T. G. C & M^r R walk part of the way to Ullin. On the way they see a stag & feel that they have not lost this day at any rate.

[Tuesday] 8th [October 1872] Lunch at Ardtornish Tower. Drive to Loch Teachus afterwards with Mrs Smith.

[Wednesday] 9th [October 1872] They devote their minds to doing nothing all day & succeed wonderfully. Mr Rutson departs.

[Thursday 10 October 1872] Directly after lunch they all start in the boat & row across to Salen in Mull. There they land & are walking along the road very happily when an individual appears approaching them! Who is it. Mr Sellar says he knows him. General desire to hide or fly but hearing he is Lord MacKenzie their curiosity to see a live law lord overcomes their terror & they advance boldly.[1] Mr Sellar & Gertrude are carried into the inn to see Mrs MacKenzie & the other three sit meekly on a wall outside. When the two join them they walk on to Duart to see the Guthries[2] They arrive exhausted with much laughing & their hearts sink within them when they find the Guthries out & the inhospitable butler offers them no tea. They trudge back again, meeting M^rs G on the way with whom they walk until the steamer appears. They are safely picked up & find Mr Tom Sellar[3] on board & they all reach Ardtornish House about 8.

[Friday] 11th [October 1872] Happy day. G & C's wandering portmanteau returns to the bosom of its family. The whole family drive over to D^r McCleod's[4] & dine & sleep at Ardtornish Tower.

[Saturday] 12th [October 1872] They return to Ardtornish House.

[Sunday] 13th [October 1872] M^r T Sellar, Miss T & G go to Kirk. They are supported under their sufferings by feeling that they are keeping up the character of the family. It is a most glorious day & they all have a delicious walk along the top of the Cliffs, in the evening.

[Monday] 14th [October 1872] Walk & ride across the hill to Ardtornish [Tower]. An inroad of visitors from whom Miss T & G take refuge in Kin Lochaline Castle. Drive home in the evening.

[Tuesday] 15th [October 1872] Day of woe & lamentation. Mr Sellar Miss Tollemache Mr Tom Sellar & Mr Shaw Smith[5] all go South by the

---

[1] Donald MacKenzie, appointed Lord MacKenzie 1872, d. 1875. Craig Sellar was Legal Secretary to the Lord Advocate for Scotland at this time.
[2] A. C. Guthrie and his wife (née Anne Chamberlain) lived at Torosay Castle, which was then known as Duart House.
[3] Tom Sellar was Alex Craig Sellar's eldest brother.
[4] John MacLeod, D.D., the minister, who lived at Fiunary.
[5] W. Shore Smith, a nephew of Octavius Smith.

Clansman. The horrid boat appears about 5 & the 2 G's & C are left dis consolate on the shore. For their feelings on this mournful occasion see the celebrated poem "The Cow & the Ferry Boat" "A night on the Clansman" also refers to this occasion, being some of the adventures of Miss Tollemache.[1]—G & C come to Ardtornish Tower. M[rs] Smith keeps Gertrude & the Baby[2] company at Ardtornish House.

[Wednesday] 16th [October 1872] Flora G & C (the 3 Kilkenny cats) cut down trees & disport themselves in an innocent way.

[Thursday] 17th [October 1872] The 3 Kilkenny Cats walk up to Ardtornish House, dine there & return by moonlight. The most lovely day & night possible. —Splendid Aurora Borealis.

[Friday] 18th [October 1872] G & C drive over to breakfast at Ardtornish House. Directly afterwards, they, M[rs] Smith & Gertrude start in the boat for Eigneig. When they get into the Linnhe Loch they find the wind too strong & are obliged to stop at MacKinnan's Bay, a most lovely place with high wooded cliffs coming close to the shore.[3] The 2 G's & C wander along the shore & then try to climb up the said cliffs. Gertrude S & C try in one place, G in another. The former give it up for want of time, but G succeeds by going up on her hands & knees. She however mentally vows that she will not attempt it again but leave such freaks to the rising generation. They return some what dishevelled to the boat & have a delicious sail back—Flora joins them at Ardtornish House & they spend some days there.

[Saturday] 19th [October 1872] G takes a solitary promenade to the Tower & back—the others dawdle about.

[Sunday] 20th [October 1872] Walk along the Ennimore path.

[Monday] 21st [October 1872] The three kilkenny cats return to Ardtornish Tower.

[Tuesday] 22nd [October 1872] Uneventful.

[Wednesday] 23rd [October 1872] Baby, M[rs] Smith, & Gertrude come home The three Kilkenny cats go down to meet them at a bridge which is supposed to be impassible. Two carriages are therefore brought to this side of the bridge to assist the transit but finding it quite safe they

---

[1] There are actually three separate pieces in the diary referring to the departures of 15 October: 'The cow in the ferry boat', a poem by the Astley girls; 'A night on board the "Clansman"', a prose description by Julia Tollemache; and 'A sigh from the swamp', a poem, also by Miss Tollemache.

[2] The baby was Gerard Craig Sellar, 1871–1929.

[3] The bay still known as MacKinnon's is at 754412; the MacKinnon family left it between 1841 and 1851.

cross & meet the procession from Ardtornish House. Then they all turn & proceed majestically to the Tower; the luggage cart, the pony carriage with Mrs Smith, Gertrude & Baby, the pony carriage with nobody, the dog-cart with the maids & man, the dog cart without the maids and man, Flora in her carriage with G & C in attendance, men & boys scattered along the road in picturesque groups, dogs ad libitum. His Imperial Highness The Baby reaches the Tower in safety about 5 p.m.

[Thursday] 24th [October 1872] A most lovely day. Mrs Smith, the two G's & C drive to Ullin. The road is rather the worse for wear; the bog of the country appearing in some places through the metal. However by getting out at the bad places they succeed in reaching their destination without going in very deep.

[Friday] 25th [October 1872] C objects to the statement that they dawdle as she says she never dawdled in her life; therefore the description of this day cannot be written.

[Saturday] 26th [October 1872] Gertrude, C, G & Bluebell start to Corospin a shepherds cottage about 3 miles up a glen.[1] They have a lovely walk through the woods & up a very wild pass. They cross the river quite easily on foot & are received at the cottage by innumerable dogs & children. Coming back Bluebell thinks nothing of walking through bogs & up the hills at such a pace that the others can hardly keep up with her.

[Sunday] 27th [October 1872] They walk about in short snatches. The weather is more beautiful than ever.

[Monday] 28th [October 1872] The day looks rather dark but the glass is going up & they determine to go to Eignaig which is only 8 miles by road.[2] Accordingly Gertrude, Bluebell the pony, G & C with the man James in attendance start at ¼ to 11. G remarks that this being the third attempt to get to Eignaig she thinks it will succeed, for which superstition she is properly laughed at by the others The road is very boggy & Bluebell takes every opportunity of objecting hoping to be allowed to go home but they persevere. At last it begins to pour & they hold a council of war in which they decide to go on to Turnet about half way & if it does not clear then to return. However at Turnet the sun shines out gloriously & the deluded beings continue on their way rejoicing. But again about 2 miles from Eignaig the clouds gather & the rain descends.

[1] They walked up the Black Glen on the old Crosben track to Crosben (2) (see pp. 144, 172). Sam Henry was living at the old cottage with his wife, seven children and an assistant shepherd (*Census*, 1871, 1881).

[2] The 'road' to Eignaig (which is actually about seven miles long) was in fact the most rudimentary of tracks.

They trudge steadily on the water above making them quite callous to the water beneath though the path has long since turned into a water course. For the view from Eignaig & their appearance on getting there see illustrations. They eat their lunch very hurriedly feeling painfully conscious of the large puddles of water they are making on the floor of the cottage. After partially drying their pocket handkerchiefs gloves etc they retrace their steps G & C feeling as if their petticoats were lined with lead. They reach home in very good time having had plenty of light for the road which after all the rain is nearly impassable. The pleasure of feeling clothed & in their right mind again quite compensates them for their wetting.

[Tuesday] 29th [October 1872] Blowing a furious gale from the south west with torrents of rain. Gertrude spends the day at Ardtornish House intent on household matters. G & C walk down to meet her & are nearly blown away.

[Wednesday] 30th [October 1872] Blowing harder than ever. Less rain but "whiles it hails" for a variety with loud peals of thunder between times. Gertrude, G & C drive up to Ardtornish House to see the Sound. Coming back they are caught in a hail storm & console themselves by hoping it is wholesome, if not exactly pleasant.

[Thursday] 31st [October 1872] The gale shews little signs of abating. Mrs Smith, Gertrude & G feel it their duty to take an airing in the carriage. They therefore drive to the Ullin waterfall & back & feel most thoroughly aired by the time they get back. His Imperial Highness the Baby also drives out accompanied by Flora & C.

Novber 1st [Friday] [1872] The wind has gone down, but the clouds come down also. It pours steadily the whole day & nobody but C ventures out. In the evening they take a little exercise as shewn in the illustration.

[Saturday] 2nd [November 1872] Showery. The 2 G's & C walk up the hill above Kinlochaline Castle to see an old woman who pitied them greatly for coming out on such a day. She supposed "they were so used to company that now they were that dull in the house alone they must just take a walk"! The box with the the clouds arrives [*sic*].

[Sunday] 3rd [November 1872] A lovely day frosty & bright. The Loch looks more lovely that in has ever done before; at low tide there appears a beautiful rim of olive green sea-weed beyond the orange. C. expresses a strong desire to sit on the shore & contemplate the scene for ever but the 2 G's forcibly drag her away.

[Monday] 4th [November 1872] The whole family devote themselves to knitting & crochet till serious fears are entertained as to what the result may be on their brain[s]. They endeavour to counteract the effects by playing billiards. Gertrude & G play C & the most remarkable feature of the game is that for the first half of it they give their opponents more than they score for themselves. Later it holds up enough to allow them to rush out for a blow.

[Tuesday] 5th [November 1872] Flora spends great part of the day superintending the demolition of the terrace wall in front of the drawing-room windows. The others look on with mingled admiration & terror & only entreat her not to begin undermining the foundations of the house itself while the unsettled weather lasts. The 2 G's & C go for a walk & are relieved to find the house still standing when they return.

[Wednesday] 6th [November 1872] Another hurricane from the south west with torrents of rain in the morning. After lunch it clears up & Gertrude G & C go out for a little air & exercise. It blows in a continuous white squall but they struggle on to the Ferry, only being blown off the road once or twice. Coming back however it is much worse. C's hat is blown off but marvellous to say she retrieves it. G's net & bow are blown off & she carries her hat under her arm. Gertrude is blown about like a leaf & the others are in momentary expectation of seeing her whirled into the air. However by sitting down on the road or clinging to the trees in the worst squalls they all manage to get safely home, but declare unanimously that they will not go out again in a heavy gale.

[Thursday] 7th [November 1872] The day is spent in speculations about the post which does not arrive. They all feel much aggrieved at being deprived of their letters & determine to go to bed early so as to make the time till tomorrow morning, shorter, when they agree the letters *must* come. NB They do not exactly follow out their resolution as they do not go upstairs till 11.30.

[Friday] 8th [November 1872] The letters justify their faith & appear about breakfast time. In the afternoon Mrs Smith Gertrude G & C drive up to Ardtornish House to see how it has survived the storms. They find everything in good order & no trees blown down. G & C take a sad farewell of the house garden etc as the next time they see them will be from the deck of the Clansman, ah bitter thought, on their way south.

[Saturday] 9th [November 1872] The knitting & crochet fever still rages. Somebody is always being wound up in somebody else's wool & nothing is to be seen but shawls, Lady Janets & stockings of the most varied & brilliant colors. Gertrude C & G take a constitutional in the afternoon along the road above the Castle, to soothe their nerves after many hours incessant knitting.

[Sunday] 10th [November 1872] Heavy snow & sleat storms. Everybody makes up their mind for a day in the house but about 12 it clears up & after lunch Gertrude G & C rush out for a walk up the Turnate Road. The hills look lovely with their fresh coating of snow & the colors of the trees etc brighter than ever from the contrast.

[Monday] 11th [November 1872] G & C's last day at Ardtornish. They are too low to do anything in particular & in the afternoon Dr MacColl[1] comes over from Mull & deprives them of at least half an hour of Gertrude's dear society. However after his departure they have a delightful walk by the lake & see a most lovely sunset.

[Thursday] 12th [November 1872] The most perfect day & G & C feel more than ever that they are leaving Paradise. After lunch Gertrude drives with them to Ardtornish House where they look out for the hateful steamer. She appears about 3.30 going into Salen. The sun disappears in a perfect glory of orange light & the moon rises brighter & brighter & at last about 6 pm the black sea-serpent-like monster steams slowly to the mouth of Loch Aline. The fatal moment has arrived. G C, maid & boxes get into the boat (not the red boat) & are rowed away Gertrude faithful to the last watching them from the shore. As soon as they get on board their melancholy thoughts are much aggravated by finding the whole steamer crammed with steerage passengers, cows, sheep, horses etc. The upper deck is so covered with luggage that they cannot get from one side to the other & the last straw is added when they find that the deck cabins are both taken. They spend about an hour at Craignure taking in three boat loads of sheep. By the time they reach Oban, about 9 pm all hope of catching the early train from Greenock next morning is gone, so they console themselves with the prospect of seeing Mr Sellar. They meet two Arisaig men who with their daughters are going to Glasgow, & have a long talk about Arisaig matters. C delights them greatly by saying something in Gaelic; under their protection she remains on deck tempted by the glorious moon, hours after G has retired to their state cabin which they find nearly as comfortable as a deck cabin.

[Wednesday] 13th [November 1872] When they appear on deck the next day there is a most bitter wind blowing & everybody looks most miserable. On reaching Greenock about 10.30 am they discover the occupant of *their* deck cabin, a lady with 5 small children 2 nurses, 17 large packages & ten small. They watch her standing pencil & notebook in hand directing a porter whom she has captured to put the children, nurses & small parcels into one fly & then return for the 17 large packages! G.

---

[1] Dr Hector MacColl was called over from Tobermory as occasion demanded, there being no medical practitioner in Morvern.

over hears her at the last moment giving minute directions to nurse in case one of the children has the croup. On arriving at the station they see her standing triumphant with all her belongings around her. About 12 30 G & C start for Edinburgh leaving the maid to go straight to London by the night train. At E they find M*r* Sellar waiting for them who promptly carries them off to his mother's house where they are most warmly welcomed.[1] About three they have a heavy lunch 4.30 tea, 6.30 dinner! At this last meal they make the acquaintance of M*r* William Sellar[2] & his eldest daughter & also see Miss Clémandot their old governess whom they have not met for years. At 8 they start again M*rs* Sellar insisting on their taking innumerable packets of food. M*r* Sellar sees them safely into the train & makes such a fuss about them that the guard evidently looks upon them as royalties in disguise. They have the carriage to themselves & at Carlisle where the guards are changed the old one duly introduces the new one to them & most solemnly puts them under his care.

1873

Oban [Wednesday] 3*rd* [September 1873]...[The sisters (now calling themselves Flotsam and Jetsam, or F and J) arrive at Oban from Fort William, where] they find Friend-in-Law who carries them off to the Fenella[3] where are Gertrude 2 Miss Nicholsons, Miss & M*r* Bonham Carter & M*r* J Sellar.[4] They are so wet & dirty that they won't stay on board so G[5] accompanies them to the Alexandra Hotel, where they are dried & fed. The others come ashore later & after some trouble G sees her flock safely to their respective bedrooms. The gentlemen sleep on board.

[Thursday] 4*th* [September 1873] A most lovely morning. F & J behave in the most exemplary manner & do not move out of their room till their chaperone fetches them. Then they all descend demurely to the coffee room & have breakfast after which the Fenella's come on shore & carry them all off to the "Julia".[6] There F & J meet Adams their old

---

[1] This was Alexander Craig Sellar, their host, taking them to visit the widow of Patrick Sellar.

[2] William Young Sellar (1825–90), Patrick Sellar's third son, Professor of Humanity at Edinburgh University.

[3] The schooner *Fenella* was a yacht belonging to John A. Sellar, Patrick Sellar's fifth son.

[4] Gertrude Craig Sellar; May and Helen Nicholson, great-grand-daughters of William Smith, and sisters of Gertrude Astley's future husband, now aged 23 and 17; John Bonham Carter (1817–84, grandson of William Smith, married his first cousin Laura Nicholson) and his daughter Edith; and John A. Sellar, the owner of *Fenella*.

[5] Gertrude Craig Sellar, who acted as chaperone ("chap") to the five young ladies at the Argyllshire Gathering: she was herself only 29 years old.
Another sailing yacht (a yawl) belonging to J. Dennistoun, a relation of Mrs W. Y. Sellar.

Capt[n] who is in command of the J; he is delighted to see them & enquires tenderly after Frank.[1] Having duly admired the Julia & watched some of the boat races they go off to the Fenella have a light lunch & then row ashore again to see the games. These are held in a field with a rocky mound on one side & cornfields on the others. The "chap" [i.e. chaperone] & her 5 young ladies perch themselves on the slope like puffins as J says. It is a commanding situation & they see beautifully, but it has its disadvantages, the stones being very hard & insecure & the sun being very hot. The first performance is the competition for the prize for the best "piobaireachd" playing. The first quarter of an hour of this is not unpleasant but when it has lasted an hour & $\frac{1}{2}$ it becomes slightly monotonous & irritating. While this is going on with the players dressed with the utmost magnificence in full Highland costume others are putting the stone, throwing the caber etc. To do these properly the great thing seems to be to take off as many garments as possible & when they get to the races their costume is of the simplest no shoes or stockings, only a scanty kilt & a shirt. An Ardtornish man is the only one who succeeds in throwing the caber & before he can do it 2 pieces have to be cut off.[2] All this time the pio-b-dchs have been going on but at least even they come to an end, & then begins the sword dance. This is most interesting; there are only three competitors & two of them are most beautiful performers. By this time all the puffins on the rock are getting roasted so there is a general move onto the grass. The 2 "chaps"[3] are carried off to be photographed as members of the Club, & soon after they return there is a universal feeling in favour of a return home. When they get back the "Chap" asks for tea which at first they decline to get but finally consent to "throw it up" on the drawing room table. They then betake themselves to their rooms to rest & F & J watch anxiously for the arrival of the steamer containing Peppina & their ball dresses. Just as they are starting for an early dinner on board the "Fenella" the steamer comes in & they have the satisfaction of seeing Peppina approaching with luggage driven triumphantly before her. The "Chap's" maid had arrived in the morning & on asking for M[rs] Sellar had been told, "M[rs] Sellar? oh yes she's here but I don' know where she is; there are 6 of them all young & scattered about the house some where"! They have a very cheery dinner & friend-in-law is seized upon by the 5 young ladies & engaged by them all for many dances. Afterwards J and Miss B C row most of them about the harbour while the 2 "chaps" & F

---

[1] The sisters had cruised in *Julia* earlier in the year; Frank was their young brother Francis Dukinfield Astley, d. 1880.

[2] J. Beaton came first at tossing the caber (*Oban Times*, 6 Sept. 1873); he was a Morvern man, but not an inhabitant or an employee of Ardtornish Estate.

[3] It is clear from later references that the second "chap" was Gertrude's husband, Alexander Craig Sellar.

moralise on deck. It is a beautiful evening & the band on Mr Stevensons yacht the Northumbria[1] discourses sweet music, occasionally assisted by the bag pipes & another band on shore. As they row on shore to dress the fireworks begin; they are not very remarkable but the blue & green lights on the Northumbria are fine. About 10.15 the supreme Chap collects her 5 young ladies & marshalls them down stairs where they find the gentlemen waiting for them They walk off in procession to the ball which is only about 100 yds from the hotel in a large tent sent down specially for the purpose from Glasgow. They are rather horrified at the first sight of the room which is filled with a thick fog, so thick that they can't see from one end to the other. However it does not interfere much with the dancing though they are all turned out once into the supper room while the other is swept! Every body gets lots of dancing & there are some delicious reels which J & F enjoy immensely. The Malcolms of Poltalloch are there M^r & Mrs Robertson of Kin Loch Moidart, Sir T & Lady Riddle, Miss Wingfield etc.[2] About 2 the supreme "Chap" begins to look stern & tries to collect her flock which is rather a difficult task but she succeeds after a time & they all trot home in the wildest spirits. Mr Rutson who arrived by the steamer from the South appeared at the ball, but was not in a state to enjoy dancing as he had a bad tooth ache & swelled face. However he did his duty manfully & danced with every body. There was an infirm old gentleman hobbling about with a stick who went up to big Malcolm & said Sir I believe you have great influence in these parts; will you kindly use that influence to have that rope removed (pointing to a coil of rope round one of the supports of the tent). One of my ancestors was hung & I cannot bear the sight of a rope"! Big Malcolm declined to use his influence so the old gentleman hobbled off to Loch Buy with his petition. Those delightful bag-pipes went on play[ing] reels long after F & J were in bed but even their sweet strains could not keep them awake long.

[Friday] 5th [September 1873] J had made virtuous resolutions of going to see Aunt Clara & Co on board the steamer which stops at Oban from Banavie at 8 am but she was not called till too late & had only the satisfaction of seeing the steamer steaming away Southwards. There is a general muddle of packing as the maids start early by the Northward steamer. About 10.30 J & F descend ravenous to the coffee room & order breakfast, the others dribbling down by degrees. M^r & Mrs Robertson are just starting in their old friend the Talisman & there is a general

---

[1] *Northumbria* was a steam yacht belonging to G. R. S. Stephenson of Glen Caladh.
[2] The names of these and other notabilities—but not those of the Ardtornish party—were printed in the *Oban Times* for 6 September. William Robertson of Kinlochmoidart, and Lady Riddell (wife of Sir Thomas Riddell, Bart., of Ardnamurchan and Sunart) reappear later in the diary.

air of going away. About one they all assemble to go on board the Fenella & as the 2 "chaps" insist on paying a morning call, the others go off without them, but relent sufficiently to send the boat back for them. And certainly a chap's weather eye is very necessary for a more uproarious set of "chapees" was never seen. At last 2 of the worst J & Miss B C climb into the boat which is in the Davits & there they are comparatively out of mischief. It is dead calm & an offer of a tow from Mr Guthrie's steamer[1] is thankfully accepted. Outside there is a nice breeze which freshens to a good wind. They have to beat all the way but there is very little motion & even friend-in-law & F enjoy it. Lunch is eaten under great difficulties as the outsiders keep continually slipping to the other side of the cabin; these little interruptions do not materially damp their spirits & seem rather to increase their appetites. Coming on deck after lunch all hands are called to the wraps etc which are flying about in all directions. Every body is carefully wrapped up & made comfortable by the devoted Commander & friend-in-law & music of the spheres is heard issuing from a moving mass of wraps. Chorusses are added to every song & the effect is altogether bewitching. They anchor in Loch Aline about 5.30 & after refreshing themselves with tea they land and go off in opposite directions, the 2 Miss Nicholsons & Mr J B C going to the Tower & the others to Ardtornish House. So ends the Chaps 2nd Oban ball & J and F's 1st.

[Saturday] 6th [September 1873] The morning is passed pleasantly in declining Ego Mihi in a new & improved manner. Ego My H'eye chap's eye wink eye, weather eye. J also received a new name from Miss B C namely Popjoy, & she returns the compliment by calling her Loathèd Melancholy as being suited to her general character. In the afternoon they drive up to the Tower where they find all pretty well. They walk & drive towards Corrospin & the Chap inveigles them down a steep bank to look at a waterfall, which is very pretty but has extraordinary attractions for midges. They dine at the Tower where they meet the delightful Dr Hamilton[2] & are conducted safely back by Reconstruction and [   ] to Ardtornish.

[Sunday] 7th [September 1873] F & J break the Sabbath by playing croquet with Mr J Sellar & Mr Rutson. After a fierce struggle F & Mr S are victorious. After lunch they walk down to the Ferry where they meet the Nicholsons, Mr J B C & the Admiral. Friend-in-law having utterly disgraced himself by refusing to drive Baby in the pony carriage goes to a School board meeting; the others man or rather woman the gig & row up the Loch to the boat house. There after complicated changes

---

[1] The Guthries of Duart had a small steam yacht called *Lussa*.
[2] Edward Hamilton, a regular sporting guest at Ardtornish from 1866 to 1879.

M[rs] Smith & Flora get into the gig & another boat is started whose crew consist of Miss H Nicholson & the Admiral aged about [ ] M[r] Nicholson[1] steering. After a perilous voyage up the river the gig rows down to & races the other boat back pausing on the way to punish Friend-in-law who is sitting comfortably on a rock reckless of his heartless behaviour. Having splashed him well they row to the boat house & get in just as the other boat arrives panting & blistered. NB. Miss H N had *never* rowed before & yet she only caught one crab. After tea at the Tower they row to the Ferry & walk home. The weather is lovely.

[Monday] 8th [September 1873] A splendid sailing day & accordingly about one the 2 Miss Nicholsons & M[r] J B C appear from the Tower & they all go on board the Fenella & beat up the Sound. Their lives are for a short time entrusted to Loathed Melancholy who takes the helm but fortunately lunch soon calls her below. This meal is if possible more uproarious & more sumptuous than any previous one. Utterly exhausted by laughing they at last reappear on deck & find themselves in Loch Sunart. A council is held & they decide on getting into the gig & rowing into Loch Teagus. Unluckily it begins to rain but the view nevertheless is lovely. There is a tremendous tide running & the row back is very hard. The wind has all this time been getting beautifully less & by the time they get into the Sound again it has almost disappeared. Under these afflicting circumstances it is absolutely necessary to keep up their spirits by having tea with ideas of cake vague notions of jam etc. Thus fortified they are enabled to give their minds to the understanding of M[r] Sellar's celebrated card trick. After repeated performances Popjoy gets a glimmering of how it is done & finally M[r] Rutson works it out laboriously & logically. Meanwhile they are floating peacefully on, the Chaps retire below & are soon wrapped in soft slumber oblivious of their duties. The "Chappees" wrapped in every conceivable rug sing songs & having exhausted even their extensive repertoire, are reduced to drawing on their imaginations both for tunes & words. The effect is charming. Finally they glide smoothly & quietly into Loch Aline, the Chaps are roused, the boats brought alongside & about 10 pm the whole party is safely landed. The Tower party drive up & the others walk to Ardtornish & sit down to dinner at the fashionable hour of 10.45.

[Tuesday] 9th [September 1873] As F & J are leisurely dressing about 9.15, awful rumours are heard that the steamer which is to take them to Arisaig is in sight! The rumours are too true; she has never been known to arrive before 12 but today she chooses to appear at this hour. The Supreme Chap & every maid in the house rush frantically in to help

---

[1] William Smith Nicholson, father of May and Helen, and afterwards Gertrude Astley's father-in-law.

pack. F with one comprehensive sweep puts bracelets cuffs & neck ties into her bag, fastens her last petticoat drinks a cup of milk & jumps into the dog cart. J & Peppina follow, a miscellaneous heap of things is thrown in & Friend-in-law who has been waiting with the patience of an angel drives them down to the Ferry. There Mr Sellar & Mr Rutson are waiting & having said farewell to the "most beautiful thing in Creation" they row into the bay & wait for the Steamer. She looks dirtier than usual; however they get safely on board & Lady Rich safely into the boat & off they go. It soon begins to rain steadily, no shelter is to be had on deck so they remain in the cabin till driven away by the appearance of dinner. Fortunately there is a strong wind blowing off shore so Ardnamurchan is passed in comfort & soon after the friendly Scur of Eig comes in sight. It kindly leaves off raining while they land; at the Rhue point they find the Camerons dog cart & after about two hours drive along the well known road they reach Inverailort & are warmly welcomed by M^r & Mrs Cameron & Miss Gillespie. ...

[Entries for 10–22 September 1873 omitted]

[Roshven, Moidart] 23rd [September 1873] "TUESDAY". Breakfast punctually at "Cuckoo 9". Weather such as to cause, astonishment, & admiration, verging on awe. F & J depart at 10 with Mrs Blackburn in the Roshven gig waving a sad farewell to Lady & Roshven generally. The breeze is light, the crew good & the boat is soon off Sammelleman, a fascinating spot which they hear is to be let, & which possesses in F's eyes at least, 2 irresistible attractions Inaccessibility & a view of Rum Skye & Eigg. They round Smirsiri & say good bye to the much loved 'Scur', as they row up the narrow arm of L. Moidart & land on Chona Island. A walk of less than a mile brings them to the other side where they meet Captn Swinburne[1] & resist his hospitable invitations to his house but borrow a boat which conveys them across the other arm of L. Moidart to Castle Tirim near which Mr Robertson[2] is seen picturesquely seated on a rock with his black retriever Chloe. They all land and accompany him to the place where he has left his dog cart which he most kindly intends to employ in conveying F & J. to Salen. They have to pass in front of Dorlin & see Lord Howard's[3] immense lifeboat just putting off apparently crammed with people. It proves to be going over to Roshven so Mrs Blackburn goes on board & hands over F & J with well founded confidence to the care of the kind & attentive Mr R. with whom they have a delightful drive of 6 miles through new & enchanting scenery. F & J were amused by M^r R's account of an old Highlander who had suggested to him to row across to Drimind'arach, shoot a couple

[1] Captain T. A. Swinburne R.N., of Pontop Hall, Co. Durham, and Eilean Shona.
[2] William Robertson of Kinlochmoidart.
[3] Lord Howard of Glossop.

of deer or so & bring them away by night, remarking quite truly that nobody need know anything about it.[1] At Salen M^r R put F & J into a boat which they had ordered beforehand, insisting upon their taking two of his rugs & a basket containing delicious pears cake & gingerbreads, which excellent as they proved, could not reconcile F & J to the loss of his company.—They saw him go off in a heavily laden boat of the Talisman, which anchored in the bay just as they were rowed off by the two boatmen whose portraits appear farther on.—(J. half melted with heat, looked with astonishment at the one who pulled stroke, wearing two waistcoats and an enormous woolen comforter.)—The sight of the Talisman suggests the contrast between this return to Ardtornish & F & Js arrival last year. The stormy sunset at Tobermory,—the cold gale blowing down the Sound of Mull, the taciturn boatmen who seemed to wish to take leave of their families before starting. How different from the present scene of tranquil beauty! But extremes meet, & in this instance the point of contact is *"gingerbreads"*! ("Sich is life". Moral reflections ad lib: by J.)—About an hour's row,—during which they watch a small Steamer coming down near the opposite shore of Loch Sunart—brings them to the mouth of L. Teachus where they are able to hoist a sail. F & J had employed their time in consuming an amazing quantity of pears cake & gingerbreads nuts—more moral reflections quite thrown away upon F.) They had to 'pause in Life's pleasures & count its many tears' ie look for one of Fs diamonds which she finds has disappeared out of her ring, alas! it was seen no more. Unsuccessful attempt at moral reflec:[s] by F. ...Arrived at the Head of L. Teachus, they fall in again with the little Steamer whose vagaries arrest their attention. After turning about in a curious & uncertain way it comes straight towards their boat which had reached the shore. It seemed to be crowded with people who waved & shouted to such an extent that F & J felt constrained to wave in return though who they were they knew no more than the man in the moon.—'Could it be Mr Guthries Yacht or a party from Arisaig'—What could they know of F & J?)—Presently a voice from the Steamer—'Do you know who we are?' Their reply shouted at the top of their voice elicited a peal of laughter, & a cry of Lady Riddell—also the information that Miss Lascelles was on board.[2] NB. It is very difficult to be polite at the top of one's voice, & it is to be feared that J's 'love' fell into L. Teachus halfway between the 2 boats. Presently a majestic figure appeared at the prow of the Steamer, announcing itself as Miss Lascelles last seen by F & J at the Chatsworth Ball but

[1] Druimindarroch is just beside Arisaig House, and the point of the joke is that it was the property of the Astley family.

[2] It must have been the Riddells' yacht. Miss Lascelles is unidentified; there are several possibilities.

fondly associated by them with Poltallach. They stand at the stern of their boat to get as near as possible & a conversation ensues consisting of kind enquiries & hospitable offers on the part of Lady Riddell which are declined by F & J who announce themselves quite capable of walking 6 or 8 miles in the next 3 hours, a statement which the good people on the Yacht seemed very much to doubt. After waving an affectionate farewell, they take the road followed by the Boatmen leaving their bag & jackets which they deposit at a cottage. F & J arrive at Ardtornish Tower after a delightful walk of 2 hours. On the way they meet a note which tells them that they are to sleep at the Tower & not go on to Gertrude's & F-in-Law. They find Col Nicholson Mr Rose & Mr Harry Rose at the Tower, & receive a pile of letters.[1]

Ardtornish [Wednesday] Sept^m 24th [1873] Another lovely day. F & J walk over to Ardtornish House before lunch & find the "Chap" only pretty well. They spend the afternoon with her & walk back over the hill, differing decidedly as to the right way. Each takes her own path & eventually arrive just at the same time.

[Thursday] 25 [September 1873] F walked & drove to Ardtornish House in alternate bits with Mrs Smith & Mr Willy.[2] Friend-in-law walked back one of the bits with her Much talk about the advisability of taking Sammelemon.[3]

[Friday] 26th [September 1873] J went to stay a few days at Ardtornish House to help entertain M^r and Mrs Edward Lushington[4] who arrived by the steamer from Oban. Mrs Smith & F accompanied her & gave her over to the Chap.

[Saturday] 27th [September 1873] M^r & M^{rs} E L & Friend-in-Law come to lunch. Afterwards F Mr Rose & M^r L walk to Arianus. It begins to pour & M^r L finds the pace rather too much for him so coming back he is picked up by the carriage & Mr Rose & F return the way they came. Col Nicholson was more amusing than ever & F & he have a grand fight on the subject of "Women's Rights".

[Sunday] 28th [September 1873] Gloriously fine. Flora & F lunched at Ardtornish House; everybody pretty well. In the afternoon Col Nicholson, Mr Rose & M^r H Rose drive up in the Car. Flora returns early but F

---

[1] Lothian Nicholson (1837–93), brother of William Smith Nicholson, died a full General, KCB and Governor of Gibraltar; the Roses are unidentified.

[2] William Smith (*c.* 1828–99), Octavius Smith's youngest son.

[3] Samalaman House in north-west Moidart; see above, p. 202.

[4] Probably a mistake for the Edmund Lushingtons; Lushington (1811–93), a brother-in-law of Lord Tennyson, was Professor of Greek at Glasgow University and a life-long friend of the William Sellars. There was an Edward Lushington (son of C. M. Lushington) but he did not marry until 1877.

only allows herself just time to walk over the hill before dressing time. Mʳ Rose returns with her & J & Mʳ L accompany them part of the way. F & J start their usual pace, the 2 gentlemen following. The path is rather boggy & gradually the distance between them gets greater & greater. At last when they are almost out of sight a faint entreaty to stop is borne on the wind, so they sit on a stone & wait till Mʳ Rose catches them up, Mʳ L being visible in the distance. J returns & Escorts him home while F & Mʳ R make their way to the Tower arriving just in time to dress.

[Monday] 29ᵗʰ [September 1873] Col Nicholson departs this morning amidst general lamentations; Mʳ Rose declares the sunshine of the house has gone. To console him Flora takes him to the waterfall on the way to Corrospin & makes him cut down trees while she & F stand on the bank & direct. Having made a great hole through the wood they return & find the 2 "Chaps" & Mʳ & Mʳˢ Lushington at home they having come to stay. J is walking over across the hill, but Mʳ L did not offer to accompany her today.

[Tuesday] 30ᵗʰ [September 1873] Mʳ & Mʳˢ Lushington start this morning just as it begins to rain. It continues more or less the whole [day] & Flora is the only person energetic enough to go out. The others play pyramids one game at which last[s] the whole afternoon. Flora & F play billiards afterwards & F is quite surprised how much the darkness improves her play.

[Wednesday] Octᵇᵉʳ 1ˢᵗ [1873] Trice's birthday.[1] Rather wetter than yesterday. Friend-in-law goes out stalking but returns wet & miserable about 4 with no results. The Chap Mʳˢ Smith & F inspect the new cottages[2] & puddle about a little J takes a constitutional up the Tirnate Road.

[Thursday] 2ⁿᵈ [October 1873] Rain again. As J says it begins every morning with such an air or originality that it quite takes one in & one begins to think that it has never done such a thing before. It clears a little in the afternoon & Flora & F go round by Claggan discoursing of trees. There they see Mʳ H Rose who has just caught his first salmon 7 lbs.[3]

[Friday] 3ʳᵈ [October 1873] Rain again, but about 4 it cleared up beautifully & the colors in the hills were too heavenly. The lake was dead calm & the reflections in it perfect. After lunch the Chap read to them about the Ashantee Exhibition & the *pinnacles* on board

---

[1] The fifteenth birthday of their sister Beatrice Astley, who had remained at home.
[2] Almost certainly Castle cottage, a double house.
[3] The Game book says that this fish was caught on 1 October.

the men-of-war & the Chappees declared it must have been the result of the toast & water.[1] Friend-in-law started about 4 with a rod & George to go & fish. J started a few minutes later & pursued him coming in sight of the 2 shortly before they reached Dalglish's cottage.[2] She soon saw by their behaviour that something exciting had occurred. F-in-law's face said before the words were out of his mouth "A Stag". They crossed the bridge & getting into the field on the other side of the river took a rest against a hay cock to look at him. But the "cannie beast" suspected something & only just gave J time to see that he was a splendid creature with a very large & beautiful 6 pt head as he stood in front of a rock in the wood above the cottage & then bounded away.—F-in-law was much disappointed at the stag's taking fright & tried in vain to bring his mind back to fishing. He asked George when they got to Claggan whether they would be likely to see deer from a hill near the road. George was strongly of opinion that they would so off they started & were rewarded by a goodly sight, nothing less than their friend the 6 pt[er] trotting majestically along the side of the opposite hill rejoicing in his strength. Suddenly a deep & awful sound is heard proceeding from the flat sort of Strath which stretches between them & the stag. It sends a thrill of excitement through them & the 6 pt[er] suddenly pauses & listens. They creep a little further forward & behold the Big Stag!—Far be it from this pen to describe the Monarch of the Morvern Hills. [*The last sentence is apparently an addition; it seems likely that the following passage, written on an odd quarter-sheet and tipped in (back to front) a dozen pages earlier, was originally intended to end this entry.*] F-in-law & J gasp & murmur ecstatically "What horns! What music!"[3] For a full hour & ½ they lie on the hill enjoying the exciting spectacle of this despot surrounded by his wives challenging all comers, chasing the foolhardy youngsters who ventured to come between the wind & his nobility. The 6 pt[er] great as he was & F-in-law thought him almost as big as *the* Stag, dared not approach him. One little one in particular was retreating as fast as he could when the big one taking round the other side of knoll almost cut him off & a regular chase ensued, the fugitive making at first straight for F-in-law & J who were breathless with excitement. He however turned off up a steep hill closely followed by the big one who after one emphatic roar was reduced by want of breath to abuse his enemy in such terms as are expressed in stag language by grunts. He wisely contented himself with this assertion of his superiority & proceeded to devote his attention to carrying off 2 hinds who were

---

[1] Jokes lost beyond recall.
[2] George Dalgleish the under-keeper, then aged 18, lived with his widowed mother at Craigendarroch.
[3] The manuscript appears to read '"What na horns! What na music!"'.

protected by several small stags. This he achieved in a masterly manner with the aid of much dignified eloquence.—Both space & power are wanting to tell how later, from the corries of Meal Damh came the distant answer to the challenge of the mighty one.—Twilight was rapidly turning to darkness when Friend-in-law & Jetsam arose—stiff— somewhat damp about the knees & elbows, but edified & exultant!— F-in-law remarked to Jetsam when he bade her good night in the evening "We feel that today we have not lived in vain."

Oct^{ber} 4 Saturday [1873] A heaven descended day. After all the rain the air is as clear as possible & the sun is so hot that friend-in-law declares it is too hot to walk to Ardtornish. After rather an unsatisfactory post F & J start off with Flora who becomes so engrossed in Goldoni's plays that she very nearly allows Tiny to get off the road at a place where there is a deep ditch. Just before the short cut she stops & F & J having eaten a great many blackberries & nuts they part, Flora returning to the Tower & F & J going on to the house. J presents a somewhat peculiar appearance with 4 or 5 pockets full of nuts, a paint box slung over her shoulder, 3 or 4 books stuck about her promiscuously & a cloak gracefully hanging over one shoulder. In the afternoon they encamp on the gravel outside the house & spend a very happy 2 hours doing absolutely nothing but watch the gambols of Baby Crusty & the Cats. Then F-in-law & F walk down to the Castle & inspect the mason's work[1] & then walk along the path to the kitchen garden & round the other way home.

5th [October 1873] Sunday. Stormy. Every body rather low. What Friend-in-law calls a suicidal letter from Mr Willy Smith saying he has wounded the big six pointer, *their* 6 pointer. F-in-law & J can talk of nothing else & nearly mingle their tears together. Flora appears just before lunch looking blooming & the others come in the afternoon. Between the showers they get a little airing & Baby drives Tiny about at full trot. In the evening the Chapees hear instructive stories of the Chaps early days & then they sing hymns. They go to bed with the full purpose of getting up early & rowing to Guerilas.[2]

[Monday]6th [October 1873] Rain & wind. Gillyan & Johnson[3] are of the opinion that it will clear but by the time breakfast is over it is pouring hard & looks about as bad as a day can. As nothing remarkable happened today except that it rained & blew harder every hour a story about Johnson (the Gardener) may here be put in. On being asked to what

[1] The earliest record of any restoration of Ardtornish Castle; the spurious window was not added for another forty years (see above, p. 167).
[2] Garbh Shlios.
[3] Gillean MacLean (see p. 190 n. 1 above); and Thomas Johnstone, gardener at Ardtornish House from November 1872 until May 1878.

family a certain flower belonged he said "Well I'm thinking it belongs
to the Deranged species"! He is supposed to have meant Hydrangia.—
Baby & the kittens are great fun all the afternoon. He seems to consider
their tails in the light of reins & uses them as he did Tiny's yesterday, the
kittens submitting placidly. The waterfalls on the cliffs are splendid & the
Bay looks very fine when F & J rush out for a blow late in the afternoon.

Tuesday Oct^ber 7 [1873] To-day is rather disjointed; there are so many
steamers "furraging about" as Johnson says, for one thing; the heavy
post comes in, with none of the letters F & J want, for another, Mr Shaw
Smith[1] arrives by one steamer & Mr Willy Smith goes away by another &
there are various great excitements. J is greatly interested by a black
object which is discovered in the Sound about 3 miles off; it is not a rock,
it is not a steamer—what can it be? All the telescopes are turned on it,
J rushes up the hill to see it better; at last somebody suggests it is a gang
way floated off by the extraordinary high tide of last evening & with this
solution they are obliged to be content tho' J declares it is much more
like a four post bed! [*Original footnote:* It was afterwards proved to have
been a pier.] All the Tower party came to lunch & after many false
alarms the steamer is seen going into Salen & M^r W Smith accompanied
by most of the family goes down to the Ferry, gets into the boat & rows
off to the steamer & everybody goes home by various ways.

8th [October 1873] Wednesday. Friend-in-law announces at breakfast
his intention of attacking the trees near the big waterfall so that it may
be better seen from the garden. Accordingly about 12 they all start
armed with the small axe & rifle It is a beautiful day quite hot in the sun
& the Chap F & J spend some time on a mossy bank eating nuts which
abound in such quantities that J wonders how any children ever survive
such a year. The walking up to the waterfall is by no means pleasant or
easy as it combines the difficulties of wood bog & hill However they get
up and find F-in-law with signs of many falls on his clothes hard at work.
After making what seems to them a great clearance F-in-law & F return
home to lunch leaving Gillyan who has joined them with many implements & J who scorns lunch hard at work. On looking from the garden for
their hole not a sign is visible & the melancholy conviction forces itself
on them that their labour has been all thrown away. It is rather difficult
to screw up their energies to going back to work after lunch but after
a little mutual encouragement they start taking a little food for the
ascetic J. They find a perfect forest cut down & having made more havoc
F in law & J go up to the upper fall to do the same there. F returns home
& about 6.30 the other 2 make their appearance J looking as if she had
just returned from a free fight at an election.

[1] W. Shore Smith again.

9th [October 1873] Thursday. The whole party were to go over to the Tower today but the weather looks very unpromising in the morning & only improves for the worse. Nobody stirs out till evening when the storm having lulled a little, those two foolish young people, F-in-law & J go out & play croquet! F takes a constitutional round the premises. The lull is soon over & the wind which had been blowing a gale from the S.E. now comes from exactly the opposite quarter & brings back all the rain it had so carefully taken with it. F-in-law & J overcome by their exertion at croquet sleep most of the evening so does the Chap & F is only awake enough to be dreadfully puzzled over a sum.

10th [October 1873] Friday. Today looks much like yesterday but it does clear up a little about [   ] though still blowing a gale F-in-law & J have another very close & exciting game at croquet. Mrs Smith drives up early greatly to every body's astonishment; she was nearly blown [away] carriage & all coming up the hill. After lunch she G & F in law drive back & F & J walk. The wind is tremendous. Just as it is getting dark Mr Shore Smith comes in with the dismal intelligence that he has wounded a stag! Oh horrors![1]

Octber 11th [1873] Saturday. A fearfully stormy night & early morning but friend-in-law nothing daunted starts about 8 determined to do or die. The rain comes down in sheets & the wind blows & every body is full of commiseration for him. The post brings a letter from Miss Courtenay which decides F & J to start South next Friday with F-in-law by the swift boat. In the afternoon they all sally forth Flora in her carriage, F & J with implements to wage war against the trees. They have a splendid opportunity of testing the waterproof qualities of their garments as one of the very heaviest showers comes on soon after leaving the house. They do a great deal of execution among the trees in the plantation at Claggan & return so wet that they have to [go] & dress immediately. On coming into the drawing room an air of depression and melancholy is on every face and a dismal silence reigns only broken by the words "The big Stag—missed"!!!!!! After that even the announcement that Peppina makes that she is going to be married can only make the gloom a little deeper.

[Sunday] 12th [October 1873] The "chap" devotes the whole morning to making out F & J's journey for them. Three ways are at last found & after much discussion they are persuaded to take what is declared by every body to be the most reasonable but is certainly the longest. Smoke

---

[1] This is presumably the 16-stone switch-horn shot by Shore Smith on Tearnait near the Glensanda march (Game book, 10 October), but not found until 15 October (see below).

pervades the house & they wander about from room to room trying which is the pleasantest wood or coal smoke. In the afternoon they all go for a Sunday walk.

13ᵗʰ [October 1873] Monday. Some talk of going to Tiernet this morning but Flora's carriage is broken so they have to give it up. It rains with great steadiness in the afternoon but the "Chap" F J & Mʳ Rose go out for their usual wetting. For the stalkers adventures see poem [*lost*].

14ᵗʰ [October 1873] Tuesday. Showery. Much hesitation about Tiernet but at last it is decided that F & J shall sleep tonight at the Tower instead of going up to the other house with the "Chap" & F-in-law. The great Mʳ Brown pays them a visit in the Mountaineer[1] & as he is going back to Oban Mʳ Rose & Harry go with him instead of waiting for the Clansman. In the afternoon Flora & J go towards Achahn to see the trees & on the way they meet a cart with a stag in it being brought home. It was wounded the day before.—Murder will out.[2]—J rides Bluebell up to Ardtornish in the evening to relieve F in law's mind & dines & sleeps there. [*The following addition by Conny is on a separate sheet.*]

Jetsam was warmly welcomed by the 2 "Chaps" on her arrival at Ardtornish, & was rewarded by a detailed account of F in-laws stalking adventures & mis adventures, by which she is confirmed in her opinion about stalking too late in the season. The 2 Chaps first insist on her stopping to dine & then to sleep Gertrude supplying the necessaries or rather luxuries of the toilet. On retiring to rest J. perceived a garment the like of which she had never before beheld.—Delicately soft & warm to the touch,—in colour of a delicious creamy white.—trimmed with ancient & costly lace on a blue ground! And then the buttons—smooth round—mother of pearl—inviting the eye to dwell upon them in a dreamy repose, & soothing it like moonlight on a sleeping sea.—

The loose & flowing folds of the exquisite work of Art were confined round the waist by a girdle which developed at the back into an elaborate and Artistic Sash! Such was the garment provided for a *Jetsam* to wrap herself in!! It was some time before she could persuade herself that this was not the Chap's wedding dress which Sarah by mistake had laid over the back of the chair, and as to the idea of doing one's hair in it—perish the thought! as soon think of blacking a grate in a coronation robe!

At 8.30 next morning Bluebell was brought to the door & taking an affecting farewell of the "Chap" J. rode up to the Tower arriving just in time for Breakfast. Never did Ardtornish better deserve J R's emphatic name of "that Heaven" than on this lovely morning. L. Aline may truly be said to have *given itself up* to reproducing the glory of the

---

[1] Mr Brown is unidentified.

[2] A 16-stone six-pointer shot on Uileann by Alex Sellar on 13 October (Game book).

hills & woods, seeming with a wonderful & subtle appreciation to give back each delicate shade of beauty, from the faintest mist of blue smoke to the hues of a bit of rainbow nestling in the hollow of a hill Whence came this bit of rainbow in a clear & cloudless atmosphere? This might be a problem in England. Perhaps as the Philosophers say it had only a '*subjective existence*'—but J inclined to the opinion that it was 'taking a holiday', as she afterwards saw what she took to be its "chap" stretching with brazen audacity across the cloudless blue sky!

Oct^ber 15 [1873] Wednesday. J arrives on Bluebell just as it strikes 9.30. It is a most beautiful morning & again Tiernit is talked of but Flora has not had a good night & there is a little shower just as they are thinking of starting so it is finally given up. The dismal preparations for departure are completed, Mrs Smith & Flora are just starting to drive up to Ardtornish & F & J to walk when they are electrified by the announcement "He has got him"! How are the mighty fallen! The big stag will roar defiance no more from the Morvern hills. Mr Shore Smith killed him just where F-in-law & J had seen him.[1] As soon as F-in-law hears of it he rushes down to the Tower to see him. He has 11 pts & weighs 16st. 12^lbs —he *ought* to have weighed 20st. Mr S. Smith's wounded stag has been found & Mr Willie's is reported to be frisking about as well as ever.[2] The Chap F & J spend a quiet evening & F in-law returns after dinner with the stag fever strong upon him.

16th [October 1873] Thursday. The last day! Alack & well a day. F & J drive up to the Tower to pay a farewell visit & M^r S Smith comes up to the House to talk more stags with F-in-law.

[Friday] 17th [October 1873] At 5 am inexorable fate in the shape of Peppina & the housemaid rouse F & she wakes with a start to the consciousness that the fatal moment has come. After dressing & breakfasting by candlelight they take a sad farewell of the Chap & start in the grey light for the ferry. Reconstruction is all too swift today; in one moment it seems they are in the boat & out in the Sound waiting for the steamer. It is a lovely morning the mist gradually floating away from the hills, Loch Aline without a ripple & color stealing into everything. Just as they pass the house in the steamer the sun strikes upon [it] & they pass by into the mist leaving it bathed in light & the "Chap" waving from the window. At Craignuir Miss McKenzie (daughter of the "real law lord")[3] comes on board full of a stag weighing 20st she declares, which her sister

---

[1] I.e. in the plantation above Craigendarroch.

[2] Willie Smith's poor marksmanship was a family joke. The stalking journal records six misses at stags on one day in 1883, with Alex Sellar's pencilled annotation "Oh Willie!".

[3] See above, p. 191.

is taking round the Mull whole; at Duart, Mʳ Guthrie & Sir Nevil Chamberlain[1] row out with a stranger who is carefully put on board. At Oban a whole room full of stags horns rivet Friend-in-Law's & J's attention and they gaze fondly at them thro' opera glasses. Just as they are leaving Oban, a lady comes up to J & says, How do you do; I think we met at Duart. J smiles blandly without the vaguest notion who she is & after a little conversation they discover the lady mistakes them for the Nicholsons who had been to Duart in the yacht. After some puzzling they decide she must be a Miss Chamberlain; she is very pleasant as is also the stranger who turns out to be a Mʳ Fane. F & J's sympathies are much excited by a small pup Sky by name the plaything of at least 6 children. The sufferings of Baby's "Poosies" are as nothing compared to his for they were 2 to 1 and he is one among 6. How he survives the journey is a mystery. After the Crinan F-in-law F & J spend most of their time eating grapes & pears & sadly gazing at the villas on the shores of the Clyde, the like of which F-in-Law declares will soon be seen on the shores of Morvern.[2] They arrive at Greenock without any adventures, in time to catch the 5.40 train to Edinburgh. This ought to get in at 8 but does not arrive till 9.15, more resembling Reconstruction as to pace & power of standing still many hours without moving a muscle, than an express train. At last they get in, F-in-law puts them into a cab & they drive off to the Clarendon very tired & rather cross.

[1] Sir Nevile Chamberlain (1820–1902) was A. C. Guthrie's brother-in-law, and a friend of the William Sellars.

[2] A prediction which happily remained unfulfilled.

II. EXTRACTS FROM WRITINGS OF
JOHN MACDONALD, 1882, 1883

[None of the letters and statements from which the following extracts are taken were explicitly signed by MacDonald; but his authorship of the statements to the Napier Commission is established by *Napier Commission evidence* (1884), III, 2301–6; while identity of phrasing and other internal evidence makes it virtually certain that he was also the author of the two earlier letters, which were in any case signed "J.M.D." and "MacDhomhnuill" respectively. See also pp. 94–6 above.]

(1) Extract from a letter headed 'The truth about Skye' published in the *North British Daily Mail* on 2 May 1882 and in the *Oban Times* on 6 May 1882.[1]

...Another charge which is being brought against Highland crofters is that they do not make the most of their buildings; that they do not improve the land nor attempt to build comfortable dwellings for themselves. Is this the fault of the crofters themselves or of the system of tenure on which they hold their lands? But notwithstanding that they are tenants from year to year crofters in many places do improve their holdings, and the factors and landlords are not slow to take advantage accordingly where such improvements are made by raising the rent, which if they refuse to pay they are very soon improved off the land altogether to make room for some one else. To show how this is done let me mention a case in point which came under my own observation not many years ago. On the estate of Drimnin, in the parish of Morven, then owned by the widow of the late Sir Charles Gordon, some crofters were removed from their holdings to make room for a large sheep farm, the sheep mania being then at its height.[2] This farm the factor or estate manager took into his own hands, and, as a matter of course, his first proceeding was to get the crofters out of his way, consequently the people were warned out. Some of them removed to the small town of Tobermory, some came to Glasgow, but three or four of them, rather than leave the place altogether, accepted an offer given them by the factor to remove to an island of some extent on the Loch Sunart side of the estate.[3] This island

---

[1] Text from the *North British Daily Mail*; the text in the *Oban Times* varies only in minor detail.

[2] See above, pp. 94–5, for a summary of the Drimnin evictions. MacDonald's dates are contradictory, but it seems most likely that the removal of a few families from Auliston and Carraig to Oronsay took place in about 1843, *before* the death of Sir Charles Gordon; and that some of the same people were evicted from Oronsay after a stay of twenty-five years, in about 1868. Two facts which do not emerge from MacDonald's accounts are that Oronsay was inhabited before the Auliston people went there (it appears to have been inhabited by 1801, and it had a population of 42 in 1841), and that the main eviction from Auliston did not take place until 1855.

[3] Oronsay.

consisted of little else than rocks and heather, with stretches of unreclaimed moss. Here the poor people took up their abode, and with years of hard and unremitting toil made this barren spot a fairly productive farm. The consequence of this was that the rent was raised on them twice in twenty years. At last when the families grew up, and they came to be fairly prosperous by their industry in fishing and by every other available means, they bethought them of building better houses. This they did at a cost of from £50 to £60, never for a moment imagining that they would be required to remove, as they always paid their rents punctually. But they little knew what was in store for them. The neighbouring sheep farmer wanted their land, the fruit of years of hard toil, to add to his already extensive run.[1] He knew well it would not be a very easy task to get it, as the people were paying a pretty high rent and were in no arrears. He also knew they were in favour with the proprietrix as being her oldest tenants, and unless some very plausible excuse could be trumped up he could not gain what he set his heart on. This he set about in a way which, for its diabolic malignity and cruelty, could not be surpassed. He pretended to be missing large numbers of his sheep, and insinuated that as his neighbours were prosperous of late years they must have something to do with it. (The people's prosperity, it being well known, was from a different cause, their own industry.) This statement was never made in such a way that the people could lay any hold of it, or in a manner in which they could put him to the proof and so clear themselves. The result was that the proprietrix's mind was poisoned by these insinuations conveyed in an indirect manner, and probably also by the fear of losing a tenant who held the best farm on her estate. As the tenant's lease was out, the only condition on which he would retake his farm was that the small farmers were to be removed from the neighbourhood; and they were removed from the place which, by their industry, they reclaimed from being a barren wilderness to a comparatively fertile farm, without compensation being given for improving the land, or for the houses they built about two years previously.[2] All the

[1] The identity of this sheep farmer is not known; he may have been John MacPhail, tenant of Druimbuidhe in 1871.

[2] When this charge was repeated in evidence to the Napier Commissioners (pp. 220–1 below) it was denied by J. C. Gordon of Drimnin: "It was stated that the houses and improvements were not paid for when the tenants left, which is not correct, as I have documents in the house to prove that. I hold the receipts for the houses and improvements. They were all paid for. The houses were paid for when they left. There were three tenants, and all three were paid for their houses; and the improvements were done by my mother's money. She borrowed money, and the people were paid wages for these improvements.
—What was the name of the place?—The island of Oronsay. That is the only thing in the evidence I have to say anything against. They were paid for by Government money.
—They were done by the tenants themselves, and paid for?—Yes." (*Napier Commission evidence* (1884), III, 2321–2).

compensation they got was an attempt to destroy their character as honest men, so that no other proprietor would give them shelter. I think it would be an act of justice in Lady Gordon's son and successor to give these men compensation even yet, as he is now in a manner reaping the benefit of their toil. I would not enter into the details of this case so fully—I would be inclined to let bygones be bygones—were it not that I consider it a good case to show the sort of encouragement given by landlords to crofters who improved their holdings; and as so much is made just now of the laziness òf our people and their disinclination to better their condition, I think it shows that a premium was put upon laziness by landlords who acted as was done in this case, and it is not by any means a solitary instance. I am sure there are other Highlanders in Glasgow who could give similar cases. A worse case, I believe, it would be impossible to give. Trusting that, in the interests of truth and justice, you will give this space in an early issue, I am &c.

J.M.D.

(2) Extract from a letter headed 'Land allocation in Morvern', dated Glasgow, 20 Feb. 1883, published in the *Oban Times* on 3 March 1883.

...Your correspondent "Argyllshire", in your issue of last week, draws attention to the state of Morvern.[1] Let me now follow up what he has already advanced. Between forty and fifty years ago the population of this parish was 2000; at the last census it stood at 828, being a decrease of over 50 per cent of the whole population. In this district there never was what may be termed a crofter population. It consisted chiefly of well-to-do small farmers, and the land was principally held on what is known as the club-farm system. Within the memory of a few old people yet living in the district, there were at Gleann Geal (White Glen), that is, from the bridge of Acharn to Clonlaid, 60 families, which would amount, giving an average of five persons to every family, to 300 souls. On the farm of Achana-gamhna, 6 well-to-do tenants, each holding a stock of eight cows and followers with 100 sheep. At Aoinebeag and Aoinemor [Unibeg and Unimore] there was between 20 and 30 families equally well-to-do. Perhaps they were not possessed of much "hard cash", but they had plenty to eat and drink. They were a contented and hospitable people, and the stranger or wanderer was never turned away from their door. At this time the sum of £11 sterling per annum from the collection at the church-door was sufficient for the support of all the poor people within the bounds of the parish, and now with a population of about 800 the rates amount to between six and seven hundred pounds

[1] "Argyllshire"'s letter appeared on 10 Feb. 1883; it stated that Morvern had been depopulated by eviction, but gave no details.

a year. At the time the people were cleared off the land by that ruthless evictor Sellar they owed not a single penny of rent. The land held by so many families is now inhabited by three or four shepherds. The greater part of the estate has lately been turned into a deer forest by the proprietor T. V. Smith, of Ardtornish. The overplus of stock sold off each year by these tenants, combined with what was sold off the adjoining farms of Ternaid, Eignaig, and Ardtornish, at that time in the hands of Sheriff Gregerson, could not have been under 1000 sheep and from 200 to 300 cattle. But to-day it is of no use to any one unless that it affords a few months sport to Mr Smith and *his party* during the shooting season. Mr Smith does not let the shootings so that he receives no revenue whatever from the greater part of his estate. Will any sane man assert that this sort of policy has been productive of good to the people or the State? when good land (better there is not in the district) has been laid waste for the pleasure of one single individual, and those whom he may delight to honour.[1] . . .

Let me now refer to what was done in another part of the parish, on the estate of the late Lady Gordon, of Drimnin, there was about 30 years ago in the crofts of Aulistan and Carrick 10 families, each having a stock of three or four cows, and a number of sheep. When the sheep farming craze took a hold of so many people, the factor on the estate took the hill grazing from the crofters, and annexed it to his own large farm. The people were still left on their crofts, but when the hill pasture was taken from them they were no longer able to make both ends meet. Some got disheartened and left the place of their own accord. Others rather than leave their native place, took an offer then given them, of going to live on an island on the Lochsunart side of the estate. This same island was about as unlikely a place for any person to think of being able to live on as possible, as it was mostly rocks and heather, with some patches of bog. The people, however, went to work with a will, and in a few years had all that was possible to reclaim under cultivation. In full expectation that their tenure was secure they latterly built good houses, each costing from £50 to £60. About this time the adjoining sheep farmer coveted the holdings held by the people, offered to give more rent, and as a matter of course, the interests of the people were sacrificed. They had to leave this place, which, by their industry, they had redeemed from a state of nature, without a farthing of compensation for land relaimed or houses built. There was in connection with this eviction, which took place only 14 years [ago], circumstances of peculiar

---

[1] In fact only just over a third of Smith's estate was cleared for deer, and it was of course the most barren part that became forest, land such as Garbh Shlios which had never had an agricultural population and which could not possibly have supported crofters at a late-nineteenth-century standard of living.

cruelty and hardship, but as all the details were published in the *North British Daily Mail,* and also in your own columns twelve months ago, it is unnecessary to repeat it here. Suffice to say that of all the evictions which took place throughout the Highlands, there were none in my opinion more unjust than this case. There was about the same time another eviction which took place in the district. When the late Mrs Campbell Paterson came into possession of the estate of Lochaline there was between the burn of Savary and the Bridge of Achaforsa, 38 families in possession of moderate sized crofts, with hill grazing. The proprietrix took it into her head that it would be an improvement to have the people removed, and turn the whole property into an extensive sheep farm. This was immediately effected, although the late Dr John MacLeod, to his honour be it said, did all in his power to prevent it. The summonses of removal came, and at the Whitsunday term the crowbar and faggot made short work of the crofters' dwellings. To me it is a never-to-be-forgotten scene. The burning cottages, the roofs falling in, and the sods which formed the covering of the roof under the thatch continued to smoulder for days. The faithful collie still lingering about the smouldering ruins of his former master's dwelling, howling pitifully, and would not for a time be comforted—and be it remembered this happened only 15 years ago.[1] Some of the people here referrred to were huddled together in the village of Lochaline. The young and the able-bodied scattered to all parts, some went to the cities of the south, some went abroad. The old people were left behind in this miserable village to become a burden to the parish, which they soon did. And now the Parochial Board, composed of proprietors and sheep farmers of course, refuse to give relief to some poor widows, which their own or their predecessors' misdeeds have rendered destitute. The poor people's natural protectors (their sons and daughters) were driven away, and scattered, and now they are deprived of the poor pittance the law of the land allows to such as have no other means of living—

"Verily the tender mercies of the wicked are cruel." . . .

I am, &c.,   MacDhomhnuill.

(3) Statements prepared by MacDonald on behalf of the people of Lochaline, of Barr and of Bonnavoulin, and read to Lord Napier and his fellow Commissioners at Lochaline on 11 August 1883.[2]

[1] MacDonald implies that the people of Lochaline Estate were forced out by the burning and demolition of their houses. In fact they left peacefully after being given more than a year's notice; and the houses were not demolished for at least a fortnight after they had gone (*Napier Commission evidence* (1884), III, 2306, 2292; *Oban Times,* 20 Dec. 1884).

[2] *Napier Commission evidence* (1884), III, 2287–9, 2294–5, 2297. The Barr and Bonnavoulin statements were partly written by the crofters of those districts, but MacDonald agreed that he had assisted in their preparation (*ibid.* 2306).

Appendix E

'Statement of Grievances by Crofters and Cottars in the district of Morven, Argyllshire.'

[a] *Lochaline.*—Our principal grievances are as follows:—1st, That we have been removed from lands occupied by ourselves and our fore-fathers, and that we have been huddled together in this miserable village; and through that and several other causes we have been reduced to great poverty; and were it not for the kindness of the late Mr Smith, and of his son, the proprietor of the adjoining estates of Acharn and Ardtornish, who, for more than thirty years, gave work to as many of us as he could, we do not know how we could have existed. We consider it a great hardship that we cannot get any land to cultivate, although abundance of good land, formerly under cultivation, is going to waste at our very doors. This land from which some of us have been evicted about seventeen years ago, we are sorry to see going back again into a state of nature, and overgrown with heather and rushes. We feel very much the want of milk for our families. Many of us would be very glad if we could get a cow's grass even without arable land at a reasonable rent which we could pay. The rent for a cow's grass, without any arable land, charged by the late proprietrix is £3 a year, which we consider an intentional discouragement against any one aspiring to the dignity of keeping a cow. We know that the want of good milk, such as most of us have been accustomed to in our younger days, has a deteriorating in-fluence upon ourselves, and more especially upon our children. We are aware that a certain medical gentleman in another part, while being examined before the Commission, recommended cheap beer as a substi-tute for milk. The use and introduction of such a substitute for milk in rearing our offspring we, and we are sure all Highlanders, will repudiate with scorn. We look upon such a suggestion as an insult to us; and we cannot perceive why we should be deprived of having a supply of good milk, so that the proprietor may obtain a few pounds more rent. 2nd, Our next grievance is in regard to fuel. Under former proprietors, the poorest of us had the privilege of cutting peats on the hill as near hand as we could find them; but now we are prevented from doing this, and compelled to go to the top of the hill to cut them. The poorest and most destitute of us dare not gather a few tufts of heather to keep up the fire in case the game be interfered with, or be put to the least inconvenience. Our Lord and Saviour said, "How much more valuable is a man than a sheep?"[1] But our landlords say, "How much more valuable is, *not even a sheep*, but a game bird than a man?" In consequence of the above restrictions as to fuel, we are at all seasons of the year under the neces-

---

[1] "How much then is a man better than a sheep?" (Matt. xii. 12). Jesus was talking about sabbatarianism, not eviction.

sity of buying coal, and in this remote district, so far situated from the coal centres of the south, coal is a luxury which some of us can ill afford.[1] As an instance of the petty tyranny exercised over us regarding these matters, we wish to refer to a case which happened about two years ago, when a man belonging to our village, who is both a cripple and in receipt of parochial aid, was found on the road with a bundle of heather for his fire, and was unmercifully deprived of his heather by one of the estate gamekeepers and shoved along the road. We therefore consider it a great grievance that we, being loyal subjects of Her Majesty, living under what we are taught to believe to be the glorious British Constitution, living in a country which is supposed to be the best governed country in the world, should be left so much to the mercy of landed proprietors, and, still worse, their factors, that we can scarcely call our souls our own. We cannot reconcile all the boasted freedom to be enjoyed by all Her Majesty's subjects alike with what we know to be the truth in our own case. From our experience, we are more inclined to believe with Lord Macaulay, that the country, and Scotland especially, has the worst constitution in Europe, at least so far as the land laws are concerned. We therefore trust that Her Majesty's Commissioners shall take our case into consideration. 3rd, Evictions. We specially beg to direct the attention of Her Majesty's Commissioners to the miserable condition of this district compared to what it was forty or fifty years ago. The population of the parish at that time was over 2000. At last census it stood at 828. Fifty years ago, with such a large population, £11 sterling per annum from the collection at the church door was sufficient for the support of all the poor and destitute people within the district, and now, with a population of 828, the poor rates amount to over £600 a year. These facts we leave to the consideration and wisdom of the Commissioners, as we consider they require no comment from us beyond showing the benefits conferred upon this district by what the Duke of Argyll calls in scientific language "economic conditions," and that we are not to be bamboozled by his Grace's scientific conundrums.[2] The first eviction which took place in this district happened between fifty and sixty years ago, when the late Miss Stewart evicted all the tenants in the township of Ferinish, Mangostell, Barr, and Innemore, numbering

---

[1] Coal was available at 15*s*. a ton. (The 15,000 peats required annually by the average crofter family took about a month to cut and prepare, say twenty-four working days, which at 2*s*. a day would buy three tons of coal; a low-paid labourer might therefore still prefer peats to coal, especially if he was occasionally unemployed.) Hardie stated in evidence that the people were allowed to cut peats, but not so as to bare the rock (*Napier Commission evidence* (1884), III, 2306).

[2] This is a reference to a perceptive article by the eighth Duke of Argyll, 'On the economic conditions of the highlands of Scotland', which had appeared in *The nineteenth century* for February 1883 (Campbell, G. D. (1883)).

in all twenty-five families.[1] The second eviction happened between forty and fifty years ago, when the tenants of several townships on the estates of Acharn and Ardtornish received summonses of removal from the proprietors before they sold the estates to Mr Patrick Sellar of Sutherlandshire. There were forty-eight families evicted at this time, so that the loss of population sustained by the parish must have been considerable.[2] There was another cruel and very harsh eviction which took place in this district about seventeen years ago. When the late Mrs Paterson came into possession of the estate of Lochaline, there were in the townships of Achabeg and Knock a well-to-do crofter population, consisting of between twenty-five and thirty families. The families, owing to some whim of the proprietrix, were evicted wholesale, notwithstanding the oft-repeated remonstrances of the late Dr John M'Leod, the minister of the parish. The crowbar and faggot were here, let us hope for the last time in the history of the Highland peasant, brought into requisition to demolish the dwellings of men whose forefathers occupied the land long before Mrs Paterson came into the district, or had the means which gave her the power of buying the land and turning out the people.[3] There was yet another eviction on the estate of the late Lady Gordon of Drimnin, and as this was a peculiarly hard case, which took place only about fifteen years ago, we feel in duty bound to refer to it as showing how completely the Highland crofter is in the power of his landlord, and however unscrupulous the landlord may be in the present circumstances there is no redress. The circumstances are as follows:—About forty years ago, when the sheep farming craze was at its height, some families were removed from the townships of Aulistan and Carrick on Lady Gordon's estate, as their places were to be added to the adjoining sheep farm. The people were removed on to the most barren spot on the whole estate, where there was no road or any possibility of making one. They had to carry all manure and sea-ware on their backs, as the place was so rocky that a horse would be of no use. Notwithstanding all these disadvantages, they contrived through time to improve the place very much by draining and reclaiming mossy patches, and by carrying soil to be placed on rocky places where there was no soil. During the twenty-five years they occupied this place their rents were raised twice. Latterly, with full confidence of their tenure being secure, they built better houses at their own expense, and two or three years afterwards they were turned out of their holdings on the usual six

[1] 1824. Not all the small tenants on these farms were evicted; and at the time of the Napier Commission there were still 23 crofters at Barr, Fernish and Bonnavoulin (Mungasdail).

[2] The Acharn eviction, involving 44 families, took place in 1838; that at Ardtornish involved only 4 families, and took place in 1844.

[3] 1866.

week's notice, without a farthing of compensation for land reclaimed.[1] In justice to the present proprietor, Joseph [Clement] Gordon, Esq., we wish to state our conviction that such an injustice would not have been permitted on the estate since he came into possession, as we regard him as a kind and considerate landlord to the few crofters on his estate. It has often been advanced by landlords, factors, and others that the Highland crofters are lazy and do not improve their holdings; but where is the inducement to improvements under such circumstances as we have here related? and as the Commissioners are well aware that this case is not a solitary instance, as it is quite common in every district throughout the Highlands, that if a crofter improves his holding he has to pay for it by having his rent raised, or his holding being given to the first man who offers more rent on account of such improvements. 4th, The remedy which we in this district would respectfully suggest for the improvement of our condition is, that the land which is lying waste on every side of us, that is to say, the townships of Achabeg, Keil, and Knock, at present in the hands of Mrs Paterson's trustees, and entirely out of cultivation, should be divided into suitable lots; that the trustees build suitable cottages on such lots. We consider they have a right to do so, seeing the proprietrix caused all the houses to be destroyed seventeen years ago; that these lots be let to us at a reasonable rent, such rent, in cases where the landlord and tenant cannot agree, to be fixed by arbitration, or such other arrangement as the wisdom of Parliament may see proper. While much preferring to have the State as our landlord, and while thoroughly convinced that the land question shall never be properly settled until it is settled on that basis, we should still be glad, in the meantime, to have matters settled on the lines indicated above; that is, a re-allotment of the land in suitable portions, security against arbitrary evictions, compensation for improvement in case of removal, a fair rent, and arbitration in case of disagreement between landlord and tenant. We have heard this statement read, and we agree with all it contains.

[*b*] *Barr.* The crofts of Barr are situated on the western shore of Lochteagus, an arm of Lochsunart, which penetrates about three miles inland in a southerly direction. These crofts are on the estate of Glenmorven, now in the hands of Miss Beattie's trustees. The whole of this estate, with the exception of a few worthless patches held by crofters, is one large sheep farm,[2] presently occupied by Captain Shaw, son of Sheriff Shaw of Lochmaddy. Our grievance is that the small spots of arable land held by us is becoming quite worthless through overcropping. It is now about eighty years since our fathers settled in this place,

---

[1] See above, p. 214 n. 2.

[2] The Commissioners particularly objected to this sentence, pointing out that Unimore, Carnacailliche and Achnasaul, which were not part of Captain Shaw's farm, could not be described as worthless.

whither they were removed from good land to make room for sheep. They reclaimed the land, such as it is, from being a miserable patch of bog. The water is carried away by open drains, which must be dug very deep. We would improve the land by stone drains, but, as we are tenants at will and can be removed at any time, we are prevented from making many improvements. Our summing is two cows with followers, and we pay a rent of £7 sterling for that and our miserable patches of land. The produce of our crofts will not feed us more than three months of the year. We plant five barrels of potatoes and four bushels of corn; but the land is so much exhausted that it will not yield a good crop. We want to get as much land as we can make a living by, which if we get we are able to stock. There is nothing to be made by herring fishing in this district now, as owing to the way the fishing is prosecuted on the west coast it never comes into Lochsunart. We get work for about fifty days throughout the year from Captain Shaw the farmer; we are paid at the rate of two shillings a day.[1] We have also to complain of having to live in very bad houses, which if we are to live here any longer we should like repaired or rebuilt. We consider our rent is excessive, and would beg respectfully to draw the attention of the Commission to the rents we pay and to our summing, which, taken along with the quality of the arable land we hold, we consider that no capitalist farmer in the Highlands pays the same rent in proportion.

[c] *Bunavullin.* This township is also on the estate of Glenmorven under Beattie's trustees. Our grievances are—(1) That we have too little hill pasture for the summer grazing of our cattle. Our summing is two cows and one calf, which must be sold when a year old for want of grazing. (2) Our arable land is so small that we cannot provide fodder for wintering our beasts. We have to buy for them, which we consider a great hardship, as there is plenty of good land close beside us very suitable for us if we could get it at a reasonable rent. (3) The extent of arable land held by each of us is about $1\frac{3}{4}$ acre of very inferior land. We pay a rent of £6, exclusive of taxes, which we consider far too high. We cannot get a day's work on the estate from one year's end to another, but have to go about here and there where we can get work. Our houses are built too near the sea-shore, and in winter time are very damp because of the sea spray.[2] There is a piece of land adjoining us between Glenmorven shooting lodge and our crofts, which if given to us we are willing to pay a fair rent for it. We have no special complaint against either the proprietrix or her factor, but we wish to have more hill pasture and our crofts enlarged. We are able to stock more land if we could get it. We have at present three horses, but owing to our restricted grazing we cannot keep but inferior animals. Our delegate will be glad to answer any questions.

[1] Ardtornish day-labourers were getting from 2*s*. 6*d*. to 3*s*. a day by this date.
[2] This is the Bonnavoulin terrace at 559537.

III. EXTRACTS FROM MISS AGNES KING'S
MEMOIRS, *c.* 1902

[The following extracts are taken from a typescript in the possession of Mrs C. Harcourt of Windlesham, Surrey, headed 'Remembrances of Long Ago. Copied from Agnes R. King's, "Little Sketch of Those who are gone, and Scenes of Long Ago"'. The original manuscript (the *See p. vii* present whereabouts of which is unknown) is dated by a reference to the coronation "the other day" of Edward VII (p. 7 of the typescript, not transcribed here). The Kings' eight-years' residence at Lochaline House lasted probably from 1855 until 1863; Agnes King was probably born in about 1844.]

...My mother, Margaret Campbell Sinclair was the daughter of John Sinclair of Lochaline.

Left fatherless at an early age John Sinclair had taken upon himself the care of his mother, sisters and younger brothers, and step by step had risen by his own integrity and high business qualities to a position of affluence and importance in the County of Argyle, and purchased the property of Lochaline in the parish of Morvern.

From an entry in an old note-book written by him I copy the following extract:

"John Sinclair of Lochaline, son of Duncan Sinclair was born at Dirinasaor, Glenkinlas, Argyleshire[1] in November 1770. His father, Duncan Sinclair died before his grandfather, John Sinclair, who lived to the advanced age of near 100 years, after he and his predecessors had possessed the lands of Glenkinlas previous to, and after it became the property of the Campbells of Lochnell. The Sinclairs of Glenkinlas were descended from the family of St. Clair of Roslyn". ...

My grandfather, John Sinclair left Glenkinlas and settled in Mull, at Tobermory, where he carried on business of various kinds. He had a distillery there for some time, and kelp was also manufactured by him. He imported seed-corn and many other things. He had smacks and sloops, if not a steamer which traded between Mull and Glasgow, (and Liverpool also sometimes I think). He was most enterprizing, and was the means of opening up the country for the benefit of others, as well as himself, and was much beloved and respected by all classes in the district. It used to be said that "Mr. Sinclair's word was as good as his Bond." He was long a deputy Lieutenant for the County, and being a practical business man was much consulted and referred to by the other proprietors of Argyleshire.

He was not in his first youth when he married Catherine McLachlan,

[1] Doire nan Saor (the site of Glen Kinglass Lodge), Glen Kinglass, Loch Etive.

eldest daughter of Robert McLachlan of Dunad, Taxman of Rahoy.[1] The family long possessed Dunad, a large estate in Argyleshire, but my great-grandfather had to sell it, as there were many burdens upon it when he came into its possession. The Coat-of-Arms, carved in stone, and brought from above the entrance of the old Castle of Dunad to Rahoy, was for long at Lochaline. I remember galleys in full sail in one of the quarterings, which, I think, denotes a Chief.

Robert McLachlan married at 21, Margaret Campbell aged 19. They had 16 of a family, 12 of whom grew up to be men and women. Several of them married, but of them all none left any family except my grandmother. ...

Rahoy, where they lived, is a farm on the other side of the hill from Lochaline, it is a most lovely spot situated on the banks of Loch Tiachkish—an arm of the sea opening out of Loch Sunart.

It must have been a patriarchal establishment, for besides the large family there were also Grannie, Grand-Aunt and Aunt, who were Mrs. Campbell, her sister and daughter, the mother, sister and aunt of Mrs. McLachlan all living under the same roof. My mother often used to tell us of the lovely flower garden that flourished there under the hand of Grand-Aunt. Mother always spoke of Rahoy with great affection—many happy days of her youth were spent there. Once and once only was I at Rahoy when it was occupied by Mr. Hugh Maclean, formerly of Killundine, just for a few days.[2] It was long ride over the hill, for road there was none—a shepherd guided us. When we got to the side of Loch Tiachkish the shepherd "put up smoke" by lighting a bonfire. This was a signal for a boat to be sent across. We were quickly rowed over to the house on the other side while the shepherd led the horses round the head of the Loch to Rahoy—a long distance.

The house was picturesque and straggling owing to many additions having been built on to it from time to time. One portion had many pointed windows in the roof, with deep thatch forming eaves over them—the other and more modern part was slated. It was more like a mansion house than a farm house. A green sward sloped down from the house to the Loch, and almost fringing the water was a long row of beautiful lime trees skirting the lawn, their branches sweeping to the ground. The situation is beautiful, and the views on all sides most exquisite—wood and water, hill and dale. Behind the house on the hill above is a vitrified fort.[3]

The sons of the house had a tutor, and Catherine being the eldest girl with many brothers between her and the next sister, was educated six months

[1] Robert MacLachlan was tacksman of Rahoy from 1791 until it was sold by Argyll as part of the Glencripesdale lot in 1821 (see pp. 161–2 above).
[2] Hugh MacLean, tenant of Rahoy, was 36 in 1861 (*Census*).
[3] Excavated in 1936 and 1937 by Professor Gordon Childe; see Childe, V. G. and Thorneycroft, W. (1938).

of the year at home by a governess, and the six other months at Aross, in Mull, with her friend Miss Maxwell (afterwards Mrs Norman Macleod),[1] the governess being half her time at each house, as also the two girls.

The sons were all over six feet in height and all good looking. Some of the daughters were beautiful. They were a very handsome family. . . .

My grandfather continued to live at Tobermory after he had bought Lochaline, but for several years, during the summer, he, with his wife and family, occupied one of the farm houses on the estate while the Mansion House was being built.

His property extended from the old Castle of Kinlochaline down the Loch on that side for four miles to the village of Lochaline at the mouth of the Loch, and from that, the land bordering on the Sound of Mull for five miles on the coast, and extending inland all the way. It covered 6,000 acres.[2]

The Kinlochaline river divided it from Achranich and Ardtornish on the one side, and Sallachan river from Kinlochaline [*sic*, for Killundine] on the other. It is an enchanting district for beauty and scenery, and romantic and historical interest. Fingal, Ossian, the very "Halls of Selma" seem to permeate the whole of it. . . .

Lochaline House stands about a quarter of a mile up from the shore of the Sound of Mull, and facing the mountains of Mull; Benmore with its double peaks being a beautiful object. The house consists of a large centre block with wings in each side, large and commodious—built for comfort more than appearance, though it looks handsome from the Sound. In front of it is a large lawn with a belting of trees all around, and a wood behind with the hills rising beyond. A pathway skirts the lawn under the trees, and the view from this path up and down the Sound of Mull is most extensive and exquisite. Oban is seen on the one side and Ardnamurchan on the other,[3] with the green isles, Aross, Durat [Duart] and Ardtornish Castles.

Near the house and reached by this same path is the flower garden, made in an old quarry, a sheltered and sunny situation. Did ever such profusion of flowers grow anywhere else? The sweet scents filled the air, and the blaze of flowers was so unexpected that all were struck by it— you came upon the garden suddenly. The large garden with quantities of fruit and vegetables was some distance from the house. Flowers were in it also—such roses, rocket phloxes and every sweet smelling thing, balm, southernwood, lavendar—and immense hydrangeas and fuchsia. I never

---

[1] Agnes Maxwell, the daughter of Argyll's Chamberlain of Mull and Morvern James Maxwell of Aros, married in 1811 Norman MacLeod, later of St Columba's, eldest son of the 'old minister'.

[2] Actually 8,550 acres.

[3] It is quite impossible to see Ardnamurchan from anywhere near Lochaline House.

see the same lovely old white low-growing Provence rose now, that used to flourish there.

I think the family occupied the house for one summer before it was quite finished, going back to Tobermory for the winter before moving the household permanently into it. But alas! before the next summer came my grandmother was dead, she and the baby Robert being buried in the same grave. She lies in Keil churchyard beside her husband, she aged 39, he 93—the numbers reversed.[1]

It must indeed have been a sad entrance to the new and beautiful home when he came into it with his five motherless children, my mother, the eldest, being only ten years old, instead of with Her for whom he had prepared it all. I have heard that everything was in the utmost order, left by her in readiness for the family returning permanently to the house. There were four girls, all of whom married, and one son, John, who grew up, but died unmarried.

Grandfather's sister, Mrs. Campbell, kept house for him till my mother was seventeen, when she took the head of it on her return from school in Edinburgh. And well she filled the difficult post, for it was no ordinary household she was called upon to manage. Hospitality was the rule of the house, and there was scarcely a day but what some strangers unexpectedly came. In those days neither by road or water was there regular communication with the south, as there is now in that district, and so people travelled very much in their own sailing boats from place to place. Indeed there was no house of any pretentions without its boathouse. It was as necessary as stables, and more so.

The cooking of a Highland kitchen was a continual process, like that on a passenger steamer on a long journey. Different classes had to be served at different periods of the day, from early morn till night. Dairymaids, and all sorts of maids with shepherds, farm servants, and herd-lads, often strangers also, were fed in the large hall adjoining the kitchen. Upstairs in the dining room the family, and visitors in the house were always a goodly number, while often a boat load of people were landed for the night, from stress of weather or other cause.

Ducks, hens, geese, and turkeys, all supplied from the home farm—in such quantities as would terrify the modern cook and landlady if required to provide them daily from the market, and sheep and lambs from the hills, with a bullock now and then, game from the moors and fish from the rivers and sea, made a plentiful supply for all. So abundant was the supply of salmon there at that time that servants when engaged, stipulated not to have it served more than so many days a week.

[1] Catherine Sinclair died on 23 November 1825, which dates the completion of the house in its original form (see above, p. 30); it was probably begun soon after Sinclair bought Fiunary and Savary in 1821.

Much forethought was always required in the ordering of such a household. When one thinks of the comfort and plenty which reigned in that home one can scarcely believe that there were no shops or markets to draw upon. Twice a year stores were ordered from Glasgow, and the store-room filled, and what a business was that! Medicines too were ordered at the same time, kept locked up in the "Medicine Press", from which the whole community were supplied with physic.

My grandfather retired from business entirely on settling at Lochaline, and devoted his time to improving his property. He planted much wood which now beautifies the place, built farm steadings, and kept the home farm in his own hands, as he believed in the landlord setting an example to his tenants. Whatever he did was thorough. He also had a fold of Highland cattle which he spent much upon.[1]

When mother married, her next sister took her place as mistress of Lochaline, and so on in rotation. It was always an open house for all the daughters to come and go after they were married.

While my parents were living in Liverpool Grandfather came to them and underwent an operation on his eye for cataract. The operation was a success, and he saw for five years after.

When my youngest Aunt, Mary, married, Grandfather had become quite blind again by that time, so Father and Mother went to live with him with their family at Lochaline. Mother once more managed the house and Father acted as land-steward or factor. For eight happy years we lived there. Not many young people are so fortunate as to spend their youth amid such pleasant surroundings as my sisters and I did there. There were five girls of us, when we went there—Agnes, Margaret, Mary, Jemima and Catherine—but Mary died after a short illness. She was the brightest and best, the "flower of the family", intelligent and clever beyond her years.[2]

Lochaline House was still the hospitable home it had always been. The daughters with their families came and went at all times, besides many visitors during the summer months.

In the house during all those years there was one gentle presence, unobtrusive but always felt, and the house would not have been like itself, without her pervading influence. Dear old Belle![3] What soothing and

---

[1] It is possible that Sinclair's fold of Highland cattle survived to become the nucleus many years later of the Ardtornish herd; see above, p. 106; and cf. p. 183.

[2] The *Census* of 1861 showed that, besides John Sinclair, aged 91, and his son John, 38, there were in residence at Lochaline House James King, 54 (son-in-law and factor, born at Port Glasgow); Margaret King, 44; Maggy S. King, 15; Mary King, 13; Jemima King, 9; Catherine King, 7; and various visitors and servants making the total number up to 26 under the one roof. Agnes King herself was evidently away but, supposing that she was then aged about 17, she was about 58 when she wrote the *Memoirs*.

[3] Isabella Sinclair, b. *c.* 1800 (*Census*).

sacred memories cluster round her very name! She had come to the family as a nurse-maid before her mistress died, and there she had remained all her life. For forty-seven years she had served her family, but at the same time she was the gentle guide, counsellor and friend of her young mistresses, and the faithful steward of her master's goods. She carried the key of the lower store-room and acted as housekeeper in the servant's region. She was the trusted friend and confidante of all and no trust was ever betrayed by her. I can see her now with her kindly face and stately presence, matronly and motherly she was—though an "old maid" and indeed she was a mother to many. There was a quiet dignity surrounding her against which no inferior ever presumed, and though so intimate with all the members of the family there was never any familiarity on her part. She was most intelligent, with an air of the gentlewoman about her and refinement in all her ways as is so often the case with Highlanders, whose good-breeding strikes all who come into contact with them.

"Belle's room" was a centre of attraction to the whole household, and there she entertained comers and goers, who were too good for the servant's hall and not good enough for the dining room, and many of such people there were. In the winter evenings she had the young servants to her room to spin—the many wheels whirring merrily. There were no drones in that household and all worked harmoniously together. There were always at least two young girls in the house being trained under Belle's hand as servants. It was a position much coveted by all the young girls in the district.

"Lochaline House was a colony that ever preached sermons, on weekdays as well as Sundays, of industry and frugality, of courteous hospitality and bountiful charity, and of the domestic peace, contentment and cheerfulness of a happy Christian home."[1]

I would like now to give a few remembrances of what is more known to myself of those far away days. The old home was indeed a busy, happy household.

When I went to the Scilly Isles and saw carved over the entrance to the Mansion of Tresco Abbey the motto "Sic vos non vobis" ("Man does not work for himself alone, but for others") by Mr. Augustus Smith, to indicate his principle of government, I could not but think that was the principle which moved the happy household long ago at Lochaline. From the blind master and my father and mother down to the scullery-maid, all worked for one another. Consideration for others, kindness towards all, bearing and forebearing, and "Kindlie courtesie" was the rule.

I can remember my blind grandfather calling "Margaret" to my mother and asking her, "What rooms are you giving to the Landle

---

[1] The source of this quotation is not known.

[Laudale] Gentlemen?" When she named the rooms he said, "That's right, see and pay them every attention for fear they should feel that their circumstances are now changed from what they were, poor fellows." "The Landle Gentlemen" as they were called, were two brothers, Colin and Hugh MacLachlan, (but no relation of our family) who owned property called Landle in Morvern.[1] In an evil moment they went security for some relative, with the result that their property had to be sold to meet the demand, and little indeed was left for them to live upon. They used to arrive as if to make a call, but it was well understood that a visit of a week or two was intended, and when they went they never went empty handed.

There were several such visitors in my remembrance. Another was a clergyman—he had been licensed, though never had a charge—of the name of Fraser. He had a slight claim to the Lovat estates, and went to law about it, but lost his plea. He was sane enough on most subjects clever and very entertaining, but if ever law or law-suits were spoken of, he seemed at once to lose his head. His visits sometimes extended rather far, and with great difficulty, after putting it off from day to day, it had to be hinted to him that other visitors were expected. He was great amusement to the young people. He cut little figures out of pasteboard and made them dance by an ingenious method of his own, while he whistled sprightly tunes, reels, etc.

Then downstairs there were several visitors who used to come regularly from time to time for a night or two (a bed in one of the out-houses being ready for them), but they did not call themselves beggars, and none of the household did either.

I can remember two of the "fools" for which the district was once famous, before District Asylums were known. One of them was Donald Tirish, Donald Tiree—he had a sort of St. Vitus' Dance and walked with an unsteady gait. Once he went to Drimnin, a neighbouring property, but found Lady Gordon out, and was not well received. On coming down the avenue he met Lady Gordon with a friend, and overheard her saying when passing him, "the man is drunk", so he looked round after them and said, "Then it would not be on your Ladyship's charity that I would get fu'." He was a poor, harmless creature, more a kind of idiot and not fit for work, so he just went round the country from house to house.

The other was "Samuel". I know not what surname. He belonged to Ross of Mull, and after the Poor Law was enforced he had to be sent back to his native Parish. A Policeman took him to Bunethan and, as he

[1] Colin and Ewan MacLachlan, who were aged 40 and 35 respectively in 1841 (*Census*), were not in fact the proprietors of Laudale, which belonged from 1825 until 1851 to Dugald MacLachlan (and later his trustees), and was then sold to John Johnston of Hunterheck. They appear as tenant-farmers of Laudale in the *Census* of 1841, but had been replaced by another tenant by 1851.

thought, left him there, but when he returned to Lochaline who was the first person he saw on the pier but Samuel—capering and smiling, and quite delighted to have out-witted the policeman. He was allowed to remain, and Mr. Smith of Anchranich made him his post runner, and very important he looked in a postman's cast off uniform.[1]

Many women used to come, crofter's wives and daughters mostly, bringing chickens or a few eggs, and always expected to have given to them tea and sugar and a little money in return. There is a Gaelic word for such presents, but I forget it now.

Many people came for medicines as they could not be produced elsewhere. Mother or Belle gave them out from the medicine press, and both must have had some idea of doctoring—which they doubtless derived from Dr. John of Rahoy who always made Lochaline his head-quarters.[2] I remember a servant coming to tell mother one day that a woman was in the kitchen wanting medicine for her husband who was ill. "She says he is ill with flation, but I know she means inflation" (inflammation.)

The household washing of linen was a great undertaking. The clothes were taken in a cart to the washing ground which was about half a mile from the house. It was beside a burn, where the ground seems scooped out and a flat grassy place left between the river and the higher bank. It was all done in the open air, as in Allan Ramsay's "Gentle Shepherd", a huge cauldron being fixed with fire under it in the shelter of the bank above.

There was a shepherd's house close by and there the servants took their food—provisions being sent over with the clothes. The washing took several days to accomplish. When the things were all bleached and dried, they were carted back to the house where in the laundry it was again some days before they were all got out of hand. A heavy box mangle was used with stones inside it, and rollers underneath, round which the clothes were tightly wound, and placed under the box. After the mangle had been turned over them they were removed from off the rollers, and others put on. Eventually a wash house was arranged close to the house, but the servants took badly to it. Though they must often have had to stand washing in the rain, they all preferred the old way.

Going to Church with Belle as we children usually did, is another remembrance. We went in a cart—straw was spread on the bottom of it, and two sacks stuffed with straw formed the seats, while all over rugs

---

[1] Samuel Cameron was paid for carrying letters for Ardtornish Estate in 1862 and 1864 (Ledgers, *AP*).

See p. vii [2] Dr John MacLachlan, Sinclair's brother-in-law, was a Gaelic poet and a physician practising in Mull and Ardnamurchan as well as in his native Morvern. Although 'Dr John' was traditionally supposed to have studied medicine at Glasgow University (*King's memoirs*, p. 5, not transcribed here), he did not in fact matriculate or graduate there (or, apparently, anywhere else in Scotland).

were spread. It was a great treat to us, but a rough journey enough. This was a drive of four miles to Keil church. In the summer time Belle carried, besides her Bible and a folded handkerchief, a posy of sweet smelling flowers. The gallery on one side of the church was allotted to the Lochaline estate, and all the dwellers thereupon filled it, the family and household occupying the front seats.

Although my Grandfather was the largest heritor in the parish he "came out" at the Disruption. He was the only Proprietor in the district who did so, and many a minister of the Church he entertained, and helped. Notwithstanding this he and Dr. Macleod, the minister of the Parish, remained fast and intimate friends for life—which says a great deal for both of them.

When Grandfather died he left Dr. Macleod one of his Trustees.

My Grandfather built a small Free Church just outside the village of Lochaline, and has left the ground on which it stood with the Manse, in perpetuity to the Free Church,[1] but as there was no stated minister there for some years, the family except when there was a preacher there, went to the Parish Church. I think that we should be proud that our families on both sides were of the Free Church. In no country but Scotland would such a step have been taken, involving as it did so much self-sacrifice and suffering, both to ministers and people. . . .

I remember the fold of Highland cattle. The cows were always milked just where they happened to be grazing at the time in the green open pasture. It was the last of such in the district and considered a very fine one. We used to be sent to the evening milking with our nurse, each with a "tumie" in our hand, into which the dairy-maid milked the foaming fluid. Such milk as it was! Like cream, sweet as a nut, a veritable nectar. The Highland cows gave little milk, but of the richest quality. Often there was a "camsleery" beast which, though its hind legs were fastened together with a kind of throng, would kick maid and stool over, but there was never damage done after all.

I also remember the post. He was never called postman. Donald the Post.[2] He rode on a shaggy and very small pony, both man and beast being of a very low order. There is a story of a man being found sleeping on the roadside by someone who, after shaking the sleeper asked, "Are you the post?". "No Sir, I am the Express." Donald was something of this sort. Someone called him the tea-pot, for his face was long and narrow, with a very pronounced nose which did bear some little resemblance to the spout of a tea-pot. He was of a most grave and melancholy aspect, and looked as if he carried the weight and responsibility

[1] See above, pp. 50, 168.
[2] This runner carried the mails on from Lochaline, whither they had been brought from Kingairloch by Hector Currie; see above, p. 55.

of the whole Kingdom on his back. He had a high idea of his office, and was a most upright and steady man, quite a character in his way. He always dined at Lochaline House on post days, which were only three times a week then, and the mails went by a very long and round about way, vastly different from what they do now, when there is a railway to Oban, and swift steamers through the Sound of Mull twice a day.

I can remember going to Lochaline from Oban in an open boat with four oars, and arriving in the middle of the night and being carried up to the house from the shore.

In Mother's youth, Thomas Campbell, the Poet was tutor at Ardtornish when that property belonged to the Gregorson family.[1]

Then, and later, there was a very pleasant society of various proprietors and their families, and visitors both in Morvern and in Mull. In those days there was more time for intercourse, and people became more intimate.

When I can remember Killundine belonged to the Maclaine family who were resident there summer and winter, as also was Lady Gordon at Drimnin, and the Macleods at the Manse of Morvern, while on the other side of us towards Oban were the Sellars of Ardtornish, and Smiths of Achranich, but those two families were only there in the summer.

Dr. Macleod was our nearest neighbour. He stood six feet seven in height[2] and on this account was called the "high Priest" of Morvern. He did not look so tall, being well proportioned. I always think that his wife had the sweetest and most beautiful face that I have ever seen. There was constant intercourse between Lochaline and the Manse. All who made that district dear are gone now!

At present Achranich, Ardtornish and Lochaline all belong to Mr. Smith, who has turned the whole into a huge deer-forest. Twice I have been back since we left, just to see the church-yard, and the graves in passing.

Many were still in the village who knew me, and weep we all did together when we thought of the happy long ago. "Lochaber no More."

These may seem trifling remembrances, not worth the telling, but to me they are "Embalmed in Memory with things that are Holy."

The time now came for the dear old Master to leave his family and numerous dependents. Except for his blindness he remained hale and hearty for all his weight of years. With silvery locks in plenty on his head, and a ruddy complexion, he did not look nearly so old as he was by many years, and his young appearance was greatly caused by the fact that not only had he all his teeth, but every one of them sound, and that at 93! He used to crack nuts with his teeth when others waited for the crackers.

[1] See above, p. 28 n. 3.
[2] His nephew, in an obituary notice, put his height at six feet nine: *Good words* (1882), 546.

He retained all his faculties, except sight, till within a year of his death, when he took to his bed and slowly and quietly passed away. By the will the property was sold at once. After it was advertised for sale Belle wept and prayed that she might not live to see strangers in the dear old home. Her prayer was answered, and she too was laid by loving hands in the old church-yard.

The departure of the family from the house which had been for so long a blessing to the whole district, was a source of distress and lamentation to all, but especially to the poor, to whom it had constantly been an open door of escape in time of need, for none were sent away without comfort to mind and body. I cannot forget one old man on the day we left weeping as he wrung his hands saying, "Morvern is a widow to-day." In the Gaelic language many of them expressed their sorrow to Mother in words untranslateable—so full of anguish were they—in that most expressive of all languages.

Appendix E

IV. EXTRACTS FROM
DONALD MACKICHAN'S MEMOIRS, c. 1944

[Donald MacKichan (1858–1954) was joiner at Ardtornish Estate in succession to his father Charles MacKichan, who had first come to Achranich in 1853 and had resided there permanently from 1856. The MacKichans lived first in a small cottage 300 yards south of Craigendarroch, but moved to Rose Cottage when it was built for them in about 1872, where Donald stayed for most of the rest of his life. Donald (who had been an office-bearer in the H.L.L.R.A. in the 1880s) dictated his memoirs from notes in about 1944 to his niece, Mrs Charlotte Cameron, and her daughter, Miss Catherine Cameron. The untitled manuscript, which was lost for some years after MacKichan's death, is now in *AP*.]

...Many years ago...[I was] in conversation with a man the name of MacIntyre a native of Morvern, who had served as a Constable in the Glasgow Police Force until he reached the age limit to retire, and in which he was held as a highly respected member.[1] He was also noted as one who had a very retentive memory. After retiring from the Force, he returned home in order to spend the remainder of his life in his native place. While in life he took a keen interest in the affairs of the Parish, and was for a number of years a member of the Parish Council. Before joining the Police Force, he was employed as a Shepherd for a few years on the Ardtornish Estate. He was keenly interested in Sheep Stock, and was very much surprised to find on his return, that the number of Sheep on Ardtornish, and Achranich Estates, had decreased so very much. He said he could give me the number that were on each Hirsel, on both Estates, when he went to Old Ardtornish in the year 1860, of which I took note at the time. The numbers were

Ardtornish	1,000	Ullin	600
Inniemore	550	Cloinlaid	900
Eignaig	500	Ulladale	500
Ternait	900	Corrospine & Acharn	1,500
Achranich	1,300	Bein-na-h'uamh	700
Claish, or Dhugary	500	Inniebeg & Inniemore	600
Claggan	500	Achnagaun	600
		Total	10,650

[1] Hugh MacIntyre (1845–1922); herd-boy at Claggan 1859; assistant shepherd at Old Ardtornish, 1860–9; Glasgow Police Force, 1869–1903 (retiring as Constable, Merit Grade); pensioner, 1903–22, living in Lochaline village (*Census*, 1861; Journals and Ledgers, *AP*; Corporation of Glasgow, Police and Superannuation Records; *VR*).

Diaries, memoirs, etc.

This large number of sheep (if correct) goes to prove how very much the land has deteriorated in the short space of a life time.[1] I remember when at school in Lochaline, a large Paddle Steamer named the Montague,[2] with two main decks, fitted up, and penned off, suitable for carrying sheep stock, used to come from Liverpool to the old Pier at Lochaline in the Autumn, in order to take away the sheep that are usually sold off, at that time of the year. I remember it being said at the time that she was capable of carrying between 2 & 3 thousand sheep. The cargo was made up of sheep from Ardtornish, Achranich, and one or two of the neighbouring Estates.

To us boys who were at School at the time, the coming of the Montague, and the Cattle Market which was held twice a year (in May and November) were the three chief events of the year, events which were greatly enjoyed by us.

The Cattle Market was held about 200 yd[s] above the high road and in line with the D[rs] House at Knock.[3] The Market Stance was partly enclosed by a stone dyke, and partly by turf walling. On one occasion when in company with other boys at the market, I found to my surprise that two Tents (one large) had been put up at the stance, by two of the local Merchants who were catering for the people that attended the Market. At one time a large number of Cattle were sent to the Market, but as years went on the number became gradually less, until in the year 1876 or –77 the holding of the Market was discontinued.

Acharn Estate Club Farm

The boundary of this Farm included both hill and lower ground from the march at Larachbeg, to the march at the head of Loch-Arienas, between Acharn, and Glenmorven Estates. There were six Tenants on the Farm, and the stock allowed for each Tenant was 8 cows and their followers, one horse, and 140 sheep. There was also a Shepherd to look after the sheep and Cattle, and two or three Cottars with a cows grass each, about Larachbeg. At the Arienas end of the Farm and on the

---

[1] Where MacIntyre's figures can be checked they are found to be fairly accurate; on the Ardtornish hirsels, the average clipping accounts for 1853–7 and the numbers of sheep actually delivered to Smith in 1860 were as follows: Ardtornish, 922/886; Inninmore, 497/409; Eignaig, 509/406; Tearnait, 715/700; Clounlaid, 942/955; Uladail, 469/363; Crosben, 909/1,227; Durinemast (Beinn na h-Uamha), 574/525; Unibeg–Unimore, 544/545; Achadh nan Gamhna, 524/545 (Ardtornish clipping journal 1851–7, *AP*; *Case for Thomas Valentine Smith, Esq. . . . 1885*, 31, *AP*). But MacIntyre's figures for the Achranich hirsels must be too large, for they come to a total of 2,900 sheep, whereas we know that there was a total of only 2,013 sheep on these same hirsels at 31 Dec. 1859 (ledger, *AP*).

[2] *Montague* is not known to Mr Graham Langmuir, who thinks that she may have been an ex-blockade-runner of the American Civil War.

[3] The old market place at 678458 is now covered by forestry plantation, but the air photographs taken in 1946 before the trees were planted show no sign of it.

Glenmorven side of the march, there were fully more people than there were on the Club Farm. I was told by a Grandson of one of those that was brought up there, when his Grandfather was a young lad, there were 29 able bodied young men in Achnagaun Club-Farm, and 29 as strong and as capable, in the little Hamlet, on the other side of the March at Inniemore.

Soon after the Tenants had left the Club Farm, the Acharn Estate was sold to Mr P. Sellar. This took place in the year 1838.

He bought Ulladale and Cloinlaid in 1841 and Ardtornish Estate in 1843 [actually 1844].

Meal Mills

There were three Meal Mills in the Parish of Morven, one at Drimnin [Mungasdail], one at Savary, and one at Acharn. The system of payment which was common at the time for the milling of the grain was in kind, not in money. The Miller got in return for every boll of grain that he milled one half peck of meal, and the Acharn Millers share for the milling of the grain from White Glen alone came to 16 Bolls. This means that a very large quantity of grain was raised in the White Glen at one time and I was told that this information could be found in the old records of the Parish.[1]

Conversation with Sea Captain

Many years ago I met a Captain and Owner of a Sailing Ship at Lochaline, with his three sons who were on their way to Stornoway with a cargo of salt for the fish Curers. He was an old man (an Irishman) to my surprise he asked if there were any people at Achabeg, which is about 2 miles from Lochaline in the Fuinary direction. I said there were a few, then he said, when I was a boy I used to come with my Father to Achabeg for a cargo of potatoes in the Autumn. Cultivation must have been very largely engaged in, and the potatoe crop a great success, when they could afford to sell as many over and above their own requirements.

Roads & Bridges

...The old Public Road which ran along all the way from Lochaline to Ardgour has been in use for a very long time back. Improvements have been made to it on different Occasions, parts of which were either raised up, or lowered down, as required. The old track can easily be followed yet, where any change was made. There were also a few branch roads (or tracks) which were joined up to the main road, and were called public right of ways. The first of these branch roads, after leaving Lochaline was almost at the very top of the steep hill above Kinlochaline, it branched

[1] No such records appear to have survived.

off at right angles from the main road, ran down to the foot of the rocks, then round the Druidical Circle, which is on the left hand, and down on the low side of the arrable land towards the back of the old Castle. From there it turned to the left at right angles down towards the tree root Ford (Ath-Stoc-an) which is immediately opposite the little Garage at Rose Cottage.[1] After crossing the Ford the road turned to the left towards Claggan, and to the right towards Achranich House, much on the same track as it is on now, only when rounding the head of the Loch, it turned to more the left hand and was kept well above high water mark, right through the (now private grounds) along past Cnoc-an-or (the Golden Hillock) on which the Mansion House is built, and round by the old stone Bridge to Achranich House which was the terminus in that direction at the time.

On the left hand to about half way between the Ford and Claggan, it was much on the same track as now also, but on reaching half-way up, it turned a little to the right, and kept higher up all the way until it joined the main road at Claggan Cottage.

In going along the main road towards Acharn the Ford on the Acharn River, which is about half way down the Avenue is passed as one enters the wood on the way to the Bridge.

Before the Acharn Stone Bridge was built, the road at the near end of the Bridge, turned to the right round the rock, and ran along a little way back from the river, to the Ford at (Ath-buie) Yellow Ford in Ulladale.[2] From the river-bank on the opposite side, it was carried up to, and joined to the main road running through the White Glen.

There was also an old road (or track) which ran down the black Glen from Corrospine, before coming quite as far down as the present one is, it turned to the left down towards Ulladale, and along to the Ford, where any person from the Glens had to cross in order to get to Lochaline, as there was no Bridge across the river at Acharn, at that time.[3]

A pass or Track which struck off from the left side of the road when within, about 100 yards of the second mile stone, from Lochaline, ran along above the rocks on Kinlochaline Hill, then down the Corrie at Achnagaun and joined the road almost at Ath-corrie Bridge, at Loch-Arienas. This shortened the road considerably for people who had to

---

[1] This road is shown on *OS 1872*, and is still mostly traceable.

[2] This road can still be followed from the southern arch of Acharn bridge to Ath Buidhe.

[3] The track from the old Crosben road to Uladail is still just traceable, but Mac-Kichan is wrong in thinking that people from the glens had to cross the White Water at Ath Buidhe; the main road actually continued westwards from Uladail, forded the Black Water just above the confluence at Acharn and then forded the mouth of Loch Arienas at 696506, swung out westwards to take in Achadh nan Gamhna and joined the route of the present main road under Sithean Achadh nan Gamhna; parts of this old road, and the ford at Arienas, are still traceable.

walk to, and from Barr, and Kinloch to Lochaline. This was called a public right of way, all of which is now under Afforestation.[1]

...The stone Bridge at Acharn could not have been built until about the year 1850–51, because in September 1848, when Mr O. H. Smith and one of his Daughters went on horseback to pay their first visit to Mr Forbes, of Kingairloch. They went up by the old road to the Ford at Ulladale, and crossed over to the other side of the river, then on to Kingairloch, through the White Glen. ...

Dispute between Mr O. H. Smith, & Mr P. Sellar[2]

About the end of Autumn 1848, Mr P. Sellar made arrangements to transfer some sheep from Acharn to Ternate, on a certain date, with Tar and Tallow, for the smearing of the sheep, all of which were to be taken across the Ford at Ulladale, then on to Ternate. On hearing of this intended procedure, Mr Smith decided to meet Mr Sellar on the day in question, and protest against such an order being carried into effect, without due notice having been given to him, as Proprietor of the neighbouring Estate, over which the sheep would have to travel half-way before reaching Ternate. They met on the hill, and after having a lengthy discussion about the matter parted without having come to any decision. However it was arranged that they should meet on the following day, which they did, and having then discussed the matter more fully they came to the conclusion that unless free access to, and from the different Estates were agreed to, sheep, stock, and cattle, could never be looked after properly.

They parted in quite a friendly way, and for years after leaving Ardtornish, members of Mr Sellar's Family were regular visitors to Ardtornish Tower.

Upkeep of Roads and Bridges

Shortly after roads were made, and Bridges erected in the district, Toll money was charged on all users of the road who passed through the Toll gate with Vehicles, the gate which was placed across the road about one hundred yards north, of the D[rs] House at Knock, was attended too, by a man the name of Cameron, whose house was quite close to where the gate was placed. The road Tax in the course of a few years, was withdrawn. The man who was collecting the road Tax, was one of the Tenants that left the Club Farm of Achnagaun and Inniebeg in 1838.

[1] This track is marked on *OS 1872*, and most of it is visible in *Air photographs 1946*; it has now disappeared under forestry plantation.

[2] This is an interestingly simplified version of the complicated dispute described above (pp. 63–4), omitting the question of the fishing rights; Mrs W. Y. Sellar's version (Sellar, E. M. (1907), 43), equally simplified, refers only to the fishing question and says nothing about the rights of way.

Diaries, memoirs, etc.

Achranich Old House

The Old House at Achranich which was a two story Building, was built with stone and lime, and slated. It stood about three to four feet back from, and ran parallel with, the front of the present Building.[1] It had a small Porch on the side facing the new stone Bridge, in which was the front door entrance into the house. The side facing the old stone Bridge was the front of the house (proper) the reason being, any traffic to, or— from Achranich, was round by the old Bridge, there being no roadway to the Ferry at that time. The only other means of approach to the house, was by crossing at the Ford on the Rannoch, which was about half way between the new stone Bridge, and the little suspension Bridge at the Farm.

When M[r] Smith bought the Estate in 1848 [actually 1845] he put an addition of Timber to the Gable end of the house next the road, with a doorway slapped through the wall from the floor above, in order to give more sleeping accomodation upstairs. The lower part being used as a store. There was also a lean-to addition of stone and lime put to the end next the river, in which the Manager lived for a number of years. A small Building was also put up against the Garden Wall, near to where the Meat Safes now are, but on a lower level, and was used as a Kitchen etc for the Shepherd and farm workers. Another small building of Wood and Corr-Iron, was run along from the Kitchen towards the River, and against the Garden Wall, and was used as a Laundry for quite a number of years. The Kitchen in the course of time, was not required, and was handed over to the School Managers, to be used as a side School for the benefit of the young Children about the head of the Loch, in which they were taught, until old enough to be able to walk to Lochaline School.

The long Building at the steading, built with stone and lime which formed the Barn, Byre, and Stable, with Dairy and Cheese store on the ground floor of the near end, and with sleeping accomodation above, for the men servants from the Mansion House, excepting the Butler, was built in 1851.[2] At the other end of the Building there was also sleeping accomodation for one or two Shepherds, a young Ploughman, and a herd boy. The Barn in its original form would hold a large quantity of Hay, or Corn. There was only one large double door on the high side of the Building, and on the level of the main floor, through which a horse and cart, fully loaded with hay or corn, could pass through and turn round on the floor in any direction as required. The roadway leading up to the door was built up at the sides with stone and lime, with cope on the top, and ran well back, in order to give a very gradual rise up towards the door-way.

[1] I.e. the manager's house at Achranich with the estate office. See Plates 14a and 14b.
[2] Plate 2a.

Appendix E

Boathouse and Road to Ferry

The old Boathouse at the head of Lochaline was built by Mr O. H. Smith in the year 1852. Boating was very much engaged in at that time, on account of no road being on either side of the Loch, but in 1853–4 he made a road from Achranich along the seashore to the march between Ardtornish and Achranich Estates. By an arrangement between him, and Mr Sellar the road was carried on all the way to the Ferry.[1] This opening up of the way between the two Estates was a great benefit to both families.

Mr Smith drove to Ardtornish, for the first time, in the season of 1855; and Mr Sellar[2] was now, also, able to drive to Achranich, and Acharn.

The River Aline

...The Kinlochaline Proprietor used to let the salmon fishing along the shore from the march at Achaforse Burn to the mouth of the river. The salmon chest was placed at the lower end of the little island below Rose Cottage which is about as far up as the salt water goes during a high spring tide. The Fisherman's house was on the same site as Castle Cottages are on now. His name was Alex[r] McPherson (better known locally as the Skipper).

In the year 1851–52 Mr Sinclair who was now Proprietor of the Kinlochaline Estate sold his fishing rights on the river Aline, with the Fisherman's House and site, to Mr O. H. Smith. It was then that Mr Smith put the Log Bridge across the river immediately below the present stone Bridge this was a great benefit to the workers, and others who had occasion to cross the river at anytime.[3]

Oak Cutting on Lochaline and Kinlochaline Estates

About the year 1868–70, soon after the late Mrs Campbell Paterson became Proprietrix of the Lochaline Estate and that part of Kinlochaline Estate from Achaforse burn to the march at Larachbeg, the whole of the young oak from the shore to the foot of the rocks, along the embankment from the head of the Loch to Lochaline, was cut down and after a good beating the bark was ripped off. This work was done by

[1] This was part of the settlement of 1850; see above, p. 180.
[2] Patrick Sellar himself had died in 1851.
[3] MacKichan is mistaken. Patrick Sellar owned the whole of the fishings of Kinlochaline from 1841 until he sold the fishing rights on the east bank of the Aline to Smith in 1850 (see above, pp. 135, 180). The Sellars continued in possession of the fishing rights on the west bank of the Aline, and the fishing station by the Castle, until Ardtornish Estate was sold to Smith in 1860. From 1857 to 1859 the Sellars let what had been the fisherman's cottage to Smith for 5s. a year; it may have been then that the log bridge was built (ledgers, *AP*).

contract during the summer months when the young oak was full of sap, by men, women and boys. The bark and the dressed oak was put in separate heaps along the seashore ready for shipment to the southern markets. The bark was largely used in the tanning of leather, and the dressed oak in the process of smelting iron. At a much earlier date, the oak on Acharn Estate on the north east side of Locharienas was cut down for the same purpose, and I was told that bark to the amount of 60 Tons was got from the cutting of the oak there. This work was done by contract, by a man the name of Malcolm Sinclair.

The Village of Lochaline

When I went to Lochaline School about the year 1868 there were 14 slated houses in the village, and a large number of thatched houses also. The Hotel,[1] the largest of a row of houses which ran along from very near the shop, on the high side of the road towards the Lodge, consisted of ground floor, first-floor, and attics, with store accomodation at end and stable D° at back. The house adjoining the Hotel, both of which were built by a man the name of Cameron, consisted of a General Store and Post Office on ground floor. The first floor and attics being let to tenants. The next, a two storey building built by a man the name of Angus Morrison, the ground floor of which was let to a Publican the name of McInnes and the upper floor to tenants. The last in the row a small cottage of one storey occupied by, and belonged to a man the name of Angus M^{ac}Vicar.

There were 5 Grocer's shops in the village, one of which had a grocer's License, also a large number of people, among whom were a Cart and wheel-wright working on his own account, with Journey-man and an apprentice. Two joiners, Three Builders, Three Shoemakers, Three Tailors, and a Blacksmith at the crossroads at Kiel. Almost all of them Descendants of those who had a small farm or holding in the Parish at one time. Trade on two days of the week Tuesday or Friday was usually busy. These were usually the days on which goods were landed at Lochaline by the Cargo boats from Glasgow, it being the only port of call in the Parish at that time.

Lochaline School

When I went to School in the year 1868 there were a large number of Schollars in Lochaline, and district. Between 50 and 60 Schollars attended School, and only one Schoolmaster. (The late and very much respected Mr J. Cameron.) He occasionally complained of headache—and no wonder. He had far too much to do. Some of the young men in the

---

[1] The Cameron Arms hotel, built by John Cameron, merchant (*c.* 1848), was bought by T. V. Smith in 1877, and was demolished in 1913–14 (Conveyances, etc., *AP*; *VR*).

district who had grown up to full manhood, when at home in Winter and early Spring, attended School regularly, one of whom had a heavy whisker and moustache.

A number of them were so successful with their studies that they went from the School here to the Training College in Glasgow, and finally to the Glasgow University. Three of them were members of one family, two of whom followed the Ministry, and the third, the Medical Profession. Those three were at a disadvantage during their studying period on account of their Father not being able to assist financially. He being paid only at the rate of 15/- a week for his labour yet both parents were in character and example a credit to any community, of which they were members.

There were other three who were very successful with their studies also, two of whom followed the Medical Profession. The other a class mate of my own, turned out such a brilliant Schollar, that at the end of his University Career, he was appointed Master of Methods in the Glasgow University, a position which he held with distinction, until he reached the age limit to retire. He was a son of the last Millar who had the Croft, and Meal Mill at Savary, which is about two miles from Lochaline.[1]

Others distinguished themselves in Commerce, Industry and the Merchant Service.

Trip to Staffa and Iona

In the end of September 1865 [actually 1866] Mr O. H. Smith chartered the Paddle Steamer Pioneer, from David Hutcheson & Co., in order to give a trip to all the Employees on the Ardtornish, and Achranich Estates, and others from about Lochaline. He also invited Mr & Mrs Gordon Drimnin, Colonel & Mrs Cheape Killundine, and a Shooting Tenant—Mr McNichol who was in Garmony Mull,[2] to accompany him and his Son and Daughter on the day's outing. After getting the Party on board they sailed along the Sound past Tobermory, and on rounding Ardmore Point fell in with a Shoal of Porpoise to the number of about four or five hundred. They formed up in line and kept abreast of the Steamer—neck & neck, for four or five miles, to the great amusement of all on board, some of whom had never been on board ship or seen

[1] Hugh MacCallum (1858–1935), b. Knock (Mull); family at Savary c. 1872–88; encouraged by Dr John MacLeod to become assistant teacher at Bonnavoulin School (c. 1874), and to go on to Glasgow University (1880); M.A. 1888; successively schoolteacher, and lecturer in education at the University and at Jordanhill; retired 1924, but did not return to Morvern (University records; information from his son, Mr H. S. MacCallum of Bearsden).

[2] John MacNichol was tenant of Garmony at least from 1862 to 1872 (Haliburton's *County Directory of Scotland*); he appears in the Ardtornish game books in 1867 and 1868, and was photographed in kilt and bonnet outside Ardtornish Tower in 1867 (*Photographs (Gertrude Smith)*). The Smiths never had shooting tenants at Ardtornish, and MacNichol was their guest, e.g. at the Estate Ball in 1867.

porpoise before. On reaching near Staffa the first detachment went down to Lunch, and the second—immediately after leaving Staffa, for Iona.

During the time the party were ashore at Iona, Mr Smith and two of the other Gentlemen went across to see the Granite Quarries at Bunessan, from whence the Thames Bank, and Albert Memorial, were being supplied. After returning from Bunessan, and when all were safely on board, they resumed the journey home, landing their Guests at the various ports of call, and arrived in Lochaline early in the evening, after having a most enjoyable days outing. The weather conditions were all that could be desired, being as calm as glass, all day long.

After the Party had landed and three ringing cheers were accorded to Mr Smith for his great kindness, and a Volley from the old Cannon on the look-out hill, by old Murdoch the Ferry-man, thus ended a memorable days Trip.

The Bridge near Entrance Gate to Mansion House

This Bridge which was erected in the early sixties was all of iron, with sides framed up to carry joists, cover plates, and asphalting. It was partly suspended by heavy wire ropes taken over massive stone pillars with cope on top, placed at each end of the Bridge, and with heavy iron rods from top of pillars run well back into the ground and securely fixed there. There were also smaller iron rods suspended from the wire ropes, and fixed to the top of the side railings all of which gave a very attractive appearance to the whole bridge.

The Bridge and abutments with retaining wall and filling in of the roadway round the head of the Loch was rather a costly undertaking. All the material required was taken in trucks from the free stone quarry which was about one hundred yards higher up than the old boathouse. A temporary timber bridge was put across the river in order to carry sleepers and rails, for the light railway which was laid down from the quarry to the river, across the bridge, and along to the end of the road, as the wall and filling in of the roadway proceeded. Originally the course of the river when nearing the bridge turned to the right, and ran in a semi-circular way towards the old boathouse, the old course of which can easily be followed yet. When the course was changed and ran along more in line with the boathouse, this meant that an extra supply of stone was required for it also amounting in all approximately to about two thousand five hundred tons.

This railway can undoubtedly be claimed as the first that ever was constructed in Morven.[1]

---

[1] The bridge can be seen under construction in *Photographs (Gertrude Smith)*, 48 and 49, the second of which also shows the light railway track; it seems likely that these photographs were taken *c.* 1870, not in the early 1860s.

Appendix E

Ardtornish Tower

When Mr O. H. Smith decided to build a house at Achranich he had no intentions of doing so hurriedly. For a number of years after the building of the house began, the work was only carried on during the late summer and autumn when he was here in residence. After purchasing the Ardtornish and Acharn Estates in 1859 [actually 1860] the building of the new house was stopped, and all attention given to the repairing, and improving of the old house and steading at Ardtornish. After a lapse of about three years, the building of the new house was resumed again and was ready for occupation in the end of July 1866.[1] The Clock Tower was also carried on then, and was finished at the same time as the Mansion House.

In the year 1884 Mr T. V. Smith decided to build a larger house, as he thought the accomodation in the old Mansion House was not sufficient to accomodate the number of guests he might have on occasion, therefore the work of taking down the old house was commenced at once and carried on without delay until the whole building was down. Soon after arrangements were made for the building of the new house by contract. The mason work by a Tobermory contractor, and Joiner work by an Oban contractor. Shortly after a start was made with the building of the house, Mr Smith changed his mind and thought that the work would be done better privately. The contractors were allowed to go, but of course were well compensated for non-fulfillment of contract. Then the building of the house was carried on under Estate Management, and was finished and ready for occupation about the end of July 1890.[2]

The Old Mansion House Ardtornish

It is difficult to know who was the owner of Ardtornish Estate when the house was built, more than likely it was owned by the Duke of Argyll at the time, because the Campbell of Argyll owned the whole of Morvern at one time. The house was one of the best built houses in the Parish.[3] The mortar with which the walls were built must have been exceptionally strong, because when the walls were being taken down, blasting with powder had to be used in order to get them down more quickly. It was Mr T. V. Smith who ordered this old house to be taken down about the year 1895.[4] So far as I am aware, his object in doing so, was to avoid having to pay taxes on unoccupied house property.

[1] The family moved into the new house on 11 Oct. 1866 (Game book, *AP*). See Plate 5.   [2] Plate 13.
[3] For details of Ardtornish House, see above, p. 168, and Plate 12.
[4] Ardtornish House was 'dismantled' in 1896, but was not pulled down until 1907, and then apparently for sentimental reasons, not in order to save money (see above, p. 186 n. 3).

Diaries, memoirs, etc.

Lochaline House Fuinary

It was Mr J. Sinclair Sen[r] and his brother-in-law Mr King that built the Mansion house at Fuinary about the year 1848.[1] The ground floor of the house had very low ceilings, but the upper parts in many respects were quite modern. The late Mr G. Sellar in 1910 gave instructions to take the house down,[2] but to save lead, or any other material that would be of any use. It was understood at the time that his reason for doing so, was to avoid paying taxes for a house that was unlikely to be of any further use.

Heaviest flood within living Memory in the River Aline

About the end of November 1868 a severe frost came on which lasted about a week, then a heavy fall of snow which did not last long. This change was followed by a rapid thaw with rain coming down in torrents. In a short time the river began to rise quickly and soon overflowed its banks. We were living at that time in the old house which stood about 20 yards in from the gate in the middle of the field between Rose Cottage and Craigendarroch.[3] In a few hours time the water had risen to the level of the roadway, and soon found its way across to the cottage. Finally it reached half way up the kitchen grate, and right up into the wood behind the Cottage. All of us had to leave the house when the water came over the door step, a few of us were taken to the Mansion House, others to the Gamekeepers cottage, and two to the Managers house at Achranich. We had to remain there for a few days until the house was again put in order. To give an idea of the extent to which the river had been flooded, the Postman (Hector Currie) who was on the run home with the Mails from Kingairloch, when he reached Claggan Bridge found he could not cross over to the other side owing to the depth of water and running stream at the low end of the Bridge. He continued the journey along the road to Craigendarroch Bridge, part of which he had to walk on top of the stone dyke which ran along on the high side of the road, on reaching the bridge he found the water was too deep here also, and could not get across. He then came along to the log bridge at the Old Castle, and had to wait there until the tide, and flood receeded before he could cross to the other side and resume his journey to Lochaline Post Office where he arrived at a belated hour, an unusual experience for Hector.

[1] Lochaline House was built in 1821–5 by Sinclair. James King was Sinclair's son-in-law, who acted as factor at Lochaline Estate from about 1855 to 1863. See above, p. 169, and Plate 4.
[2] Date confirmed by *VR*.
[3] These cottages were not of course built until after 1868.

Appendix E

The next highest flood which I have seen in the River Aline during my lifetime, took place at the end of July 1882. After having very heavy rain which lasted fully a week, the river began to rise, and rose steadily until it reached the level of the roadway at the old cottage, but not any higher. The two fishing bridges on the upper reaches of the river, the timber for which was all laid on the ground ready for assembling[1] was swept out into the river and carried right down into Lochaline. Fortunately there was a strong breeze of south west wind blowing up the Loch at the time which helped to keep the timber from being carried down by the ebb tide, and right into the Sound of Mull. Boats were got ready by the Employees, and after a dilligent search in and around both sides of the Loch, all the timber was got with the exception of a few small pieces which was easily replaced.

Storms and high Tides

One of the most violent storms ever experienced on the west coast of Scotland took place on Sunday the 28th Dec 1879 with the result that great damage was done to house property, and plantations. On the Ardtornish, Achranich, and Acharn Estates 8000 trees were blown down. All the trees which ran along above the fields at Old Ardtornish, lay flat as if it were a field of corn, after being cut by the scythe. Owing to the unusual height to which the tide had risen, during the storm, roads running along near the shore were badly damaged also. Huge gaps were made in the retaining wall of the roadway round the head of Lochaline, and also much damage to the lower parts of the road towards the Ferry. The log bridge across the river below the Old Castle was carried away by the high tide and thrown up on the old road near by. An old Lean too building which stood about 20 or 30 yards south of Castle Cottage and supposed to have been above high water mark, was occupied by two women one of whom was within a year or two of her hundredth birthday. When the tide had come up almost to the door, and the storm still increasing the two women were taken away to one of the neighbouring houses. Shortly after they had left a big wave came in with the rising tide, rolled up against the door and window, and threw them both inside the house. In a short time almost all they possessed was washed out by suction from the back wash of the waves. On the following morning Mary Cameron the youngest of the two women who lived there, was early on the scene. She had a small chest in which she kept a few articles of clothing and a little money amounting in all to fully £3. 0. 0. to her great surprise the chest and all it contained was washed away, and no where to be seen. However, a dilligent search was made along a huge roll

[1] Both these fishing bridges are marked on *OS 1872*; presumably they were being rebuilt in 1882.

of seaweed which lay on the shore in front of the two cottages, and when near the far away end, the chest was found with the lid open, and nothing in it. The search was continued a little farther on, and when almost at the end of the roll, the little bag containing the money was found, for which poor Mary felt very thankful.[1]

Highest Tide ever recorded on the west coast of Scotland

This extraordinary high tide, accompanied by a westerly gale of wind, which took place during the winter of 1881 badly damaged the Lismore Lighthouse and adjoining buildings. ...In order to indicate the height to which the tide had risen too at the head of Lochaline, it may be mentioned that a large rowing boat which had been drawn up on the north east side of the old Boathouse and placed on the ground close to the high side of the road, was found when the tide receded, within a short distance of the fence that runs along the bottom of the wood towards the stone Bridge. Also at the entrance Gate to the Mansion-House, seaweed was found right along the top railing of the Gate, which no doubt was washed up by the waves, and remained there. It may be said that the Gate at that time, was of iron, and 4 ft 6″ high. The tide mark could also be seen a little way up on the bottom of the newly sloped embankment in front of Achranich House.

[1] Following the loss of her bothy, Mary Cameron moved into Kinlochaline Castle, which was then an unrestored ruin (no more is heard of her elderly companion). "It may be stated", wrote a correspondent to the *Oban Times* of 22 Sept. 1883, "that the woman has a great aversion to go to live in the Village, and she cannot be greatly blamed, as a more miserable place does not exist. It would also remove her too far from Mr Smith's estate on which she obtains work." She was still squatting in the Castle in 1885, when *The Highland Magazine* remarked (i, 72–4): "Her sleeping apartment is unmercifully exposed to the elements. ...As a rule she passes the time knitting."

APPENDIX F

GENEALOGICAL TABLES

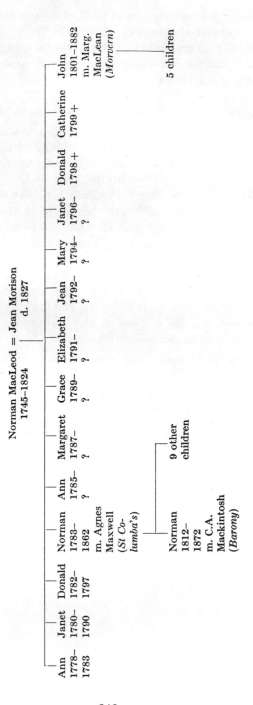

Norman MacLeod = Jean Morison
1745–1824   d. 1827

| Ann 1778–1783 | Janet 1780–1790 | Donald 1782–1797 | Norman 1783–1862 m. Agnes Maxwell (*St Columba's*) | Ann 1785– ? | Margaret 1787– ? | Grace 1789– ? | Elizabeth 1791– ? | Jean 1792– ? | Mary 1794– ? | Janet 1796– ? | Donald 1798 + | Catherine 1799 + | John 1801–1882 m. Marg. MacLean (*Morvern*) |

Norman 1812–1872 m. C.A. Mackintosh (*Barony*)

9 other children

5 children

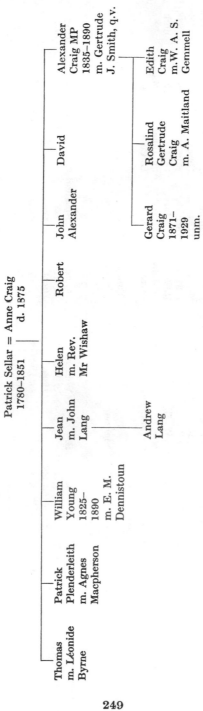

Patrick Sellar = Anne Craig
1780–1851   d. 1875

Thomas
m. Léonide
Byrne

Patrick
Plenderleith
m. Agnes
Macpherson

William
Young
1825–
1890
m. E. M.
Dennistoun

Jean
m. John
Lang

Helen
m. Rev.
Mr Wishaw

Robert

John
Alexander

David

Alexander
Craig MP
1835–1890
m. Gertrude
J. Smith, q.v.

Andrew
Lang

Gerard
Craig
1871–
1929
unm.

Rosalind
Gertrude
Craig
m. A. Maitland

Edith
Craig
m.W. A. S.
Gemmell

William Smith MP = Frances Coape
1756–1835   1758–1840

Martha Frances 1782–1870 unm.

Benjamin MP 1783–1860

Ann Elizabeth 1786–1854 m. G. T. Nicholson — Nicholsons

Frances 1788–1880 m. W. E. Shore (Nightingale) — Nightingales

William Adams 1789–1870 unm.

Joanna Maria 1791–1884 m. John Carter — Bonham Carters

Samuel 1794–1880 m. Mary Shore — Shore Smiths

Octavius Henry 1796–1871 m. Jane G. Cooke

Frederick Coape 1798–1882 m. Margaret Yates

Julia 1799–1883 unm.

Leigh Smiths

Frederic Cooke 1821–1839 unm.

Thomas Valentine 1825–1906 twice m. no issue

Gerard B. c. 1827–1858 unm.

William c. 1828–1899 m. Harriet Cook

Flora Maria 1834–1919 unm.

Rosalind ?–1853 unm.

Edith ?–1855 unm.

Gertrude Joanna 1844–1929 m. A.C. Sellar, q.v.

BIBLIOGRAPHY

MANUSCRIPTS, MAPS AND PHOTOGRAPHS

I. Public records
II. Estate papers
III. Memoirs, diaries, etc.
IV. Maps, plans and atlases
V. Photographs
VI. Thesis

I. PUBLIC RECORDS

SRO   *Scottish record office*, General Register House, Edinburgh 2.

GRS   *General register of sasines*, 1781–1868 (references are to volume-number and folio).

GR   *General register of sasines* (*Argyll*), 1868–   (references are to volume-
(Argyll)   number and folio).
      Plans: see section IV below

RSA   *Register of sasines abridgments* (*Argyll*), 1781–   (references are to the year of entry and the serial number of the abridgment).

VR   *Valuation roll of the County of Argyll*, Parish of Morvern, 1855–   (MS 1855–74, printed thereafter).

RGO   *Registrar-General's Office*, New Register House, Edinburgh 2.

Census   *Census of Scotland*, 1841–91, Parish of Morvern, enumeration schedules (Parish of Strontian, 1841–51 for Liddisdale/Achagavel).
      Parochial registers, Parish of Morvern.
        Births, 1803–.
        Marriages, 1804–.
        Deaths, 1855–.

ACOL   *Argyllshire County Offices*, Lochgilphead.
      Minute books of the Parochial Board of Morvern, 1845–1930.
      Minute books of the District Committee of Ardnamurchan, 1890–1930.
      Minute books of the Argyleshire Road Trustees, 1775–1890 (lacking vols. for 1794–1802, 1818–27).
      Minute book of the Morvern District Road Trustees, 1864–90 (earlier volume missing).

VR   *Valuation roll of the County of Argyll*, 1688 (transcript), 1751, 1802, 1855–.

II. ESTATE PAPERS

AP   *Ardtornish papers:* Mrs O. H. Smith, Ardtornish, Morvern.
      Estate and farm records
        Account sheets, 1909–18.
        Cash books, bought and sold books, 1890– .
        Journals, 1850–80 (Achranich Estate, 1850–9; Artornish Estate, 1860–80).
        Ledgers, 1853–74, 1890–1908 (Achranich Estate, 1853–9; Ardtornish Estate, 1860–74, 1890–1908. Includes annual trading accounts in 1853–74, and annual balance sheets in 1890–1908).
        Letter books, and files of correspondence, 1882–.
        Sheep accounts: Ardtornish clipping journal, 1851–7; Ardtornish Estate herding books, 1880–4, 1885–.
        Time and pay books, Ardtornish Estate labourers, 1875–.

251

Bibliography

Game books
> Game and fishing books, 1853–80 (lacking 1855, 1858, 1869–71 (part)).
> Gamekeepers' journals, 1883, 1887–1905.
> Game books, 1907–15, 1915–25, 1925–36, 1937–.
> Stalking journal, 1870–84.

Plans
> Plans and diagrams of buildings, bridges, etc., 1871–.
> Plans and maps of the estate: see section IV below.

Miscellaneous documents
> A collection of letters, memoranda, notebooks, etc., dating from 1850 up to the present day.

Titles and other deeds
> The titles and other deeds of the Estates of Ardtornish, Kinlochaline, Acharn and Lochaline, 1703–1888 (held hitherto by the solicitors to the owner of Ardtornish Estate in Edinburgh; now deposited in the Scottish Record Office).

Inventory 1872
> *Inventory of the title deeds of the Estates of Achranich, Ardtornish and others belonging to Thomas Valentine Smith Esquire*, 1872–88 (now *SRO*).

ICP   *Inveraray Castle papers:* The Duke of Argyll, Inveraray Castle, Inveraray, Argyll.
> *Instructions to Chamberlains* (Mull and Morvern), 1750–62, 1804–9 (see also Cregeen, E. R. (1964)).
> *Plans:* see section IV below.

Rent rolls
> Sett and rental of Mull and Morvern, 1744, etc.

Tack books
> *Book of Mull and Morvern tacks*, vols. '0', '1', '2', '3', '4'. (Vol. '0' is an unnumbered general collection of copies covering 1769–1807; the volumes numbered '1' to '4' are later copies of the same documents, with a few omissions and additions; vol. '4' carries the Morvern tacks up to 1813.)

Miscellaneous documents
> A very large collection of Argyll documents, with references to Morvern up to 1819.

NOTE: *ICP* is at present undergoing reorganisation, and further references to Morvern may be found in the future.

III. MEMOIRS, DIARIES, ETC.

Astley diary
See p. vii   Astley, Gertrude and Constance, *First Journal*, 1872–3 (Mrs John Lipscomb, Chilham, Canterbury).

King's memoirs
> King, Agnes R., *Little sketch of those who are gone, and scenes of long ago*, c. 1902 (typescript; Mrs Harcourt, Windlesham, Surrey; location of original unknown).

MacKichan's memoirs
> MacKichan, Donald, untitled memoirs written at his dictation, c. 1944 (*AP*).

NOTE: See above, p. 82 n. 2 and p. 89 n. 3 concerning the destruction of the Smith family papers and business records.

IV. MAPS, PLANS AND ATLASES (MSS. and printed)

Acharn plan 1815
> *Plan of the estate of Acharn, surveyed 1815*; MS., 1865, *AP*.

Achranich plan 1815
> *Plan of the lands of Achranich...belonging to John MacDonald Esqr. Borrodale, surveyed 1815, by Alexander Langlands*; lithograph, *AP*, *SRO*.

Bibliography

Ainslie's Scotland 1789
>Ainslie, John, *Scotland drawn from a series of...observations*; copper-plate, Edin., 1789.

Argyll estate plans 1770
>Richmond, James, *Plans of Mull and Morvern*, 1770; MS., *ICP*.

Argyll farms plan 1819
>*Plan of the farms in Morvern Argyll Shire the property of His Grace the Duke of Argyll, David Crawford Surveyor Edinr. 1819*; MS., *SRO* RH 3260.

Argyll farms plan (copy)
>Copy of *Argyll farms plan 1819*, with additions; MS., *SRO* RH 3033.

Clounlaid plan 1833
>*Plan of the farm of Claonlaid...surveyed 1833*; MS., 1865, *AP*.

Drimnin plan 1836
>*Plan of the Estate of Drimnin the property of Sir Charles Gordon 1836, David Wilson L-s-r*; MS., *SRO* RH 3258.

Knock plan 1788
>*Plan of Achnahaw Achabeg Keil and Knock in Morvern belonging to his Grace the Duke of Argyll taken in July 1788 By George Langlands*; MS., *SRO* RH 2971.

Knock plan 1815
>*Plan by Alexr. Langlands in Summer 1815* (of area covered by *Knock plan 1788*); MS., *SRO* RH 2993.

Langlands' Argyll 1801
>Langlands, George, and sons, *Map of Argyleshire*; copper-plate, 1801.

Morvern map 1865
>*Sketch of the Parish of Morvern*; MS., 1865, *AP*.

OS 1872
>*Ordnance survey of Argyleshire and Buteshire*, 6 inches to 1 mile, surveyed 1872 etc.

OS 1872 NB
>*Name books 60, 69 and 70 (Parish of Morvern)*, 1872, MS., Ordnance Survey, Edinburgh.

OS 1 inch 3rd ed.
>*Ordnance survey of Scotland*, 1 inch to 1 mile, 3rd ed., rev. 1904.

OS 1 inch 7th S.
>*Ordnance survey of Great Britain*, 1 inch to 1 mile, 7th series, rev. 1954 (6-figure map references are to sheets 45 and 46, grid square NM).

Roy's Scotland 1747–55
>Roy, William, *Map of Scotland*, 1747–55; MS., draft and finished version, BM K.XLVIII.25.8.

Thomson's atlas 1824
>Thomson, John, *The atlas of Scotland*; copper-plate, Edin. 1832; Morvern on plate 17, part 1, dated 1824.

Uladail plan 1833
>*Plan of the farm of Ulladal...surveyed 1833*; MS., 1865. *AP*.

V. PHOTOGRAPHS

Album of 60 photographs, taken c. 1865–75, by Gertrude Smith and 'S.S.'; formerly Gertrude's property; now Mrs Donald Cameron, Larachbeg, Morvern.
Photographs (Gertrude Smith)

Album of 61 photographs, 39 of which are duplicates of those in *Photographs (Gertrude Smith)*, and the remainder other photographs from the same series and by the same photographers; formerly the property of Flora Smith; now Colonel Arthur Gemmell, Ingarsby, Leicestershire.
Photographs (Flora Smith)

Collection of 6 photographs of old Ardtornish House, etc., taken c. 1884 by Miss H. M. Nicholson; Miss Joan Becher, Arisaig House.
Photographs (Arisaig)

Bibliography

Album of box-camera snaps, taken *c.* 1911 in and around Lochaline, by members of
the Sinclair family, together with earlier loose prints of Knock and Lochaline;
Mrs Robert Simpson (formerly Mrs Duncan Sinclair), Lochaline.

Photographs (Sinclair)

Air photographs (RAF) 1946; Scottish Development Dept., Queen St., Edinburgh
(B 95/CPE/SCOT/UK 197; C 55/CPE/SCOT/UK 195). *Air photographs 1946*

VI. THESIS

Storrie, Margaret C., *Landholdings, land utilisation and settlement in certain isolated
areas of Western Scotland*; University of Glasgow, Ph.D., 1962.

PARLIAMENTARY PAPERS

1804 etc.	Highland roads and bridges, Reports of Commissioners.
1841	Emigration, Scotland, First and second reports of the Select Committee.
	Emigration (Scotland) report (1841)
1846 etc.	Relief of the poor in Scotland, Annual reports of the Board of super-vision.
	Poor board reports
1848 etc.	Statute labour trusts (Scotland), Abstracts of returns.
1851	Western highlands and islands, Report to the Board of supervision by Sir John M'Neill.
1874	Owners of lands and heritages 1872–73 (Scotland), Return.
1879	Parochial boards (Scotland), Return.
1884	Condition of the crofters and cottars in the highlands and islands of Scotland, Report of her Majesty's Commission of inquiry; Evidence.
	Napier Commission report and *evidence* (1884)
1894	Royal Commission (Highlands and islands 1892), Report; Evidence; Maps ('Deer-forest Commission').
1895 etc.	Local government board for Scotland, Annual reports.
1922	Deer forests, Report of the Departmental committee.
1954	Close seasons for deer in Scotland, Report of the Committee.
1963	Scottish salmon and trout fisheries, Report of the Committee.
1964	Land use in the highlands and islands, Report of the Advisory panel.

PRINTED BOOKS AND PERIODICALS

With cross-references to the abbreviations for MSS., etc.,
in previous sections of the bibliography

Abbott, E. and Campbell, L. (1897). *The life and letters of Benjamin Jowett M.A.*
2 vols. London, 1897.

—— (1899). *Letters of Benjamin Jowett M.A.* London, 1899.

Acharn plan 1815. See p. 252.

Achranich plan 1815. See p. 252.

ACOL. See p. 251.

Ainslie's Scotland 1789. See p. 253.

Air photographs 1946. See above.

Annan, N. G. (1955). 'The intellectual aristocracy', in *Studies in social history: a
tribute to G. M. Trevelyan* (ed. J. H. Plumb). London, 1955.

AP. See pp. 251–2.

APS. 'Acta parliamentorum Caroli II; 1681, third Parliament of Charles II', in
The acts of Parliament of Scotland, VIII (London, 1820), 257–9.

Bibliography

Argyll estate plans 1770. See p. 253.
Argyll farms plan 1819 (and copy). See p. 253.
Astley diary. See p. 252.
Beattie, W. (1849). *Life and letters of Thomas Campbell.* 3 vols. London, 1849.
Blackie, J. S. (1885). *The Scottish highlanders and the land laws.* London, 1885.
Blaikie, W. B. (1916). *Origins of the 'forty-five (PSHS,* 2nd ser. II). Edinburgh, 1916.
Bonham Carter, V. (1960). *In a liberal tradition.* London, 1960.
Brown, P. H. (1902–9). *History of Scotland.* 3 vols. Cambridge, 1902–9.
Burke's landed gentry. History of the landed gentry of Great Britain and Ireland (ed. Burke, Sir Bernard). London.
Cameron, J. A. (1884). 'Storm-clouds in the highlands', *The nineteenth century,* XVI, no. 91 (London, Sept. 1884), 379–95.
Campbell, G. D., 8th Duke of Argyll (1883). 'On the economic conditions of the highlands of Scotland', *The nineteenth century,* XIII, no. 72 (London, Feb. 1883), 173–98.
—— (1884). 'A corrected picture of the highlands', *The nineteenth century,* XVI, no. 93 (London, Nov. 1884), 681–701.
—— (1906). *Autobiography and memoirs.* 2 vols. London, 1906.
Campbell, R. H. (1965). *Scotland since 1707.* Oxford, 1965.
Census. See p. 251.
Childe, V. G. (1935). *The prehistory of Scotland.* London, 1935.
Childe, V. G. and Thorneycroft, W. (1938). 'The vitrified fort at Rahoy, Morvern, Argyll', *PSAS,* LXXII (1938), 23–43.
Clerk, D. (1878). 'On the agriculture of the county of Argyll', *THASS,* 4th ser. X (1878), 1–105.
Clounlaid plan 1833. See p. 253.
Cokayne, G. E. and Gibbs, V. (1910). *The complete peerage.* London, 1910–.
Collier, A. (1953). *The crofting problem.* Cambridge, 1953.
Cook, Sir E. T. (1913). *The life of Florence Nightingale.* 2 vols. London, 1913.
County families. The county families of the United Kingdom (ed. Walford, E.). London.
Cregeen, E. R. (1963). *Inhabitants of the Argyll Estate 1779* (Scottish Record Society). Edinburgh, 1963.
—— (1964). *Argyll Estate instructions: Mull, Morvern, Tiree: 1771–1805 (PSHS).* Edinburgh, 1964.
Crowley, D. W. (1956). 'The "Crofters' Party", 1885–1892', *Scottish historical review,* XXXV (Edinburgh, 1956), 110–26.
Cruden, S. H. (1960, 1963). *The Scottish castle.* Edinburgh, 1960, rev. 1963.
Darling, F. F. (1947). *Natural history in the highlands and islands.* London, 1947; reissued as *The highlands and islands* (with Boyd, J. M.). London, 1964.
—— (1955). *West highland survey.* Oxford, 1955.
Dewar, J. (1962). *The Dewar manuscripts* (ed. J. Mackechnie). Glasgow, 1962.
Donaldson, M. E. M. (n.d.). *Further wanderings—mainly in Argyll.* Paisley, [1926].
Drimnin plan 1836. See p. 253.
Duckworth, C. L. D. and Langmuir, G. E. (1950). *West highland steamers* (2nd ed.). London, 1950.
Duncan, D. (1908). *The life and letters of Herbert Spencer.* London, 1908.
Emigration (Scotland) report (1841). See p. 254.
Ensor, R. C. K. (1936). *England 1870–1914.* Oxford, 1936.
Fasti. See Scott, H. (1915–28).
Feachem, R. (1963). *A guide to prehistoric Scotland.* London, 1963.
Fergusson, Sir J. (1951). *Argyll in the forty-five.* London, 1951.
Free Church destitution committee (1847). *First [second] statement of the destitution committee of the Free Church.* Glasgow, 1847.
Good words. Good words, a weekly magazine. Edinburgh and London, 1860–1906.
Graham, H. G. (1899). *The social life of Scotland in the eighteenth century.* 2 vols. London, 1899.
Grant, I. F. (1924). *Everyday life on an old highland farm.* London, 1924.

Bibliography

Grant, I. F. (1935). *The Lordship of the Isles; wanderings in the lost Lordship.* Edinburgh, 1935.

—— (1961). *Highland folk ways.* London, 1961.

GR (Argyll). See p. 251.

Gray, M. (1955). 'The highland potato famine of the 1840s', *Economic history review,* 2nd ser. VII (Cambridge, 1954–5), 357–68.

—— (1957). *The highland economy 1750–1850.* Edinburgh, 1957.

Gregory, D. (1881). *The history of the western highlands and isles of Scotland* (2nd ed.). London, 1881.

Grey, Sir G. (1841). *Journals of two expeditions of discovery in north-west and western Australia, during the years 1837, 1838 and 1839.* 2 vols. London, 1841.

Grimble, I. (1962). *The trial of Patrick Sellar.* London, 1962.

GRS. See p. 251.

Haldane, A. R. B. (1952). *The drove roads of Scotland.* Edinburgh, 1952.

—— (1962). *New ways through the glens.* Edinburgh, 1962.

Halliburton's county directory. The county directory of Scotland (ed. W. W. Halliburton, etc.). Edinburgh.

Harkness, T. (1835). 'Remarks on the smearing of sheep', *THASS,* n.s. IV (1835), 125–30.

Highland relief board reports. First [etc.] *report by the central board of management of the fund raised for the relief of the destitute inhabitants of the highlands and islands of Scotland.* Glasgow, 1847, etc.

Inglis, H. R. G., etc. (1936). *The early maps of Scotland* (2nd. ed.). Edinburgh, 1936.

Inventory 1872. See p. 252.

Johnston, Sir C. N., Lord Sands (1931). *Kinlochmoidart's dirk.* Edinburgh, 1931.

Johnston, J. B. (1934). *Place-names of Scotland.* London, 1934.

Kelly's titled classes. Kelly's handbook to the titled, landed and official classes. London.

King's memoirs. See p. 252.

Knock plans 1788 and *1815.* See p. 253.

Kyd, J. G. (1952). *Scottish population statistics (PSHS).* Edinburgh, 1952.

Lamont, W. D. (1957–8). 'Old land denominations and "Old extent" in Islay', *Scottish studies,* I (Edinburgh, 1957), 183–210; II (Edinburgh, 1958), 86–106.

Lang, A. (1898). *The highlands of Scotland in 1750.* Edinburgh, 1898.

Langlands' Argyll 1801. See p. 253.

Lloyd's register. Lloyd's register of British and foreign shipping. London, 1834–.

Lloyd's yacht register. Lloyd's register of British and foreign shipping: yacht register. London, 1878–.

MacConnochie, A. I. (1923). *The deer and deer forests of Scotland.* London, 1923.

MacCulloch, J. (1824). *The highlands and western islands of Scotland.* 4 vols. London, 1824.

MacDonald, C. M. ([1950]). *The history of Argyll.* Glasgow ([1950]).

—— (1961). *The county of Argyll* (3rd Statistical account). Glasgow, 1961.

MacGibbon, D. and Ross, T. (1887–92). *The castellated and domestic architecture of Scotland.* 5 vols. Edinburgh, 1887–92.

MacKenzie, A. (1883). *The history of the highland clearances.* Inverness, 1883.

MacKenzie, D. (1954). *Farmer in the western isles.* London, 1954.

MacKichan's memoirs. See p. 252.

MacLennan, Rhona M. (1953). 'The liassic sequence in Morvern', *Transactions of the geological society of Glasgow,* XXI (Glasgow, 1953), 447–55.

MacLeod, J. (1843). 'Parish of Morvern', *NSA,* VII (1845, written 1843), 163–95.

MacLeod, J. N. (1898). *Memorials of the Rev. Norman MacLeod (Senr) D.D. Minister of St Columba's Church, Glasgow.* Edinburgh, 1898.

MacLeod, N. (1794). 'Parish of Morvern', *OSA,* X (1794), 262–76.

MacLeod, N.[2] (1847). *Extracts from letters to the Rev. Dr M'Leod, Glasgow, regarding the famine and destitution in the highlands and islands of Scotland.* Glasgow, 1847.

Bibliography

MacLeod, N.[3] (1863). *Reminiscences of a highland parish*; orig. pub. as a serial in *Good words*, III (London, 1863); refs. are to the 2nd ed. London, 1868.

MacPhail, J. R. N. (1914). 'Papers relating to the MacLeans of Duart, 1670–1680', in *Highland papers I*, ed. J. R. N. MacPhail (*PSHS*). Edinburgh, 1914.

MacSween, M. D. (1960). 'Transhumance in North Skye', *Scottish geographical magazine*, LXXV (Rotterdam, 1960), 75–88.

Morvern map 1865. See p. 253.

Murray, Sir A. (1740). *The true interest of Great Britain, Ireland and our plantations.* London, 1740.

Napier Commission evidence and *report* (1884). See p. 254.

North British Daily Mail. Glasgow.

NSA. The new statistical account of Scotland. Edinburgh, 1845.

Oban Times. Oban.

O'Dell, A. C. and Walton, K. (1962). *The highlands and islands of Scotland.* London, 1962.

Oliver and Boyd. The Edinburgh almanac. Edinburgh.

OPS. Origines parochiales Scotiae, ed. C. Innes, 3 vols. in 2. Edinburgh, 1851–5.

OS 1872, etc. See p. 253.

OSA. The statistical account of Scotland. Edinburgh, 1791–8.

Pearsall, W. H. (1950). *Mountains and moorlands.* London, 1950.

Pennant, T. (1772). *A tour in Scotland and voyage to the Hebrides.* 2 vols. Chester, 1772.

PGSS. The public general statutes affecting Scotland. Edinburgh, 1849, etc.

Phemister, J. (1960). *Scotland: the northern highlands* (British regional geology). Edinburgh, 1960

Photographs (Gertrude Smith, etc.). See pp. 253–4.

Poor board reports. See p. 254.

Prebble, J. (1961). *Culloden.* London, 1961.

—— (1963). *The highland clearances.* London, 1963.

PSAS. Proceedings of the society of antiquaries of Scotland. Edinburgh.

PSHS. Publications of the Scottish history society.

Rainsford-Hannay, F. (1957). *Dry stone walling.* London, 1957.

RGO. See p. 251.

Richey, J. E. (1960). *Scotland: the tertiary volcanic districts* (British regional geology). Edinburgh, 1960.

Robson, J. (1794). *General view of the agriculture in the county of Argyll.* London, 1794.

Ross, A. M. (1932). *History of the clan Ross.* Dingwall, 1932.

Roy's Scotland 1747–55. See p. 253.

RSA. See p. 251.

Sands, Lord. See Johnston, Sir C. N.

Savage, D. C. (1961). 'Scottish politics, 1885–6', *The Scottish historical review*, XL (Edinburgh, 1961), 118–35.

Scott, H. (1915–28). *Fasti ecclesiae Scoticanae*, new ed. Edinburgh, 1915–28.

Scott, J. F. (1931). 'General geology and physiography of Morvern', *Transactions of the geological society of Glasgow*, XVIII (Glasgow, 1931), 149–89.

—— (1956). 'The parish of Morvern', *The Scottish geographical magazine*, LXX (Edinburgh, 1956), 79–92.

Scrope, W. (1838). *The art of deer stalking.* London, 1838.

—— (1843). *Days and nights of salmon fishing.* London, 1843.

Sellar, E. M. (1907). *Recollections and impressions.* 3rd imp. Edinburgh, 1907.

Sellar, T. (1883). *The Sutherland evictions of 1814.* Edinburgh, 1883.

Sinclair, A. M. (1899). *The clan Gillean.* Charlottetown, 1899.

Sinclair, Sir J. (1831). *Analysis of the statistical account of Scotland.* 2 vols. Edinburgh, 1831.

Slater's directory. Slater's royal national commercial directory of Scotland. Manchester.

Smith, A. (1865). *A summer in Skye.* 2 vols. Edinburgh, 1865; refs. are to 1-vol. ed. Edinburgh, 1866.

Smith, J. (1813). *General view of the agriculture of the county of Argyle.* London, 1813.

Spencer, H. (1904). *An autobiography.* 2 vols. London, 1904.

Sportsman's guide. The sportsman's, tourist's and general time-tables and guide to the rivers, lochs [etc.] *of Scotland.* London, 1873–1915.

SRO. See p. 251.

Stewart, N. P. and Laidlaw, R. (1871). 'On dipping, pouring and smearing sheep', *THASS*, 4th ser. iii (1871), 260–73.

Stuart, M. (1930). *Scottish family history.* Edinburgh, 1930.

Symon, J. A. (1959). *Scottish farming, past and present.* Edinburgh, 1959.

THASS. Transactions of the highland and agricultural society of Scotland. Edinburgh.

Thomson's atlas 1824. See p. 253.

Tweedsmuir, S. (1947). *John Buchan by his wife and friends.* London, 1947.

Uladail plan 1833. See p. 253.

VR. See p. 251.

Wallace, R. (1923). *Farm live stock of Great Britain* (5th ed.). Edinburgh, 1923.

Whitehead, G. K. (1960). *The deer stalking grounds of Great Britain and Ireland.* London, 1960.

Wilkie, T. (1895). *The representation of Scotland.* Paisley, 1895.

Wilson, J. (1842). *A voyage round the coasts of Scotland.* 2 vols. Edinburgh, 1842.

Wilson, G. V. (1921). *The lead, zinc, copper and nickel ores of Scotland* (Memoirs of the geological survey, Scotland). Edinburgh, 1921.

Wood, G. H. (1909). 'Real wages and the standard of comfort since 1850', *Journal of the royal statistical society,* LXXII (London, 1909), 91–103.

Woodward, E. L. (1938). *The age of reform 1815–1870.* Oxford, 1938.

1 Remains of some of the houses of Auliston settlement in the north-west corner of Morvern, from which more than 100 people were evicted in 1855; in the background are Ardmore Point, Mull, on the left, and the tip of the Ardnamurchan peninsula on the right.

2a The east end of Octavius Smith's barn at Achranich, dated 1851.

2b The old boat-house, Achranich, dated 1853. The large house in the background is Ross's Ardtornish Tower II of 1884–91, with the clock-tower of 1856–66, re-roofed, rising behind it.

3a Uileann shepherd's cottage and byre, dated 1857. The corrugated-iron of the gable-end and the composition roofing-tiles are not original.

3b Durinemast shepherd's cottage, dated 1861.

4 The ruins of Lochaline House. This façade was probably added by Mrs Paterson in the 1870s to the house completed in 1825 by John Sinclair. The building was deliberately destroyed by fire in 1910.

5 Ardtornish Tower I, 1856–66, from a photograph taken *c.* 1867 by Gertrude Smith. The clock-tower, re-roofed in 1884–91, still stands, but the house was demolished in 1884. (*Photographs (Gertrude Smith)*, 19.)

6a Inninmore shepherd's cottage and byre, 1862.

6b Old Ardtornish shepherd's cottage, probably in the 1890s. The lower part of the building, on the right, is half of a double cottage built *c.* 1840, of which the other half was replaced *c.* 1862–3 by the larger, two-storey building in the middle. The seated couple are probably the shepherd William Nichol and his wife. (*AP*)

7a Eignaig shepherd's cottage and byre, 1864.

7b Keeper's cottage, Achranich, *c.* 1867–8.

8 Octavius Smith at Ardtornish Tower in 1867 with his daughter Gertrude, his son **Willie** and his nephew William Smith Nicholson (holding gun), from a photograph taken by 'S.S.'. (*Photographs* (*Flora Smith*), unnumbered.)

9 Mrs Octavius Smith in the drawing-room at Ardtornish Tower, from a photograph taken *c.* 1870 by her daughter Gertrude. (*Photographs* (*Gertrude Smith*), 59.)

10a Castle cottages, Kinlochaline, by Samuel Barham, 1873.

10b Terrace of six houses at Larachbeg by Samuel Barham, 1875.

11a Claggan school house by Samuel Barham, 1877–8.

11b Caolas ferry house and stables by Samuel Barham, 1879. The stables building was later converted into a shepherd's cottage.

12 Ardtornish House, 1755–70, from a photograph taken c. 1864 by Gertrude Smith; Octavius Smith and his wife face each other by the porch, Flora Smith stands on the lawn. (*Photographs* (*Gertrude Smith*), 13.) The house was completely demolished in 1907.

13 Ardtornish Tower II by Alexander Ross of Inverness, 1884–91.

14a Achranich farm-house (1815–24), from a photograph taken *c.* 1867 by Gertrude Smith. The object just visible amongst the trees between the main chimney-stacks appears to be the keeper's cottage under construction. (*Photographs (Gertrude Smith)*, 31.)

14b The manager's house at Achranich by Samuel Barham, which replaced the old farm-house (shown above) in 1880.

15a Lochaline high street in the 1890s. These thatched houses of *c.* 1840 were replaced by Barham's terrace in 1899 (from a photograph of unknown provenance in the possession of Mrs Mary Wilson, Lochaline).

15b The pier-master's house and post office, Lochaline, probably by Samuel Barham, 1898–9. The pier building on the left faces out towards Mull.

16 Stalking at Ardtornish in the early 1870s, from a photograph by Gertrude Smith. Two of the figures are probably gamekeepers (John Ross kneeling by the stag and George Dalgleish standing with a knife); the man with the fun is probably Willie Smith, and it may be Alexander Craig Sellar, seated, pouring a dram. (*Photographs* (*Flora Smith*), **13.**)

INDEX

References to main entries are in bold figures

Index

Bonnavoulin, Morvern, 21, 33, 33 n., 48, 49, 54, 55, 74, 154–5, 157, 217, 217 n., 220 n., 222, 222 n.; map 10/84
  fish trap, 170; school, 50, 242 n.; smithy, 170
Bow Brewery, 89 n.
bridges, *see* roads, tracks and bridges
Brown, Mr –, 210
Buchan, John, Lord Tweedsmuir (1875–1940), 58, 92 n., 107
  Mr Standfast, 107; *John MacNab*, 107
Buchan, Susan, Lady Tweedsmuir, 107
Bunessan, Mull, 229, 243

Callander and Oban Railway, 110
Camas Glas, Morvern, 161; map 10/118
Camas Gorm, Morvern, 131
Camas na h-Airdhe, Morvern, 162; map 10/123
Camas Salach, Morvern, 15, 19, 50, 112, 124, 127, 162; map 10/122
Cameron, Alexander, lodge-keeper (b. 1834), 99, 104–5
Cameron, Allan, of Glendessary, 12, 134, 135, 137, 145, 147, 148, 149; map 1
Cameron Arms inn, Lochaline, 56, 99, 241, 241 n.
Cameron, Catherine, 234
Cameron, Dr Charles, of the *North British Daily Mail*, 111 n.
Cameron, Charlotte, 234
Cameron clan, 3, 4, 33 n.
Cameron, Donald, of Lochiel (1695–1748), 3
Cameron, Donald, crofter (*c.* 1798–1855), 69
Cameron, Duncan, sen., of the *Oban Times*, 111
Cameron, Duncan, jun., of the *Oban Times* (1861–1954), 96, 111, 111 n.
Cameron, Duncan, police constable, 112
Cameron, Hugh, residenter of Arienas, 69 n.
Cameron, Hugh 'Crosag', crofter and estate labourer (1816–83), 69–70, 78, 90
Cameron, Jean, tenant of Unimore, 124, 150, 166
Cameron, John, merchant and inn-keeper, 56, 241, 241 n.
Cameron, John, schoolmaster, 50, 56, 241
Cameron, John, tenant of Keil, 125
Cameron, Mary, crofter's daughter, 69
Cameron, Mary, Kinlochaline, 246–7, 247 n.
Cameron (?), Mary, Unimore, 33–4
Cameron, Peter, crofter's son, 69
Cameron, Samuel, fool and post-runner, 229–30
Cameron, –, of Inverailort, 202
Cameron, –, toll-keeper, 238
Campbell, Alexander, tenant of Killundine, 124, 152
Campbell, Lieut. Archibald, tenant of Laudale, 163

Campbell, Archibald, tenant of Rahoy, 124, 161
Campbell, Charles, of Combie and Achranich, 141, 142
Campbell, Lord Colin, M.P. for Argyllshire, 99
Campbell, Colin, tenant of Kinlochteacuis, 124, 161
Campbell, Lieut. Colin, tenant of Liddesdale, 124, 125, 164, 168
Campbell, Donald, of Airds, 5, 28, 124, 125, 133
Campbell, Donald, of Killundine, 46, 151, 153
Campbell, Dugald, of Craignish, 3
Campbell, Duncan, of Glenure, tenant of Glencripesdale, 161
Campbell, Duncan, tenant of Barr, 124, 156
Campbell family, *see* Argyll, Dukes of
Campbell, Hugh, tenant of Killundine, 152
Campbell, John, of Ardslignish, 124, 134, 148, 149, 163
Campbell, John, tenant of Lagan, 124, 152
Campbell, John, tenant of Liddesdale, 165
Campbell of Lochnell family, 223
Campbell, Thomas (1777–1844), poet, 28 n., 232
Campbell, Mrs – (*née* Sinclair), 224, 226
Caolas, Morvern, 41, 131, 180; map 10/4; plate 11*b*
  see ferries
Caol Bheinn, Morvern, 59
Caol Charna, Morvern, 161; map 10/117
Carabinier, P.S., 110
Carnacailliche, Morvern, 127, 154, 221 n.; map 10/79
Carna island, Morvern, 127, 165–6; map 10
Carnliath, Morvern, 161; map 10/119–20
Carraig, Morvern, 36, 129, 157, 213, 213 n., 216, 220; map 10/93
Carron, Loch, 87
Carter, Alfred Bonham, 77
Carter, Edith Joanna Bonham (d. 1899), 197–201, 197 n.
Carter, Hugh Bonham, 77–8
Carter, Joanna Maria (*née* Smith, 1791–1884), 57, 250
Carter, John Bonham (1788–1838), 57, 250
Carter, John Bonham (1817–84), 197–201, 197 n.
Castle cottages, Kinlochaline, 90–1, 135, 136, 205, 205 n., 240, 246; plate 10*a*
Castle of Dogs, *see* Killundine Castle
castles, 167
cattle, 6, 26, 218, 222, 227, 227 n., 231
  in 1800–10, 13–14, 125–6; in 1850, 52; droving, 21–2, map 7; Achranich, 61, 173–4; Ardtornish, 106, 106 n., 173–4, 182–3, 186; Lochaline cattle market, 235, 235 n.

261

Index

Doire nan Saor, Glen Kinglass, 29, 223, 223 n.
Doirlinn, Morvern, 110, **157**; map 10/97 ferry, *see* ferries
Donald of Tiree, fool, 229
Donald the post, 230–1, 231 n.
Donaldson, M. E. M., travel-journalist, 102 n.
Dorlin, Ardnamurchan, 202
Dounanlui, Morvern, **147**; map 10/55
Drimnin, Morvern, 3, 4, 5, 6, 12, 21, 24, 55, 110, 111, 115, 127, **157**, 229, 232, 236; map 10/94–5
Castle, 35, **167**, map 10/138; chapel, 35, 168; Cottage, 157; Mains, 36; pier, 172; *see* MacLean of Drimnin
Drimnin Crofts, Morvern, **157**; map 10/96
Drimnin Estate, 35–7, 48, 52, 94–5, 94 n., 100, 118, 129, **156–9**, 213–17, 220–1; maps 3, 4
Drimnin House, 35–6, 157
Druimbuidhe, Morvern, 36, **157**; map 10/98
Druim Cracaig, Morvern, 124, 127, **154–5**; map 10/85
Druimindarroch, Arisaig, 203
Duart Castle, Mull, 225
Duart House, Mull, *see* Torosay Castle
Dubh Dhoire, Morvern, 18, 68, 77, 134, **140–1**, 179, 180, 234; map 10/36
Duff, Robert, Captain R.N., 3–4
Dunad, Argyll, 224
Duncan, James, of Altachonaich, 166
Durinemast, Morvern, 50, 75, 105 n., 115, 127, **144**, 235 n.; maps 9, 10/45–6; plate 3*b*
Durran, Argyll, 28
dykes, 169

Edinburgh, 84, 94, 188, 197, 212
Clarendon Hotel, 212
education: in 1800, 11; in 1850, 50; schools, 12, 50, 90–1, 239, 241–2; tutors, 28, 28 n., 50, 224–5; illiteracy, 50; at Achranich, 79, 239
Eigg, Inverness, 202
Eignaig, Morvern, 15, 21, 28, 29 n., 71, 75, 83, 85, 106, 127, **132**, 192, 193–4, 216, 234, 235 n.; maps 9, 10/11; plate 7*a*
Eilean Musdile light-house, Lismore, 171, 247
Eilean nan Eildean, Morvern, **154**; map 10/75
Eilean Shona, Inverness, 202
Elgin, Moray, 42
Elliot, Walter, manager of Ardtornish (1852–1906), 77 n., 82 n., **92–3**, 102, 108, 113, **114**, 114 n., 176, **180–3**, 186 n.
emigration, 25–7, 47, 49, 68, 123, 213, 215, 219
English language, 50–1
evictions, *see* clearances

famines of 1836, 1846–7, 47–8
Fane, Mr – , 212
Fenella, yacht, 85, 197–201
Ferguson, Alexander, merchant in Lochaline, 61
Fernish, Morvern, 11, 15, 21, 24, 33, 49, 51, 124, 127, **154**, 172, 219–20, 220 n.; map 10/80–1
change-house, 124, 155; *see* churches; ferries; Glenmorvern Estate
ferries, maps 7, 8
Caolas, 11, 48, 55, 90–1; Corran, 20, 22, 55, 189 n.; Doirlinn–Glen Borrodale, 11, 22; Fernish (Rhemore)–Mull, 11, 22, 172; Knock–Fishnish (Bailemeonach), 55, 172
feu-duties, 3 n.
'Fiddler's burn', Morvern, 68
Finlay and Wilson, solicitors, Edinburgh, 183, 185
fishing: in 1800, 19; commercial, 19, 222, 240, 240 n.; Achranich Estate, 63–5, 178, 240; Sellar–Smith dispute, 63–4, 179–80; salmon pass, 65; Ardtornish Estate, 71, 77–8, 88, 106, 107, 178–9, 187, 205, 240; by women, 84; fish traps, 19, 170
fishing rights, *see* Kinlochaline, fishings of
fishing station, Aline river, 19, **135–6**, 180, 240, 240 n.; map 10/16
see Kinlochaline, fishings of
Fishnish, Mull, 22
fish traps, tidal, 19, **170**
Fiunary, Morvern, 11, 15, 30, 31, 118, 124, 127, **150–1**, 169, 170, 184, 186, 226 n.; maps 9, 10/61
cottage, 46; pier, 172
Fiunary Forest, 149
Fiunary House, *see* Lochaline House
Fiunary Manse and glebe, 11, 49, 86, 93, 150, 232
floods, 245–7
'Flotsam', *see* Nicholson, Gertrude Susan
'fools', 229–30
Forbes, Charles H., of Kingairloch, 141, 166, 238; map 3
Forbes, Duncan, of Culloden (1685–1747), 2–3, 8, 160
Forbes, James, of Kingairloch, 127, 166; map 2
fords, 172; map 7
Acharn, 237, 237 n.; Achranich, 239; Arienas, 171, 237 n.; Ath Buidhe, 179, 237, 237 n., 238; Ath-stoc-an, 21 n., 237; Uileann, 180
Forestry Commission, 118, 133, 149, 153, 156, 162, 169, 172, 238
see woods and timber
Fort William, Inverness, 55, 197
market, 73
Forty-five, the, 2, 3–5
'Fossil burn' (Allt na Samhnachain), Morvern, 69

263

Oronsay island, Morvern, 19, 36, 51, 52, 94–5, 94 n., 111, 129, **158**, 213–14, 213 n., 216, 220–1; map 10/101–4
fish trap, 170

Palgrave, Francis Turner (1824–97), 41–2
parliamentary elections: 1885, 1886, 99; 1892, 99 n.
Parochial Board, Morvern, *see* Morvern parish
Paterson, Campbell, banker and factor, 42, 149
Paterson, Magdalene, of Lochaline (1812–80), 27, 30, **42–6**, 52, 55, 93, 102, 105, 110, 112, 128–9, 146, 149, 150, 217, 220, 221, 240
paupers: in 1800, 11; in 1850, 48; in 1900, 113; and clearances, 215, 217, 219
Pennygowan, Morvern, 164
Peppina –, the Astleys' maid, 198, 202, 209, 211
pheasants, *see* shooting
Phineas Finn (1867–9), 87
photography, 76
piermaster's house, Lochaline, 103, 104
piers, **172**
    Lochaline, 48, 53, 103, 104, 110, 172, 185, 186, 235
Pilkington, Irma H., of Glenmorvern, 156
Pioneer, P.S., 80, 110, 242–3
Poll Luachrain, Morvern, 8 n., 35, 124, 127, **158**; map 10/105
Poltalloch, Argyll, 204
population, 6–7, 36, 47, 93, 111, 116–18, 121–3, 215, 219
    see emigration; settlements
Portabhata, Morvern, 8 n., 15, 35, 36, 48, 124, 127, **158**, 170; map 10/106
Port Glasgow, Renfrewshire, 87, 88
postal services: in 1800, 22, map 7; mid-19th-cent., 55–6, 231–2, 231 n., 245; in 1900, 110–11, map 8; telegraph, 111; private, 230
post office, Lochaline, 103, 104, 241
potato famine of 1846–7, 47–8, 68–9
Pouligou, Poulivaan shielings, 147
Prebble, J., 38 n.
Princess Ann, H.M.S., 3
productivity: 1750–1850, 52–3; Achranich and Ardtornish, 60, 72; summary to 1900, 115–17; statistics, 121–2; *see* agriculture; sheep and wool
proprietors: defined, 3 n.; in 1800, 12–13, 23–4; and clearances, 25–7; in 1850, 46; rights and duties of, 44–5, 49, 113–14; 'enlarge' properties, 31 n., 103–4, 180, 180 n., 181, 181 n., 185, 185 n.; new type of, 41–2, 58–9, 70, 86–7; pleasures of, 86–7, 103; animosity towards, 80, 98, 100; and Land League, 100; contribution of, 108, 113–15; power of, 114; kindly feeling towards, 114–15; summary to 1900, 115–17; maps 1, 2, 3, 4

quarries, *see* mines and quarries
Quinish, Mull, 84, 189, 189 n.

rabbit trapping, 78
Radio Times, 38 n., 112, 112 n.
Rahoy, Morvern, 15, 16, 17 n., 19, 24, 50, 110, 118, 124, 125–6, 127, 143, 159, 161, 169, 224; map 10/121
    vitrified fort, 224, 224 n.
railways: Callander and Oban, 110; Achranich, 243
Ramage, John, tenant of Achleanan, 36
Rannoch cottage, Achranich, 103
Rannoch river, Morvern, 66, 67, 186, 239
Rannoch, S.Y., 108, 187
Reconstruction, *see* horses
Reform bills, 1832, 1868, 1884, 96–7
rentals, Argyll estate, 124–6
Representation of the people Acts, 1832, 1868, 1884, 97
Rhemore, Morvern, 11, 33, **154**, 172; map 10/81
Rhifail, Strathnaver, 83
Rhum, Inverness, 65, 202
Rich, Lady –, 202
Riddell, James, of Ardnamurchan, 136
Riddell, Mary Ann, Lady (*née* Hodgson), 199, 199 n., 203–4
Riddell, Sir Thomas M., Bart (1822–83), 199, 199 n.
Riverside cottage, Achranich, 103
Road Trustees, Morvern, *see* Morvern parish
roads, tracks and bridges, **20–2**, 48, 54–5, 91, 104, 110, **171**–2, 179, 180, 236–8, 240; maps 7, 8
    statute labour system, 20; the Commissioners' plans, 21; tracks, 21, 236–8; drove roads, 21–2; new roads built, 48, 54–5, 110; private roads, 55, 91; remains of old roads, 171–2; bridges, 20, 54, 238; *see* ferries; fords; shielings
Robertson, William, of Kinlochmoidart (b. 1802), 199, 199 n., 202–3
Rose cottage, Achranich, 90–1, 135, 141, 234, 237, 240, 245
Rose, Harry, 204, 204 n., 205, 210
Rose, Mr –, 204, 204 n., 205, 210
Roshven, Inverness, 202
Ross, Alexander, architect (1834–1925), 67, 101, 101 n., 103, 104, 167
Ross and Macbeth, architects, Inverness, 167
Ross, John, gamekeeper (b. 1844), plate 16
Roundell, Charles Saville, M.P., 190 n.
Roundell, Julia Elizabeth Anne (*née* Tollemache, d. 1931), 80, 86, 189 n., 190–2 and nn., 210